Emerging Intersections

Emerging Intersections

Race, Class, and Gender
in Theory, Policy, and Practice

Edited by

BONNIE THORNTON DILL and
RUTH ENID ZAMBRANA

Foreword by PATRICIA HILL COLLINS

RUTGERS UNIVERSITY PRESS

NEW BRUNSWICK, NEW JERSEY, AND LONDON

LIBRARY OF CONGRESS CATALOGING-IN-PUBLICATION DATA

Emerging intersections: race, class, and gender in theory, policy, and practice / edited by Bonnie Thornton Dill and Ruth Enid Zambrana ; foreword by Patricia Hill Collins.
    p. cm.
Includes bibliographical references and index.
ISBN 978–0–8135–4454–0 (hardcover : alk. paper)
ISBN 978–0–8135–4455–7 (pbk. : alk. paper)
    1. United States—Social conditions—1980– 2. United States—Race relations.
3. Social classes—United States. 4. Sex role—United States.
5. Homosexuality—United States. 6. Discrimination—United States.
7. Poverty—United States. I. Dill, Bonnie Thornton. II. Zambrana, Ruth E.
HN59.2.E334 2008
306.0973'09045—dc22   2008011238

Visit our Web site: http://rutgerspress.rutgers.edu

Manufactured in the United States of America

CONTENTS

FOREWORD

Emerging Intersections–Building Knowledge and Transforming Institutions

PATRICIA HILL COLLINS

As thinkers and practitioners, Bonnie Thornton Dill and Ruth E. Zambrana have been actively engaged in nurturing intersectionality since its inception. For Dill and Zambrana, intersectionality constitutes "an innovative and emerging field of study that provides a critical analytic lens to interrogate racial, ethnic, class, ability, age, sexuality, and gender disparities and to contest existing ways of looking at these structures of inequality, transforming knowledges as well as the social institutions in which they have found themselves." This expansive definition, one that links knowledge and power, research and policy, the individual and the collective, captures the spirit of intersectionality as it unfolded in the last three decades of the twentieth century. Unlike scholarly dilettantes who perpetually chase scholarly fads, Dill and Zambrana have been patiently, and some would say heroically, laboring for several decades to develop our understanding of intersectionality as a critical analytic lens that serves social justice. *Emerging Intersections* encompasses one important project that reflects the larger corpus of their work.

Despite the widespread belief that intersectionality has arrived, I think that it is important to stop and recognize that this way of looking at and living within the world constitutes a new area of inquiry that is still in its infancy. Moreover, because this field remains both staunchly interdisciplinary and committed to claiming the much-neglected space of praxis (one where transforming ideas and institutions inform one another), from its inception intersectionality set a seemingly impossible high bar for itself. Given its high initial aspirations and the way they have played out, *Emerging Intersections* can serve as an important guidepost to mark the trajectory of intersectional scholarship and practice. This volume can help us look backward in order to interrogate past ideals and practices as well as forward in order to imagine potential directions and future achievements. In short, the volume raises three core questions. What have we learned from the early decades of the field of intersectionality? Given its past, what directions might this field that is still in its infancy now take? Furthermore how might practitioners who are doing intersectional scholarship and/or activism continue to move the field forward?

As to the first core question, what might *Emerging Intersections* tell us about past practices of intersectional inquiry? In the greatly changed political and intellectual context of the early twenty-first century, revisiting and clarifying the initial impetus and vision that accompanied this critical analytic lens of intersectionality becomes especially prescient. We need to remember that such a wide range of scholar/activists developed various aspects of this approach through the 1970s and 1980s that, when Kimberlé Crenshaw penned the term "intersectionality" in 1991, she basically named a heterogeneous set of practices that had gone on for some time (Crenshaw, 1991). She argued, quite convincingly, that understandings of violence against women would be limited unless one took into consideration the race, ethnicity, immigrant status, and class of women who were targets of violence. Crenshaw pointed out how programs that were developed via gender-only frameworks were narrow at best, and deeply flawed at worst, because they failed to take into consideration how intersecting power relations of race, class, immigrant status, and gender affected women's options. More importantly, Crenshaw saw knowledge and hierarchical power relations as co-constituted—the very frameworks that shaped understandings of violence against women simultaneously influenced both the violence itself as well as organizational responses to it. In this regard, social institutions were limited if they did not take intersectional analyses into account.

Crenshaw was not alone in calling for intersectional analyses of social problems and the knowledge/power relations that catalyzed them. As discussed in Dill and Zambrana's introduction to this volume, many thinkers and activists set out to transform a host of institutional practices and knowledges via a newfound and seemingly expansive framework of intersectionality. From its inception, intersectionality took up the social problems that most affected those most harmed by inequalities—poverty, poor education, substandard healthcare, inadequate housing, and violence all became rethought through a lens of intersecting power relations of race, class, and gender. It soon became apparent that it was not enough to use an intersectional framework to understand specific social problems—one could also begin to ask the big questions of how racism and sexism were co-constituted, how class and heterosexism mutually constructed one another, and how citizenship status (nationality) articulated with issues of ability and age. In essence, intersectionality increasingly took on the big question of the very meaning of power itself. Intersectionality also went beyond simple understanding of either social issues or social structures. Its focus remained staunchly on engaging in a host of projects that might foster social justice. Thus, from its inception, intersectionality was not a theory of truth, a form of academic currency to be brokered for the next scholarly publication, with the implications of scholarship neatly severed from the lives of the people who were forced to live with its consequences. Instead intersectionality mattered in real people's lives and tried to keep this expansive understanding of social relations in mind.

For me, the 1970s and 1980s were the heady days of intersectional scholarship, a time when the critical analytical lens of intersectionality was attuned to assessing significant social issues, thinking through the mechanisms of intersecting systems of power themselves, and/or trying to do something about social inequalities. Ironically some view Crenshaw's 1991 piece coining the term "intersectionality" as intersectionality's coming of age, yet this moment can also be interpreted as launching a decade where the initial vision of intersectionality became increasingly drowned out by a new set of social meanings and practitioners. Today, for many practitioners, the spirit of adhering to an intersectional framework may remain the same, yet both the interpretive context in which such work occurs as well as the object of analysis has shifted. In recent years, intersectional analyses have far too often turned inward, to the level of personal identity narratives, in part, because intersectionality can be grasped far more easily when constructing one's own autobiography. This stress on identity narratives, especially individual identity narratives, does provide an important contribution to fleshing out our understandings of how people experience and construct identities within intersecting systems of power. Yet this turning inward also reflects the shift within American society away from social structural analyses of social problems, for example, the role of schools, prisons, and workplace practices in producing poverty, and the growing rejection of institutional responses to social inequalities, e.g., how governmental social policies might address this intractable social problem. Unfortunately the ascendancy in the 1990s within the American academy of poststructuralist social theory has of yet done little to slow down this erasure of social structure. Despite their appeal, ideas of performativity, social constructionism, and discourse analysis have not garnered any substantive changes in the organizations and social institutions that continue to reproduce racism, sexism, class exploitation, heterosexism, and the like.

Emerging Intersections appears within these crosscutting political and intellectual trends and thus debuts during a critical historical moment for the field of intersectionality. By showcasing in one place how social science research might continue to use the critical analytical lens provided by intersectionality, this volume refocuses attention to social structural analysis of inequality, in particular, the organizational and institutional manifestations of power hierarchies and their effects upon individuals and groups. Taking this stance during the contemporary period is not easy—theoretical arguments about the workings of power as being "everywhere" abound; yet ironically, terms such as inequality, hierarchy, racism, sexism, exploitation, and oppression remain noticeably absent from discussions of power. Understandings of power in the broader American context fare little better—because as individuals, we are each deemed to be the sole cause of our own successes or failures, each individual is responsible for fixing any problems he or she may have. This is a long way from Crenshaw's analysis of the social causes of violence against women and the need for social remedies for such violence. In this context, Dill and Zambrana's focus on social inequalities constitutes a bold move; it is refreshing yet sobering to return to the important contributions of social science research in pointing out how unjust power relations are organized and operate. They refocus our attention to neglected objects of analysis, namely, the social structural processes by which inequality is organized as well as the mechanisms that can be used to change, address, or transform these structures.

Given this recent history, I think that it is important to return to the initial spirit of scholarly activism/activist scholarship that catalyzed attention to building knowledge and transforming institutions in the first place. In this regard, let me move on to the second core question raised by *Emerging Intersections*, namely, what directions might this field that is still in its infancy now take? This question in turn, raises a series of derivative ones for which there is now no clear answer. For example, is it enough to return to the initial vision that catalyzed the field in the hopes of replicating it under current conditions? Or does such a return constitute a form of myopic nostalgia that is no match for current intellectual and political realities? What have we learned from the many contributions and omissions to the field as it has emerged during its formative years and how might we put this learning to good use today? Is the vision of intersectionality detailed by Dill and Zambrana fundamentally flawed, or merely troubled in its execution?

There are no easy answers to these questions, yet I encourage readers to pay careful attention to Dill and Zambrana's introductory chapter. There they offer a solid synthesis of some of the best practices of the field and, by doing so, provide a clearer roadmap for intersectional projects than those that were available to either the field at its inception or to former practitioners. Specifically Dill and Zambrana identify four theoretical interventions of advocacy, analysis, theorizing, and pedagogy that they argue are basic components essential to the production of knowledge as well as the pursuit of social justice and equality. They also argue that intersectionality challenges the traditional ways that knowledge has been produced in the United States and illustrates how this theory provides an alternative model that is foundational to this interdisciplinary intellectual enterprise. The ideas from this introductory chapter constitute a solid summary not simply of the articles included in *Emerging Intersections* but also provide us with a place to start answering some of the thorny questions of today.

This brings me to the third and final core question catalyzed by this volume, namely, how might we continue to move the field forward from here? Dill and Zambrana provide a compelling case for continuing to build alternative explanations for existing phenomena by bringing contemporary disparities into view, analyzing those that were hidden and unknown, and, in other cases, reformulating thinking about the seemingly familiar, e.g., single mothers. In a context of practices such as proclaiming that racism is dead under the banner of colorblind racism, of claiming that women are equal to men because gender-neutral social policies seem to be in force, and the erasure of poverty as a social problem via mass-media amnesia, it becomes even more important to cast the critical analytical lens of intersectionality on prevailing social inequalities. By approaching some of the most significant social science research through intersectional frameworks, *Emerging Intersections* raises a clarion call for the next generation of scholar/activists who inherit the very large task of using it to foster social justice. As long as social inequalities persist, scholar/activists using intersectionality will have plenty of material to keep us busy. This is not glamorous work, but it is important work because people's lives depend on it. For example, can we ever develop a comprehensive, effective set of social practices that would head off the disgrace brought on by Hurricane Katrina without attention to intersecting power relations of race, class, gender, regionalism, age, and disability and the placement of varying social groups within them? If scholar/activists do not take on the big challenge of thinking through and challenging social inequalities such as this, then who will?

Beyond the simple advice that we continue to do competent social science research that is informed by the critical analytical lens of intersectionality (which is by no means easy), we might also ask what criteria might fine-tune emerging work in the field of intersectionality? As I see it, such scholarship would reject the false binary of choosing either the deterministic scientific models of the past (for example, the legions of social science studies that were dedicated to proving women's emotional inferiority to men, African American's propensity to violence, the basic perversion of homosexuals, or the damaged culture of Chicanos and Puerto Ricans), or the poststructuralist correctives of the recent past (creating space for individual expression and creativity via interpretive, narrative traditions). Instead intersectional scholarship would choose to place these social structural and interpretative/narrative approaches to social reality in dialogue with one another. More importantly, scholars engaged in intersectional work would be constantly cognizant of and vigilant about the social and political conditions that house their work—even the so-called best work on racism rings hollow when no

African Americans, Chicanos, Puerto Ricans, Native Americans, or other historically oppressed ethno/racial groups are part of the research team. Seemingly inclusionary knowledge produced in exclusionary contexts remains suspect, no matter how well intentioned its practitioners might be. Dill and Zambrana's four theoretical interventions of advocacy, analysis, theorizing, and pedagogy do not come with a set of specific instructions that one can follow in setting up a community center, doing evaluation research for a governmental agency, drafting a proposal for a foundation, or writing a dissertation. Instead the guiding principles that they identify in their introduction and that reappear in varying formats through all of the essays in the volume, encourage the next generation of scholar/activists to use the framework of intersectionality to respond to and hopefully address existing disparities and those that might come.

Despite this vision, continuing to move the field forward requires that the expansive approach to intersectionality engage some thorny questions. For one, can the expansive approach taken to intersectionality that seemingly emerges from and remains central to interdisciplinary endeavors work within traditional disciplines? Is intersectionality inherently oppositional to traditional disciplinary approaches to knowledge production and the social conditions that accompany them? Or can intersectionality be recast solely as a theoretical frame that might reform existing disciplinary paradigms? Under what conditions does this kind of scholarship and praxis flourish, and what conditions foster its demise?

For another, can this version of intersectionality's trajectory, namely, its visibility within the American context, be fruitfully used in other Western societies as well as within non-Western settings? As a Western social theory and set of social practices, intersectionality contains numerous blind spots that make it less applicable to non-Western societies, but only if the specificity of the Western experience continues to stand in for everyone else. One would hate to see intersectionality make the same mistake defining the experiences of a small group of humanity, in this case, oppressed groups within Western societies, as representative of all of humanity, in particular the much larger population that lives in non-Western societies. This need not be the case, but it does require a perpetual energy applied to intersectional work that does not affect scholars and practitioners who simply assume that their way is best. Transnational feminist communities come closest to approximating the radical potential of intersectionality, yet this work is demanding and never-ending. In essence, intersectionality's strength may be its self-reflexivity, but this same self-reflexivity comes with the cost of acting more cautiously, slowly, and, sadly, often ineffectively.

Yet another question concerns the status of the field of intersectionality itself. Will intersectional scholarship become tarred with the brush of being reduced to theories for the oppressed, or can intersectionality make the leap to emerge as a universal way of building knowledge and transforming institutions? Negotiating this dilemma requires addressing two challenges. On the one hand, because intersectionality was launched in the United States by less powerful social actors, it runs the risk of being recast as a form of special interest politics, especially those versions that persist in continuing to lobby for social justice. In essence, a more robust version of intersectionality, the kind presented here by Dill and Zambrana, can be discredited as being too closely tied to the concerns of African Americans, Latinos, and other disempowered groups. On the other hand, a sanitized, depoliticized version of intersectionality may prevail because it is more in tune with current social and political realities. Unlike the invisibility that plagued the field of intersectionality at its inception, it now faces an entirely new challenge of being hypervisible within equally novel conditions of global, commodity capitalism. In U.S. academic settings, a superficial version of intersectionality is routinely packaged, circulated, and sold to faculty and students alike, only to be prematurely discarded when the product's performance fails to match the promises on the package. In this consumer context of accelerated packages of ideas, intersectionality becomes just another theory vying for attention in the universe of its competitors. In brief, the placement of the field of intersectionality and its practitioners within the very power relations that they study and aim to transform continues to have a far-reaching effect on not only what is practiced, but also what can be imagined.

As we move through the early decades of the twenty-first century, Dill and Zambrana remind us that the growing quiescence about social inequality neither means that disparities have disappeared nor that social hierarchies have atrophied. Moreover, in the current context whereby social justice initiatives have been roundly severed from academic scholarship and where the pressures to keep ideas and politics separate seemingly prevail, it remains difficult to retain the robust, initial vision of social justice that catalyzed intersectionality's origins. Thus, at this particular historical moment, one characterized by deeply entrenched and seemingly growing inequalities of race, class, gender, sexuality, ethnicity, ability, and citizenship-status, the critical analytic lens provided by intersectionality may be more needed than ever.

Reference

Crenshaw, K. (1991). Mapping the Margins: Intersectionality, Identity Politics, and Violence against Women of Color. *Stanford Law Review*, 43(6), 1241–1299.

ACKNOWLEDGMENTS

In many ways this book has been in the making since we first met and participated in a small research group exploring the "intersections" of gender, race,
and ethnicity in 1978. Since then, contributing to a growing scholarship on
intersectionality has been both a compelling intellectual enterprise and a personal passion that is reflected in all of our scholarship. This collection, however,
is more immediately an outgrowth of our collaborative work in developing the
Consortium on Race, Gender and Ethnicity (CRGE) at the University of Maryland. Founded in 1998 and directed first by Bonnie Thornton Dill and now by
Ruth Enid Zambrana, CRGE's mission is to promote, advance, and conduct
research, scholarship, and both faculty and student development that examines
the intersections of race, gender, and ethnicity with other dimensions of difference and inequality.

In the process of developing the scholarly directions of CRGE, we have had
the opportunity to meet and interact with a number of outstanding scholars,
"fellow travelers" who embrace the explanatory potential of intersectional
theory and share our commitment to social justice and social change. The contributors to this collection have all expressed a belief that this book is essential and would make an important contribution to the different disciplines it
represents. We would like to thank each of them for their exemplary scholarship, cooperation, and patience in the writing experience. We would especially like to thank Patricia Hill Collins for writing the foreword to this book.
Her voice has provided important theoretical foundations for our scholarship
and inspiration in fostering the empowerment of people of color.

In the process of implementing CRGE's research mission, we sought and
received funding to undertake several important initiatives. A number of the
chapters in this collection are the product of those initiatives and we are particularly grateful to the institutions that provided the financial support to
undertake this work. Funding from the Ford Foundation supported the establishment and maintenance of CRGE and a number of the initiatives that
resulted in chapters for this book, including both the work on intersectionality in higher education and a set of commissioned papers on poverty and
intersectionality. We wish to acknowledge the visionary support of Margaret

Wilkerson and Cynthia M. Duncan, the program officers who helped us develop these projects and Janice Petrovich, who recognized innovative merit in our efforts. Grants from the Annie E. Casey Foundation supported a series of research and action briefs, included in this volume, which synthesized data documenting disparities in key areas of the foundation's work to improve systems serving disadvantaged children and transform neighborhoods. The briefs were designed to give a nuanced understanding of the policies, practices, ideologies, and interactions that produce racial, ethnic, gender, and class disparities as well as information about strategies, tools, interventions, and other resources that can be effective in reducing their influence. We are especially grateful to Senior Vice President Ralph Smith whose vision created the opportunity and to Paula Dressel, the program officer, for her abiding confidence in our capability to carry out the assignment. We also acknowledge with gratitude a grant from the Institute for Women's Leadership at Rutgers University that contributed to the research on our own institution as well as the UCLA faculty awards program and Institutes of American Cultures grant that supported the original data collection for research on Mexican American and African American women in higher education. Over the years, offices and institutes at the University of Maryland have also funded the work of CRGE and we are grateful to Dean James F. Harris of the College of Arts and Humanities for his support of and confidence in our leadership and vision, the Office of the Provost, and the Maryland Population Research Institute in the College of Behavioral and Social Sciences for their ongoing support. We would also like to acknowledge the fact that CRGE is an association of academic units and individual faculty on the University of Maryland campus and thus there are many places in the institution that have and continue to support and enhance our work, most notable among these are the African American Studies Department and the Curriculum Transformation Project, collaborators in several of the Ford Foundation Grants. We are particularly grateful to our colleagues in the Department of Women's Studies for championing the work and mission of CRGE and providing ongoing encouragement of and engagement in our work in both locations.

In the end, we could not have completed the process of writing and editing this manuscript without the indefatigable work of two women. We are indebted to and deeply appreciate our trusted and invaluable coworker, Wendy Hall, program management specialist of the Consortium on Race, Gender, and Ethnicity for her skilled and careful work in formatting and preparing the manuscript and serving as the hub from which all activity, not only for this book, but for all aspects of CRGE's administrative management and budget emanated. Wendy's quiet, calm, and steadfast manner combined with her complete reliability made an often overwhelming workload bearable. We are also indebted and deeply grateful to Laura A. Logie, our research assistant who was completing her doctoral work in women's studies, for her thorough edit-ing, commentary, reference checks, and attention to detail in preparing the entire manuscript and especially the chapters that we authored. Laura's sense of humor combined with her blunt and direct feedback, kept us humble, hon-est, and in good humor as we wrote and revised multiple drafts of the manu-script. Working with these two women has been a privilege.

Finally we dedicate this book to our brilliant and talented colleague, Linda Faye Williams (1949–2006) whose life and work exemplified engaged scholar-ship, a passionate commitment to social justice, and unerring focus on the eradication of social inequality.

Bonnie Thornton Dill
Ruth Enid Zambrana
December 1, 2007

Emerging Intersections

1

Critical Thinking about Inequality

An Emerging Lens

BONNIE THORNTON DILL AND RUTH ENID ZAMBRANA

Inequality and oppression are deeply woven into the tapestry of American life. As a result large disparities exist on measures of income, wealth, education, housing, occupation, and social benefits. These disparities are neither new nor randomly distributed throughout the population, but occur in patterns along such major social divisions as race, gender, class, sexuality, nationality, and physical ability. Social scientists have traditionally analyzed inequalities by isolating these factors and treating them as if they are independent of one another. Even when their interactions are discussed they are still conceptualized as if they are largely independent forces that happen to overlap under specific conditions. For example, studies of race often focus upon contrasting Whites with Blacks and other racially identifiable groups without taking into account historical modes of incorporation of each group. Historical linkages and systemic interrelationships that reveal the underlying ways any one dimension of inequality is shaped by another are rarely fully examined. A problematic result is that the experiences of whole groups are ignored, misunderstood, or erased, particularly those of women of color.

This chapter discusses intersectionality as an innovative and emerging field of study that provides a critical analytic lens to interrogate racial, ethnic, class, physical ability, age, sexuality, and gender disparities and to contest existing ways of looking at these structures of inequality. It identifies and discusses four theoretical interventions that we consider foundational to this interdisciplinary intellectual enterprise. We argue that intersectionality challenges traditional modes of knowledge production in the United States and illustrate how this theory provides an alternative model that combines advocacy, analysis, theorizing, and pedagogy—basic components essential to the production of knowledge as well as the pursuit of social justice and equality.

Research and teaching that focuses on the intersections of race, ethnicity, gender, and other dimensions of identity is a relatively new approach to studying inequality. (Inequality for these purposes is defined as institutionalized patterns of unequal control over and distribution of a society's valued goods and resources such as land, property, money, employment, education, healthcare, and housing.) Intersectionality has gained its greatest influence in the post–civil rights era and has been developed and utilized most prominently in the new scholarship created in the interdisciplinary fields of ethnic studies,[1] women's studies, area studies, and, more recently, lesbian, gay, bisexual, and transgender studies, cultural studies, critical legal studies, labor studies, multicultural studies, American studies, and social justice education. Intersectional analysis begins with the experiences of groups that occupy multiple social locations and finds approaches and ideas that focus on the complexity rather than the singularity of human experience.

Traditional disciplinary boundaries and the compartmentalization and fixity of ideas are challenged by these emerging interdisciplinary fields. These fields seek not only to reexamine old issues in new ways, but also to shift the lens through which humanity and social life are viewed—identifying new issues, new forms, and new ways of viewing them. Thus intersectional scholarship reflects an ongoing intellectual and social justice mission that seeks to: (1) reformulate the world of ideas so that it incorporates the many contradictory and overlapping ways that human life is experienced; (2) convey this knowledge by rethinking curricula and promoting institutional change in higher education institutions; (3) apply the knowledge in an effort to create a society in which all voices are heard; and (4) advocate for public policies that are responsive to multiple voices.

THIS BOOK HAS FIVE OBJECTIVES:

- To demonstrate that intersectionality is a critical analytic interdisciplinary tool to interrogate racial, ethnic, class, and gender disparities and to contest existing ways of looking at these disparities.
- To provide examples of the use of an intersectional framework in the analysis of a variety of social issues.
- To illustrate the strategic importance of intersectional analysis as a mechanism for developing social policy that promotes social justice.
- To demonstrate the importance of comparisons among U.S. social groups (racial, ethnic, class, and gender) as a way of providing a fuller understanding of the nature of dominance, subordination, and inequality.
- To illustrate ways intersectional analysis is a tool for linking theory and practice in higher education.

The Intersectional Lens: An Emerging Perspective

Discussion of the origins of intersectionality most often begins with the research, writings, and teaching by and about women of color in the United States (both native and migrant). Women of color scholars have used the idea of intersections to explain our own lives and to critique the exclusion of our experiences, needs, and perspectives from both White, Eurocentric, middle-class conceptualizations of feminism and male dominated models of ethnic studies. We have laid claim to a U.S. scholarly tradition that began in the nineteenth century with women like Maria Stewart and men like W.E.B. DuBois, whose work of "cultural social analysis," according to ethnic studies scholar Johnella Butler, claimed the right to articulate a sense of self and act on it.[2] Contemporary women of color have continued this legacy by locating ideas that explore the intersections of race, gender, ethnicity, and sexuality at the center of their thinking about their own lives and those of women, men and families of color (Baca Zinn & Dill, 1994; Collins, 1998, 2000; Crenshaw, 1993a and b; Davis, 1983; Anzaldua, 1999; Dill, 1983; hooks, 1992; Moraga & Anzaldua, 2002; Hull, Bell Scott, & Smith, 2003). Intersectionality is a product of seeking to have our voices heard and lives acknowledged.

Although considerable ground work for this kind of scholarship was laid first in the fields of ethnic and women's studies—areas that perhaps have the longest published record of grappling with these issues—as this body of ideas and knowledge grew and developed, new ways of thinking, which were emerging in other fields, began to influence one another, broadening the intellectual appeal and practical applicability of intersectional approaches to questions of identity and social life.

In addition to its academic and intellectual concerns, intersectional scholarship matters outside the academy because day-to-day life and lived experience is the primary domain in which the conceptualization and understanding of these constructs is and has been grounded. Scholars emphasize that the work itself grew out of movements with a social justice agenda such as those focused on civil rights, women's rights, and the struggles to include ethnic studies within university curricula. Thus this work is not seen as emanating solely from a series of linked theoretical propositions but from an effort to improve society, in part, by understanding and explaining the lives and experiences of marginalized people and by examining the constraints and demands of the many social structures that influence their options and opportunities. For example, rather than think that one could understand the responses of young Black women to hip-hop music merely through an analysis that focuses on race, an intersectional framework would analyze the relationships among sexuality, gender, class, and popular culture, within an historical as well as a contemporary framework, in order to shed light on this phenomenon (Crenshaw, 1993a; Rose, 1994; Morgan, 1999; Pough, 2004).

One point of general agreement among intersectional scholars is that the experiences and texts of traditionally marginalized groups were not considered knowledge thirty years ago. Yet the writings, ideas, experiences, and perspectives of people whose lives were once considered unimportant are increasingly influencing traditional disciplines. In the field of sociology, for example, intersectional analysis has extended and combined traditional subareas of stratification, race and ethnicity, and family by drawing on conflict theory, theories of racialization (Omi & Winant, 1994; Oliver & Shapiro, 1995; Massey & Denton, 1993) and gender stratification (Lorber, 1994, 1998; Gardiner, 2002; Kimmel, 2000; Myers, Anderson, & Risman, 1998). These subareas, combined with ideas drawn from ethnic studies, critical legal theory, and postmodernism, explore the ways identity flows from and is entangled in those relationships and how systems of inequality (race, ethnicity, class, gender, physical ability, and sexuality) are embedded in and shape one another. Intersectionality is both a reflection of and influence upon some of the newer directions in fields such as history, sociology, legal studies, and anthropology to name a few. It does this by examining relationships and interactions between multiple axes of identity and multiple dimensions of social organization—at the same time.

Throughout this book, we treat intersectionality as an analytical strategy—a systematic approach to understanding human life and behavior that is rooted in the experiences and struggles of marginalized people. The premises and assumptions that underlie this approach are: inequalities derived from race, ethnicity, class, gender, and their intersections place specific groups of the population in a privileged position with respect to other groups and offer individuals unearned benefits based solely on group membership; historical and systemic patterns of disinvestment in nonprivileged groups are major contributors to the low social and economic position of those groups; representations of groups and individuals in media, art, music, and other cultural forms create and sustain ideologies of group and individual inferiority/superiority and support the use of these factors to explain both individual and group behavior; and individual identity exists within and draws from a web of socially defined statuses some of which may be more salient than others in specific situations or at specific historical moments.

As Weber (2001) points out, intersectional analysis operates on two levels: at the individual level, it reveals the way the intermeshing of these systems creates a broad range of opportunities for the expression and performance of individual identities. At the societal/structural level, it reveals the ways systems of power are implicated in the development, organization, and maintenance of inequalities and social injustice. In both writing and teaching, scholars engaged in this work are challenged to think in complex and nuanced ways about identity and to look at both the points of cohesion and fracture within groups (Dill & Johnson, 2002; Weber, 2001) as they seek to capture and convey dynamic social processes in which individual identities and group formations grow and shift in continuous interaction with one another, within specific historical periods and geographic locations.

Additionally intersectional analysis provides an important lens for reframing and creating new knowledge because it asserts new ways of studying power and inequality and challenges conventional understandings of oppressed and excluded groups and individuals. Collins (2000) in her discussion of Black feminist thought as critical social theory states:

> For African American women, the knowledge gained at intersecting oppressions of race, class and gender, provides the stimulus for crafting and passing on the subjugated knowledge of Black women's critical social theory. As a historically oppressed group, U.S. Black women have produced social thought designed to oppose oppression.

Thus, to use Collins's language, intersectional analysis is a tool that reveals the subjugated knowledges of people of color and produces social thought that can be considered critical social theory. One of the key ways this is accomplished is through the unveiling of power in interconnected structures of inequality/Intersectional analysis explores and unpacks relations of domination and subordination, privilege and agency, in the structural arrangements through which various services, resources, and other social rewards are delivered; in the interpersonal experiences of individuals and groups; in the practices that characterize and sustain bureaucratic hierarchies; and in the ideas, images, symbols and ideologies that shape social consciousness (Collins, 2000)/It is characterized by the following four theoretical interventions: (1) Placing the lived experiences and struggles of people of color and other marginalized groups as a starting point for the development of theory; (2) Exploring the complexities not only of individual identities but also group identity, recognizing that variations within groups are often ignored and essentialized; (3) Unveiling the ways interconnected domains of power organize and structure inequality and oppression; and (4) Promoting social justice and social change by linking research and practice to create a holistic approach to the eradication of disparities and to changing social and higher education institutions.

Intersectionality's Theoretical Interventions

Centering the Experiences of People of Color

The intersectional approach to the study of inequality, as it has developed in U.S. social thought, is rooted in illuminating the complexities of race and ethnicity as it intersects with other dimensions of difference. In doing this, the multiple and intersectional influences of these characteristics become clear. For example, for African American men and women, if we begin with their own understandings of the ways race is used to limit their life choices and chances, we see that opportunity is not just structured by race, but by the confluence of race, class, gender, and other dimensions of difference. Similarly the opportunity for a college preparatory K–12 education is influenced by one's race but also by class position in the society and within that racial group, as well as by gender and the perceptions and expectations of one's gender based on class, race, region, ability, and so on. (A low-income woman from Appalachia, who is White, faces a different set of opportunities and constraints on the path to a college degree than a middle-income woman who is White and living in New York City.)

As discussed earlier, intersectional knowledge is distinctive knowledge generated by the experiences of previously excluded communities and multiply oppressed groups. It tells, interprets, and analyzes the stories of Black, Latino/a,[3] Asian American, and Native American Indian women and/or of gay men, lesbians, and transgender people of all racial and ethnic groups in the United States.[4] It is knowledge based upon and derived from what intersectional scholars have called the "outsider-within," "subaltern," and "borderland"[5] voices of society, creating counterhistories and counternarratives to those based primarily on the experiences of social elites/ Importantly this approach focuses on the relationships of opportunity and constraint created by the dimensions of inequality so that racism, for example, is analyzed not only in terms of the constraints it produces in the lives of people of color but also in terms of the privileges it creates for Whites./

An example can be found in some of the earliest work in what has come to be termed "Whiteness studies." Other scholars (Frankenberg, 1993; Waters, 1990; Brodkin, 1998; Lipsitz, 1998; Roediger, 1991) have extended the concept of race to Whites and revealed the unacknowledged privilege that is derived from White skin, a privilege that is taken for granted and remains invisible.

Complicating Identity

Both individual and group identity are complex—influenced and shaped not simply by a person's race, class, ethnicity, gender, physical ability, sexuality, religion, or nationality—but by a combination of all of those characteristics. Nevertheless, in a hierarchically organized society, some statuses are more valued than others. Within groups, there is far greater diversity than appears when, for analytical purposes people are classified with a single term.

For example, the term Latino/a—as a gendered, ethnic, and racial construct—is interconnected with multiple discourses on social stratification and political/national identity. Its meaning varies depending on the social context in which it is employed and the political meanings associated with its usage.

The term Latino/a challenges the privileging of Spanish or Hispanic lineage over the other indigenous and African lineages of Spanish-speaking individuals in the United States. Nevertheless Latino/a as a social construct needs to be problematized because its underlying political discourse seeks to disrupt "neat" categories of what is now perceived as the Latino or brown race. Thus, by homogenizing all Latino/as into one category, the discourse on national identity is dismissed and the effects of the intersection of race, ethnic subgroup, and socioeconomic status on Latinas are overlooked.[6]

Identity for Latinos, African Americans, Asian, and Native Americans, is complicated by differences in national origin or tribal group, citizenship, class (both within the sending and host countries—for recent migrants), gender as well as race and ethnicity. A contemporary example is found in the controversy surrounding whether or not Black students who migrated from Africa or the West Indies to the United States should be permitted to take advantage of scholarships designed for historically underrepresented African Americans. In several articles it has been argued that in their pursuit of diversity, universities have redefined the original remedies of civil rights law to include immigrant Africans and Afro-Caribbean's as substitutes for native born African American Blacks (Guinier, 2004; Bell, 2004). An intersectional approach necessitates acknowledging such intragroup differences in order to address them.

Unveiling Power in Interconnected Structures of Inequality

Collins, in *Black Feminist Thought* (2000, 275) conveys a complex understanding of power by describing it as *both* a force that some groups use to oppress others *and* "an intangible entity that operates throughout a society and is organized in particular domains." This complex notion of power provides tools for examining the ways that people experience inequalities are organized and maintained through four interrelated domains:

1. the structural domain, which consists of the institutional structures of the society including government, the legal system, housing patterns, economic traditions, and educational structure;
2. the disciplinary domain, which consists of the ideas and practices that characterize and sustain bureaucratic hierarchies;
3. the hegemonic domain, which consists of the images, symbols, ideas, and ideologies that shape social consciousness (Collins, 2000).
4. the interpersonal domain, which consists of patterns of interaction between individuals and groups.

Intersectional analyses, as knowledge generated from and about oppressed groups, unveil these domains of power and reveal how oppression is constructed and maintained through multiple aspects of identity simultaneously. Understanding these aspects of power draws on knowledge of the historical legacies of people who have experienced inequality due to discriminatory practices and policies based on combinations of race, class, gender, ethnicity, and other dimensions of difference. Because arrangements of power shift and change over time and in different cultural contexts, individuals and groups experience oppression and inequalities differently according to their social, geographic, historical, and cultural location (Weber, 2001).

STRUCTURAL POWER. Within the structural domain, we are particularly interested in the ways "institutions are organized to reproduce subordination over time" (Collins, 2000, 277). In U.S. history, people of color have been controlled by policies in every institution of the society. These included, but are not limited to, racial segregation, exclusion acts, internment, forced relocation, denial of the right to own property, and denial of the right to marry and form stable families. Within each of these forms of institutional subordination, the various categories intersect to provide distinctive experiences for groups of individuals.

For example, in a recent essay using an intersectional approach to Latina health, we argue that the location of health services in relationship to low-income Latino communities structures access to healthcare and is a major factor affecting the health of Latino women, children, and families. The distribution of governmental resources, ranging from funding for research to the provision of public health services, is examined in terms of historical patterns and political considerations, which have led to a concentration of health resources in middle- and upper-income communities and the prioritization of research on diseases and illnesses, which are more prevalent in those populations (Zambrana & Dill, 2006).

Intersectional analysis also directs us to look at structural inequities by examining questions of social and economic justice, both to reveal the sources of these inequities and to begin to redress them. Poverty is primarily the result of the unequal distribution of society's goods and resources and the concentration of wealth in the hands of a few. When one examines the interaction of poverty with race/ethnicity and gender, it is apparent that these factors, taken together, have a disproportionately negative effect on people of color, especially women (Higginbotham & Romero, 1997; Williams & Collins, 1995), and result in an over concentration of detrimental social, economic, and political outcomes for them and their families.

Race, ethnicity, and geography matter, as they are all determinants of access to social capital or social resources (Massey & Denton, 1993).[7] Intersectional analysis draws attention to the policies, practices, and outcomes of institutional racism and discrimination, one result of which is the concentration of low-income people of color in resource poor neighborhoods with poorly financed and underdeveloped public systems such as schools and public health services.

DISCIPLINARY POWER. In addition to formal policies or the location of resources away from some communities, intersectional analyses draw attention to the bureaucratic practices that perpetuate and maintain inequality. Linda Gordon, in her book: *Pitied but Not Entitled: Single Mothers and the History of Welfare, 1890–1935* (1994) provides an analysis that illustrates the intertwining of structural and disciplinary power. The book focuses upon the ways in which U.S. social welfare policies and their implementation have resulted in the impoverishment of single mothers. Gordon's history outlines the development during the New Deal of a two-tier welfare system; a nationally supported social insurance system of generous benefits for workers who were disproportionately White and male, and a poorly funded, state supported system of "means-tested" morally evaluated benefits for those who were irregularly employed, a disproportionate number of whom were women and minorities. In her telling of this story, Gordon reveals the behind the scenes politics, rivalries, and values within the Children's Bureau in which "feminist" social workers of the progressive era became the advocates of a system of maternal and child health that gave primacy to women's role as mother and advocated for states to implement these policies. An unintended consequence was that the primary program for single mothers, Aid to Families with Dependent Children (AFDC), became subject to state politics and local bureaucratic practices. It was, therefore, more likely to be governed by state legislation that openly discriminated on the basis of race or immigrant status and to bureaucratic practices that gave or denied benefits on the basis of morality, political loyalty, and the value judgments of individual caseworkers.

In sum, Gordon's work shows how disciplinary power administered through case workers at the national and state levels combined with structural power organized in state and federal legislation shaped historical patterns of racial and gender relations within the U.S. system of social welfare. This example is repeated throughout the society not only in public welfare systems but across all public systems including education, housing, and employment.

HEGEMONIC POWER. Hegemonic power refers to the cultural ideologies, images, and representations that shape group and individual consciousness and support or justify policies and practices in the structural and disciplinary domains. Through the manipulation of ideology it links social institutions—structural power, organizational practices—disciplinary power, and everyday experiences—interpersonal power (Collins, 2000, 284). These ideas influence the ways members of various social groups are viewed and depicted in the society at large and the expectations associated with these depictions (hooks, 1992; Chin & Humikowski, 2002; Zambrana, Mogel, & Scrimshaw, 1987). Intersectional analyses challenge us to interrogate those ideologies and representations, to locate and uncover their origins and multiple meanings, and to examine the reasons for their existence and persistence.

For example, dominant representations of people of color build upon and elaborate ideas, images, and stereotypes that are deeply rooted in American history and become the rationale for the differential treatment of groups and individuals (Portes, 2000). In the case of Latinas, scholars have argued that stereotypes of Latinas as aliens, hypersexual, exotic, and passive promote the myth that they need to be controlled by state institutions through such policies as those that deny prenatal care or force sterilization. These false representations affect not only the ways dominant culture healthcare providers treat their Latina patients but the kinds of public policies that are designed to determine access to healthcare. (Silliman, et al., 2004, 216).

Welfare reform provides another example of the ways stereotypes and representations affect social policies, access to services, and the location of groups within the social structure. An essay written by Dill, Baca Zinn, and Patton examines this issue in depth. This essay demonstrates that representations of single motherhood as the cause of delinquency, crime, violence, abandonment, abuse, and gangs and depictions of single mothers as self-centered, freeloading, idle, and sexually promiscuous, have been nationally linked to Black women, Latinas—especially on the West Coast and in the Mexican border states—and Native American women in the West. These representations have been used to justify welfare reform strategies specifically designed to promote work and decrease childbirth among low-income women. In the essay we argue that a major source of the power and appeal of welfare reform was its effort to discipline and control the behavior of Black women, other women of color, and by example, White women (1999).

These stereotypes exist, are interpreted, understood, and reinscribed within larger social and historical narratives that have a long history in U.S. society. Another example discussed at length in the Dill, Baca Zinn, and Patton essay cited above, relies heavily on scholar Rickie Solinger's book, *Wake up Little Susie: Single Pregnancy and Race before* Roe v. Wade (1992).

According to Solinger, social services available to pregnant single women in the post–World War II era were strikingly dissimilar based on race. Young, White, middle-class women who got pregnant during this era were typically sent to homes for unwed mothers far away from their communities where they were heavily counseled that giving up their children for adoption and "forgetting" the experience was the only psychologically acceptable thing to do (Cole & Donley, 1990; Solinger, 1992). During this same time period, however, she shows that African American women were excluded from most homes for unwed mothers on the basis of race, and there were very few all-Black homes. In contrast to White women, African American women went virtually unserved in the child welfare system. Black women were frequently turned away from adoption agencies (Day, 1979) and directed to public welfare departments. Thus the stereotype of the Black welfare mother was both drawn on and enforced by policies that limited African American women's access to social resources while maintaining the myth of White moral superiority (Dill, Baca Zinn, & Patton, 1999).

/INTERPERSONAL POWER/ Interpersonal power refers to "routinized, day-to-day practices of how people treat one another. Such practices are systematic, recurrent and so familiar that they often go unnoticed." They have been referred to as everyday racism or everyday sexism, etc. and are powerful "in the production and reinforcement of the status quo" (Collins, 2000, 287; Bonilla Silva, 2006, 26; Essed, 1991). Everyday racism is entwined with the implementation of disciplinary and hegemonic power. It is exemplified in the simple acts of referring to White men as "men" and men of color with a racial modifier in news reports; or reports by White women of experiencing feelings of threat or fear when encountering a Black man on the street in the evening.

In her book, *Understanding Everyday Racism*, Essed analyzes interviews with fifty-five women of African descent in the Netherlands and the United States who recount experiences of everyday racism. She argues that these accounts are not ad hoc stories but have a specific structure with several recurring elements and reflect the fact that Whites in the Netherlands and the United States have very different and narrower definitions of racism than Blacks. For Whites, racism is seen as extreme beliefs or actions that endorse White supremacy. For Blacks, the emphasis is on a wide variety of actions including White supremacy as well as Eurocentrism, avoidance of contact with other ethnic groups, underestimating the abilities of minorities, and passive tolerance of racist behavior by others.

Within intersectional analyses, unveiling the workings of power, which is understood as both pervasive and oppressive, is vitally important. It reveals both the sources of inequality and its multiple and often conflicting manifestations. It provides a way to examine how different identity markers overlay or intersect with one another at all levels of social relations (structural/institutional/ideological/macro and interpersonal/everyday/micro) in different historical and geographical, contexts (Collins, 1998; Crenshaw, 1993b; Weber, 2001).

Promoting Social Justice and Social Change

Grounded in the everyday lives of people of diverse backgrounds, intersectional knowledge reveals the various impacts of the presence of racial and gender disparities, and is a critical first step toward eliminating inequality. The social justice agenda of the intersectional approach is inextricably linked to its

utility in unveiling power. It also provides an analytical framework for combining the different kinds of work that need to be included in the pursuit of
social justice: advocacy, analysis, policy development, theorizing, and education. Because intersectional work validates the lives and stories of previously
ignored groups of people, it is seen as a tool that can be used to help empower
communities and the people in them. Implicitly the production of this knowledge offers the potential for creating greater understanding among groups
of people.

The Declaration of the NGO (nongovernmental) Forum of the UN Conference on Racism in 2001 included in its opening statement the following under
the topic gender:

> 119. An intersectional approach to discrimination acknowledges that
> every person be it man or woman exists in a framework of multiple
> identities, with factors such as race, class, ethnicity, religion, sexual ori-
> entation, gender identity, age, disability, citizenship, national identity,
> geopolitical context, health, including HIV/AIDS status and any other
> status are all determinants in one's experiences of racism, racial dis-
> crimination, xenophobia and related intolerances. An intersectional
> approach highlights the way in which there is a simultaneous interac-
> tion of discrimination as a result of multiple identities. (Declaration &
> Programme of Action, 2001)

This statement, in an international document that begins with an assessment of the contemporary circumstances of discrimination in a global context
and continues by laying out a program of action that individual nation-states
are encouraged to follow is an excellent example of the ways the ideas of intersectionality are linked to social action. In this case, the statement about gender immediately links gender issues to a variety of other issues for which
specific action steps are delineated. In effect, it is argued that gender, as part
of a complex set of relationships, must be also considered within each of the
concerns delineated in the plan of action.

A second example of the link between intersectional thinking, social justice, and social change is the work of LatCrit. LatCrit, Latina and Latino Critical Legal Theory, Inc., describes itself as "an intellectual and social community
of people engaged in critical 'outsider jurisprudence' that centers Latino/as in
all of their diversity." One of its goals is "to develop a critical, activist, and
interdisciplinary discourse on law and policy toward Latinas/os and to foster
both the development of coalitional theory and practice as well as the accessi-
bility of this knowledge to agents of social and legal transformation" (www
.LatCrit.org). To accomplish these goals, LatCrit supports projects at a number
of law schools around the country. One project that exemplifies the link
between theory and activism is the Community Development Externship

Network, "an experiential learning project designed to provide legal assistance to local communities or activists working on social justice efforts in rural and urban sites in the U.S. and the Americas. Central to this project is that students are engaged in the work of securing material remedies to social injustices suffered both by groups and individuals, including land reclamation projects and other kinds of reparations-oriented efforts."

In conclusion, transformation of knowledge and of individual lives is a fundamental aspect of intersectional work. Strong commitments and desires to create more equitable societies that recognize and validate differences drive the research of scholars and the practice of activists. Among these scholars, discussions of social change focus not just on changing the society at large but also on changing structures of knowledge within institutions of higher learning and the relationship of colleges and universities to the society (see chapter 10). *Transformative* is perhaps one of the best words to characterize this scholarship because it is seen not only as transforming knowledge but using knowledge to transform society.

Emerging Intersections: The Anthology

This anthology is a collection of previously unpublished essays that showcase the innovative contributions that an intersectional lens can provide in expanding our understanding of: (1) how inequality shapes the lives of people of color, particularly historically underrepresented groups; (2) the ways public policies reinforce existing systems of inequality; and (3) how research and teaching using an intersectional perspective compels scholars to become agents of change within institutions. Though intersectional work has taken form in many disciplines, in this volume we examine its forms and utility predominantly from a social science perspective. The chapters here use a wide variety of social science methodological approaches to provide complex and nuanced analyses of social life through an intersectional lens. Multiple methods are represented in the volume as chapters are based on interviews, quantitative data analyses, policy analyses, syntheses, and review of empirical literature, case studies, and program evaluations.

Chapters 2 through 4 of this book provide illustrations of hegemonic power—the cultural ideologies, images, and representations that shape group and individual consciousness and support or justify the policies and practices in the structural and disciplinary domains (Collins, 2000). The majority of these articles also historicizes the topic under study and illuminates the persistent patterns of inequality in the fabric of U.S. society. The actual lived experiences of poor people and people of color are framed within an historical context as well as within their specific geographic, economic, or social locations. The authors present examples of how policy and institutional practices continue to maintain power relations of domination and subordination. They also demonstrate that the intersections of education, race, and ethnicity, and inferior public services are a result of unequal allocation of resources and stereotypic attitudes that maintain people of color in subordinate positions. These chapters reiterate in specific detail the argument that gender, race/ethnicity, and class are mutually constituted systems of power, which have material consequences in both public sector systems and social interactions (Baca Zinn & Dill, 1996; Steinbugler, Press, & Dias, 2006).

In chapter 2, Elizabeth Higginbotham examines the experiences of Black women lawyers in their transition from law school to professional employment and describes the structural barriers these women experience that shape their options and opportunities. She illustrates how race profoundly shaped the professional lives of Black lawyers by placing her contemporary findings in the context of a legacy of exclusion and racism in the law profession that was present throughout much of the twentieth century and continues today. Her study of Black women lawyers provides insight into how they negotiate discriminatory barriers of both race and gender in the past and the present, but also how their professional work impacts the Black community and the wider society. Higginbotham illuminates the institutional and bureaucratic practices that create a network of restrictions and differences in treatment, so that law schools themselves function differently and racial minorities face more hurdles to paid employment as attorneys because of representational issues combined with a lack of mentoring and networks that can be translated into human and social capital. Thus they are less likely to launch and sustain a solid private practice and encounter more difficulty in securing employment after graduation due to the combined effect of racial and gender biases. In effect, Black women lawyers are concentrated in public sector locations, where prestige and economic remuneration are much lower than in corporations and major private law firms.

Negative representations of race and class have heightened visibility in the discourse on poverty. In chapter 3, Henderson and Tickamyer interrogate the racialization of poverty as it is entrenched in public systems in rural Appalachia. Using an intersectional framework that examines the relationships between race, class, gender, space, and culture, the authors argue that poverty remains firmly entrenched as a Black and White issue, both literally and metaphorically. In their paper, the authors examine one group—poor White Appalachian women—as an entry point into deconstructing discourses of poverty and welfare policy in the United States. They discuss the complexity of the poverty discourse so as to expand understanding of the multiplicities of poverty identities, locations, and control mechanisms; and to show how the existence of this complexity nevertheless reinforces the welfare racism that underlies poverty discourse in the United States.

In the fourth chapter, Zambrana and McDonald describe the reported experiences of Mexican American women who had completed higher education in the period 1969–1980 and compare these experiences to African American and non-Hispanic White women. They examine institutional arrangements in higher education since the early twentieth century and how these arrangements have resulted in "staggered inequalities" for women by race and ethnicity. The major argument in this chapter is that for racialized women (Mexican American and African American) the race/gender imagery places them at a disadvantage from early on in their school experiences and this disadvantage is reinforced throughout their higher education experiences. For Mexican American women, multiple subordinate locations in the gender, class, and cultural hierarchies increase the material consequences of their educational disadvantage relative to other women in U.S. society.

Chapters 5 through 9 identify and discuss major contemporary social problems and their association with institutional and bureaucratic policies and practices in education, welfare reform, and political participation. They demonstrate how an intersectional analytic approach can be used to contextualize disparities within the larger matrix of power relations and formulate clear solutions at the social, community, and individual level. These chapters are most exemplary of disciplinary power, which can be viewed as the ways in which formal policies such as the location of resources outside some communities are reinforced through bureaucratic practices that perpetuate and maintain inequality. This set of articles interrogates hegemonic and disciplinary power and contests the practices that maintain dominant culture ideologies and reinforce the marginalization of people of color through specific practices in four public systems: welfare, education, employment, and civic participation. The analyses yield promising practices that support antidiscriminatory and social justice outcomes.

Gatta's major thesis, in chapter 5, is that employment in the U.S. labor market does not always translate into economic self-sufficiency, especially for marginalized groups. The author explores workforce development by addressing two broad research questions: What are the challenges single mothers confront in attaining education and training via public sector initiatives? Specifically, how do race, class, and marital status intersect with gender to limit the access of women to public sector education and training? The second question examines how the Workforce Investment Act (WIA) conceptualized single, working-poor mothers and addressed their employment and training needs. Using a case study from New Jersey, Gatta illustrates how a job training policy can be reconceptualized by attending to the multiple dimensions of women's lives in order provide real access to education and training for low wage working women.

For employed women, access to benefits is central to the economic viability of workers and their families. In chapter 6, Manuel and Zambrana examine how race, ethnicity, and class affect the employment benefit decisions that new mothers make following childbirth. Using a sample from the National Longitudinal Survey of Youth, the authors examine variations among low-wage earners who are generally assumed to have the strongest economic incentive to return promptly to work after childbirth and who are the targets of public policy efforts to encourage them to stay in the workforce. When the decision to return to work after childbirth is examined, family, economic status, and employment level variables are found to be the most important determinants. The data confirm that low-income mothers tend to take shorter leaves, are substantially less likely to have access to work supports, and particularly lack those supports that address work and family conflicts. Women with less than one year on the job (a likely circumstance for many low-income women "transitioning" off of public assistance programs) take the shortest maternity leave of all socioeconomic groups. Another finding showed that flexible hour benefits have a more dramatic impact in terms of increasing the length of leave taken by low-income mothers than maternity leave benefits. These study findings confirm that the conditions of women's lives when combined with institutional arrangements in the workplace are especially germane to women's decisions to return to work after childbirth. Given recent policy attention aimed at shaping the fertility and employment decisions of low-income women, these findings are particularly important. Further they give credence to the notion that "one-size" policies do not "fit all." That is, policies that seek to help all mothers are likely to engender a host of unintended and/or deleterious effects for different subgroups.

This insight is most evident in the implementation of the Personal Responsibility and Work Opportunity Reconciliation Act of 1996 that is discussed in chapter 7. Jones-DeWeever, Dill, and Schram seek to answer an important question regarding why people of color have become a larger proportion of the welfare caseload since the implementation of this welfare reform policy. What kinds of opportunities enhance women's successful transition from welfare to self-sufficiency? The authors review studies on the relationship between racial, ethnic, and gender disparities and access to jobs and education for welfare recipients and reveal how historical patterns of racial, ethnic, and gender discrimination result in disparities that have restructured the relationship of the welfare population to the rest of the poor. The major findings show differential treatment of welfare recipients across race and ethnicity: White recipients were more likely than their Black counterparts to receive subsidized childcare, transportation assistance, and assistance to pursue postsecondary education. Among recipients that were able to make that transition from welfare to paid employment, non-Hispanic Whites were most likely to receive critical supports such as healthcare, housing, and transportation assistance.

In chapter 8, Dance examines the characteristics of school drop-outs and conditions under which students are more likely to stay in school or be "pushed out." Her main argument is that class-based measures of dropout rates do, indeed, reveal that regardless of race or ethnicity, students from low-income backgrounds are more likely to dropout of school than their more affluent counterparts. But dropout scenarios may become graver still when race, ethnicity, gender, or other social locations intersect with class. The author examines how the intersections of multiple social locations render students from ethnic minority and low-income backgrounds vulnerable to early school leaving. Strategies to promote equality in the school system include what she labels "the 4 C's": more investment of resources (cash); more understanding and caring by teachers (care); more computer technology (computers); and more coalitions of parents (coalitions).

A major claim among mainstream scholars is that parental involvement of low-income families in schools and society would enhance their children's life choices and options and increase their integration into mainstream society. Yet as Frasure and Williams demonstrate in chapter 9, social barriers to civic and political participation at multiple levels of society are deeply embedded in the fabric of society and restrict the ways in which racial, ethnic, and class groups can engage in civic activity. The authors examine how well the United States has overcome its dismal exclusionary past in the areas of political participation and civic engagement. This thoughtful, thorough, and synthetic review of key concepts and literature details what is known about disparities in civic and political participation within a racially and ethnically specific historical context. By centering the experiences of people of color, innovations and promising practices for eradicating civic and political disparities among the nation's racial and ethnic minority groups are straightforwardly developed and presented. The authors expertly intersect policy and research and propose specific practices to decrease and eliminate civic and political disparities.

Knowledge production, and its application to individual, group, and societal problems, has an important role in shaping the attitudes of future generations as well as policymakers. The final three chapters of the book engage the discourse on the production and transmission of knowledge and its role in bringing about social change and social justice in institutions of higher learning. Nonhegemonic knowledge production is a strategy of resistance and challenges the power of institutions to "do business as usual." How these new knowledges are produced and legitimated, who the thought-leaders are and what barriers they face in gaining acceptance of these innovations are used to explain the possibilities and limits of change in institutions of higher learning and to illuminate how persistent patterns of inequality in the United States are replicated in the academy.

Dill, in chapter 10, draws on insights around knowledge production and institution building garnered through a series of conversations with intersectional scholars in academic locations across the country. Common themes found in the conversations include: the importance of institutional support as demonstrated in hiring, retention, and promotion; the costs and benefits of leadership for scholars of color; the role of alliances, networks, and multiple affiliations in promoting this work; and the need for programmatic resources to sustain and enhance this scholarship and reinforce its place in teaching and curriculum transformation. The author concludes that transformation in higher education institutions usually involves the building of alternative institutions within the larger institution. Yet these alternative spaces are often marginalized enclaves, with little or no institutional identity. Lessons and barriers to including this perspective in research and teaching in higher education institutions and strategies on affirmative college and university practices are discussed.

In chapter 11, Dill, Zambrana, and McLaughlin use a case study approach to illustrate the ways that institution building, intellectual collaboration, and mentoring can contribute to transforming a particular institution of higher education. Multiple methods were used including oral history, review of documents, and interviews with affiliated faculty of the Consortium on Race, Gender and Ethnicity (CRGE) at the University of Maryland, subject of the study. The emergence of CRGE is discussed within the institutional history of race relations. Also, its role as a mechanism for helping to implement the university's mission and goals around diversity as a project designed to integrate and coordinate diverse theoretical and pedagogical perspectives as well as mentoring activities to improve the educational pipeline for historically underrepresented graduate students and faculty of color is explored. The findings confirm the themes articulated in chapter 10 by intersectional scholars nationwide: that institutional support needs to move beyond short-term funding of units which remain marginalized and financially unstable but must be part of a broad commitment on the part of colleges and universities to transforming their cultures of power to be truly inclusive of diverse perspectives and identities.

The concluding chapter by Zambrana and Dill engages the numerous critical debates and major intellectual challenges about the scope, purpose, place, meaning, and future of intersectional analyses. It engages arguments about the rigidity of intersectional categories, its limited use as an analytical construct, its relationship to identity studies, and claims that it privileges race and presumes a hierarchy of oppressions. It also examines the contribution of intersectionality to the new scholarship on queer/sexuality, globalization, and Latino/a and Asian Pacific Islanders and critical race theory. As an emerging lens, the foundational construct of intersectional analysis is the unveiling of hegemonic power and the ways in which it historically and currently maintains subordinate groups.

NOTES

1. Throughout this book we often use the term "ethnic studies" to refer to the group of departments and programs that include African American (Black) studies, Chicano (Mexican American) studies, Puerto Rican studies, American Indian studies, and Asian American studies. In some institutions all of these programs are combined into a department called American Ethnic Studies. In other universities some exist as separate departments.

2. Johnella Butler, Spelman College, personal communication.

3. The term Latina/o is used interchangeably with Hispanics, consistent with federal standards. Under the category of Hispanic/Latino are included persons of Spanish-speaking origin from the Spanish-speaking Caribbean, Central America, Mexico, and Latin America. Hispanics/Latinos may be of any race and/or mixed race but have a preference for identifying with their national origin.

4. Examples include: E. N. Glenn, *Unequal Citizens*; R. Ferguson, *Aberrations in Black*, P. Hondagneu-Sotelo, *Domestica*, Audre Lorde, *Sister Outsider*, P. H. Collins, *Black Feminist Thought*, A. Hurtado, *The Color of Privilege*, among many others.

5. These terms are drawn from the work of Patricia Hill Collins, Gayatri Spivak, and Gloria Anzaldua, respectively.

6. For an excellent historical account of the role of race and class and exclusionary racial practices in the United States and Latin American countries, see C. E. Rodriguez, 2000.

7. Social capital broadly refers to access to resources that improve educational, economic, and social position in society (Bourdieu, 1985; Ellen & Turner, 1997).

References

Anzaldua, G. (1999). *Borderlands La Frontera: The New Mestiza*. Second edition. San Francisco: Aunt Lute Book.

Baca Zinn, M., & Dill, B. T. (Eds.). (1994). *Women of Color in U.S. Society*. Philadelphia: Temple University Press.

Bell, D. (2004, April 2). The Real Lessons of a "Magnificent Mirage." *Chronicle of Higher Education*.

Brodkin, K. (1998). *How Jews Became White Folks and What That Says about Race in America*. New Brunswick, NJ: Rutgers University Press.

Bonilla Silva, E. (2006). *Racism without Racists: Color-Blind Racism and the Persistence of Racial Inequality in the United States*. Second Edition. Lanham: Rowman & Littlefield Publishers, Inc.

Bourdieu, P. (1985). The Social Space and the Genesis of Groups. *Social Science Information, 24*(2), 195–220.

Chin, M. H., & Humikowski, C. A. (2002). When is Risk Stratification by Race or Ethnicity Justified in Medical Care? *Academic Medicine, 77*(3), 202–208.

Cole, E. S., & Donley, K. S. (1990). History, Values, and Placement Policy Issues in Adoption. In D. M. Brodzinsky & M. Schechter (Eds.), *The Psychology of Adoption*. New York: Oxford University Press, 273–294.

Collins, P. H. (2000). *Black Feminist Thought: Knowledge, Consciousness, and the Politics of Empowerment*. New York: Routledge Press.

Collins, P. H. (1998). *Fighting Words: Black Women and The Search for Justice*. Minneapolis: University of Minnesota Press.

Crenshaw, K. W. (1993a). Beyond Racism and Misogyny: Black Feminism and 2 Live Crew. In M. J. Matsuda, K. W. Crenshaw, R. Delgado, & C. R. Lawrence (Eds.), *Words That Wound: Critical Race Theory, Assaultive Speech, and the First Amendment*. Boulder, Colorado: Westview Press.

Crenshaw, K. W. (1993b). Mapping the Margins: Intersectionality, Identity Politics, and Violence against Women. *Stanford Law Review, 43*, 1241–1299.

Davis, A. (1983). *Women, Race, and Class*. New York: Vintage Books.

Day, C. (1979). Access to Birth Records: General Register Office Study. *Adoption and Fostering, 98*, 17–28.

Dill, B. T. (1983). Race, Class and Gender: Prospects for an All-Inclusive Sisterhood. *Feminist Studies, 9*(1), 131–150.

Dill, B. T. (1994) *Across the Boundaries of Race and Class and Exploration of Work and Family among Black Female Domestic Servants*. New York: Garland.

Dill, B. T., & Johnson, T. (2002). Between a Rock and a Hard Place: Mothering, Work, and Welfare in the Rural South. In S. Harley (Ed.), *Sister Circle: Black Women and Work*. New Brunswick, NJ: Rutgers University Press.

Dill, B. T., Baca Zinn, M., & Patton, S. L. (1999). Race, Family Values and Welfare Reform. In L. Kushnick & J. Jennings (Eds.), *A New Introduction to Poverty, The Role of Race, Power and Politics* (pp. 263–286). New York: New York University Press.

Ellen, I. G., & Turner, M. A. (1997). Does Neighborhood Matter? Assessing Recent Evidence. *Housing Policy Debate, 8*, 833–866.

Essed, P. (1991). *Understanding Everyday Racism: An Interdisciplinary Theory*. Thousand Oaks, CA: Sage.

Frankenberg, R. (1993). *White Women Race Matters: The Social Construction of Whiteness*. Minneapolis: University of Minnesota Press.

Guinier, L. (2004, June 24). Top Colleges Take More Blacks, but Which Ones? *New York Times* (Rimer & Arenson).

Gardiner, J. K. (Ed.). (2002). *Masculinity Studies and Feminist Theory: New Directions*. New York: Columbia University Press.

Gordon, L. (1994). *Pitied but Not Entitled: Single Mothers and the History of Welfare, 1890–1935*. New York: Free Press.

Higginbotham, E., & Romero, M. (Eds.). (1997). *Women and Work: Exploring Race, Ethnicity, and Class*. Thousand Oaks, CA: Sage.

hooks, b. (1992). *Black Looks: Race and Representation*. Boston: South End Press.

Hull, G. T., Bell S. P., & Smith, B. (Eds.). (2003). *All the Women are White, All the Blacks are Men, But Some of Us are Brave*. New York: The Feminist Press.

Kimmel, M. (2000). *The Gendered Society*. Oxford University Press.

LatCrit. (2006). Retrieved June 18, 2007, from www.arts.cornell.edu/latcrit/PortfolioOfProjects/ LCPortfolio9_29_2006.pdf.

Lipsitz, G. (1998). *The Possessive Investment in Whiteness*. Philadelphia: Temple University Press.

Lorber, J. (1994). *Paradoxes of Gender*. New Haven, CT: Yale University Press.

Lorber, J. (1998). *Gender Inequality: Feminist Theories and Politics*. Los Angeles: Roxbury.

Massey, D., & Denton, N. (1993). *American Apartheid*. Cambridge, MA: Harvard University Press.

Moraga, C., & Anzaldua, G. (2002). *This Bridge Called My Back: Writings by Radical Women of Color*. Third edition. Berkeley, CA: Third Woman Press.

Morgan, J. (1999). *When Chickenheads Come Home to Roost: My Life as a Hip-hop Feminist*. New York: Simon & Schuster.

Myers, K. A., Anderson, C. D., & Risman, B. J. (Eds.). (1998). *Feminist Foundations: Towards Transforming Sociology*. Thousand Oaks, CA: Sage Publications.

The Declaration and Programme of Action, NGO Forum of the United Nations World Conference against Racism, September 3, 2001.

Oliver, M., & Shapiro, T. M. (1995). *Black Wealth/White Wealth: A New Perspective on Racial Inequality*. New York: Routledge Press.

Omi, M., & Winant, H. (1994). *Racial Formation in the United States: From the 1960s to the 1990s*. Second edition. New York: Routledge Press.

Portes, A. (2000). The Resilient Significance of Class: A Nominalist Interpretation. *Political Power and Social Theory*, *14*, 249–284.

Pough, G. D. (2004) *Check It While I Wreck It: Black Womanhood, Hip-hop Culture, and the Public Sphere*. Boston: Northeastern University Press.

Roediger, D. R. (1991). *The Wages of Whiteness: Race and the Making of the American Working Class*. New York: Verso Books.

Rodriguez, C. E. (2000). *Changing Race: Latinos, The Census, and the History of Ethnicity in the United States*. New York: New York University Press.

Rose, T. (1994) *Black Noise: Rap Music and Black Culture in Contemporary America*. Hanover, NH: University Press of New England.

Silliman, J., Gerber Fried, M., Ross, L., & Gutierrez, R. (2004). *Undivided Rights: Women of Color Organize for Reproductive Justice*. Cambridge, MA: South End Press.

Solinger, R. (1992). *Wake up Little Susie: Single Pregnancy and Race Before Roe v. Wade*. New York: Routledge Press.

Spivak, G. (1988). Can the Subaltern Speak? In C. Nelson & L. Grossberg (Eds.), *Marxism and the Interpretation of Culture* (pp. 271–313). Chicago: University of Illinois Press.

Steinbugler, A., Press, J. E., & Dias, J. J. (2006). Gender, Race, and Affirmative Action: Operationalizing Intersectionality in Survey Research. *Gender & Society*, *20*, 805–825.

Waters, M. C. (1990). *Ethnic Options: Choosing Identities in America*. Berkeley: University of California Press.

Weber, L. (2001). *Understanding Race, Class, Gender, and Sexuality: A Conceptual Framework*. New York: McGraw-Hill Higher Education.

Williams, D., & Collins, C. (1995). US Socioeconomic and Racial Differences in Health: Patterns and Explanations. *Annual Review of Sociology*, *21*, 349–386.

Zambrana, R. E., & Dill, B. T. (2006). Disparities in Latina Health: An Intersectional Analysis. In A. J. Schulz & L. Mullings (Eds.), *Gender, Race Class & Health*. San Francisco, CA: Jossey-Bass.

Zambrana, R. E, Mogel, W., & Scrimshaw, S.C.M. (1987). Gender and Level of Training Differences in Obstetricians' Attitudes towards Patients in Childbirth. *Women & Health*, *12*(1), 5–24.

2

Entering a Profession

Race, Gender, and Class in the Lives of Black Women Attorneys

ELIZABETH HIGGINBOTHAM

In the era of Jim Crow, racial barriers limited the production of Black professionals, the spheres where they could operate, and their abilities to influence their fields. Have these trends changed in the post–civil rights era? This chapter looks at the historical record and interviews with Black women attorneys to examine their progress in the profession. I focus on the experience of Black women within the wider context of recent changes in the legal profession in the United States, particularly the expansion of large firms (thirty people or more) and declining percentages in solo practices (Heinz, et al., 2005). These trends only further complicate the entrance of Black women graduates of law school into the field. More knowledge is needed on the progress of Black women law school graduates and how they enter the mainstream of the legal profession. Given the legacy of biases in the practice of law, how are their race, gender, and social-class backgrounds important in their ability to enter this profession? I begin by looking at their educational experiences, and then examine the transition from law school to where and how they practice law to provide a context for understanding the meaning of their social characteristics. I am interested in uncovering how discrimination in the training and hiring of African American female law students has changed from outright exclusion to more subtle and pernicious forms that are increasingly difficult to measure and articulate.

Many scholars have written about the lives of Black men and women professionals in the age of segregation. Kevin Gaines (1996), Darlene Clark Hine (1989, 2003), Stephanie Shaw (1996), and Francille Wilson (2002, 2006), to name just a few, have documented how people faced the challenges of segregation, built careers, and worked to make a difference. These scholars provide me with key questions to explore as I examine changes after civil rights legislation that opened new doors, but did not eliminate inequalities in occupational placements, many of which continue to this day. We often use the language of either discrimination or choice to make sense of people's locations. This chapter advocates for a more complex understanding of how discrimination shapes choices that take into account the different sets of advantages and disadvantages that individuals face once they obtain their occupational training. This perspective gives more agency to the subjects, rather than assuming that everyone is choosing from the same set of options or that they have the same occupational goals.

Historical Background

Professions are occupations requiring skilled work that is often abstract in nature and requires advance schooling and licensure to enter. There are various barriers to entry into this exclusive group, where members are then governed by a code of ethics. Much scholarship on professions has looked at their development, the disputes between areas of expertise and how people maintain the boundaries or as Andrew Abbott (1988) notes, matters of jurisdiction in professions. These questions are separate from the actual task of earning a living in a profession. In the case of law, passing the bar and securing a position are two initial barriers to entering the profession. Professional training and securing the opportunity to practice law are distinct.

In the United States, there is a legacy of the segmentation or segregation of professional work, especially for Black Americans. Economic barriers and racial segregation created obstacles to securing an education and professional training for most of the twentieth century. Also during this time, the Black Americans who were able to successfully train for a profession faced employment restrictions. As educated and skilled persons, most were limited to practices within their own communities. Exclusion from the larger public sector curtailed their economic earnings, because the majority of the Black population early in the twentieth century was poor and working class. Only professionals in urban areas were able to develop financially lucrative practices, but that did not mean there were no obstacles to serving their clients' needs. For example, Black physicians faced problems with access to hospitals; Black lawyers struggled in courtrooms with a racist judicial system; and so forth. Each profession encountered a unique set of restrictions shaped by the wider public environment. More scholarly attention needs to be paid to analyses of these experiences as their progress is important to all and their struggles worthy of study.

White male professionals, in order to maintain control over their fields, sought to distance themselves from groups they viewed as inferior. Denial of access to professional bodies limited the abilities of Black professionals to shape the very professions to which they belonged. Black professionals established parallel organizations to improve their own skills and keep up with developments in their fields. Black attorneys founded the National Bar Association (NBA) in 1925, because they were barred from membership in the American Bar Association (ABA) until 1943. Yet variations in state bar associations' practices meant that it was really in the early 1960s that the ABA dropped all barriers to access for Black Americans (Blackwell, 1981). The NBA and other professional organizations like the National Medical Association and National Dental Association, and many other units helped professionals network. These were also sites of advocacy for social change as they operated independently and linked with formal civil rights groups to secure political power and end discrimination.

Racial segregation in the era of Jim Crow meant that few Black Americans had access to higher education and professional training. Prior to major changes during the civil rights movement, it was Historically Black Colleges and Universities (HBCUs) that educated the majority of Black professionals, that is physicians, dentists, pharmacists, veterinarians, and lawyers, as well as teachers, social workers, and nurses (Blackwell, 1981). For decades, these institutions that were producing and reproducing a Black middle class lacked the funding to adequately meet the task. Katznelson (2005) and Onkst (1998) have discussed how segregation prohibited many Black veterans and their families from using the very educational benefits they had earned through military service. After World War II, established Negro institutions in the South could not meet the educational needs of their communities. Consequently many in the Black community were not able to take full advantage of education benefits of the G.I. Bill, while more White Americans, including the descendants of eastern and southern European immigrants did. The mainstreaming of professional African Americans would not seriously begin until the mid-1960s, after passage of the Civil Rights Act.

Understanding this legacy is important for grasping how race profoundly shaped the professional lives of people of color. Throughout much of the twentieth century and even now in the twenty-first century, only a minority of Black Americans works as professionals. Studying them enables us to see not only how they negotiate discriminatory barriers in the past and the present, but also how their professional work impacts the Black community and the wider society.

J. Clay Smith, Jr. (1993) documents the first century of Black lawyers in the nation and tells a sad tale of exclusion and struggle for work and respect. He writes, "Black lawyers survived by necessity, serving a restricted market within the black community which itself often used white lawyers at higher legal fees" (11). Black lawyers had a monopoly in criminal law, where the police routinely harassed the Black community. Across the nation, "the black community expected the black lawyer to defend any black man charged in a capital case, even if there was no money for legal fees" (12). As part of a generation that was educated to serve, many Black lawyers obliged (Gaines, 1996). During World War I, segregation worked to their advantage as they served as lawyers in the army and defended Black soldiers; some continued to do so when they returned to civilian life.

In terms of professions, the legal profession is distinctive in its history of race, gender, and religious discrimination. After World War II, with the G.I. Bill and the expansion of legal opportunities, more people, even the descendants of recent European immigrants, considered legal careers. Blackwell (1981), in *Mainstreaming Outsiders*, identifies the LSAT, developed in 1947, as an instrument of exclusion to keep this field majority male, White, and Protestant. Initially used by only eighteen law schools, the LSAT became more popular in the 1950s and 1960s, when applications to law schools increased as employment options expanded. While men of ethnic and religious minority backgrounds were able to make inroads into the field even if they rarely made it to top Wall Street law firms, women and Black attorneys remained outside the mainstream. They faced quotas in law schools and few employment options to practice law when they did pass the bar (Blackwell, 1981; Epstein, 1993). Working mostly in solo or small practices, the majority of Black attorneys struggled to earn a living (Smith, 1993; Wilson, 2002). They were not part of major law firms, nor were they legal staff at major corporations, where attorneys made significant salaries. The limited educational and employment options meant the numbers of Black practicing attorneys was small. As noted in Segal (1983), in 1963 Secretary of Labor Willard Wirtz described "the legal profession as the worst segregated group in the whole economy" (24).

The Civil Rights Act of 1964 had very real consequences for the arenas of education, employment, and public accommodations. In 1960, the majority of Black students attended Historical Black Colleges and Universities; in 1970, the majority was in enrolled in predominantly White institutions. This cohort included the first wave of the baby boomers therefore creating a significant increase in the actual numbers of Black Americans securing advanced schooling. In *Mainstreaming Outsiders*, Blackwell (1981) explores the dynamics of institutional change as both professional schools and graduate programs in predominantly White institutions opened their doors beyond a crack to admit Black students. In the 1960s, the ABA committed itself to ending discrimination based on race and ethnic origins. Working with the American Association of Law Schools (AALS), bold plans to increase enrollments and remove barriers to practicing law were made. While progress would take decades, hundreds of minority students entered law schools in the 1970s and many of them were women. The profession grew as the number of Black lawyers grew from 3,260 in 1970 to more than 11,000 in 1980 (Segal, 1983).

In her study of educated Black women in the era of Jim Crow, Shaw (1996) demonstrates that by the 1960s these women had been answering the call to service for decades. However, they faced gender barriers as well as racial restrictions. Thus, not only was securing an education an economic struggle, requiring either family resources or considerable personal sacrifices, but once their education was completed, they were channeled into professions considered to be gender appropriate in the larger community. Although Black women could find training to be a nurse, social worker, librarian, or teacher, there were still biases in these realms. For example, if White nursing schools did admit minorities, there was generally a quota of only one Negro and one Jewish nursing student in the class (Hine, 1989). Once trained, Black women could only exercise these skills within certain segregated schools, agencies, organizations, and hospitals. Black women working as nurses were in hospitals that were either segregated or had segregated wards, if they found such work at all. The only exception was the private duty nurse, who worked in White homes, but still experienced considerable social distance between herself and the family.

As I discussed in an earlier essay (Higginbotham, 1987), gender barriers in education meant that Black women were unable to prepare for professions where they could establish their own practices, as Black male professionals were more able to do. Women were dependent on the job market, thus vulnerable to discriminatory barriers. For example, a credentialed African American could teach if the public school system hired teachers to teach Negro students; if not, it was not possible to work in that market. Those few women who were pioneers in traditional male professions, like the legal field, faced multiple barriers to practicing (Smith, 1998; Wilson, 2002). Black women intent on professional careers during Jim Crow faced both racial and gender barriers, in addition to the social class hurdles of attaining higher education. New cohorts merit attention to better understand the impact of civil rights legislation, particularly the 1964 Civil Rights Act that not only made racial but also gender discrimination in education and employment illegal. Opportunities for training in professional schools expanded after 1964, and people responded with new aspirations. What has happened to those hopes?

Social class must also be considered to understand current discriminatory practices. Not only has the legal field been White, male, and Protestant, it has traditionally drawn members from the middle and upper classes. The majority of lawyers traditionally came from middle-class families, and many entered family practices or had the resources to establish a private practice. However, even for the established Black middle class, pursuing the law was a risky career choice (Segal, 1983). Training as a physician or dentist was often a more secure professional route because there were clear avenues for service to the Black community. Even if there were problems getting jobs in hospitals, in some locations such as Chicago and Atlanta, Black physicians built their own hospitals. In the legal field, Black lawyers had to go into the White controlled courtroom or halls of justice. Indeed many judges were disrespectful to Black attorneys, especially in the South. Thus even Black people of means thought they did better in court with White legal representation.

In the wake of the Civil Rights Act, which of course required more lawyers to enforce it, and the ABA's new commitment to racial justice, developing minority attorneys became a priority and required considerable outreach, including to people from nonaffluent backgrounds. To encourage racial minorities to train for legal careers, the ABA and AALS supported the Council on Legal Education Opportunity Program (CLEO), which starting in 1968 identified and assisted about two hundred minority students each year with entrance into law schools (Blackwell, 1981). In addition to offering summer skills programs for prospective students and some financial assistance, this program actively recruited racial minorities into the profession. Men and women of color, including significant numbers from the working class, answered that call. According to David Wilkins (2004a), many of the African Americans entering law schools in the late 1960s and 1970s were inspired by civil rights lawyers, like Thurgood Marshall, but many were also motivated by the television show, *Perry Mason*. To many working-class youth, watching weekly this well dressed attorney use the law to right wrongs gave them an occupational role model that was not visible in their own community.

What does this legacy of racial, gender and class bias in the legal field mean for Black women who are part of this new cohort entering the profession? Even when legal barriers are removed, institutional cultures are slow to change. After the Civil Rights Act of 1964, women and racial minorities faced many battles in their efforts to enter previously exclusionary educational institutions and employment settings, but those who entered the legal field found intense resistance. It was widely recognized that the legal field was the most segregated of many professions and this legacy means that even today, Black attorneys are a lower percentage in their profession than fields such as medicine, accounting, and managers (Chambliss, 2004). Yet there is more gender parity among the population of Black attorneys than other racial groups, as doors opened for both at the same time.

What does this legacy of segregation of professionals in the United States mean as groups once denied access begin to enter mainstream educational institutions and workplaces? Part of that legacy is the rationales that were developed to normalize and justify exclusion. Have professionals working within mainstream settings altered illusion/myths about racial inferiority? Has the old racism morphed into a new racism that still operates to limit the economic and political power of Black professionals, as well as the images and ideologies about them? If this is the case, how does that new racism manifest itself? What do people do to scale barriers?

This legacy of segregation shapes how I think about these issues in the case of Black professional women. As they engage in professional work I ask, are Black women able to maximize their economic and political power and also control the image of themselves as professionals? Unraveling these issues means that we have to examine how race, gender, and social class operate in these workplaces within a historical context. What do these issues mean ideologically, how do they affect social reception, and what is the overall influence on the shape of opportunities and rewards?

Data

This chapter builds on secondary sources as well as years of researching issues of Black professional women (Higginbotham, 1987, 1994; Higginbotham & Weber, 1999) and includes analysis of in-depth interviews with eight black women attorneys who entered the field in the post–civil rights era. Beginning in 1997, I conducted telephone interviews with three Black women who had worked in the same municipal agency in a location I referred to as North City to explore the common, but under researched population of public sector attorneys. Their careers differ in that they graduated law school in 1975, 1983, and 1986, but there are common themes. In 2001, I was able to contact two of those attorneys and follow up their telephone interviews using a formal interview schedule that considered their backgrounds, education and career decisions, and perceptions of their workplaces. In 2005, I began a pilot study with a more formal instrument focusing on attorneys in the Mid-Atlantic region. In this study, I interviewed six Black women practicing attorneys who completed law school between 1974 and 1990. The interviews cover family and educational backgrounds (particularly law school experiences), and work and legal careers. I met with each woman in this study twice, gaining in the first interview a scenario of her legal career, so that I could develop questions about the transitions and the nature of work in different arenas. In this paper eight interviews (two from the 2001 interviews and six from the pilot study) are combined to explore the law school experiences of these Black women during the 1970s and 1980s. Table 2.1 provides a profile of each respondent including details about their social class and law school education. Names given are pseudonyms to protect respondents' identities. All the women were asked to talk about law school, enabling us to see how the experience of those who began in the 1970s, when both gender and race made them a tiny minority, differs from those who entered later when law schools had a significant female population and some institutional support for racial minorities. Securing credentials is just one step in entering a profession; the interviews also provide insights about the transition to establishing a career.

TABLE 2.1

Black Women Attorneys

Name	Social-Class Background	Type of Law School	Year Graduated from Law School	Early Career
North City Study				
Helen Fleming	working-class	Regional University	1975	public/non profit sector
Rebecca Johnson	working-class	Local University	1983	public sector
Mid-Atlantic Study				
Edwina Charleston	working-class	Regional University	1977	private sector
Josephine Daniels	middle-class	Prestigious University	1979	nonprofit/ public
Carol Howard	middle-class	Regional University	1990	private
Mary Jefferson	middle-class	Prestigious University	1979	private
Brenda Scott	working-class	Prestigious University	1974	public
Irma Walker	working-class	Historically Black University	1990	public

Note: All names listed above are pseudonyms.

Opening New Doors

Law schools began to modify their established racial practices, especially Northern schools, in the 1960s. Early civil rights victories ended discrimination in state-supported graduate programs before affecting undergraduate institutions. As barriers dropped, a few Black men and women applied to law school outside of the historically Black law programs that had been serving their community for decades. Because it was also made illegal for public institutions and private graduate programs to receive federal monies if they discriminated on the grounds of sex, major law schools, which were predominantly White and male, were eager to comply with the 1972 Title IX in the Educational Amendments Act to maintain their federal funding (Epstein, 1993). As these educational doors opened, many women entered.

I turn now to the early careers of my respondents, particularly the transition from law school to a permanent position in the legal field. How did law school prepare them for a legal career? When do they begin to work? What was the climate and how did their early careers progress? What are their opportunities for employment? How does a race, class, and gender analysis help us answer these questions?

These eight Black women, born between 1946 and 1958, are part of the baby boomer generation. As such, they had greater opportunities to attend predominantly White colleges and universities than earlier cohorts. Although these women came from varied social class backgrounds, they were more likely to be either from working-class or striving middle-class families, than from very comfortable middle-class homes. Only three women were from established middle-class homes, where their parents had significant economic resources. The working-class homes also vary from stable, two-parent and modest income families to single-parent homes. The women's backgrounds are reflective of patterns identified in other discussions of the production of black professionals at that time (Blackwell, 1981; Higginbotham, 2001; Segal, 1983). In terms of educational careers, they all had experiences in integrated institutions. Of the eight women interviewed for this study, only one attended an HBCU for her legal education. The other seven women graduated from prestigious, regional, and local law schools that witnessed significant gender shifts as well as the increasing presence of racial minorities in the 1970s and 1980s. Most of the women went to law school directly after college, even if they had interrupted their college careers; only one selected law as her second professional career.

The earliest graduate in this study, Brenda Scott, finished law school in 1974. She was born in 1950 and grew up in the Mid-Atlantic region. Her father was a unionized blue-collar worker and her mother was a clerical worker in the city government. Education was a family priority and she went to a predominantly White college outside of her home community. She was part of a wave of Black students entering prestigious, predominantly White colleges in significant numbers in the mid-1960s. While Brenda had been thinking about a career as a teacher, having been encouraged by her mother, many students in her cohort were considering law school. By 1971, when she graduated college, law school was a common goal for many women graduates (Epstein, 1993). Brenda applied and was accepted at several schools; she stayed at her alma mater where she received a full scholarship.

While there were a significant number of women in her class and a number of black men, she was the only Black woman. The school was in the early stages of adjusting to a new population. Brenda thought that "law school is very isolating, it is very intensive, it was very different [from her undergraduate experience]."

As is often the case with desegregating institutions, any accommodations that are made are most often made by the new group members who enter (Feagin, Vera, & Imani, 1996; Higginbotham, 2001). While Brenda was admitted and received a scholarship, she was not strongly encouraged or mentored in law school. Brenda notes, "I was not very aware of opportunities in the legal profession. The school did not push me or encourage me to be involved in legal opportunities or clerkship." Asked about her experience learning the law, she said:

> I took it on as an intellectual challenge; in terms of the school interacting with me. I would think about it as benign neglect. I do not think they did one thing to push me towards a career, I do not think they did one thing to help me get into a career mode. So they just let me study and they paid for it. I was good for their numbers and I did not flunk out. I did relatively well. Everyone got what they wanted out of the bargain and that was it.

The doors to predominantly White law schools were opening in the 1970s, but few were genuinely inviting places. Over time more structures, like Black law student groups, would provide ways for people to network, get support and information about how to negotiate the system, but in the early 1970s, there were few, if any, Black faculty at these law schools.

Helen Fleming, born in 1950, also grew up in a working-class family in the Mid-Atlantic region. After graduating from high school in 1967, she worked as a bookkeeper and attended college part-time and later full-time. She finished college in 1972 and applied to law schools. While she was accepted at most schools, she proceeded directly to a reputable regional law school outside of her community that offered a solid financial aid package. State Law School had a reputation for having a majority of graduates pass the bar on their first attempt. When she arrived, Helen was one of seven Black students and the only Black woman in her cohort. Another Black woman was in her senior year in the school, but they did little together. As Helen recalls, White women were well represented in the school, a statement that is supported by Epstein's findings of legal careers becoming a common occupational choice for White women college graduates by that time (1993).

A solid student, Helen had done "a lot of reading around political issues, a lot of reading of Black literature. [Law school] seemed like a natural continuation. I was not really interested in going to graduate school for political science or something like that. And I had trouble linking that with an actual [sic] particular job." As part of an early cohort emerging with a college degree from a majority White college, Helen was on her own about planning for the future.

Like many others in her cohort, she thought about a visible profession. She said, "You go to law school and you're a lawyer and that is a job. It was a way of blending my studying with a career opportunity." The reality of law school was a challenge, but Helen met it. She recalls:

> I did not do well in law school with the exception of one or two classes. When I actually had to write something, then I got an A. When I did not have that opportunity, I got Bs and Cs. Because you have to function in a box and I do not function well in boxes. You have to give back what you were given; you have to just regurgitate. It does not promote any real imagination, it does not really promote thinking, it does not really encourage creativity, and it does not really expand your mind. It is just not an educational experience, it really isn't like going to college, where you really learn something, you learn to use your mind and think and be creative. Law school was not like that at all.

The regular law school channels for internships were hard to navigate and biased in many respects. However, Helen was able to use racial networks to secure work experience in the state legislature. Racial networks would also help her at other stages in her career.

Born in 1946, Edwina Charleston grew up in a working-class family in the Mid-Atlantic region. While education was stressed in her family, new employment options for Black women in the 1960s made working attractive. After graduating from an integrated high school in 1963, Edwina worked in business and attended a couple of predominantly White colleges before finishing a business degree at an HBCU. She graduated in 1974, which seemed to be a time when new corporate doors were opening for Black women. Edwina took a position with a major bank in commercial finance, but when her job was changed without her consent, she decided to go to law school. She thought that combining her business experience with legal training would give her security in a fast changing business world. She went to Middle State Law School, a regional law school, where she was part of a cohort of nineteen Black students on the campus. This was the first year that this law school had a double-digit enrollment of Black law students, thus they were still a tiny minority, but a critical mass for their own networking. While Black students were a presence on the campus (and Middle State Law School was complying with federal law), the law school was not very welcoming. There was rhetoric, but in reality the school did little to facilitate the students' adjustment and success. In fact, Edwina, a successful student, said, "In many ways it was a very sad time for me, since I saw the departure of friends who lost it. People do get hurt in this game." One institutional response to the increasing number of Black students was to hire a Black attorney, from a local law firm, to tell them what do to. According to Edwina, his stance was one of accommodation and assimilation rather than supporting the students or challenging institutionalized racism. Few people talked about challenging institutionalized racism in law schools in the 1970s.

Edwina noted: "I was president of [the local] BALSA, the Black American Law Student Association, now it has changed its name, it is BLSA. So as president I met with him, since he was sort of the liaison [with the students], since Lord knows the dean did not have time for that stuff. I remember our meeting when he sat me down and explained this stuff about 'If you do not have your helmet, you shouldn't play the game, because you are going to get hurt.'" Only ten of the nineteen Black students in Edwina's cohort finished; some receiving mentoring by working with the National Bar Association and support from Black attorneys in the city. However, they mostly supported each other. She recalled, "We pretty much became a family."

The other two graduates in the 1970s, Josephine Daniels and Mary Jefferson, tell a similar tale. However, there were more organizations on campus and opportunities to gain legal experiences by the late 1970s. We learn from their experiences that the law school environment improved over time, so the women entering in the 1980s found more institutional support as well as more gender balance and larger racial cohort groups than in the 1970s. In contrast to the scene in majority White law schools, we can look at the one woman who went to a historically Black law school.

Irma Walker, whose parents migrated from the South, was born in 1957 in a major Northern city. She was in majority Black public schools until she attended a private predominantly White college in her region. She faced racism from other students and did not get much individual attention from faculty. After graduation, she worked as a professional in the institution where she had worked part-time as an undergraduate. Later that year, Irma, who had been a criminal justice major, decided to attend law school. She applied and was accepted at a historically Black law school in 1979.

As a working-class student, Irma was overwhelmed by the people with more polish and resources at this historically Black law school, which was in a Southern city. She wanted to return home, but the student assigned to mentor her spent three hours convincing her to stay. She stayed and during that first year in law school, she volunteered at the office of a local attorney in private practice and really learned much of the details of doing legal work. Her law school socialized students into a tradition of social service that had been the hallmark of Black attorneys in the past. Irma received more mentoring and support than the women in predominantly White law schools at that time. She was more connected to legal circles because she attended a historically Black law school, than the other Black women interviewed. After law school Irma, like many Black women lawyers, found a position in the public sector. While Black women's experiences in law schools are mixed and generally improve over time as later cohorts had more institutional support. In the case of these eight women, their law schools were slow to facilitate these Black female law graduates' entry into the profession.

Many people argue that the goals of predominantly White law schools, which gained support from major corporations in terms of funding programs like CLEO, were that these racial minority lawyers would graduate and then return to serve their communities (Wilkins, 2004b). The experiences of exclusion of Black students within their law schools support such a claim. The development of larger cohorts meant that they began to build more institutional support, like the chapters of Black Law Students Association. As the critical mass of practicing attorneys grew, Black attorneys begin to enter more previously unexplored areas of law. Yet these developments in White law schools took time. As we look at various groups, White women were more likely to be mainstreamed into the regular channels for law school students, internships, law reviews, and other venues that lead to opening doors in the profession (Chambliss, 2004). With law degrees, but with minimal support from their law schools, these Black women, especially the 1970s' graduates, entered the world of employment.

First Jobs

While the doors of law schools opened, the larger profession did not move at the same pace. Speaking at a 2006 meeting of the American Sociological Association, Ruth Bader Ginsburg said, "Even today women are not entering a bias free profession." Think about the challenge of entering this profession three decades earlier. For the 1970s cohort, their exclusion from the regular channels for mainstreaming and directing law students to careers meant they had to sort out their own paths to employment in the public and private sectors. Many were motivated by social concerns and even majority White law schools had students with interests in public-interest law in the 1960s and 1970s. Most of these women, however, would find their employment niche in the public sector (Segal, 1983). Of the eight women, only one had her total career in the private sector and then entered the public sector on a part-time basis after she retired. The earliest law school graduates were more likely to have careers within the public sector and the world of nonprofits. After working in these arenas, one woman left the public sector to pursue a solo practice, the most common employment setting for attorneys, but less common for Black attorneys. The other four women moved between the two sectors. Such movement between sectors is common. David Wilkins (2004a) who studies the careers of Black attorneys in corporate law, finds many worked in government during their careers: 48 percent of the Black women and 40 percent of the Black men. Thus the Black attorneys who get to the private sector, often spent time in the public sector, working in government at various levels and often developing reputations that make them attractive to firms and corporations. Early career experiences, particularly in the first five years, speak to the difficulties of the transition from law school to employment as an attorney.

Public Sector Careers

Graduating with a law degree in 1974, Brenda entered a job market with limited options. She commented: "I guess I saw and became aware of some opportunities. Some of them were more the District Attorney's office (DAs) and Legal Aid (LA) and that type of thing. I did not see law firms as an option. I knew that one person from the neighborhood was at a law firm and then I remember thinking that they were not ready for a Black woman." As Epstein (1993) notes from her groundbreaking study of women attorneys, the impact of informal social controls was powerful. Some law firms clearly discriminated, but for women coming out of law schools an awareness of discrimination often meant that they resigned themselves to what were real options. Epstein also notes that: "Individuals also learn to work within and to manipulate the system that surrounds them" (91). We find a similar pattern among Black women law school graduates in the 1970s and 1980s as discriminatory patterns shape the nature of their choices.

Which doors were open to Black women law school graduates in the early 1970s? In Brenda's case it was the DAs office in her city that was slowly hiring more women and racial minorities. When she went to work for the DAs office, Brenda was the second Black woman hired. She started as a criminal law investigator and when she passed the bar, she was an assistant district attorney. Brenda spent the first five years of her legal career prosecuting cases for the city, working on general cases and then in homicide and the sex crimes units. It was innovative for Brenda to be a litigator, when many women attorneys had been hidden in law libraries and/or researching cases for decades; now in the mid-1970s women entering the courtroom began to become more common (Epstein, 1993; Pierce, 1996).

While hiring women and racial minorities made political and financial sense for urban district attorneys around the nation in the 1970s, it was up to these individuals to either change this White and male culture or fit in. As part of this early group, Brenda had to cope with the larger legal system's lack of readiness for change. Brenda recalled:

> I did find that there was a lot of sexism in the prosecutor's office. Guys did not want women there, and they made it very clear. Even the attorneys, they were nasty and mean. They would say things like you're stupid and you can't do this and ... This went on; they really tried to

demoralize us. But you had a bunch of pretty tough ladies. At this point they [the men] were just trying to hold back the tide and they could not. You had investigators and police officers, who would have girlie pin-ups in their offices and all that. Again this was a time when people were beginning to speak up and women would say, "that's inappropriate" and they did not understand it, so there were a lot of clashes as well.

Over time many of these attitudes would change because these attorneys worked together and in the process shared and came to appreciate each other as people. Later in the interview, Brenda talked about the collegial work atmosphere, where attorneys shared information and suggestions on how to address problems in cases, such as dealing with uncooperative witnesses. Changes occurred because this office continued to hire more women and racial minorities to meet the challenge of fighting crime and drugs in the 1970s and 1980s.

Brenda not only faced challenges in the office, but also in the courtroom. As a young Black woman doing litigation, the courtroom was a battleground where she could be personally attacked or demeaned.

I had one [defense] attorney during his closing argument refer to me as a Black Farah Fawcett. Just trying to marginalize me to the jury, but ignoring any argument I was going to make to convict somebody. People were just not ready. Judges, many judges called you "girlie" and things like that. They were not ready. I remember one time I wore a white pantsuit and this judge thought I was a nurse accompanying somebody. [I told him] "No, I am the prosecutor."

Her position required her to work to be accepted as legitimate by colleagues, coworkers, and others in the justice system, including the members of the jury. These transitions did not all happen at the same pace.

Helen Fleming completed law school and passed the bar in 1975. She won a fellowship that took her to a different state, where she had to pass another bar, and worked with a legal service agency. Like many Black women law graduates, Helen thought that "Most of the opportunities that I've had have been in public sector legal services, legal aid types of jobs." These positions did give her opportunities to master her craft:

I've had some really good successes with legal services. I remember even making an argument in traffic court, where an older White male attorney followed me outside of the courtroom and actually congratulated me for the argument that I made. That felt really good. My one big victory was winning a social security appeal in federal court, where I felt I was literally raked over the coals by this appellate judge. My opponents were these well-paid federal attorneys. I went in there with my little organized argument; I had a loose leaf with everything. I went outside and sat in my car and cried since I was so physically and mentally exhausted. Then I found out two weeks later that I had won.

In these early jobs, many people had to make their own way without clear mentors and/or career ladders. While not the topic of this chapter, more research is needed on how Black women translate such experiences into wider employment options.

Brenda and Helen are the success stories. It was critical for these women to be able to move from law school into paid employment, because they were the first generation in their families to attend college and lacked the wealth to establish private practices. They are part of a trend in which Black attorneys were moving from small firms into government service and public-interest firms (Segal, 1983). They also emerged from law school with minimal debt, as they were scholarship students and in the early period when law schools were complying with Title IX such financial support was available. In later years, as more Black women enter law schools, they pay a larger share of the tuition for their education, but still face bias in the legal job market and the potential for greater economic stress.

Rebecca Johnson was born in 1958 and grew up in a Mid-Atlantic city. She knew that she wanted to be an attorney. She took the LSATs, graduated college in 1980, and entered a local law school that was her first choice. Her law school experience was positive and she had an internship with a nonprofit agency, as the paths to legal career opportunities were more apparent to Black students at that time. When she graduated in 1983, it was difficult to find a position as a practicing attorney. She could have worked for the nonprofit agency where she had interned, but they could not pay her the money she needed. With student loans, she felt pressured to find work at a salary that would help her meet her obligations. It took her two years to find a job where she could actually practice law. Rebecca recalled those years: "I took a job as an investigator. I did other things to find a job that was paying me enough so I could pay my student loans back and still afford to live. . . . And then I finally got with a new union. And the union allowed me my first legal job in terms of actually working."

The union offered discounted legal services to union members, so Rebecca's work was quite varied. Nonprofit agencies, along with the public sector, are critical sources of employment for Black women who were not considered appropriate for the private positions that dominate the field. Just as was the case with Helen, Rebecca was in a job where she had to find her own way; there were no clear avenues to pursue and mentors to aid her career. She was in a small office providing legal services to union members; thus she had to learn what she needed to do for a variety of clients. After working outside of her field, Rebecca was grateful for the opportunity. She said, "The thing that I

liked about the union was that it gave me a very strong foundation in matri-
monial and family law. Because it was a growing union at that time, I did a little more. I got a little exposure to real estate and bankruptcy." She worked for
the union and then went on maternity leave. Her next legal position would be
working for a city agency, but her first opportunity to practice law was with an
organization that was committed to racial and gender equality.

Many Black women attorneys begin their careers in the public sector. Of
the eight women's careers explored here, five begin their legal careers in
either nonprofit or public-sector positions. We could attribute this pattern to
the fact that these subjects were raised working class and did not attend prestigious law schools, but the next case shows how common these patterns are
for Black women entering the profession. Josephine Daniels, born in 1954, was
raised in a middle-class family. She is currently a partner in a major East Coast
law firm, but her first real legal position was in the public sector. After graduating from a private high school in her native city, Josephine attended an elite
New England college. Her parents insisted that she begin working or continue
her education upon graduation. Rather than pursue a doctorate, Josephine
thought that she could handle three years of law school. She attended a prestigious law school in a major city and graduated in 1979. She accepted a legal
position in a nonprofit agency, but they lost funding for the position between
the time she accepted and started the job. She found her position evaporating
around her as her salary was cut; after six months the position disappeared
and she was out of a job.

Asked about her sense of options as a Black woman who had passed the
bar and held an Ivy League law degree in 1980, Josephine noted: "I did not see
any and I did not like law. I was thinking about, should I go back to school, but
at this point, no, I had loans. I did not have loans after undergraduate, but I
had loans after law school." After six months, Josephine found a job in the City
Solicitor's Office, through a connection with a Puerto Rican woman, Maria,
who had also graduated from her law school. Josephine commented:

> We were the only women of color in our department, which was the
> largest department. A lot of the guys had graduated from Regional Law
> School, which had just gotten their accreditation, and State Law School.
> And they were offended by the fact that we had gone to an Ivy League
> [law school]. Maria would say, "Do not worry we did not take your place,
> you were not getting in anyway."

It is funny, but also sad, that these two women of color needed an Ivy
League law degree to secure the job that White males got with degrees from a
state or regional institution. While there was some tension with male coworkers, Josephine, like other Black women in the public sector, found the workplace changed over time as more people of color were hired and the gender

balance continued to shift. Talking about those years, she notes: "In ways it was an extension of school, since many people were very young. I socialized with a number of the people from work."

In her position, Josephine worked hard. As a new attorney for the city she went into court against some of the strongest defense attorneys in the area. She says, "You were out-experienced." There were very few structures in place to guide these young lawyers. Talking about those early days, Josephine recalled:

> I had a trial and at the end of the trial, I knew I was supposed to ask for some motion, but I had no idea what it was. So I came back to the office, since it did not make sense and asked, "I'm supposed to ask for something, what is it?" At the end of the plaintiff's case, you are supposed to ask for something and I thought it was a summary judgment and then they would dismiss the case. We were there looking it up in the rule book and at that point, somebody who had two years of experience came by and heard what we were doing. He fell out laughing, "No, you dummy." He wrote it down and I ran back to court and said whatever and the judge denied it, which I knew he would do, but I had to say it.

Even without solid mentoring, Josephine developed the skills that enabled her to move from general trials, protecting the city against people who fall on the sidewalks and other cases valued as less than $50,000, to major trials. While there are many people, especially racial minorities whose careers end in litigation, and they do not advance (Wilkins, 2004a), that was not her case. Josephine spent about four years working for the city and then entered the private sector as part of the legal staff of an insurance company, where she had to master a different type of law. Like many Black women who work in the private sector, she did not enter it directly out of law school.

Private-Sector Careers

Three of the practicing attorneys began their careers in the private sector as part of the legal staff for corporations and companies, "in-house" attorneys, or in a law firm. Their stories and their workplace settings are very different from each other; however, they are useful in revealing the importance of time in that the women who graduated in the 1970s, experienced a very different climate than the later graduates. The stories also show that the work environment is also very critical to well-being. The private legal field includes small practices, medium-sized practices, and major law firms (approximately more than twenty-five attorneys). People can also hold positions on the legal staff of corporations and companies, which range from small to medium to large.

A recent study by the ABA Commission on Women in the Profession (2006), *Visible Invisibility: Women of Color in Law Firms*, identifies how racial minority women are leaving major law firms in droves. These women, recruited from the prestigious law schools such as Harvard, Yale, Michigan, and Berkeley, tend to leave within five years. The study respondents identify the lack of mentoring in these firms, something they were more likely to have in law school as they met the criteria for entry in the first place. They also cite differential assignments, as well as overtly racist and sexist comments from other attorneys. For many, such demeaning comments are shocking after participating in a liberal law school program. And finally, these attorneys find it difficult to balance the demands of work with having a personal life (Chanen, 2006). The three women who began their careers in the private sector in this investigation echoed the concerns found among more recent graduates.

After graduating from a reputable law school in 1978, Edwina Charleston secured a position as a part of the legal staff for a major corporation. She had interned at Corporate during the summers, so she had a foot in the door.[1] Corporate began growing their own legal staff rather than hiring attorneys who had not made partner in law firms. This new route was obviously less expensive than if you hired people right out of law school, which is now a more standard practice. Once hired, Edwina was one of the few people of color in a huge legal department. She began her job in limbo because like many law school graduates, she had taken the bar but did not know if she had passed it yet. Many public-sector positions have a status for people who have not passed the bar, and in many cases they allow one or two years to pass the bar. In the private sector, there is no margin for error, which makes this waiting period very tense. Talking about her status, Edwina noted:

> No, I didn't go having passed the bar. I had taken the bar, but I started working before the results were out. It was a very interesting thing because a requirement of the job was that you had to pass the bar. So, I make the distinction that I had not passed it, because as news came in [on the status of other recent graduates who had taken the bar] the managing counselor in my department would come to my room almost everyday and sit, like "Is there any news?" Like I would be holding out on them. They could have called Middle State, they did not have to come in and look at me. They could have asked if they had published the results, but instead . . . It was a very strange place.

In those days, Corporate had a legal staff of over two hundred attorneys and about one hundred other legal staff, but only a handful of Black attorneys and a support staff that included about three or five Black people working as legal secretaries or clerks. Many private sector corporations had been majority White not only in their professional staff, but in clerical staff as well. The public sector had more diversity in the 1970s, with people of color in support staff positions, while the professional ranks had remained majority White. The private sector was a place where people faced racism on many levels. Edwina had a secretary who was hostile to her and that added to the tensions on the job. Asked about the challenges she faced in the workplace, Edwina said:

> The pressure of being under a microscope and the pressure of not knowing what I was doing on top of it. The culture was not—if a culture is ever—ready for that experience. Corporate had just begun its journey to try and address these issues of race. It had a poor history. It did not rely on government contracts, so it did not need to . . . that came later, when the patent position began to crack and they had to look at other sources of money and they had to look at government contracts. That led them to have to deal more realistically with race issues. But prior to that they did not have to deal. I think Dick Williams was the first professional Black they hired. Dick said to me, just before he left, that "Things had changed, but yet they are still the same." So they had not had a long history of having professional Blacks, they had the men who ran the elevators and the like, but [they had done] nothing brave. So I came into what was still very much that blindness, so the challenge was keeping yourself sane.

Like other Black women attorneys starting in the late 1970s, Edwina was not mentored when she began working at Corporate. "I met a mentor as my career was ending. I acquired a mentor and I often said to this man, 'Boy, I sure wish I had you at the beginning. I might have done things differently.'" Her mentor was a White male, reflecting how, by the late 1980s and 1990s, more White men were advocating for racial minorities in the world of corporations and law firms. However, the 1970s and early 1980s were rough times considering that there were few opportunities in White corporations and many Black people faced hostility. Blacks were an unwelcome presence. There was much pressure to assimilate, but insiders were not reaching out to show newcomers the way.

Unlike the public sector, where, due to changing urban demographics and political pressure, legal services were becoming more gender and racially balanced, the private sector was not following the same pattern. So while Edwina entered the legal counsel of a company with a clear structure for socializing attorneys and training them for advancement, she was not part of this system. What Edwina shares with the Black women attorneys in the public sector and small nonprofit organizations is that she had to find her own way.

Mary Jefferson was born in 1954, grew up in the Mid-Atlantic region in a striving middle-class family, where after a divorce, her mother, a registered nurse, provided her children with a parochial school education. After high school, Mary secured a scholarship and went away to an elite women's college and then applied to law schools. She attended an Ivy League law school in another city and graduated in 1979. One of a few minorities from an elite law school, Mary secured a position as in-house attorney for a corporation. Like Edwina, Mary faced many pressures to prove herself in a work setting that was hostile.

In her early years at Corporate, Edwina did not think she received assignments that challenged her or enabled her to advance. In contrast, Mary thought she was getting appropriate assignments, but the racism took another form. She recalled: "My position involved research and advising clients at the Company on regulations and anti-trust. I was getting good assignments, but it was just that when you did well, people were surprised." Commenting about the type of racism where people's expectations for you are low, she only said, "It gets very old." She was not happy in her job and left after a year and a half. She had been looking for another position in her home city, because she was socially isolated, but workplace dynamics at the Company also pushed her to leave. "I was working on a project and someone else took credit for what I did. And let it stand. So I said, 'I'm out of here' and I went to Southern City for two years."

Her second position took Mary to a new city where she worked for a New York City law firm that was establishing an office in Southern City. Moving after such a short time, she had to take the bar examination for her new state. Mary relocated to another state again when she married in 1982, which meant that she had to take a third bar examination. After this final move, she was on the legal staff for a bank. This group of in- house counsel was a small operation of six attorneys and she was the only Black attorney. She was positive about the compensation, but she did not like the culture. Not only was the legal department majority White, but it was hostile in many respects to her own values. When she became a mother, another woman attorney resented her commitment to her son. At that point, she left to work with her husband who had launched his own public relations firm after frustrations of working in his field for a major corporation and a large firm. Unlike the public sector, where, in the late 1970s and 1980s, the racial and gender composition changed as more women and minorities secured positions and slowly moved into leadership positions, the private sector seems to let a few people in without making changes in their general structure and operation.

Our final case shows some of the larger changes that were happening in the overall field, as law firms that have significant numbers of women do change the opportunities for some women of color. Carole Howard was born in 1957 in a middle-class family that resided in the Mid-Atlantic region. She grew up in a suburban community and attended integrated schools. After high school, she went to college and then graduate school in the social sciences and began work as a college professor. She was troubled by trends in her field and decided to go to law school to more directly address issues of justice. Entering a regional law school in 1987, she was pleased with the gender and racial diversity of her cohort and found that she was one of many students who were pursuing law as a second career.

Returning to school, Carole was clear about using her law degree for advancing social justice. While in law school, Carole interned for a small firm. Upon graduation in 1990, she worked in a small firm and then joined a major firm that actually created a position for her to work in both family and environmental law. In addition to having strong mentors in her graduate program, she was mentored at her law firm by a White woman. While Carole was the only Black attorney in this firm, she found people willing to help her advance her career. While this particular firm might have been a positive workplace in the 1970s, it did not hire a Black woman attorney until the 1990s. Carole's experience differs from Black women in earlier cohorts who had to make their own way without mentoring or support.

In this small law firm, there was clear strength in family law; consequently many women were present. This private-sector location can be very different from the typical male dominated law firms that the ABA study found women of color leaving (2006). Carole had the benefit of a firm where women were in leadership positions, a developing pattern now that it has been three decades that White women have been graduating law schools in significant numbers. Edwina and Mary never had such advantages, because in their locations they were minorities in both race and gender and were working in cultures that were resistant to change. In addition to coming to law as a second career, so that she understood many of the logistics of building a professional life, Carole's middle-class background gave her cultural capital that women with even prestigious law degrees, but from marginally middle-class or working-class roots lacked.

Edwina, Mary, and Carole all began their careers in the private sector, but entering in the 1990s is very different from the challenges those Black women faced in the 1970s and early 1980s. However, access into this sector depends greatly on law school rank, law review experience, moot court participation, and other issues related to mastering the formal structure of professional socialization in law school. Thus we observe how Black women over time began to benefit from new organizations in law schools, like BLSA, for mentoring and help in navigating the law school.

Conclusion

In conclusion, examining the entrance of Black women law graduates into the legal profession enables us to see the difficulties and challenges of social change. Even with qualifications, Black women with law degrees have limited employment options. Their educational qualifications do not immediately open doors. These stories reveal that the historical moment when a Black woman completes her law degree and enters a labor market is important. In the 1970s only a few doors were open, while some might be revolving and others remained shut. The experience of recent law graduates shows that some progress has been made. Yet limited options are shared by many Black law school graduates who, according to an American Bar Association report, are less likely than White law school graduates to enter private law firms and therefore earn less over their careers than most White attorneys (Chambliss, 2004). Many of the women of color who do secure positions in private law firms experience a kind of second-class citizenship that is not only stressful, but it motivates them to reevaluate their career choices, as did Mary Jefferson in this study (ABA Commission on Women in the Profession, 2006).

Rather than a simple explanation of discrimination, we can first identify problems in law schools, where compliance with new legal standards does not mean that a real invitation or welcome is extended to a new group. It was common, especially in the early years, to just admit and if possible fund people, without any other accommodations. As a result, it was incumbent upon these new law students to learn on their own how to best use their years in law school effectively to gain entry into one of the most exclusive professions in the nation. Again the historical moment is important, because as a result of years of restrictions, there were few Black attorneys in the era before the Civil Rights Act. As majority White law schools opened their doors to racial minorities, the production of Black attorneys increased, which meant there were more colleagues who could support each other and serve as mentors. A critical mass of racial and gender pioneers makes a difference in helping a Black woman navigate the profession as she can now develop networks and a support system. Institutions like the BLSA and links with the National Bar Association and local Black attorneys increased over time, enabling the later graduates to learn more about the field and how to negotiate within it.

Yet such connections can only carry Black women so far. Using a person's law school class rank, law review and moot court participation, and clerkship to recruit associates as many private law firms do opens the process to much influence. Research suggests that firms might rely more heavily on such credentials "when screening minority candidates, creating an invisible double standard" (Chambliss, 2004, 33). As we saw in the cases described above, within prestigious law schools, these Black women were not encouraged to participate in such activities. They concentrated on coursework and lacked mentors to inform them about what experiences you need in law school to secure such positions. Students from middle-class families might have a greater understanding of these social norms, but that was more the case with later cohorts of Black women in law schools. In regard to historically Black law schools, these schools cannot necessarily provide avenues to major predominantly White law firms or in-house positions with major corporations. Over time many predominantly White law schools would change their practices, with respect to the diversity of faculty and students. Thus more recent work does demonstrate that more racial minority women graduates from elite law schools do access law firms, but many encounter problems at this level of professional development (ABA Commission on Women in the Profession, 2006; Chanen, 2006; Wilkins, 2004a).

Second, making the transition to paid employment is particularly troubling, but again we have seen changes over time. For the early 1970s graduates, there was little help from their law schools. Josephine, Mary, and Brenda went to schools that recruited for major law firms, but they were not the types of candidates such firms were seeking. At that time, women were more likely to secure employment in the public sector, also a new avenue of employment since previous generations of Black women attorneys struggled for work in public offices often entering the family court system via social work careers (Smith, 1998). Working in more high profile places like the district attorney's office and the city solicitors' office were groundbreaking achievements for racial minorities.

We must consider these developments within the context of a changing occupation. The legal field was expanding in the 1970s and 1980s. In their study of the lawyers in Chicago, Heinz, et al., (2005) found that while the percentage of lawyers in large law firms increased, many were high-end attorneys with elite educations' working in expanding corporate and financial institutions. The authors find that social class background provides access to educational preparation for elite training and that type of legal training is the path to elite positions in specialized firms and practices.

This story is also about race and gender. This picture of Chicago could be repeated in other cities. The expansion of the high end of the profession in Chicago, according to Heinz, et al. (2005) means that "[as] women and racial minorities entered the profession in substantial numbers, they tended to replace the Catholics and Jews on the lower rungs of the ladder" (72). They overwhelmingly work in public-sector enterprises, servicing the state or perhaps servicing poor clients. This pattern is reflective of what is happening in the wider field of law, but we see that the options for women and racial minorities are shaped by race, gender, and social class background.

In an earlier era, Black women could not readily secure an education to enter a profession that enabled them to pursue an independent career. As teachers, social workers, nurses, and librarians, they had to work for others. Now that this supposedly entrepreneurial profession is open to women, including Black women, their own social class position and the changing occupational structure make it hard to secure a living. Ideally, after passing the bar, any lawyer can open an office, put up a sign, and, since 1977, advertise their services to the public. But the question about making a living is crucial.

Increasingly lawyers work for others, and those employment options are strat-ified by social class, gender and race. Black women, even as professionals have long found employment in the public sector. Where once they were teachers, social workers, nurses, and librarians, they now are attorneys, accountants, and managers just as these positions decline in status, working conditions, and earnings because of limited public funding.

This is a story about discrimination, but not the simple picture of specific individuals being denied certain jobs by people with the intent to discrimi-nate. It is instead a story about a network of restrictions and differences in treatment, so that law schools themselves function differently and racial minorities face more hurdles to paid employment as an attorney because they cannot readily turn a law degree into a solid private practice. After obtaining an education, racial and gender biases make it difficult to secure work in the field. Rebecca was delighted to work for a union that initially paid her enough to meet her obligations, even though this position did not offer any real chance of advancement. After one position in the nonprofit sector disap-peared, it took Josephine six months to find a public-sector position, where she joined men with lesser legal credentials. She found this position via per-sonal connections. As we look across the spectrum, we see that women and racial minorities, particularly Black women are increasing in the public sector, and many find it difficult to transition into private firms.

Those few women who did begin in the private sector in those early years of the 1970s had very difficult experiences as the firms were not welcoming locales. Looking to move into this sector in the mid-1980s, Josephine inter-viewed at some firms. She recalled, "One firm told me that they had never hired a Black before, for anything, including a secretary." The world that Edwina, Mary, and Carole entered was majority White with few faces of color, but for early cohorts like Edwina and Mary these were hostile environments where they had to make most of the accommodations. These women are qual-ified, but their experiences varied in whether supervisors recognized their tal-ents, which directly impacted their assignments and ability to move up in the company or firm. The fact that the racial composition of attorneys in the pri-vate sector changed little means that Black women in these settings faced var-ious forms of racism for longer time periods than their counterparts in the public sector.

This historical analysis and the interviews with Black women attorneys suggest that the legacy of segregation is important. The ideologies that justi-fied their exclusion from mainstream educational institutions hindered them when they first arrived in the legal profession. They were not immediately accepted as equals and incorporated into the professional socialization aspects of law schools. It was necessary to create organizations that helped to combat their exclusion in law school to improve the transition to practicing law. It would take time before some law schools would treat racial minority law students as equals with White peers.

Yet this legacy does interact with changes in the profession, where the route to solo law practices becomes more difficult and social class, gender, and race influence access to elite law schools and firms and practices. The growth of the field has presented opportunities at the bottom of the ladder, in public-sector locations, where people work hard on various sides of the law, but do not earn the income of lawyers placed in corporations and major law firms. In private and public positions, Black women have to work to demonstrate that they can be attorneys, often in settings with little assistance and mentoring. While we hear accounts of affirmative action letting nonqualified Black women into professional settings, these interviews as well as earlier studies (Higginbotham & Weber, 1999) show that Black women are indeed well qualified and might have to have more qualifications for positions than those who have race and gender privileges. Prestigious law school attendance can ensure a job in public-sector settings, but these same credentials would likely enable a male to move into private-sector employment as an attorney, bringing more opportunities for advancement and earnings. Some Black women are able to convert early public-sector employment, where they obtain litigation experience, into new employment options; but this is not always the case (Wilkins, 2004a).

Private-sector legal employment similarly does not offer the same advantages to Black women as it may to White attorneys, as Black women are less likely to make partner (Heinz, et al., 2005) and recent studies show they leave due to a hostile climate (ABA Commission on Women in the Legal Profession, 2006). The women in Heinz's study voiced complaints that are echoed in other scholarship about the hostility and chilly climate as well as the lack of mentoring. Their incorporation into mentoring relationships is not immediate, but came only after they had demonstrated their abilities and learned the ropes on their own.

The practice of law is a public service, as well as an occupation, so that the larger changes in the field impact who gets legal representation and the quality of that representation. We have moved from the early days when the barriers to securing an education and obstacles to practicing law were huge, but we continue to have race, gender, and social class operating as barriers to who can become a practicing attorney and the employment options he/she finds available. As Black women enter the profession of law in significant numbers, they find many bridges to cross to reach parity in political power and earnings, as well as respect for the work they do in the field.

NOTE

1. "Corporate," "Company," and "Southern City" are used as a pseudonyms to protect the identities of sources.

References

Abbott, A. (1988). *The System of Professions: An Essay on the Division of Expert Labor.* Chicago: University of Chicago Press.

ABA Commission on Women in the Legal Profession. (2006). *Visible Invisibility: Women of Color in Law Firms.* Washington: American Bar Association.

Blackwell, J. E. (1981). *Mainstreaming Outsiders: The Production of Black Professionals.* Bayside, NY: General Hall, Inc.

Chanen, J. S. (2006, August). Early Exits: Women of Color at Large Law Firms Tell ABA Researchers They Are Overlooked and Undervalued—Maybe That's Why They Are Leaving in Droves. *ABA Journal.*

Chambliss, E. (2004). *Miles to Go: Progress of Minorities in the Legal Profession.* Washington: American Bar Association Commission on Racial and Ethnic Diversity in the Legal Profession.

Epstein, C. F. (1993). *Women in Law.* Second edition. Urbana: University of Illinois Press.

Feagin, J. R., Vera, H., & Imani, N. (1996). *The Agony of Education: Black Students in White Colleges and Universities.* New York: Routledge Press.

Gaines, K. (1996). *Uplifting the Race: Black Leadership, Politics, and Culture in the Twentieth Century.* Chapel Hill: University of North Carolina Press.

Heinz, J. P, Nelson, R. L., Sandefur, R. L., & Laumann, E. O. (2005). *Urban Lawyers: The New Social Structure of the Bar.* Chicago: University of Chicago Press.

Higginbotham, E. (1987). Employment for Professional Black Women in the Twentieth Century. In C. Bose & G. Spitze (Eds.), *Ingredients for Women's Employment Policy* (pp. 73–91). Albany, NY: SUNY Press.

Higginbotham, E. (1994). Black Professional Women: Job Ceiling and Employment Sectors. In M. B. Zinn & B. T. Dill (Eds.), *Women of Color in U.S. Society* (pp. 113–131). Philadelphia: Temple University Press.

Higginbotham, E. (2001). *Too Much to Ask: Black Women in the Era of Integration.* Chapel Hill: University of North Carolina Press.

Higginbotham, E. & Weber, L. (1999). Perceptions of Workplace Discrimination among Black and White Professional-Managerial Women. In Irene Browne (Ed.), *Latinas and African American Women at Work: Race, Gender, and Economic Inequality* (pp. 327–353). New York: Russell Sage Publications.

Hine, D. C. (1989). *Black Women in White: Racial Conflict and Cooperation in the Nursing Profession.* Bloomington: Indiana University Press.

Hine, D. C. (2003). Black Professional and Race Consciousness: Origins of the Civil Rights Movement, 1890–1950. *Journal of American History, 78,* 1279–1294.

Katznelson, I. (2005). *When Affirmative Action Was White.* New York: Norton.

Onkst, D. (1998). First a Negro . . . Incidentally a Veteran: Black World War II Veterans and the G.I. Bill of Rights in the Deep South, 1944–1948. *Journal of Social History, 31,* 517–538.

Pierce, J. (1996). *Gender Trials.* Berkeley: University of California Press.

Segal, G. R. (1983). *Blacks in the Law: Philadelphia and the Nation.* Philadelphia: University of Pennsylvania Press.

Shaw, S. J. (1996). *What a Woman Ought to Be and to Do: Black Professional Women Workers during the Jim Crow Era.* Chicago: University of Chicago Press.

Smith, J. C., Jr. (1993). *Emancipation: The Making of the Black Lawyer, 1844–1944.* Philadelphia: University of Pennsylvania Press.

Smith, J. C., Jr. (Ed.) (1998). *Rebels in Law: Voices of Black Women Lawyers.* Ann Arbor: University of Michigan Press.

Wilkins, D. B. (2004a). Doing Well by Doing Good? The Role of Public Service in the Careers of Black Corporate Lawyers. *Houston Law Review*, *41*, 1–91.

Wilkins, D. B. (2004b, March). From "Separate in Inherently Unequal" to Diversity is Good for Business: The Rise of Market-Based Diversity Arguments and the Fate of the Black Corporate Bar. *Harvard Law Review*, *117*(5), 1548–1615.

Wilson, F. R. (2002). "All the Glory . . . Faded Quickly": Sadie T. M. Alexander and Black Professional Women, 1920–1950. In S. Harley & the Black Women and Work Collective (Eds.), *Sister Circle: Black Women and Work* (pp. 164–183). New Brunswick, NJ: Rutgers University Press.

Wilson, F. R. (2006). *The Segregated Scholars: Black Social Scientists and the Creation of Black Labor Studies, 1890–1950*. Charlottesville: University of Virginia Press.

3

The Intersection of Poverty Discourses

Race, Class, Culture, and Gender

DEBRA HENDERSON AND ANN TICKAMYER

Hurricane Katrina and its aftermath present a timely window on the contradictory inner dynamics of race, class, gender, and poverty in America. The exposure of extreme poverty, closely associated with an urban Black underclass, stranded by natural disaster and political neglect, was both a reminder of the existence of deprivation that the public is reluctant to acknowledge and a reinforcement of popular prejudices and stereotypes about poverty that the same public is all too ready to espouse. In the United States, poverty is commonly given a Black and disreputable face and then alternately ignored and demonized, part of a legacy of institutionalized racism that obscures the complexity of its demographics, causes, and consequences. Media coverage of the disaster followed a familiar script: surprise and discovery, followed by efforts to classify victims and victimizers, deserving and undeserving, laced with a little sympathy for the former and moral outrage at the latter. Regardless of whether Katrina actually generates new concern, policy, or programs for the poor or just represents one of the periodic rediscoveries of poverty, the portrayal of its ravages graphically reinforces popular views of who is poor and why that underlies much of public opinion and policy.

Yet the reality of poverty is much more complex. Across the country, although African Americans are overrepresented among the poor, they are not the majority or the only high visibility group among the poor. Whites make up the majority of all persons below the poverty line, and depending on location, pockets of White, Black, Latino, Asian, or Native American poverty dominate local landscapes.[1] Yet poverty remains firmly entrenched as a Black and White issue, both literally and metaphorically. In this chapter, we examine one group—poor White Appalachian women—as an entry point into deconstructing discourses of poverty and welfare policy in the United States, looking at the

50

intersections of race, class, gender, space, and culture. The purpose is twofold: to expand understanding of the multiplicities of poverty identities, locations, and control mechanisms; and to show how the existence of this complexity nevertheless reinforces the welfare racism that underlies poverty discourse. We use an intersectional framework built on feminist and critical race perspectives to accomplish these tasks.

Overview

Poverty discourse, both academic and popular, highlights race and implies "Blackness" as the primary racial identity when examining welfare policy. This body of research rarely considers identities that are attributed to other racial, ethnic, or cultural groups. In her early work on Black feminism, Collins (1990) argues that the stereotypical representation of the "welfare mother" is an ideological image used to control Black women. Similarly the stereotypical perception of the "hillbilly" and "White trash" creates an image in rural Appalachian communities that serves to control and exploit poor, White women receiving public assistance. While welfare racism clearly exists in racially heterogeneous communities, in rural Appalachia where the population is primarily White, other sources of disadvantage and difference exist. By examining the intersections of culture, class, and gender along with race, we argue that poor Appalachian women experience a form of "welfare culturalism" that has similarities to the welfare racism experienced by poor Black women. In addition, we argue that not only do the negative stereotypes fostered in Appalachia serve to control poor rural White women, but they sustain a broader system of welfare racism that impacts poor minority women.

In the rest of this chapter we deconstruct the discourses on poverty and welfare provision in conjunction with an intersectional framework to demonstrate the ways that class, race, space, and culture intersect with gender to create the politics of current welfare policy. We begin by examining beliefs about poverty and welfare and how these engage different social locations and identities. We then turn to a critical view of intersectionality theories to determine whether and to what extent they privilege some social locations over others and how this is relevant for analyzing poverty politics. This analysis is informed by our research on the impacts of welfare reform on poor individuals, families, and communities in rural Appalachia (Tickamyer, et al., 2006; Tickamyer, et al., 2000; Henderson, et al., 2002). Based on the juxtaposition of the experiences of poor women across race, place, and culture, we end by evaluating the implications for poverty discourse and welfare policy.

Poverty and Welfare Discourse

In the United States the official poverty measure is defined by failure to meet an income threshold based on a formula to determine a minimum subsistence level constructed from cost of living data, adjusted for family size and composition and adjusted annually for inflation (U.S. Census Bureau, 2000). Poverty in this formulation is conceptualized as an objective condition, defined by a scientifically devised, politically neutral formula that can then document differential impacts on some individuals and groups compared to others. Gender and race are correlates of poverty.

At the same time, there are deeply embedded beliefs about poverty and the poor that belie this technocratic view and create a subtext that forms the foundation for political action. Specifically poverty has long been associated with social values and judgments of worth and worthiness that determine welfare policy. Both historically and currently poverty status has been accompanied by beliefs about moral worth that attribute responsibility for the condition. Thus the notions of "deserving" and "undeserving" poor can be found in poverty discourse dating as far back as the English poor laws and by some accounts much longer (Katz, 1990). Attribution of deservingness has varied by time and place with changing views of morality and social justice, but the fundamental construction has retained its potency despite repeated efforts to debunk its claims.

The basic component of deserving status revolves around beliefs about responsibility for poverty status coupled with value for particular social identity. When poverty is seen as an accident of fate, through no fault of the individual to otherwise worthy and productive citizens, there is much greater likelihood of attribution of deservingness and a greater willingness to commit public resources to its alleviation. Alternatively when the individual is viewed with suspicion of moral slackness, there is much less willingness to take a charitable view. Women have been particularly targeted by these changing notions of morality. Categories of "deserving" have focused on normative behavior and sexuality. The White war widow with young children and working- or middle-class origins represents the quintessential stereotype of deservingness that all other categories are measured against. It is no accident that U.S. welfare programs have historical roots in widow's pensions (Gordon, 1990; Orloff, 1993).

Just as income and poverty are highly correlated with demographic characteristics such as gender and race, so are attributions of social worth. Popular views of who is deserving and who is not follow societal prejudices and stereotypes. The same dynamics that economically disadvantage women, race and ethnic minorities, the lower class, and so on are at play in creating the representations that denigrate these identities, branding them as undeserving in popular perception. It is a short step from creating categories and labels of moral worth to attaching them to particular configurations of gender, race, class, and culture with consequences for political action and public policy. Public opinion about deservingness is quickly transformed into welfare racism and culturalism.

Welfare Racism and Culturalism

In most instances, the images associated with poverty have become synonymous with those of African Americans, although other race and ethnic minorities may be similarly vulnerable. The media plays a role in racializing welfare policy, and the subsequent perceptions of broader society, by disproportionately presenting images of African Americans in missives on poverty (Avery & Peffley, 2003). However, the pejorative race/poverty connection can be linked to a history of influential racially biased policy analysis and subsequent welfare policy.

During the 1960s' war on poverty, Moynihan (1965) systematically linked poverty in the inner cities to the deterioration of the Black family. Rather than address structural causes of poverty, he argued that economically disadvantaged Blacks were caught in a "tangle of pathology" and blamed inner-city poverty on a Black culture that embraced broken families, illegitimacy, and intergenerational dependency on welfare. Much of Moynihan's work was rejected by social scientists; however, current welfare reform policy rests on his and subsequent analysts' "culture of poverty" arguments that blame the poor for their own poverty (Murray, 1984). Proponents of welfare reform have argued that the "problem" with welfare lies not with broader structural constraints but with the inability of poor people to take personal responsibility for themselves and their families, resulting in denial of "traditional family values," lack of a strong work ethic, inability to delay personal gratification, and, ultimately, the long term dependency on public assistance (Reese, 2005; Hays, 2003).

Blaming welfare recipients for their poverty was part of a discourse imbued with racism that represented recipients, particularly African Americans, as welfare cheats and perpetuated racial stereotypes that produced controlling images such as the "welfare queen." As a result, the ghost of Moynihan's "tangle of pathology" view of the Black family was covertly reintroduced into the debate on welfare reform. This discourse "relied on and reinforced racist views of people of color in general, and African Americans in particular" (Sparks, 2003, 178).

The role of racism in the development and implementation of welfare policy indicates that the social welfare system is not color-blind, but systematically discriminates against people of color (Schram, Soss, & Fording, 2003; Roberts, 2003; Piven, 2003; Dill, Baca Zinn, & Patton, 1998). Socially and politically we "whitewash poverty" by reporting that the majority of welfare recipients are

White. However, due to racialized media presentations, the persistence of explanations founded in a culture of poverty, and the strength of race-based stereotypes such as "welfare queen," the face of welfare is Black (Dill, Baca Zinn, & Patton, 1998; Schram, 2003). More importantly, racism not only informs and molds public assistance policies, but it also results in outcomes that significantly impact the life chances of poor people of color.

By disregarding race-based prejudices and discrimination in broader society, people of color are placed at a disadvantage in terms of successfully leaving public assistance programs and obtaining self-sufficiency. Welfare reform policy does not take into account that racial discrimination impacts the likelihood that recipients of color will be able to secure employment that pays a living wage or obtain safe, affordable housing and childcare (Neubeck & Cazenave, 2001). A growing body of research reports the existence of "racial disparities" in the implementation and outcomes of welfare reform policy, as well as the treatment of Black recipients in comparison to White recipients (Schram, 2005, 253). For example, it appears that as the percentage of people of color increases there is a higher likelihood of stricter welfare reform restrictions and enforcement (Soss, et al., 2001; Fellowes & Rowe, 2004). Furthermore White recipients are more likely than Black recipients to successfully leave welfare (Finegold & Staveteig, 2002), to stay off of assistance once they have left (Loprest, 1999), and to have better options and referrals for education/training (Gooden, 2003).

Current discussions of welfare racism often devolve into analyses of the Black experience. However, other racial/ethnic minorities have also experienced the impact of welfare racism via the implementation and outcomes of welfare reform legislation. This is particularly apparent among immigrant groups seeking new opportunities in the United States and those minorities that live in isolated geographic locations. Empirical evidence suggests that the welfare system has been grounded in a "history of exclusion" and that welfare reform legislation works to further the disenfranchisement of other people of color in the United States (Fujiwara, 1998, 2005; Weinberg, 1998, 2000).

Prior to the implementation of welfare reform, growing anti-immigration sentiment responded to arguments that immigrants were taking jobs away from U.S. citizens (Fujiwara, 2005) and immigrant women were taking advantage of an overly indulgent welfare system (Fujiwara, 2005; Lindsley, 2002; Roberts, 1997) by restricting the access of legal immigrants to need based public assistance such as Supplemental Security Income, food stamps, and services provided by Temporary Aid to Needy Families (Fix & Zimmerman, 1995). While there has been a partial restoration of need based assistance to noncitizen immigrants, this mandate placed them at the center of a racially charged political debate and cast them as members of the undeserving poor, further bolstering anti-immigrant bias and stereotypes (Fujiwara, 2005).

Similarly the racial politics underlying welfare reform had a significant negative impact on the life chances of other racial/ethnic minorities. The limited research on poor Hispanic recipients in the United States suggests that their welfare experiences may be similar to those of African American recipients (Dill, Baca Zinn, & Patton, 1998; McPhee & Bronstein, 2003; Lee & Abrams, 2001; Weinberg, 1998). Furthermore the image of the "welfare queen" that has haunted African American women is also a prominent controlling image for poor Hispanic women (Briggs, 2002). Hispanics also face difficulties that are distinct to their racial/ethnic background when attempting to meet the mandates of welfare reform. For example, language barriers and conflicting cultural demands play an important role in the distribution of assistance, opportunities for further education, and successful entry into the labor market (Allegro, 2005; Bok, 2004; Briggs, 2002; Burnham, 2002; Cattan & Girard, 2004).

Other minorities residing in isolated communities have also been disproportionately impacted by welfare reform policy. This is particularly the case for reservation bound Native Americans. Given the extreme poverty on reservations, the high unemployment rates, and the lack of employment opportunities, tribal governments found themselves without the social capital or economic resources necessary to successfully implement welfare reform (Pandey, et al., 1999; Stromwall, et al., 1998). Yet, when recipients were unsuccessful in entering the labor force the stereotypical image of the "lazy, alcoholic Indian" was evoked as explanation for the inability to achieve personal responsibility.

In summary, welfare reform has consistently been tied to racial politics and has significantly impacted the life chances of racial/ethnic minorities across the country. Missing from this discussion is an analysis of how White poverty fits into the system of welfare racism. There is a need to examine White women's experiences with the welfare system, especially in racially homogeneous rural areas such as Appalachia where clear spatial inequalities exist (Tickamyer, et al., 2006) and cultural stereotypes that create stigma and controlling images (Billings, Norman, & Ledford, 1999). Appalachian scholarship suggests that the construction of an Appalachian identity and a rigid two-class system often parallels, and is as enduring, as race disadvantage (Duncan, 2000). Thus the construction of a rural Appalachian identity creates a dimension of difference that is denigrated by policy makers and represented as culturally inferior (Billings, Norman, & Ledford, 1999), which in turn has a material reality for poor women in the region (Duncan, 2000; Billings & Blee, 2000; Lichter & Jensen, 2002; Tickamyer, et al., 2004).

We synthesize theory and research on welfare racism produced by "intersectional analysis" (Dill, 2002; Dill, Jones-Deweever, & Schram, 2004) with our empirical research on Appalachian poverty (Tickamyer, et al., 2006, 2000) to show that the facade of a universal social welfare system and policies disguises discourses that reinforce the real disadvantages that different race and ethnic groups experience, including White Appalachian women. Appalachian women, as a cultural minority and a segment of the lower socioeconomic class, are twice exploited by the stereotypical images of welfare recipients. First, in isolated rural Appalachia the stereotypical images of White poverty—"hillbilly" and "White trash"—and belief in a culture of poverty serve to define poverty in the area and foster hostility from working- and middle-class Whites. These images influence economic development within the region with impacts on employment opportunities. At an individual level they stigmatize recipients, making it difficult for women to leave welfare and enter the workforce. Second, at the same time that poor Appalachian women are denigrated as yet another example of the deficiencies attributed to welfare dependency, their Whiteness becomes the means to argue that the welfare system is bias-free regarding race. Thus these stereotypical images serve to control the opportunities of both White Appalachian women and women of color as they attempt to negotiate the welfare system.

The existence of rural White poverty reinforces the claim that public policy is a universal that does not discriminate by gender, race, or any other salient category. The realities are that these dimensions of difference are reinforced by the pretense that poverty policy is unbiased and gender/race neutral. Poverty policy is neither culturally nor gender/race neutral, but the existence of pockets of poor White women in rural Appalachia provides a convenient way for policy makers to argue that neutrality exists with detrimental outcomes for all poor women.

Theoretical Framework: The Intersections of Feminist Perspectives

An intersectional perspective examines "the relationships and interactions between multiple axes of identity and multiple dimensions of social organization—at the same time" (Dill, 2002, 4). To understand the impact of structured inequality on individual lives requires scrutiny of overlapping categories (e.g., race, class, gender) and multiple sources of power and privilege (Dill, 2002; Dill, Baca Zinn, & Patton, 1998; Weber, 2001). This perspective has been particularly important when examining the intersecting systems of domination that impact the opportunities for women of color in the United States (Dill, 1988, 2002; Gilkes, 1994; Higginbotham, 1994; Weber, 2001).

Collins (2004, 351) provides a concise statement of the meaning of intersectionality as "analysis claiming that systems of race, economic class, gender, sexuality, ethnicity, nation, and age form mutually constructing features of social organization, which shape African American experiences and, in turn, are shaped by African Americans." Oppression and exploitation can be best understood through an evaluation of how varying statuses within a hierarchical social system are intertwined to produce a matrix of domination whereby the experiences of individuals are bound by their specific social locations (Collins, 1990). Intersectionality captures the dynamic and relational nature of interconnected status and power hierarchies for defining group experience and opportunities.

One issue for intersectional analysis is how to evaluate contradictory social locations. In most formulations of intersectional frameworks, even recognizing the complexity of different combinations, there is at least implicit but more often, explicit assertion of a dominant identity, what in other contexts has been called a "master status." Race in U.S. society, by virtue of its historical, political, and legal legacies of exploitation and repression, usually is accorded primacy. For example, in their analysis of multiracial feminism and the difficulties confronted by women of color, Baca Zinn and Dill (1996) argue that race is the primary structure of power and social segmentation and "even cultural and group differences among women are produced through interaction within a racially stratified social order" (203). Collins (1998, 211) similarly privileges race when she dispels the "myth of equivalent oppressions" arguing, for example, that the position and life experiences of Black women are not comparable to gay White men or similar nonequivalent combinations of advantage and hardship. In her early influential writings, hooks (1981, 1989) focuses on the unique hardships produced for African American women in the systematic acts of terrorism embedded in slavery and Jim Crow. Guinier and Torres (2002) assert the power of "political race" as both a defining and liberating condition. In these formulations, racial dynamics trump other group identities even as they forge unique perspectives in their intersections.

The focus on race extends from the binary of Black and White to include multiple racial categories and experience. Influential work by and about Latinas, Asian Americans, Native Americans, and immigrant and native-born women of various ethnicities and nationalities augments primary work on African American experience and extends empirical and theoretical understanding of difference and diversity for women of color in a variety of hues (Collins, 2004; Cole & Guy-Sheftall, 2003; Bettie, 2003; Hurtado, 1996; hooks, 1990; Mihesuah, 2003; Romero, 2002; Shah, 1997). Within this rainbow approach, the analytic category that remains problematic is Whiteness, because White denotes the privileged and majority end of racial categorization. When White women are part of an underclass, the contradiction between racial privilege and other subordinate positions presents the problem of contradictory social location.

Yet the existence of groups with contradictory positions is both real and important for understanding the "mutual construction" of intersecting systems of domination and subordination. In recent writings, hooks (2000) argues that "class matters" to both Whites and Blacks and Collins (2004) focuses on how the "new racism" embodying elements of class, culture, and dominant notions of sexuality differentially but adversely affect both women and men. Each gives voice to more nuanced depictions of the shifting meanings of different combinations of social locations that may include nominally privileged positions. Poor White Appalachian women on welfare embody this type of contradictory location.

Consensus versus Crosscutting Intersections

A useful means of organizing forms of intersectionality is suggested by Collins (2004, 47) when she describes a model used by Cohen (1999) to examine the politics of intersectional identities. This model distinguishes between consensus and crosscutting political issues. Consensus issues affect all group members, although not necessarily in the same way. Crosscutting issues are perceived to affect one subgroup more than another. In Collins's examples, race is a consensus issue for African Americans; gender and sexuality are crosscutting issues perceived by Blacks as only relevant for women and lesbian, gay, bisexual, and transgendered (LGBT) individuals respectively. If we turn this formulation around and ask how it applies to Whites, the facile answer is that Whiteness mirrors Black experience: it is also a consensus issue, although often an unexamined one given the invisibility and taken for granted nature of Whiteness for Whites; gender and sexuality are similarly largely segregated to women and LGBT individuals.

If this model is extended by analogy to consider class, the picture gets murkier, although, for both Whites and Blacks, class has a somewhat equivocal position. Within African American communities class has traditionally been subsumed to race, at least as far as political behavior goes, reinforcing the notion that race serves as the organizing status, despite the existence of significant class differences (Collins, 2004). Part of the dynamics of racial politics is that Whites too often perceive all Blacks as being lower-class, and much of the poverty and welfare racism endemic to U.S. politics is based on this stereotype (Schram, 2005). In other words, class is conflated with race for African Americans both within and outside African American communities, although for different reasons, making it a consensus issue. For Whites, however, class may be defined as crosscutting, viewed as applicable only to Blacks and to "underclass" Whites, a group pejoratively labeled in the vernacular with terms such as "White trash" and "hillbilly." The result is to ignore poor Whites, rendering them as aberrant anomalies in the infrequent case when they are visible in the public eye.

The exception to this neglect is where the racial homogeneity of the population combined with historic and identifiable local cultural forms and practices creates a unique social location associated with poverty. Poor Appalachians, the "hillbillies" of popular culture, have assumed this role both locally and in the larger society, and as such, form an interesting test group for understanding welfare politics. We argue that to extend the analytic power of intersectional analysis, it is important to examine the intertwined statuses of race, class, and culture with gender, whereby culture is the key structure of power and social division and "Whiteness" as informed by culture becomes the primary racial categorization.

Whiteness as Race and Culture

The study of "Whiteness" emerged in response to its absence in scholarly investigations of race and current concerns about the "end of Whiteness" as the result of accepted multiracial identities (Hill, 2004). Frankenberg (1993) was one of the first scholars to address the significance of Whiteness in understanding the broader construction of racial categories. She stated, "Whiteness signals the production and reproduction of dominance rather than subordination, normativity rather than marginality, and privilege rather than disadvantage" (236). White privilege has certainly shaped much of our society and has systematically sustained an ideological and material system of power resulting in racial oppression (Jensen, 2003; McIntosh, 2002). However, it is also a perplexing and complicated social phenomenon that is confounded by distinct class and cultural differences. Hartigan (1999) argues that Whiteness is constructed just as other racial categorizations and White privilege is not normative or absolute, but is shaped by class dynamics as well as geographic and cultural labels. Newitz (1997, 148) notes that Whiteness as a racial construct is an "oppressive ideological construct that promotes and maintains social inequalities." However, even as a dominant culture, Whiteness does not always result in privilege and power. Thus race may define Whiteness, but distinctions in class and culture determine boundaries of privilege. Frankenberg states that there are primarily two types of Whites "those who are truly or only White, and those who are White but also something more—or is it something less" (1993, 198). Thus there are Whites of privilege and Whites that are marginalized and defined as "other" (Allison, 1998; Newitz & Wray, 1997). This is particularly noteworthy in rural Appalachia where significant class divisions exist within predominantly White communities (Duncan, 2000), and a White identity often gives sway to a perceived Appalachian cultural identity that is rife with stereotypes and misconceptions.

In deconstructing Whiteness and White privilege, there is also a strong oppositional argument. According to Wiegman (1999), there is potential harm in giving minority status to what is a historical and contemporary majority. By advancing Whites the same minority status as people of color, a "mutuality-of-harm hypothesis" is constructed whereby Whites are said to experience racial oppression similar to that experienced by people of color (144). This is especially problematic, according to Wiegman, when the category of White trash is brought into play. The origins of this stereotype can be traced to the "Eugenic Family Studies" project, which tried to prove through scientific investigation that poor Whites in rural areas were genetically defective (Rafter, 1988). In so doing, they fostered a stereotype that remains today of "rural poor Whites as incestuous and sexually promiscuous, violent, alcoholic, lazy, and stupid" (Wray & Newitz, 1997, 2). By accepting that Whiteness is always equated with power and privilege, Wray and Newitz (1997) argue that the logical corollary is that poor White people are responsible for their poverty and oppression. However, Wiegman (1999) asserts that one must question the logic that equates class oppression with racial oppression (145).

We argue that the failure to evaluate the intersections of race and class results in a misunderstanding of the duality of Whiteness. The stereotypical representation of Whites, in conjunction with physical and spatial location, plays a prominent role in the marginalization of rural Appalachians. In the isolated communities of Appalachia, the conceptualization of White trash is often used synonymously with the term hillbilly, both of which play a significant role in the development and perpetuation of social statuses, identity politics, and a perceived Appalachian culture. While cultural studies and identity scholars are attempting to deconstruct Whiteness and address the rapidly changing face of racial/ethnic identity in the United States, we believe it is important to evaluate the intersections of race, class, culture, and gender in spatial locations where systems of dominance exist that result in White on White oppression.

Appalachian Culture and Controlling Images

The Appalachian region is one of the poorest geographic locations in the nation (Billings & Blee, 2000; The State of Poverty in Ohio, 2004), and lags other regions in economic development, employment rates, and per capita income (Appalachian Regional Commission, 2005). Rural Appalachia has a long history of high unemployment and persistent, severe poverty that is equal to, or worse than, that in urban areas (Rural Sociological Task Force on Persistent Rural Poverty, 1993; Lichter & Jensen, 2002). While those receiving public assistance in both rural and urban areas may confront similar problems in terms of making ends meet and complying with the mandates of welfare reform, empirical evidence indicates that the constraints experienced by welfare recipients in rural areas are distinct from those in urban areas (U.S. Department of Health and Human Services, 2002).

Rural communities are often perceived by broader society as idyllic settings that offer a stable, wholesome environment in which to live and raise a family (Brown & Swanson, 2003; Logan, 1996; National Rural Electric Cooperative Association, 1992; Seebach, 1992). However, these views rarely acknowledge the true nature or conditions of the region (Logan, 1996; Brown & Swanson, 2003). The extreme level of spatial inequality in rural Appalachia, particularly in isolated communities, has a significant impact on the ability of poor people to leave welfare and successfully enter the labor market (Tickamyer, et al., 2006; Zimmerman & Hirschi, 2003). Leaving welfare and achieving self-sufficiency through employment is hindered by the lack of job opportunities and the social/human capital required to facilitate the transition (Parisi, et al., 2003; Tickamyer, et al., 2006; Weber, Duncan, & Whitener, 2002). Unlike their urban counterparts, those in these isolated rural communities often confront an absolute lack of resources such as economic assets, childcare, transportation, healthcare, and housing (Henderson, et al., 2002; Rural Policy Research Institute, 1999; Zimmerman & Hirschi, 2003). Consequently, in comparison to those in urban areas, poor women living in rural communities often encounter more hardship (Brown & Lichter, 2004; Snyder & McLaughlin, 2004).

Spatial inequality in rural communities has a tremendous impact on the experiences of welfare recipients, particularly poor women. However, when examining causes and consequences of rural poverty, the structural constraints are often overlooked in favor of "culture of poverty" explanations. In rural Appalachia, poverty is not blamed on the lack of economic development and viable job opportunities, but on a culture where poor people lack the mainstream values of personal responsibility, a strong work ethic, and the ability to delay gratification (Lewis & Billings, 1997). In this region, a culture of poverty is often translated into an "Appalachian culture." People in isolated rural communities are thought to be so out of sync with the norms and values of broader society that they create a "culture" based in psychological dysfunction and social disassociation (Lewis & Billings, 1997; Ball, 1968). As a result, they foster generational poverty by perpetuating norms and values that embrace laziness, a lack of ambition, pathological tendencies, and welfare dependency. Just as the majority of scholars have renounced the existence of a culture of poverty in urban locales, an "Appalachian culture" of poverty has also been invalidated in rural communities (Billings & Blee, 2000; Billings, Norman, & Ledford, 1999; Lewis & Billings, 1997). This explanation of poverty perseveres in rural Appalachia and in its wake we find misrepresentations of a population that is replete with stereotypical images of White trash and hillbilly (Denham, 2005; Harkins, 2004). The persistence of a culture of poverty explanation in rural Appalachia, and the accompanying cultural stereotypes, serve to parallel race in creating stigma and controlling images (Billings, Norman, & Ledford, 1999; Duncan, 2000) that ultimately impact the livelihood and experiences of those living in this geographic region (Duncan, 2000; Billings & Blee, 2000; Lichter & Jensen, 2002; Tickamyer, et al., 2004)

With the passing of welfare reform legislation, our research group (The Rural Welfare Reform Project) embarked upon an investigation of the impacts of welfare reform and devolution in four poor rural counties in Appalachian Ohio selected for their high levels of poverty and varying capacities to implement welfare reform.[2] The study examines three primary populations most closely affected by welfare reform: public assistance recipients, agency directors, and local employers, as well as secondary populations such as case managers, outside service providers, and county commissioners that play a significant role in the restructuring and devolution of welfare. Using a combination of existing statistics, administrative records and primary data collection consisting of focus groups, surveys, and in-depth interviews the research was designed to provide us with extensive sources of quantitative and qualitative data from each of the participating groups. By analyzing interview data from agency directors, caseworkers, and potential employers, we were able to examine welfare politics in the racially homogeneous communities of rural Appalachia and determine the role of "Appalachian culture," and the accompanying stereotypical images of White trash and hillbilly, in controlling poor White women on welfare in this locale.

By definition, welfare recipients are located in powerless positions within the welfare system as directors and case managers control the valued resources offered through public assistance programs. Similarly potential employers maintain positions of power relative to recipients in their ability to facilitate gainful employment that ultimately impacts the overall survival of recipients. Our data indicate that the perceptions of a viable Appalachian culture of poverty, and the stigmatizing images that are often associated with it, were invoked by all of the aforementioned groups when discussing Appalachian poverty and welfare recipients.

In our interviews with human service agency directors we found that most were long time residents of rural Appalachia and were very knowledgeable of structural constraints that hindered recipients from successfully negotiating welfare-to-work mandates. Yet these same directors were quick to fall back on stigmatizing stereotypes of recipients and the perceived Appalachian culture when evaluating persistent poverty in their region. For example, while explaining problems of recipients successfully leaving welfare and entering the labor market, the director from one of the poorer counties claimed that people in the area were lazy and lacked the necessary ambition to obtain jobs. However, later in the interview he clearly articulated his frustration with the limited employment opportunities in the area as well as a lack of agency resources to fund programs to assist recipients. It was at this point that he invoked the stereotypical hillbilly image regarding his lack of understanding of state regulations in the process of devolution, "What are my people to do? You tell me. I am just a dumb ole hillbilly, but I can't figure this one out."

Our data from caseworker focus groups also showed that while most were in support of welfare reform, they also had concerns similar to directors regarding local capacities to successfully move recipients from welfare to work. However, they, too, resorted to stereotypical representations and Appalachian culture of poverty explanations when discussing poverty and the inability of welfare recipients to achieve self-sufficiency. As one caseworker stated:

> I think the barriers that the workers face are just very significant. They either have legitimate barriers that the client needs to overcome in order to be employed or their attitude or you know, generational or cultural barriers that I think are equally as significant if not more so. Because how do you teach somebody whose parents and grandparents and sisters and brothers and aunts and uncles have lived through the welfare system that it not the way we want you. There is another way to do it.

Another caseworker offered a similar concern with the following comment: "Yeah, their mother was on assistance and they just don't want to work. They don't want to do anything."

Even though caseworkers were cognizant of structural obstacles that recipients face in leaving welfare or making ends meet, they were also likely to make references to a dysfunctional Appalachian culture when discussing incentives to leave welfare. One caseworker voiced the opinions of others with the following remark about the financial incentive proposed by President Bush for those recipients who married. She remarked:

> Oh my God, they're [recipients] going to get married, get divorced, get married, get divorced. Because they do work the system . . . if we could give them, you know, $500 to be married . . . they're going to get married, stay married for six months, get divorced and then get married again to get the incentive again. . . . these people have children with men that they don't know their last name, men that live in Mexico that came up and had a party and they have Internet sex, like they meet someone over the Internet, go to meet them, hop into bed with them, have a kid and can never track the person down again.

Although potential employers are external to the formal functioning of human service agencies, they were instrumental in the survival of welfare recipients as they moved from welfare-to-work. One of the mandates of welfare reform was that recipients achieve self-sufficiency through work. However, successfully moving from cash assistance into the labor market in rural areas is difficult because of the lack the jobs as well as the social/human capital to facilitate this move (Parisi, et al., 2003; Tickamyer, et al., 2006; Weber, Duncan, & Whitener, 2002). Thus the perceptions of potential employers are vitally important in determining who procures the limited jobs available. In an analysis of interviews with potential employers, we found that they, too, incorporated stereotypes and culture of poverty references into their discussions of welfare recipients (White, et al., 2003). One employer made a broad generalization that was consistent with the views of many other employers when he said:

> This is a high welfare area … it's been grandfather, father, and son right on down the line. It's been handed down you know. Ah, people around here joke when the kids aren't in school, what these kids are doing out of school. Well, they're training for when they grow up to be on welfare. That's typical in this area. You drive down the street in the daytime and mom and dad and the kids are all sitting on the front porch when they should be working around and in school … a lot of people see that as the culture and they see these people won't work. They've never worked out … he's not gonna do it cause he's been bred up not to, brought up that way and it's inbred into him.

Although this employer clearly believed in the stereotypical representations of poor people in the area, he strongly supported the existence of an Appalachian culture of poverty. Interestingly enough, in a follow-up statement during a discussion of available employment opportunities for recipients leaving welfare in his community, he said "in [our] county we probably won't be able to come up with the jobs for people [welfare recipients]." It was clear from this statement that, regardless of their work ethic or motivation, successfully entering the labor market would be difficult for recipients.

Another employer expressed the disdain of local employers toward recipients moving from welfare to work with the following comment:

> … most people equate welfare with laziness. And, a lot of people don't want lazy people in their workplace … people's opinion of anyone who's had welfare, they just think they're low lifes. I mean, I don't know how else to say that … it's just they're not worth much.

Overall the strict class dichotomy in this racially homogeneous region results in powerful groups, in this case agency directors, caseworkers, and potential employers, controlling and stigmatizing poor White women through the use of stereotypical images and a perceived Appalachian culture of poverty (Duncan, 2000; Ball, 1968). By examining the intersections of culture, class, and gender along with race our results reinforce previous research (Duncan, 2000) suggesting that poor Appalachian women experience a form of "welfare culturalism" that is similar to the welfare racism experienced by poor Black women.

Implications for Poverty Discourse and Policy

We have argued that it is important to consider the role that the existence of poor White women, and especially a clearly identifiable and visible group of poor Whites as is found in Appalachia, can play for defining the politics of poverty and welfare. At the risk of invoking outmoded forms of functional analysis, we can echo Gans (1971) by asking: What are the functions of poor Appalachian women for the society and the welfare system? Just as Gans demonstrates the social functions of the poor in undifferentiated form for affirming the moral order and maintaining status and power hierarchies, scrutiny of the uses made of different groups of poor people provides insight into the social and political systems that govern and benefit from their existence. In the case of poor Appalachian women, the answer lies in the contradictions of their positions within these systems. First, they are rendered invisible in the pervasive political discourse about poverty and welfare that blames individuals and particularly blames a demonized Black culture of poverty that appears to flaunt middle-class White values and practice for the existence of poverty and the abuse of welfare. Second, they become highly visible as the counterargument to assertions about the restricted and racist nature of the opportunity structure of U.S. society in general, and the welfare system in particular. Their existence reinforces claims for the colorblind nature of the system; whether they are stigmatized depends on context. Unlike African Americans and other racial and ethnic minorities who are invariably perceived as "undeserving," they are assigned a shifting identify as "deserving poor" when welfare racism is in question, but locally they are the underclass with all the negative implications of this status.

Of course, these are discursive functions that describe how the existence of Appalachian poverty (primarily female, White, rural, and steeped in local culture) feeds into larger public opinion and debate about the reasons and appropriate policies for poverty in a way that ultimately is detrimental to all poor people. They do not address the actual experiences of the subjects of this niche in the poverty population, nor do they suggest how the knowledge that poverty has different faces and represents the intersection of different social locations and identities can contribute positively to policy formation. Recognizing that poverty is a phenomenon rooted in many communities with different historical relationships to the larger society is one step in wresting discussion from the hands of demagogues who use poverty as a code for race and racism as the basis of public policy. The issue is not whether the experiences and poverty of White Appalachians are equivalent to, or better or worse than other groups who are stigmatized and suffer deprivation and varying forms of oppression and subordination. Rather the purpose is to recognize the existence of this particular form of poverty, to understand points of similarity and difference, and to use this knowledge to further more informed discussion of policy goals.

What are the implications for poverty and welfare policy? First, is the obvious point that political action and sound policies and programs to benefit the poor are never an easy sell, but they are made virtually impossible when successful divide and conquer strategies are applied to both the poor themselves and to how other citizens view them. Convincing the majority of voters that poverty is someone else's problem, that it is particularly a problem of a racial "other," and that it is primarily a problem created by individual and collective group failure, rather than the outcome of structural impediments and system failure has been a successful strategy for advancing the agenda of those whose goal has been to radically alter public service provision.

The war on welfare, otherwise known as welfare reform, has systematically dismantled the safety net originating in the New Deal and subsequently expanded during the War on Poverty and the civil rights movement. However minimal and inadequate these programs were, up until the last decade of the twentieth century, the trend was to expand coverage and access to previously excluded groups, including racial minorities and rural workers, both White and Black, who were previously excluded from coverage. At the same time, however, these changes opened the door to the form of victim blaming that defines Black poverty as welfare dependency and welfare use as fraud (Schram, Soss, & Fording, 2003). In the backlash, welfare has now been radically altered to eliminate entitlements that guaranteed access if economic criteria were met, a successful effort to reverse the hard won gains to expand the safety net of the previous century with disproportional impacts on African Americans but also on other lower class groups such as poor White Appalachians. The poor of all demographics are the targets of policies initially fueled by racial bias.

This is not to assert that all aspects of the efforts to restructure the welfare system are fundamentally wrong or that there are not successful and much needed changes, but we do claim that some of the underlying reasons for the particular forms they take are misguided and ill-conceived, based on misinformation, stereotypes, and racism. Additionally, in advancing arguments for the importance of scrutinizing class and culture, we are not arguing for the "declining significance of race" as Wilson (1980) and others have claimed, but rather for the necessity to recognize that "class matters" as hooks (2000) writes there are unifying interests within class categories that are important to recognize in order to transcend race and other structural barriers. While it may be utopian to expect that the poor can unite across race, gender, and cultural barriers, there is little reason to hope for change in the absence of such united purpose.

A second implication is that successful programs need to be context specific. Interventions of benefit to the urban poor may not strictly parallel those of rural residents. The hardships and experience of poverty may be similar, but the causes and remedies need to be evaluated for differences as well as similarities. Structural barriers to African American mobility are rooted in the history of slavery, de jure and de facto discrimination, and a long history of institutional racism that are now hidden in official "colorblind" policies that do not recognize these barriers. Similarly Appalachian poverty is rooted in historical forms of regional exploitation that have resulted in isolation and lack of economic development. These examples could be multiplied many times over depending upon particular social location. For example, sources of Hispanic poverty vary depending on the particular ethnicity/nationality, regional location, and so on, so that poverty among urban Puerto Ricans will have very different sources than migrant Mexican labor. The point is that regardless of the specific history and circumstances, when the outcome is disadvantage and deprivation, the current barriers, remedies, and points of leverage for change may differ and have to be addressed accordingly. Thus urban African Americans may need more vigorous forms of antidiscrimination interventions to get access to jobs (Schram, 2005); rural Appalachians may need more direct job creation (Tickamyer, et al., 2006). As primarily women with children, they both will need better childcare options and supports, but even here there can be substantial differences in delivery. In more densely populated urban areas, agency based childcare may be the most viable and desirable option, whereas in remote rural areas where there are few institutional supports, providing incentives for improving the quality of home providers may be a more feasible route.

A third implication is tied to the nature of intersectionality analysis. If this approach is to be more than a descriptive catalog of social locations, or worse a divisive call to ever more minutely subdivided categories for identity politics, it is important to find ways to move beyond the particular and to build on understanding of the structural conditions that this approach can bring. If we draw from the previous arguments the importance of clear under-standing of points of similarity and difference, it may be possible to think about ways of transcending social location to begin to see the means of creat-ing agency within categories and alliances across them. Intersectional analysis provides the means for revealing these barriers (and opportunities) and for giving voice to the varieties of experience they produce. It is the springboard for moving beyond their scripted outcomes.

The question remains of how practically this can happen? How can we overcome the scripts that gender, race, class, and culture create? Here we come full circle. Guinier and Torres (2002) argue that race is the "canary in the coal mine," the first warning that the atmosphere is too poisonous to support life. What is fatal to the canary ultimately will harm all who breathe the poi-soned air. They further argue that forms of resistance forged in racial struggle can play a leading role in seeking progressive social change, but this will require recognizing racial difference and harnessing the knowledge this pro-duces. They see the possibility of transcending racial barriers not by pretend-ing they do not exist, but by recognizing the costs, realizing that what is bad for the canary ultimately touches everyone, and using this knowledge as the means to organize for change.

The events of hurricane Katrina and their portrayal in the media are a recent manifestation of this canary, a revelation of the poisonous atmosphere that still surrounds the lives of the poor and the particular role that race plays in its detection. They are also evidence of the distance this society has to go to achieve the necessary knowledge of poverty. Only by revealing the complexities of the causes, consequences, and experiences of poverty, including the lives of poor White Appalachian women, can steps be taken toward gaining this new level of awareness.

NOTES

1. We recognize the variation in identities that are often attributed to people of color from diverse racial/ethnic backgrounds. However, for the purpose of this chapter we will use the terms Black/African American, Hispanic/Latino, and Indian/Native American interchangeably.

2. Support for this research comes from the Joyce Foundation; The National Research Initiative of the Cooperative State Research, Education and Extension Service, USDA Grant #97–35401–4561; Ohio State Legal Services and Legal Aid Society of Greater Cincinnati (OSLSA/LASGC); and Ohio University.

References

Allegro, L. (2005). Welfare Use and Political Response: Urban Narratives From First and Second-Generation Puerto Ricans and Dominicans in New York City. *Centro Journal*, 17(1), 221–241.

Allison, C. B. (1998). Okie Narratives: Agency and Whiteness. In J. L. Kinchelo, S. R. Steinbert, N. M. Rodriguez, & R. E. Chennault (Eds.), *White Reign: Deploying Whiteness in America* (pp. 229–243). New York: St. Martin's Press.

Appalachian Regional Commission. (2005). Retrieved April 14, 2005, from www.arc.gov/index.jsp.

Avery, J. M., & Peffley, M. (2003). Race Matters: The Impact of News Coverage of Welfare Reform on Public Policy. In S. Schram, J. Soss, & R. C. Fording (Eds.), *Race and the Politics of Welfare Reform* (pp. 131–150). Ann Arbor: University of Michigan Press.

Baca Zinn, M., & Dill, B. T. (1996). Theorizing Difference from Multiracial Feminism. *Feminist Studies*, 22, 323–329.

Ball, R. A. (1968). A Poverty Case: An Analgesic Subculture of the Southern Appalachians. *American Sociological Review*, (33), 885–895.

Bettie, J. (2003). *Women Without Class: Girls, Race, and Identity*. Berkeley: University of California Press.

Billings, D. B., & Blee, K. M. (2000). *The Road to Poverty: The Making of Wealth and Hardship in Appalachia*. Cambridge: Cambridge University Press.

Billings, D. B., Norman, G., & Ledford, K. (1999). *Back Talk from Appalachia: Confronting Stereotypes*. Lexington: University of Kentucky Press.

Bok, M. (2004). Education and Training for Low-Income Women: An Elusive Goal. *Affilia*, 19(1), 39–52.

Briggs, L. (2002). La Vida, Moynihan, and Other Libels: Migration, Social Science, and the Making of the Puerto Rican Welfare Queen. *Centro Journal*, 14(1), 75–101.

Brown, D. L., & Swanson, L. E. (2003). Introduction: Rural America Enters the New Millennium. In D. L. Brown & L. E. Swanson (Eds.), *Challenges for Rural America in the Twenty-First Century* (pp. 1–15). University Park: Pennsylvania State University Press.

Brown, J. B., & Lichter, D. (2004). Poverty, Welfare, and the Livelihood Strategies of Non-Metropolitan Single Mothers. *Rural Sociology, 63*(2), 282–301.

Burnham, L. (2002). Welfare Reform, Family Hardship, and Women of Color. In R. Albelda & K. Byron (Eds.), *Losing Ground* (pp. 43–56). Boston: South End Press.

Cattan, P., & Girard, C. (2004). Recent Cuban Immigrants and Native-Born African Americans Leaving Welfare. *Hispanic Journal of Behavioral Sciences, 26*(3), 312–332.

Cohen, C. J. (1999). *The Boundaries of Blackness: AIDS and the Breakdown of Black Politics.* Chicago: University of Chicago.

Cole, J., & Guy-Sheftall, B. (2003). *Gender Talk: The Struggle for Women's Equality in African American Communities.* New York: Ballantine.

Collins, P. H. (1990). *Black Feminist Thought: Knowledge, Consciousness, and the Politics of Empowerment.* Boston: Unwin Hyman.

Collins, P. H. (1998). *Fighting Words: Black Women and the Search for Justice.* Minneapolis: University of Minnesota Press.

Collins, P. H. (2004). *Black Sexual Politics: African Americans, Gender, and the New Racism.* New York: Routledge Press.

Denham, S. A. (2005). Voices at Ohio University Speak About Appalachia: Perspectives about Stereotypes. *Appalachian Faculty Learning Community.* Ohio University.

Dill, B. T. (1988). Our Mothers' Grief: Racial Ethnic Women and the Maintenance of Families. *Journal of Family History, 13*(4), 415–431.

Dill, B. T. (2002). Intersections, Identities & Inequalities in Higher Education. *Robin Williams Jr. Lecture.* Eastern Sociological Society.

Dill, B. T., Baca Zinn, M., & Patton, S. (1998). Valuing Families Differently: Race, Poverty and Welfare Reform. *Sage Race Relations Abstracts, 23*(3), 4–30.

Dill, B. T., Jones-Deweever, A., & Schram, S. (2004). Racial, Ethnic, and Gender Disparities in Access to Jobs, Education and Training under Welfare Reform. *Research and Action Briefs 1.* College Park, MD: The Consortium on Race, Gender and Ethnicity.

Duncan, C. M. (2000). *Worlds Apart: Why Poverty Persists in Rural America.* New Haven, CT: Yale University Press.

Fellowes, M. C., & Rowe, G. (2004). Politics and the New American Welfare State. *American Journal of Political Science, 48*(2), 362–373.

Finegold, K., & Staveteig, S. (2002). Race, Ethnicity, and Welfare Reform. In A. Weil & K. Finegold (Eds.), *Welfare Reform: The Next Act* (pp. 203–244). Washington, DC: Urban Institute Press.

Fix, M., & Zimmerman, W. (1995). When Should Immigrants Receive Public Benefits? In I. V. Sawhill (Ed.), *Welfare Reform: An Analysis of the Issues* (ch. 13). Retrieved April 30, 2005, from http://www.urban.org/url.cmf?ID=306620.

Frankenberg, Ruth. 1993. *White Women, Race Matters: The Social Construction of Whiteness.* Minneapolis: University of Minnesota Press.

Fujiwara, L. H. (1998). The Impact of Welfare Reform on Asian Immigrant Communities. *Social Justice, 25*(1), 82–104.

Fujiwara, L. H. (2005). Immigrant Rights are Human Rights: The Reframing of Immigrant Entitlement and Welfare. *Social Problems, 52*(1), 79–101.

Gans, H. (1971, July/August). The Uses of Poverty: The Poor Pay All. *Social Policy,* 20–24.

Gilkes, C. T. (1994). If It Wasn't for the Women . . . African American Women, Community Work, and Social Change. In M. Baca Zinn & B. Thornton Dill (Eds.), *Women of Color in U.S. Society* (pp. 229–246). Philadelphia: Temple University Press.

Gooden, S. (2003). Contemporary Approaches to Enduring Challenges: Using Performance Measures to Promote Racial Equality under TANF. In S. Schram, J. Soss, &

R. C. Fording (Eds.), *Race and the Politics of Welfare Reform* (pp. 254–275). Ann Arbor: University of Michigan Press.

Gordon, L. (Ed.). (1990). *Women, the State and Welfare*. Madison: University of Wisconsin Press.

Guinier, L., & Torres, G. (2002). *The Miner's Canary: Enlisting Race Resisting Power, Transforming Democracy*. Cambridge, MA: Harvard University Press.

Harkins, A. (2004). *Hillbilly: A Cultural History of an American Icon*. New York: Oxford University Press.

Hartigan, J. (1999). *Racial Situations: Class Predicaments of Whiteness in Detroit*. Princeton, NJ: Princeton University Press.

Hays, S. (2003). *Flat Broke with Children: Women in the Age of Welfare Reform*. New York: Oxford University Press.

Henderson, D. A., Tickamyer, A., White, J., & Tadlock, B. (2002). Rural Appalachian Families in the Wake of Welfare Reform. *Family Focus: National Conference of Family Relations Report, 47*(3), F7–F9.

Higginbotham, E. (1994). "Black Professional Women: Job Ceilings and Employment Sectors." In M. Baca Zinn & B. T. Dill (Eds.), *Women of Color in U.S. Society* (pp. 113–131). Philadelphia: Temple University Press.

Hill, M. (2004). *After Whiteness: Unmaking an American Majority*. New York: New York University Press.

hooks, b. (1981). *Ain't I a Woman: Black Women and Feminism*. Boston: South End Press.

hooks, b. (1989). *Talking Back: Thinking Feminist, Thinking Black*. Boston: South End Press.

hooks, b. (1990). *Yearning: Race, Gender, and Cultural Politics*. Boston: South End Press.

hooks, b. (2000). *Where We Stand: Class Matters*. New York: Routledge Press.

Hurtado, A. (1996). *The Color of Privilege: Three Blasphemes on Race and Feminism*. Ann Arbor: University of Michigan Press.

Jensen, R. (2003). White Privilege Shapes the U.S. In M. S. Kimmel & A. L. Ferber (Eds.), *Privilege* (pp. 79–82). Boulder, CO: Westview Press.

Katz, M. B. (1990). *The Undeserving Poor: From the War on Poverty to the War on Welfare*. New York: Pantheon Books.

Lee, S. Z., & Abrams, L. S. (2001). Challenging Depictions of Dependency: TANF Recipients React to Welfare Reform. *Journal of Poverty, 5*(1), 91–111.

Lewis, R. L., & Billings, D. B. (1997). Appalachian Culture and Economic Development: A Retrospective View of Theory and Literature. *Journal of Appalachian Studies, 3*(1), 1–31.

Lichter, D., & Jensen, L. (2002). Rural America in Transition: Poverty and Welfare at the Turn of the Twenty-First Century. In B. Weber, G. Duncan, & L. Whitener (Eds.), *Rural Dimensions of Welfare Reform* (pp. 77–110). Kalamazoo, MI: Upjohn.

Lindsley, S. (2002). The Gendered Assault on Immigrants. In J. Silliman & A. Bhattacharjee (Eds.), *Policing the National Body: Race, Gender and Criminalization* (pp. 175–196). Boston: South End Press.

Logan, J. R. (1996). Rural America as a Symbol of American Values. *Rural Development Perspectives, 12*(1), 19–21.

Loprest, P. (1999). How Families That Left Welfare are Doing: A National Picture. *Assessing the New Federalism, B-01*. Washington, DC: Urban Institute.

McIntosh, P. (2002). White Privilege: Unpacking the Invisible Knapsack. In P. S. Rothenberg (Ed.), *White Privilege* (pp. 97–101). New York: Worth Publications.

McPhee, D. M., & Bronstein, L. R. (2003). The Journey From Welfare to Work: Learning From Women Living in Poverty. *Affilia, 18*(1), 34–48.

Mihesuah, D. A. (2003). *Indigenous American Women: Decolonization Empowerment and Activism*. Lincoln: University of Nebraska Press.

Moynihan, D. P. (1965). The Negro Family: The Case for National Action. *Office of Family Planning and Research, Department of Labor*. Washington, DC.

Murray, C. (1984). *Losing Ground*. New York: Basic Books.

National Rural Electric Cooperative Association. (1992). Public Attitudes toward Rural America. CD3–46. Washington, DC: NRECA Public Relations Division.

Neubeck, K. J., & Cazenave, N. A. (2001). *Welfare Racism: Playing the Race Card against America's Poor*. New York: Routledge Press.

Newitz, A. (1997). White Savagery and Humiliation, or a New Racial Consciousness in the Media. In M. Wray & A. Newitz (Eds.), *White Trash: Race and Class in America* (pp. 131–154). New York: Routledge Press.

Newitz, A. & Wray, M. (1997). Introduction. In M. Wray & A. Newitz (Eds.), *White Trash: Race and Class in America* (pp. 1–12). New York: Routledge Press.

Orloff, A. S. (1993). *The Politics of Pensions: A Comparative Study of Britain, Canada, and the United States*. Madison: University of Wisconsin Press.

Pandey, S., Brown, E. F., Scheuler-Whitaker, L., Gundersen, B., & Eyrich, K. (1999). Promise of Welfare Reform. Development through Devolution on Indian Reservations. *Journal of Poverty, 3*(4), 37–61.

Parisi, D., McLaughlin, D., Grice, S., Taquino, M., & Gill, D. (2003). TANF Participation Rates: Do Community Conditions Matter? *Rural Sociology, 68*(4), 491–512.

Piven, F. F. (2003). Why Welfare is Racist. In S. Schram, J. Soss, & R. C. Fording (Eds.), *Race and the Politics of Welfare Reform* (pp. 323–335). Ann Arbor: University of Michigan Press.

Rafter, N. H. (Ed.). (1988). *White Trash: The Eugenic Family Studies, 1877–1919*. Boston: Northeastern University Press.

Reese, E. (2005). *Backlash against Welfare Mothers Past and Present*. Berkeley: University of California Press.

Roberts, D. (1997). Who May Give Birth to Citizens? Reproduction, Eugenics, and Immigration. In J. F. Pera (Ed.), *Immigrants Out: The New Nativism and the Anti-Immigrant Impulse in the United States* (pp. 205–219). New York: New York University Press.

Roberts, D. (2003). *Shattered Bonds: The Color of Child Welfare*. New York: Basic Books.

Romero, M. (2002). *Maid in the USA: 10th Anniversary Edition*. New York: Routledge Press.

Rural Policy Research Institute (RUPRI). (1999). *Rural America and Welfare Reform: An Overview Assessment*. Policy paper pp. 99–103, February 10, Rural Welfare Reform Initiative. Retrieved April 24, 2005, from www.rupri.org/publications/.

Rural Sociological Task Force on Persistent Rural Poverty. (1993). *Poverty in Rural America*. Boulder, CO: Westview Press.

Schram, S. (2003). Putting a Black Face on Welfare: The Good and the Bad. In S. Schram, J. Soss, and R. C. Fording (Eds.), *Race and the Politics of Welfare Reform* (pp. 196–221). Ann Arbor: University of Michigan Press.

Schram, S. (2005, June). Contextualizing Racial Disparities in American Welfare Reform: Toward a New Poverty Research. *Perspectives on Politics, 3*(2), 253–268.

Schram, S., Soss, J., & Fording, R. C. (2003). *Race and the Politics of Welfare Reform*. Ann Arbor: University of Michigan Press.

Seebach, M. (1992). Small Towns Have a Rosy Image. *American Demographics, 14*(10), 19.

Shah, S. (1997). *Dragon Ladies: Asian American Feminists Breathe Fire*. Boston: South End Press.

Snyder, A., & McLaughlin, D. (2004). Female-Headed Families and Poverty in Rural America. *Rural Sociology, 69*(1), 127–149.

Soss, J., Schram, S. F., Vartanian, T. P., & O'Brien, E. (2001). The Hard Line and the Color Line: Race, Welfare, and the Roots of Get-Tough Reform. In S. Schram, J. Soss, & R. C. Fording (Eds.), *Race and the Politics of Welfare Reform* (pp. 225–249). Ann Arbor: University of Michigan Press.

Sparks, H. (2003). Queens, Teens, and Model Mothers: Race, Gender, and the Discourse of Welfare Reform. In S. Schram, J. Soss, & R. C. Fording (Eds.), *Race and the Politics of Welfare Reform* (pp. 171–195). Ann Arbor: University of Michigan Press.

Stromwall, L. K., Brzuzy, S., Sharp, P., & Anderson, C. (1998). The Implications of "Welfare Reform" for American Indian Families and Communities. *Journal of Poverty, 2*(4), 1–15.

The State of Poverty in Ohio. (2004). Ohio Association of Community Action Agencies. *Community Action Partnership*. Retrieved August 21, 2005, from www.ceogc.org/research/contentonly.pdf.

Tickamyer, A., Henderson, D., Tadlock, B., & White, J. (2004). *The Impact of Welfare Reform on Rural Livelihood Practices*. Presented at the Rural Sociological Society Annual Meetings. Sacramento, CA.

Tickamyer, A. R., Henderson, D., White, J. A., & Tadlock, B. (2000). Voices of Welfare Reform: Bureaucratic Rationality Versus the Perceptions of Welfare Participants. *Affilia: Journal of Women and Social Work, 15*(2), 173–192.

Tickamyer, A. R., White, J., Tadlock, B., & Henderson, D. A. (2006). The Spatial Politics of Public Policy: Devolution, Development and Welfare Reform. In L. Lobao, G. Hooks, & A. Tickamyer (Eds.), *Spatial Inequality* (pp. 113–139). New York: SUNY Press.

U.S. Census Bureau. (2000). *Income 2000*. Retrieved May 25, 2002, from www.census.gov/hhes/www/income00.html.

U.S. Census Bureau. (2003). *2002 Poverty and Income Report*. Retrieved September 26, 2003, from www.census.gov/Press-Release/www/2003/IncomePoverty.html.

U.S. Department of Health and Human Services [USDHHS]. (2002). One Department Serving Rural America" HHS Rural Task Force Report to the Secretary. Retrieved from ftp://ftp.hrsa.gov/ruralhealth/PublicReportJune2002.pdf.

Weber, B. A., Duncan, G. J., & Whitener, L. A. (2002). *Rural Dimensions of Welfare Reform*. Kalamazo, MI: UpJohn Institute.

Weber, L. (2001). *Understanding Race, Class, Gender, and Sexuality*. Boston: McGraw Hill.

Weinberg, S. B. (1998). Mexican American Mothers and the Welfare Debate: A History of Exclusion. *Journal of Poverty, 2*(3), 53–75.

Weinberg, S. B. (2000). Welfare Reform and Mutual Family Support: Effects on Mother-Led Mexican American Families. *Affilia: Journal of Women and Social Work, 15*(2), 204–223.

White, J., Tickamyer, A. R., Henderson, D. A., & Tadlock, B. (2003). Does Welfare to Work Work? Rural Employers Comments. In W. W. Falk, M. D. Schulman, & A. R. Tickamyer (Eds.), *Communities of Work: Rural Restructuring in Local and Global Contexts* (pp. 240–264). Athens: Ohio University Press.

Wiegman, R. (1999). Whiteness Studies and the Paradox of Particularity. *Boundary 2, 26*(3), 115–150.

Wilson, W. J. (1980). *The Declining Significance of Race*. Chicago: University of Chicago.

Wray, M., & Newitz, A. (1997). *White Trash: Race and Class in America*. New York: Routledge Press.

Zimmerman, J. N., & Hirshl, T. A. (2003). Welfare Reform in Rural Areas: A Voyage Through Uncharted Waters. In D. L. Brown & L. E. Swanson (Eds.), *Challenges for Rural America in the Twenty-First Century* (pp. 363–374). University Park: Pennsylvania State University Press.

4

Staggered Inequalities in Access to Higher Education by Gender, Race, and Ethnicity

RUTH ENID ZAMBRANA AND VICTORIA-MARÍA MACDONALD

In institutions of higher learning, the retention and persistence of underrepresented racial and ethnic groups has come to the forefront as the economic and social value of a baccalaureate degree increases (Orfield, Marin, & Horn, 2005; Tinto, 1987, 1988).[1] After making rapid gains in the late 1960s and early 1980s, the enrollment of historically underrepresented groups, namely African Americans, Mexican Americans, and Puerto Ricans, began to stall in the late 1980s, increasing again only in the late 1990s (Price & Wohlford, 2005). Latina/o youth actually increased enrollment in higher education during the 1990s but persistence to degree remained elusive (Suro & Fry, 2005). Their enrollment is clustered disproportionately in community colleges that have a poor record of transferring students to four-year colleges. Studies on Latinos and African Americans in higher education have remained remarkably silent on gender issues. With the exception of the American Association of University Women's landmark 2001 study on Latinas in school (Ginorio & Huston, 2001), the emphasis remains upon aggregate data (e.g., Tienda & Mitchell, 2006). Gender differences have been highlighted in the past decade as a result of the growing gap between male and female baccalaureate degree holders among African Americans, Mexican American, and non-Hispanic Whites (NHW), as women outpace their male counterparts (Price & Wohlford, 2005; González, Jovel, & Stoner, 2004). However, educational disparities by socioeconomic status (SES), race, and ethnicity among women in access to U.S. higher education have been less studied but are important to illuminate factors associated with completion of higher education that are unique to women from different ethnic groups.

Among all baccalaureate degrees awarded to women in 1990, 84 percent were awarded to non-Hispanic Whites, 7 percent to African American women,

TABLE 4.1

Percent (%) of Bachelor's and Doctoral Degrees Granted to
Non-Hispanic White, African American, and Latino Women,
1980, 1990, and 2000

	1980	1990	2000	Point Change
NHW B.A.	86	84	75	−11
NHW Ph.D.	84	76	67	−17
AA B.A.	7.8	7	10.3	+2.5
AA Ph.D.	5.6	4.5	6.7	+1.1
Latina B.A.	2.4	3.5	6.5	+4.1
Latina Ph.D.	1.7	2.5	4.1	+2.4

Source: Table 261, Bachelor's degrees conferred by degree-granting institutions,
by racial/ethnic group & sex of student, 1976–77 through 2003–04 and Table
267, Doctoral degrees conferred by degree-granting institutions, by
racial/ethnic group & sex of student, 1976–77 through 2003–04, National
Center for Education Statistics (http://nces.ed.gov accessed May 16, 2007).

and only 3.5 percent to Latino women.[2] Three-quarters of all female doctoral degrees were awarded to non-Hispanic Whites in 1990, with African Americans receiving 4.5 percent and Latinas 2.5 percent.[3] By 2000 the numbers had crept up for African American and Latino women, receiving 6.7 percent and 4.1 percent, respectively, of all doctoral degrees. According to scholars examining parity in doctoral production, between 1990 and 2000, Mexican American women remain the most underrepresented group among all female doctoral recipients and have the lowest rates of degree attainment among all Latino women (Watford, et al., 2006). Among the 358 Latino women receiving doctoral degrees in 1990, less than one-fourth were Mexican American, and in 2000 less than one-third (1.6 percent vs. 4.1 percent) of all doctoral recipients were Mexican American despite their larger numbers in the general Latina population (Watford, et al., 2006). This finding is not surprising, as Mexican Americans, representing two-thirds of all Hispanics in the United States, have experienced systematic and persistent oppression and inequality since the 1848 Treaty of Guadalupe Hidalgo that ended the Mexican American War. These data emphasize the importance of examining women's experiences in sociohistorical contexts and interrogating how prior treatment has shaped barriers over time to differentially impede the educational attainment of Mexican American women in comparison to other women.

The analytic approach derives its grounding from an intersectional perspective to examine factors that facilitated or hindered higher education attainment. Using an intersectional framework allows one to examine patterns of educational attainment by taking into account historical relations of power that shape institutions in which historically underrepresented women participated, and patterns of inequality which include both hegemonic and disciplinary power in the educational pipeline (Hill-Collins, 2000; Dill & Zambrana, in this volume, chapter 1).

Five explicit assumptions are inherent in the intersectional lens. First, race, ethnicity, SES, and gender are co-constitutive and mutually reinforcing dimensions that shape one's life chances, opportunities, and, in turn, experiences in higher education. Second, access to public educational systems with limited resources and privilege is simultaneously shaped by the intersection of race, ethnicity, gender, and SES. Third, structural barriers, such as the increasingly resegregated conditions of urban majority/minority secondary schools, are limiting educational preparedness for Latino and African American youth. Fourth, stereotypic representations of students as inferior permeate the attitudes of school personnel that contribute to Mexican American and African American women seen as not desiring or wanting to succeed academically. Fifth, institutional factors such as the role of teachers and administrators in K–12 schools have contributed to the academic disengagement of Mexican American and African American youth, dampening educational expectations and aspirations. Using gender as the sole category of analysis and centering generic women's experiences in education essentializes the experiences of non-White women and masks the historic patterns of racial inequality that have shaped past and current access to and completion of higher education among historically underrepresented women. In this chapter we examine historical, social, and institutional factors among non-Hispanic White, African American, and Mexican American women who received higher education degrees during the late 1960s through the 1980s. This study aims to identify and compare pre-college experiences and reported barriers in higher education associated with perceived institutional stress and academic difficulty. These experiences are informed by the history of women in higher education in the United States.

History of U.S. Women's Access to Higher Education: Staggered Inequality

Although in the colonial period, native-born White women were denied access to colonial colleges and local schools (Solomon, 1985; Tyack & Hansot, 1990), during the nineteenth century, "social utility" arguments were used to justify higher learning for White women. Arguments for access included the need to: develop future citizens of the republic; train girls to become good mothers; train women to enter teaching; and civilize waves of immigrants entering the United States. By the early 1900s, native-born White women were entering

postsecondary institutions reaching parity in numbers with men. The prolif-
eration of state-supported normal (teaching) schools created a higher education pipeline for them, often offering free tuition in exchange for commitment
to teach for a certain period after graduation (Ogren, 2005; McCandless, 1999).

African American women in the South were denied the right to any education before 1865. At the time of emancipation, historians estimate that only
10 percent of the African American population could read or write. The federal
government's creation of the Bureau of Refugees, Freedmen, and Abandoned
Lands (Freedmen's Bureau), religious missionary organizations, and African
American communities themselves helped create hundreds of schools for children and adults in the Reconstruction period (Anderson, 1988; Williams,
2005). The establishment of Howard University in 1867 was the U.S. government's first investment in higher education for African Americans. The Second Morrill Act of 1890 required the Southern states to create segregated and
equal public universities for Blacks or to admit Blacks into Southern public
institutions. The increase in Historically Black Colleges and Universities
(HBCUs) in the early twentieth century contributed to the pool of African
American college graduates who constituted the foundation of a Black middle
class and became a vanguard in the push for civil rights in education. In addition, through the creation of sororities, African American women with college
degrees, who regarded their role as critical ones in the "racial uplift" of less
privileged women (Perkins, 1983), worked to support and further education for
their communities. Given formal status at the Howard University campus in
1908, Alpha Kappa Alpha (AKA) was the first Black sorority, founded fifty-
seven years after the country's first White sorority, Alpha Delta Pi (Gasman,
2005). For Black women, HBCUs and sororities became the "purveyors" of
social capital and vocal supporters of increasing educational opportunities for
Black women (Mercomes, 1998). During the years that the African American
women in this study began college, opportunities in higher education had
expanded to include more predominantly all-White institutions (Samuels,
2004). Within these integrated yet predominantly White institutions, African
American women broke away from traditional expectations for their gender
in the Black community while simultaneously breaking racial barriers
(Higginbotham, 2001).

"Triple Oppression": Class, Gender, and Race/Ethnicity

Since the 1800s, Mexican American women's participation in higher education
has been limited. Incorporation of Mexican Americans into the United States
through conquest as a result of the Mexican American War in 1848 combined
with the federal government's legislative, judicial, and monetary power delayed
access to higher education. As a result, the initial push for educational access

among Latinos focused on the lower levels of schooling (MacDonald, Botti, & Hoffman Clark, 2007). Testimony from civil rights hearings, court depositions, and first-person interviews during the civil rights era reveal that it was an unofficial practice to bar Latinos from attending high school in the Southwest. Even until 1960, the highest level of education for the majority of Latinos in the Southwest was eighth grade (Donato, 1997), and they comprised fewer than 6 percent of entering college students in 1958 (Carter, 1970).[4] While Mexican Americans pursued equity in educational arenas during the early twentieth century through civic organizations such as the League of United Latin American Citizens (LULAC), the early desegregation cases focused on K–8 schools where Mexican American children were clustered. As a result of systematic and structured discrimination against Mexican American youth in the Southwest, Mexican American women were often excluded from government-supported programs in higher education (MacDonald, Botti, & Hoffman Clark, 2007).

When Denise Segura identified the "triple oppression" of Mexican American (Chicana) women in the labor force (1984, 1990) she was also speaking to Mexican American women entering higher education in the early 1960s hoping to broaden their horizons from those of their mothers. Mexican Americans were the last to access higher education. Their entry as a significant presence only began in the mid- to late twentieth century and is first seen in women's Catholic Colleges, two-year schools, and teacher training institutions. (MacDonald, 2004; MacDonald & Garcia, 2003).

> Fíjese Papá que entré al Student National Education Association (SNEA) porque nos dijo la monja que "it would look good in our record" pero tuvimos que pagar las "fee" y como soy miembro neuvo tengo que pagar $5.50. No lo pagui [sic] yo porque el dinero que me mando lo utilize en los libros que compre y aparte tuve que pagar un "fee" en Music Education, compre typing paper, 1 Red pencil y otras cosas que me faltaban y tenía que comprar así es que me quedé sin dinero.

> [Look Dad, I joined the Student National Education Association (SNEA) because the nun said that "it would look good in our record" but we had to pay a "fee" and since I am a new member I have to pay $5.50. I didn't pay it because the money that you sent I used it to buy books and aside from that I had to pay a "fee" in Music Education, I bought typing paper, 1 Red pencil and other things that I needed to buy and that's how I am left without money.]

Letter from Rosa C. Martinez
Our Lady of Lakes College,
San Antonio, TX, October 9, 1961.
(Papers of Mercurio Martinez, Texas A&M Archives, College Station, TX)

The student above, Rosa C. Martinez, had taken out a loan from the U.S. National Defense Student Loan Fund. Although her father was one of the first certified Mexican American teachers in Texas and a small town mayor, sending a daughter to college was almost prohibitive for the family. He exhorted her to watch her money because it was "sangre del corazon" (blood from the heart) and several family members contributed clothes and supplies for Rosa to attend (Letter from Mercurio Martinez, Laredo, Texas, October 24, 1961). Rosa's story is just one of hundreds and then thousands of stories of the first generation of Latino women to enter higher education in the 1960s and 1970s. In so doing, these pioneers faced significant barriers both institutionally and as a result of gender and race discrimination as well as socioeconomic status.

As late as 1978 when this study's cohort was in higher education, institutions with the highest numbers of Mexican Americans and Latinos were East Los Angeles College (two year); Miami Dade Community College (two year); and private schools such as Our Lady of Lakes University in Texas (Brown, Rosen, & Hill, 1980, table 3.15). Different from African American women, Mexican American women lacked successful counterparts to HBCUs and the resulting network of college graduates or sororities. In fact, the first Latina sorority in the United States, Lambda Theta Alpha at Kean University (New Jersey) was not founded until 1975. Most Latina sororities were founded in the 1990s and continue to be created as Latina women recognize the support and social capital advantages that lifelong membership in a sorority can bring (www.latinogreek.com).

Historical data support a staggered inequality model by which historically underrepresented women have attained higher education. Historicizing our understanding of access to higher education demonstrates how hegemonic power has differentially shaped access to educational institutions for African American and Mexican American women, and for non-Hispanic White women who have been beneficiaries of unacknowledged privilege. These historical patterns continue post–civil rights legislation and are embedded and reproduced in the educational pipeline.

Institutional Patterns in Pre-College Educational Pipeline

Pre-college preparation is associated with academic difficulty and stress in higher education (Capello, 1994; Reyes, 2001; Rodriguez, et al., 2000; Gandara, 2006). High school grade point average (HSGPA), advanced placement courses and the perception of an individual's ability, and prior encouragement from school personnel are major criteria of entry and access to higher education and major factors in understanding racial and ethnic disparities (Farkas, 2003; Teranishi, Allen, & Solórzano, 2004). Using HSGPA as a predictor of college performance has been well studied for non-Hispanic White students, but less so for African Americans and Mexican American students (Allen, 1985; Johnson,

1986; Smith & Allen, 1984). Using HSGPA to predict academic success in various fields shows that both non-Hispanic White and African American women tend to have higher grade point averages (GPA) than non-Hispanic White and African American men (Allen & Haniff, 1991; Solomon, 1992; Astin & Cross, 1981; Smith, 1991). HSGPA however is strongly associated with school resources, geographic location, and attitudes of high school personnel toward students of African American and Mexican American origin.

School environments for a significant number of African American and Mexican American girls are not conducive to academic achievement (Dance, in this volume, chapter 8). Experiences of Latinas from elementary to postsecondary education show that teachers often overlook, ignore, and avoid Latinas in the classroom while preferring to interact with Anglo males (Pizarro, 2005; Ginorio & Huston, 2001). Mexican American girls begin the process of leaving school earlier than African American and non-Hispanic White girls (Astin, 1982; Del Castillo, et al., 1988; Nielson & Fernandez, 1982; Rumberger, 1988; Zambrana & Zoppi, 2002) and dropout to assist families economically with childcare or because of their own pregnancies (Ginorio & Huston, 2001). Teachers, and even Mexican Americans themselves, often attribute Latino academic success to luck or to factors other than ability (Lee, 1988; Cuádraz, 1999). Mexican American girls tend to have the highest high school dropout rates as a result of the intersection of low-socioeconomic status and limited encouragement to succeed academically, which narrows their perceived life options.

Educational segregation, which characterizes many public schools in urban areas that educate the majority of Black and Latino students, is problematic (Orfield & Eaton, 1996). Segregation by race, ethnicity, and low SES all too frequently is accompanied by lack of adequate resources such as comprehensive libraries and computers, poorly qualified teachers, lack of advanced placement classes, and lack of the social and cultural capital that non-Hispanic White, middle-class students accrue in affluent suburban public schools. The absence of these resources negatively affects Latino and African American students' opportunities to access higher education (Teranishi, Allen, & Solórzano, 2004). In an influential study, Swail, Cabrera, & Lee (2004) found, among other factors, that for Latino students to persist through completion of a four-year degree they needed to have a plan by the eighth grade that included knowing that students needed to take Algebra I by the ninth grade to be competitive for college. This type of information has often been difficult for Latino parents to access, particularly because of language barriers, discrimination by school counselors and personnel, economic necessities requiring two or more jobs, and transportation problems, thus precluding attendance at school meetings (Auerbach, 2002; Zoppi, MacDonald, & Munoz, 2007; Loza, 2003). For those African American and Mexican American students who successfully navigate the pre-college pipeline, adjustment to predominantly non-Hispanic White environments present new challenges (Cuádraz, 1999). According to Higgin-botham (2001, 15), institutions of higher education are still "sites of routine and periodic trauma for African Americans and many other students of color."

Higher Education Institutions: Barriers to Adjustment

Multiple factors have been identified as important to persistence in higher education among women. These include: family socioeconomic status and gen-der discrimination (Epstein, 1970; Almquist, 1974); and lack of support from professors and financial support (Gloria, et al., 2005). Prior research on non-Hispanic White women's experiences in the 1970s confirm overt gender discrimination in admission and financial aid practices, in institutional regula-tions, and in faculty attitudes and behavior (Furniss & Graham, 1974; Kutner & Brogan, 1976; Roby, 1975). Women reported not receiving enough financial sup-port (Howard-Vital, 1987), and were often reluctant to obtain additional loans to pay for graduate education (Farley & Allen, 1987). They also reported feeling iso-lated, lonely, and invisible (Dinwiddie & Allen, 2003); less likely to be chosen as protégés of influential male faculty, thus resulting in the loss of benefits that such a relationship has on later career opportunities (Allen & Haniff, 1991; Feldman, 1974; Moses, 1989); and being harassed by the use of demeaning comments about women, sexual jokes, and outright hazing (Bernard, 1976; Holahan, 1979).

For African American and Mexican American women, race, ethnic, and gender discrimination (Jackson, 1998; Reyes, 2001) and social and academic adjustment to a predominantly White environment all may contribute to aca-demic difficulty and perceived stress (Howard-Vital, 1987; Mortenson, 1991; Solomon, 1992; Castillo, et al., 2004; Williams, 2005). Historically underrepre-sented students who come from ethnically homogenous community and school environments often experience feelings of isolation and alienation, have less contact with peers, are less often engaged in social activities (Padilla, 1997; Benjamin, 1982; Fleming, 1983; Capello, 1994), are less likely to receive encouragement from counselors and advisors to pursue graduate training (King, 2007; Howard-Vital, 1987), and may not get to know faculty members who can write letters of recommendation or help them secure financial assis-tance (Jacobs, 1981; Carroll, 1982). Banks (1988), in a study of African American female law students found that they volunteered less often in the classroom than men, believed that their professors often ignored them or overlooked them when they did volunteer, and had less access than non-Hispanic White women or racial and ethnic men to informal interaction, such as having lunch, with their advisors outside the advisor-advisee relationship.

Adjustment to college involves both an academic transition as well as a cul-tural one for racial and ethnic women (Chacon, 1982; Wolf-Wendel, 1998; Munoz & Garcia-Bahne, 1978; Squires-Nieves, 1991; Aguilar, 1996). Adjustment in higher education institutions among African American and Mexican American women is often associated with being first generation college students, perceived discrimination, personal and familial issues, and pre-college academic preparation, which may contribute to high levels of perceived stress and low levels of perceived institutional support (González, Jovel, & Stoner, 2004; Archor & Morales, 1990; Rodriguez, et al., 2000). Students who are the first generation in their families to attend college may experience higher stress, which has a negative impact upon persistence. The knowledge of parents who have attended college facilitates academic and social adjustment of their children (Choy, 2001). For example, in a study of Latino college students in 1976 living with their parents, only 11 percent of these students had parents who were college graduates compared to over one-third of the non-Hispanic White students (Brown, Rosen, & Hill, 1980, table 3.37). Another study conducted in Austin, Texas (Mendoza, 1981) found that both non-Hispanic White and Mexican American women experienced more stress than men in academic, personal and familial issues. A recent study confirmed an earlier study (Chacon, 1982) that found that comfort with White cultural values, perceived support from family, and financial support, were related to lower perceived stress among Mexican American female college students (Castillo, Conoley, & Brossart, 2004).

An additional barrier to women is the lack of female faculty role models and mentors. Tidball (1980) reported that as the proportion of women faculty relative to the number of women students increases, so does the proportion of women high achievers in professional life. Among faculty in U.S. colleges and universities, Latinos (men and women) comprise only 3.5 percent of all faculty (NCES, 2003). The relative lack of female faculty is a deterrent to women's educational and career pursuits (Mortenson, 1991; O'Donnell & Anderson, 1978; Solomon & Wingard, 1991). In 1985 while the cohort of women in this study was obtaining higher education degrees, African American women constituted only 1.9 percent of full-time faculty in higher education, 0.6 percent of full professors, 1.4 percent of associate professors, 2.7 percent of assistant professors, and 3 percent of instructors and lecturers (Cole, 1988). Gregory (2001) reports that Black women account for only 6.43 percent of all full-time faculties, and one-half of these women are employed at HBCUs. Only 1 percent of Black women PhDs teach full-time in four-year universities. Although non-Hispanic White women students and faculty have increased significantly in higher education, in 2003, African Americans and Latinos held 5.5 percent and 3.5 percent of all faculty positions respectively (NCES, 2003). Collectively African American and Latino faculty comprise only 5 percent of all full-professors nationwide (NCES, 2001). Among women as percent of all faculty, only 2.9 percent of all those with tenure were African American or Latina in 2001 in contrast to 25.9 percent of non-Hispanic White women. The numbers of tenure-track faculty for the two historically underrepresented groups in all major universities have remained stagnant for almost three decades, as has the progress made by increased enrollment of historically underrepresented students in higher education systems. Recent events suggest that the "chilly climate" for non-Hispanic Whites may be slowly experiencing a small thaw. For example, in 2007 one-half of Ivy League institutions are headed by women, six non-Hispanic Whites and one African American. Non-Hispanic White women have achieved considerable progress toward parity in higher education while African American and Mexican American women still lag noticeably behind.

The sparse data on higher education experiences of Mexican American women suggest that they may experience more stressors due to ethnic, racial, and class discrimination resulting from educators' stereotypic expectations of lower ability and performance by Latino students and the lack of Latino faculty and administrators who can provide mentorship and emotional support for them during their higher education experiences (Rodriguez, et al., 2000; Castillo, et al., 2004).

Methodology

Sample and Procedures

Data employed in this study were derived from interviews with three hundred Mexican American, one hundred African American, and one hundred non-Hispanic White women who lived in the Los Angeles area and had completed a higher education degree (ranging from a bachelor's degree to a doctorate) during the late 1960s through mid-1980s. The criteria for sample selection were: ethnicity; completion of secondary and higher education experiences in the United States; and English as the primary language. A purposive, network sampling approach was used. Study protocol and procedures were reviewed and approved by the UCLA Human Subjects Committee. Respondents were contacted by telephone and explained the nature of the study. After informed consent was provided, respondents who agreed were then administered the questionnaire during the years 1987–1990. All questionnaires were completed in English. As a nonprobability sampling method was utilized in this cross-sectional study, the population studied is not representative of all women in higher education in the three racial/ethnic groups and the findings cannot be generalized. However, the findings do suggest important descriptive results and provide a unique opportunity to look at Mexican American women who are relatively invisible in higher education in comparison to non-Hispanic White and African American women.

Measures

The questionnaire consisted of 233 items and included both open-ended and closed-ended response options. Data were obtained on current sociodemographic characteristics of respondents, private vs. public high school attended, academic predictors including high school and undergraduate GPA, work status during higher education, type of higher education institution attended, institutional resources available such as loans and scholarships, perception of institutional stressors, and perceptions of institutional or academic support.

A series of items asked the respondent to report on their high school experiences and included items on perceptions of high school performance, excellence in particular subjects, perception of teacher encouragement for college attendance, and whether they felt high school prepared them for college. Several items obtained data on residence during undergraduate education, employment status, number of hours worked, and type of institution attended. Academic performance indicators were measured by self-report of high school and college grade point average (GPA). Another series of questions asked the respondent to report on their undergraduate experiences and included items on whether they perceived racial discrimination to be a problem for women, whether they experienced racial and/or sex discrimination as a problem, and whether they perceived that the educational experience was harder for minority women. In addition, data were obtained on whether they experienced academic, emotional, and/or social difficulties.

The major dependent variables were the perception of stress and reported academic difficulty during the undergraduate experience. A stress scale consisting of sixteen items asked respondents to rate the degree of stress from 1 = not stressful to 5 = highly stressful during the pursuit of their higher education. The areas included educational demands, marital companionship pressures, immediate family pressures, financial, health, childcare, social life, and academic and institutional pressures. The reliability analysis on this scale yielded a Cronbach alpha of .85.[5] A single item asked the respondents to rate their overall academic difficulty on a four-item Likert scale, where 4 = very difficult, 3 = somewhat difficult, 2 = difficult, and 1 = not difficult. Descriptive univariate and bivariate statistics to examine similarities and differences by race/ethnicity on the major study variables were conducted. Multivariate analyses were also run to assess the relationships of selected factors on perceived academic difficulty and perceived level of stress by ethnic group.

Results

Description of the Sample

The median age of participants was thirty-five years with no significant difference across ethnic groups. A higher percentage of non-Hispanic White women were single (37 percent) or married (54 percent) while a lower percentage were separated or divorced, 9 percent as compared to 28.3 percent of the African American women and 19.6 percent of the Mexican American women. Less than

40 percent of the non-Hispanic White women had one or more children compared to almost 60 percent of African American and 50 percent of Mexican American women. The majority of all women worked full-time. Just over 65 percent of all the women had completed a masters and/or doctoral degree. Ninety percent of the respondents received their bachelor's degree by 1978. Those who pursued postbachelor's degrees received their degrees by 1988.

The current socioeconomic status (SES) of the respondents as measured by education, income, and occupation revealed that the majority of all the women were in high or high-middle SES (94.6 percent of the Mexican American women and 75.3 percent of the African American and White women). This is in sharp contrast to the socioeconomic status of their families of origin as indicated by their fathers' socioeconomic status. Fifty-six percent of the Mexican American women and 48 percent of the African American women, as compared to 20 percent of the White women, reported low-middle or low SES. Just over half of the non-Hispanic White women (52.10 percent) compared to 30 percent of the African American and 13 percent of the Mexican American women came from upper or upper-middle SES homes. It has been shown that higher SES non-Hispanic White women are more likely to volunteer for studies than non-Hispanic White women from working-class or low-SES background (Weber, Higginbotham, & Leung, 1999).

Pre-College Educational Experiences

In high school, Mexican American women were more likely to have attended parochial schools (31.3 percent) than either the African American women (11.2 percent) or the non-Hispanic White women (19 percent). As shown in table 4.2, during high school, the majority of all the women (over 80 percent) reported being in a college bound group and performing well in school, though a significantly larger number of Mexican American women reported not performing well (11 percent) compared to the other two groups. However, close to half of all respondents indicated that they did not feel that high school had prepared them well for college.

The average high school GPA (HSGPA) for all the women was 3.41. On the other hand, their experience with high school teachers varied significantly across groups. Mexican American women were less likely to have been encouraged by their teachers to go on to college and more likely to have been encouraged to go to a trade school followed by African American and then non-Hispanic White women. The majority of all the women entered college directly after high school with no significant variation across groups.

The trends change, however, at the undergraduate level. As shown in table 4.3, African American women (33 percent) were significantly most likely to have attended private colleges and Mexican Americans (18 percent) least likely. However, average college GPA scores differed across groups with non-Hispanic

TABLE 4.2

High School Experiences by Ethnic Group

High School Characteristic	Mexican American (300)	African American (100)	White (100)
Type of High School:			
Public	68.70%	88.80%	81.00%
Private	31.30%	11.20%	19.00%
$(X^2(2) = 19.76, p < .01)$			
In College Bound Group:			
Yes	83.10%	85.20%	86.50%
Performed Well: Yes	89.10%	95.90%	99.00%
$(X^2(2) = 15.68, p < .01)$			
Excelled in Subject(s):			
Particular Subject	66.90%	53.50%	38.10%
All Subjects	27.40%	41.40%	49.50%
No Subjects	5.70%	5.10%	12.40%
$(X^2(4) = 27.84, p < .01)$			
Well Prepared for College:			
Yes	51.90%	41.10%	44.90%
Grade Point Average (GPA):			
Mean	3.37	3.41	3.46
(SD)	(0.47)	(0.51)	(0.47)
Teachers:			
Encouraged Going to College:			
Yes	66.60%	86.60%	91.00%
$(X^2(2) = 35.25, p < .01)$			
Encouraged Trade School:			
Yes	26.80%	19.20%	14.00%
$(X^2(2) = 8.22, p < .05)$			

White women reporting significantly higher college GPA scores on average (3.36) than either the Mexican American (3.20) or African American (3.15) women.

During their undergraduate experience, almost twice as many Mexican American women (29 percent) as African American or non-Hispanic White women reported living with their parent(s), while more African Americans (45 percent) reported living on campus. This higher percentage of Mexican

TABLE 4.3
Undergraduate Characteristics by Ethnic Group

Undergraduate School Characteristic	Mexican American (300)	African American (100)	White (100)
Type of Institution:			
Public	82.10%	67.40%	74.20%
Private	17.90%	32.60%	25.80%
$(X^2(2) = 9.16, p = .01)$			
Grade Point Average: (GPA)			
Mean	3.20	3.15	3.36
(SD)	(0.42)	(0.42)	(0.36)
$(F(2) = 6.59, \text{Sig } F < .01)$			
Residence:			
With Parent(s)	28.90%	14.30%	15.50%
Campus Residence Hall	20.10%	44.90%	28.90%
Off Campus	51.00%	40.80%	55.70%
$(X^2(4) = 28.47, p < .01)$			
Employment:			
Full-Time	12.67%	20.60%	10.80%
Part-Time	76.33%	43.04%	66.20%
Did Not Work	11.00%	36.36%	23.00%
$(X^2(4) = 34.43, p < .01)$			
Received Scholarships:			
Yes	45.67%	49.50%	23.00%
$(X^2(2) = 39.07, p < .01)$			
Received Student Loans:			
Yes	32.33%	35.35%	22.00%
$(X^2(2) = 18.48, p < .05)$			

American women living with their parents may reflect cultural practices, which prefer keeping young women under a watchful eye, and financial concerns regarding housing on campus. The group with the largest number of women who reported working full-time during college was African American (21 percent) and that group also reported the highest percentage (36 percent) of women who did not work at all during college. Just under half of the Mexican American and African American women indicated they had received some form of financial scholarship during college as compared to 23 percent of non-Hispanic White women. Approximately one-third of the racial-ethnic women received student loans compared to 22 percent of non-Hispanic White women. This finding reflects differences in social class background.

Experiencing Higher Education: Discrimination, Difficulties, and Stress

Educational climate is critical for learning and educational success. Table 4.4 shows that Mexican American (68 percent) and particularly African American women (77 percent) reported experiencing racial discrimination in their relationships with professors and peers, compared to 19 percent of non-Hispanic White women. However, approximately half of all the women reported sex discrimination as a problem while pursuing their undergraduate education with a slightly lower percentage of African American women reporting sex discrimination (43 percent) compared to Mexican American (58 percent) and non-Hispanic White women (50 percent). On the whole, almost 90 percent of Mexican American and African American women, and 75 percent of non-Hispanic White women indicated that based on their own experience, they felt that the attainment of an education was harder for minority women than for the non-Hispanic White women.

A majority of the respondents reported experiencing difficulties while pursuing higher education, including academic, emotional, and social problems. This was especially true for Mexican Americans, over two-thirds of whom reported difficulties in all three areas. African American women were least likely to report any emotional difficulties (41 percent) and non-Hispanic White women were less likely to report academic (40 percent) or social difficulties (46 percent). Ethnic and racial group differences were significant in all three areas.

The overall greater difficulty reported by Mexican American women is likely reflected in the perceived level of stress they experienced while pursuing their educational goals. On the Stress Scale, measuring factors related to the institutional environment as well as factors related to work, family, and personal problems, Mexican American women reported significantly higher levels of stress (mean 40.9) on institutional environment than the African American (mean 35.7) or non-Hispanic White (mean 37.2) women. On the scale measuring stress factors relating solely to family, employment, and personal problems, African American women reported significantly lower scores than the other two groups. In response to a four-point item that asked how frequently the women had felt stressed during college, over half of the Mexican American women reported feeling stressed frequently or most of the time compared to 42 percent of African Americans and 36 percent of non-Hispanic White respondents. To assess whether the women perceived support in their institutional environments, they were asked whether they felt supported by

TABLE 4.4

Ethnic Differences in Perceptions of Discrimination, Stress, and Social Support by Ethnic Group

Higher Education Characteristic	Mexican American (300)	African American (100)	White (100)
Experienced Discrimination:			
Racial— Yes $(X^2(2) = 90.41, p < .01)$	68.50%	76.80%	19.20%
Gender— Yes $(X^2(2) = 7.30, p < .05)$	57.90%	42.60%	50.00%
Experienced Difficulties:			
Academic— Yes $(X^2(2) = 44.35, p < .01)$	74.40%	51.60%	40.00%
Emotional— Yes $(X^2(2) = 32.59, p < .01)$	84.90%	58.50%	67.00%
Social— Yes $(X^2(2) = 12.45, p < .01)$	63.20%	48.90%	45.50%
Reported Level of Total Stress While in School:			
Mean	40.88	35.70	37.18
(SD)	(10.19)	(9.57)	(8.88)
$(F(2) = 11.28,$ Sig F $< .01)$			
Institution Related Stress:			
Mean	23.31	20.47	19.97
(SD)	(7.28)	(6.23)	(6.11)
$(F(2) = 11.48,$ Sig F $< .01)$			
Work/Family/Personal Stress:			
Mean	17.45	15.05	17.05
(SD)	(4.68)	(5.11)	(4.47)
$(F(2) = 9.05,$ Sig F $< .01)$			
Felt Supported by Professors/ Advisors: Yes $(X^2(2) = 51.43, p < .01)$	45.10%	71.00%	81.60%

their professors and advisors while pursuing higher education. Mexican American women were more likely to report that they did not feel supported (55 percent) compared to 29 percent of African American and 18 percent of non-Hispanic White women.

Multivariate Analyses: Stress and Academic Difficulty

To examine the variation in stress experienced by the women while pursuing their higher education, as a function of predominantly institutional-related factors, multiple regression analyses were conducted with total stress score as the dependent variable, for all the women, for each ethnic group, and when controlling for the added difficulty of raising children while in school. Factors included in the model as intervening variables were: average number of hours worked weekly and level of perceived institutional support. Dummy variables were created for the following factors: financial aid (coded 1 for no aid); place of residence (coded 1 for living away from parental home); type of undergraduate institution (coded 1 for public); and the reported experience of race and sex discrimination and academic difficulty (coded 1 if experienced). The results from the analysis on the entire sample, as shown in table 4.5, demonstrate that the model was significant, accounting for 22 percent of the variation in reported stress levels (model $R^2 = .22$, Standard Error of Estimate = 8.88, signif. F < .01). Variables in the equation that significantly predicted higher stress included the experiences of race and sex discrimination, the experience of academic difficulty, the number of hours worked weekly, and place of residence.

Analyses were conducted on each ethnic group. For African American women, the only significant predictor of variation in stress was average number of hours worked per week, accounting for 8 percent of the variation. For non-Hispanic White women, the significant predictors of variation in stress were level of institutional support and sex discrimination, accounting for 14 percent of the variation. Higher perceived institutional support predicted lower stress levels. On the other hand, for Mexican American women, academic difficulty, and the experience of race and sex discrimination had significant effects on stress, together accounting for 18 percent of the variance.[6] Logistic regression analyses were conducted for the total sample and for each ethnic group, predicting academic difficulty. The dependent variable, academic difficulty, initially measured on a scale ranging from 1, not difficult, to, 4, very difficult, was recoded (1,2 = 0, no difficulty, and 3,4 = 1, difficulty). The model included the following categorical variables: high school GPA (coded 1 for scores of 3 or less); hours worked in college (coded 1 for more than 15); place of residence (coded 1 for away from parental home); type of institution (coded 1 for public); institutional support (low support coded 1); financial aid (coded 1

TABLE 4.5

Multiple Regression: Perceived Level of Stress during Higher Education

Independent Variables	Regression Coefficient	Standard Error	Correlation C/ Total Stress
(Intercept)	26.6428	3.1048	
Reported Academic Difficulty:	4.3525**	1.0717	.314
Experienced Racial Discrimination:	3.9323**	1.1798	.272
Average Weekly Hours Worked:	1.2099**	.4465	.268
Mexican American:	.7847	1.4351	.246
Experienced Sex Discrimination:	2.3350*	1.0390	.233
African American:	−3.0040	1.7589	−.161
Residence During College:	2.9480*	1.2220	.096
Financial Aid:	.1526	1.0177	−.017
Institutional Support:	.1007	.1382	.014
Type of Institution:	−1.0589	1.2107	−.003

Model R^2 = .22, Standard Error = 8.88, F = 9.61, Signif F < .01

Note: * $p < .05$; ** $p < .01$

for no aid); and the experience of race and sex discrimination (coded 1 if experienced). Ethnicity was included in the analysis for the total sample. The results (not shown) suggest that the model was a fairly good fit for the Mexican American women (model X^2 (2) = 10.87, $p < .01$) but less so for African Americans (model X^2 (1) = 6.56, $p < .05$) and not significant for Whites. For Mexican Americans, two of the predictor variables had a statistically significant effect on the likelihood of experiencing academic difficulty. Working more than fifteen hours a week during college and experiencing racial discrimination significantly increased the odds of experiencing academic difficulty by factors of 2.49 and 1.91 respectively. For African American women who worked more than fifteen hours a week during college the odds of experiencing academic difficulty increased by a factor of 4.12.

Discussion

These respondents represent an historical cohort of high achieving women who graduated between 1978 and 1988, and benefited from affirmative action. The major findings of this study show:

- Women's access to higher education followed a staggered inequality entry model.
- Pre-college academic indicators such as HSGPA and being in a college bound group were similar across non-Hispanic White, African American, and Mexican American women.
- Significant differences in pre-college experiences are found for Mexican Americans in that they are less likely to report performing well and teacher's encouragement to attend college.
- Undergraduate experiences show similarities between African American and Mexican American as they report similar college GPA's and are significantly more likely than non-Hispanic White women to receive scholarships and student loans.
- Perceptions of institutional support are more likely to be reported by non-Hispanic Whites and least likely to be reported by Mexican American women with African American women in between.
- Academic, emotional, and social difficulties are most likely to be reported by Mexican American women.

In this chapter we argue that women's access to higher education followed a staggered inequality entry model to institutions of higher learning. Theorizing with an intersectional lens, the historical data reveal that in the hierarchically organized U.S. society, educational institutions gave non-Hispanic White women a social status that was more privileged than that found among historically underrepresented women at any time in U.S. history and in all parts of the country. Only in recent American history have Mexican American women accessed higher education at a significant level and their presence in U.S. institutions at the baccalaureate, master's, and doctoral level are still at a nascent stage (American Council on Education, 2004; Swail, Cabrera, & Lee, 2004; Watford, et al., 2006). However, while non-Hispanic Whites have increased degree attainment at all levels of the educational system, African American and Mexican American women have experienced uneven patterns in the modest gains made during the 1970s and early 1980s (Trent, 1991). Identity, understood as a multidimensional category rather than a unidimensional one, challenges the applicability of the feminist model as a paradigm to understand the experiences of all women. Gender is only one dimension that needs to be examined within an intersectional historical, social, and institutional framework to move beyond individual and culturally deterministic models that

ignore the role of institutional practices in promoting or hindering performance in pre-college and college experiences by gender, race, ethnicity, and
socioeconomic status.

Pre-college educational experiences show that Mexican American women
were the least likely to be encouraged to go to college in spite of being in a
college-bound group, feeling well-prepared for college, and having similar
HSGPAs to other groups. The lack of support from school personnel is an
important determinant of a sense of self-confidence and has been found to
significantly contribute to a woman's educational attainment (Tidball, 1980).
For historically underrepresented young women, experiences in the pre-
college educational pipeline such as lack of support from high school teachers
and university professors and advisors has been found to increase stress and
decrease the sense of self-confidence (Del Castillo, et al., 1988; Allen & Haniff,
1991). Prior studies show that Mexican American women may enter the university system with lower self-confidence due to non-supportive experiences
in high schools (Lee, 1985, 1988; Zambrana & Zoppi, 2002). However, for Mexican American and African American women these influences are exacerbated
when they are compounded by low socioeconomic status of the family of
origin and limited financial resources during the college years (Zambrana,
Dorrington, & Alonzo-Bell, 1997; Cardoza, 1991; Zambrana, 1988). The majority
of Mexican American women were the first generation to attend college. Thus
it seems likely that fewer family financial resources were available to the
Mexican American women during their undergraduate experience. The data
confirm that pursuit of a college education often represents a financial hardship for Mexican American students, as evidenced by the average number of
hours worked per week, which may be associated with increased academic difficulties (Chacon, 1982; Archor & Morales, 1990; Rodriguez, et al., 2000).

In examining the respondents' perception of perceived discrimination,
academic difficulties, and institutional stress, distinct experiences emerge by
ethnicity. In this study, about 50 percent of non-Hispanic White women report
sex discrimination and two-fifths report experiencing academic difficulties.
Interestingly their ability to persist and maintain their academic averages is
perhaps mediated by a strong set of pre-college experiences that bolstered
their sense of confidence in their academic abilities. In addition, a higher perception of support from professors and advisors suggests a more welcoming
environment. These data contrast with earlier studies that found that non-
Hispanic White women did not feel encouraged or supported by the faculty
(Epstein, 1970; Feldman, 1974). Though not explored in this study, it can be
speculated that this may in part be due to the increase in non-Hispanic White
women peers and faculty at institutions of higher education during the 1970s
and 1980s. Thus throughout the educational pipeline factors such as perceptions of teacher encouragement, high academic performance, and human

and cultural capital, along with knowledge of how to interact with professors, are all highly associated with self-confidence and have a positive influence on academic achievement in college.

Not unexpectedly, the majority of the African American women report racial discrimination (77 percent), while less than 50 percent report gender discrimination. Other studies confirm that for African American and Latino women, racial discrimination is more salient than gender discrimination and represents a "double jeopardy" (Gonzales, Blanton, & Williams, 2002; Howard-Vital, 1987). This perceived discrimination might have contributed to over half of the African American women experiencing academic difficulty and report-ing significantly lower GPAs than non-Hispanic White women. Apart from the shared experience of discrimination, in contrast to the Mexican American women, African American women in this study appear more likely to experi-ence academic and social integration while in college as evidenced by greater perceived support from professors and advisors (Tinto, 1987, 1988). African American women experienced less overall stress, whether related to the insti-tution or to their work, family, and personal lives, were less likely to experi-ence academic, emotional, or social difficulties during college, and were more likely to report encouragement to go to college while in high school. For African American women, the presence of a group of African American peers during their undergraduate experience, whether they attended an Historically Black College or University or had a sorority which could provide support com-bined with financial assistance may also be associated with less perceived stress and academic difficulty.

Although the African American and Mexican American women shared similar experiences of discrimination, Mexican American women report the highest levels of sex discrimination, academic, emotional, and social diffi-culty, and the highest levels of stress and the lowest level of support from pro-fessors and advisors. Limited experience with dominant culture individuals, due to the likelihood of coming from more segregated communities and schools, from families with less education than their college counterparts, fewer social networks on campus and limited financial options may account for the differences between Mexican American women and the other two groups (Hernandez, 1990; Chacon, 1982; Gandara, 1982; Capello, 1994). These findings underscore the importance of understanding the different factors, which influence the lives of middle-class non-Hispanic White women and those of low-income and middle-income African American and Mexican American women. Further within group differences by SES of family of origin and race/ethnicity require exploration in order not to essentialize the experi-ences of all historically underrepresented women.

Extending the theoretical paradigms to include family of origin SES, pre-college experiences and perceptions of support are dimensions to be included in any further inquiry to avoid any assumptions regarding a "level playing field" for all women. These data also provide a more authentic, compelling and profound understanding of the realities of what Feagin, Vera, and Imani called "The Agony of Education" (1996). Many of the same factors historically underrepresented women identified in the 1970s and 1980s as barriers remain in place, providing additional insight into the reasons for the sustained low participation of Mexican American women, in particular, and African American women in institutions of higher education. These data challenge current university systems that maintain a status quo by advocating for an undifferentiated set of policies "for all women" or "all minorities," which has simply maintained a "survival of the fittest" policy. Institutions of higher learning have engaged in a minimal policy modifications approach that masks racial and ethnic educational disparities in retention and degree completion of historically underrepresented women. Multiple recommendations have been heralded as ways to break the disturbing and unequal historical patterns of social and racial inequality in the United States. Access to higher education is a major vehicle for social change and social justice. Bold university leadership is required to reverse entrenched patterns of inequality for historically underrepresented women.

NOTES

1. The first author gratefully acknowledges the support of the UCLA Faculty Research Awards and Institute of American Cultures grants in the original data collection of this research and the contributions of Drs. Sally Alonzo Bell and Claudia Dorrington. The authors also express gratitude to Ana Maria Perez, a graduate student in the Department of Women's Studies at the University of Maryland, and Lisa Hoffman Clark, doctoral candidate at Florida State University for their research assistance in the development of this chapter.

2. Table 261, Bachelor's Degrees Conferred by Degree-Granting Institutions, by Racial/Ethnic Group & Sex of Students, 1976–2003–04. National Center for Education Statistics.

3. Table 267, Bachelor's Degrees Conferred by Degree-Granting Institutions, by Racial/Ethnic Group & Sex of Students, 1976–2003–04. National Center for Education Statistics.

4. Thomas P. Carter, *MAs in School: A History of Educational Neglect*. New York: College Entrance Examination Board, 1970, 31; this percentage is affirmed in the comprehensive study funded by the Ford Foundation of which Thomas P. Carter also participated and published as *The Mexican-American People: The Nation's Second Largest Minority*. New York: Free Press, 1970, 142–179.

5. Cronbach's alpha is used as a measure of reliability of a psychometric instrument. A high value (close to 1.0) indicates a strong relationship among the dimensions on the scale.

6. Separate multiple regression analyses were performed to control for the added difficulty of raising children while attending college. When women with children were

excluded from the sample, significant factors predicting higher stress among women with no children during undergraduate school included, the experience of academic difficulties, race and sex discrimination, residence away from home, and Mexican American ethnicity. These variables accounted for 26 percent of the variation in stress.

References

Aguilar, M. A. (1996). Promoting the Educational Achievement of Mexican American Young Women. *Social Work in Education, 18*(3), 145–156.

Allen, W. R. (1985). Black Students, White Campus: Structural, Interpersonal, and Psychological Correlates of Success. *Journal of Negro Education, 54,* 134–147.

Allen, W. R., & Haniff, N.Z. (1991). Race, Gender, and Academic Performance in U.S. Higher Education. In W. R. Allen, E. G. Epps, & N. Z. Haniff (Eds.), *College in Black and White.* New York: State University of New York Press.

American Council on Education. (1991). *Minorities in Higher Education.* Washington, DC: American Council in Education Press.

American Council on Education. (2004). *Reflections on 20 Years of Minorities in Higher Education and the ACE Annual Status Report.* Washington, DC: ACE.

Almquist, E. M. (1974). Sex Stereotypes in Occupational Choice: The Case for College Women. *Journal of Vocational Behavior, 5,* 13–21.

Anderson, J. (1988). *The Education of Blacks in the South, 1860–1935.* Chapel Hill: University of North Carolina Press.

Archor, S., & Morales, A. (1990). Chicanas Holding Doctoral Degrees: Social Reproduction and Cultural Ecological Approaches. *Anthropology & Education Quarterly, 21*(3), 269–287.

Astin, A. W. (1982). *Minorities in American Higher Education.* San Francisco, CA: Jossey-Bass.

Astin, H., & Cross, P. H. (1981). Black Students in White Institutions. In G. E. Thomas (Ed.), *Black Students in Higher Education in the 1970's.* Westport, CT: Greenwood Press.

Auerbach, S. (2002). Why Do They Give the Good Classes to Some and Not to Others? Latino Parent Narratives of Struggle in a College Access Program. *Teachers College Record, 104,* 1369–1392.

Banks, W. M. (1988). African American Scholars in the University. *American Behavioral Scientist, 27*(3), 324–338.

Benjamin, L. (1982, Spring). Black Women Achievers: An Isolated Elite. *Sociological Inquiry, 53*(2), 141–149.

Bernard, J. (1976). Where Are We Now? Some Thoughts on the Current Scene. *Psychology of Women Quarterly, 1,* 21–37.

Brown, G. H., Rosen, N. L., & Hill, S. T. (1980). *The Condition of Education for Hispanic Americans.* Washington, DC: Government Printing Office.

Capello, D. (1994). Beyond Financial Aid: Counseling Latina Students. *Journal of Multicultural Counseling & Development, 22*(1), 28–36.

Carroll, C. (1982). Three's a Crowd: The Dilemma of the Black Woman in Higher Education. In G. T. Hull, P. B. Scott, & B. Smith (Eds.), *But Some of us are Brave.* Old Westbury, NY: The Feminist Press.

Carter, T. (1970). *Mexican Americans in School: A History of Educational Neglect.* New York: College Entrance Examination Board.

Cardoza, D. (2001). College Attendance and Persistence Among Hispanic Women: An Examination of Some Contributing Factors. *Sex Roles, 24*(3/4), 133–147.

Castillo, L. G., Conoley, C. W., & Brossart, D. F. (2004). Acculturation, White Marginalization, and Family Support as Predictors of Perceived Distress in Mexican American Female College Student. *Journal of Counseling Psychology, 51*(2), 151–157.

Chacon, M. (1982). Chicanas in Postsecondary Education. *Center for Research on Women.* Stanford, CA: Stanford University Press.

Choy, S. (2001). Students Whose Parents Did Not Go to College: Postsecondary Access, Persistence, and Attainment. *Washington, DC: U.S. Department of Education, National Center for Education Statistics, Office of Educational Research and Improvement.*

Cole, J. B. (1988). *The Education and Endowment of Black Women.* Albany, NY: Association of Black Women in Higher Education, Inc.

de la Luz Reyes, M., & Halcon, J. J. (1991). Practices of the Academy: Barriers to Access for Chicano Academics. In P. G. Altback & K. Lomotey (Eds.), *The Racial Crisis in American Higher Education* (pp. 167–186). Albany, NY: State University of New York Press.

Cuádraz, G. H. (1999). Stories of Access and "Luck": Chicana/os, Higher Education, and the Politics of Incorporation. *Latino Studies Journal, 10,* 100–123.

Del Castillo, A. R., Frederickson, J., McKenna, T., & Ortiz, F. I. (1988). The Assessment of the Status of the Education of Hispanic American Women. In T. McKenna & F. I. Ortiz (Eds.), *The Broken Web* (pp. 3–44). Claremond, CA: Floricanto Press.

Dinwiddie, G., & Allen, W. (2003). Two Steps forward, Three Steps back: Campus Climate, Gender, and African American Representation in Higher Education. In C. C. Yeakey & R. D. Henderson (Eds.), *Surmounting All Odds: Education, Opportunity, and Society in the New Millennium* vol. 2 (pp. 563–594). Greenwich, CT: Information Age Publishing.

Donato, R. (1997). *The Other Struggle for Equal Schools: Mexican Americans during the Civil Rights Era.* Albany, NY: SUNY Press.

Epstein, C. F. (1970). Encountering the Male Establishment: Sex-Status Limits on Women's Careers in the Professions. *American Journal of Sociology, 75,* 965–982.

Farkas, G. (2003). Racial Disparities and Discrimination in Education: What Do We Know, How Do We Know It, and What Do We Need to Know? *Teachers College Record, 105*(6), 1119–1146.

Farley, R., & Allen, W. (1987). *The Color Line and the Quality of Life in America.* Oxford: Oxford University Press.

Feagin, J. H., Vera, H., & Imani, N. (1996). *The Agony of Education: Black Students at Historically White Universities.* New York: Routledge.

Feldman, S. D. (1974). *Escape From the Doll's House: Women in Graduate and Professional School Education.* New York: McGraw-Hill.

Fleming, J. (1983). Black Women in Black and White College Environments: The Making of a Matriarch. *Journal of Social Issues, 39*(3), 41–54.

Fry, R. (2002). Latinos in Higher Education: Many Enroll too Few Graduate. Pew Hispanic Center Report. Retrieved from www.pewhispanic.org.

Furniss, W. T., & Graham, P. A. (1974). *Women in Higher Education.* Washington, DC: American Council on Education.

Gandara, P. C. (2006). *Fragile Futures: Risk and Vulnerability Among Latino High Achievers.* Princeton, NJ: ETS.

Gasman, M. (2005). Sisters in Service: African American Sororities and Philanthropic Support of Education. In A. Walton (Ed.), *Women and Philanthropy in Education* (pp. 194–214). Bloomington: Indiana University Press.

Gandara, P. C. (1982). Passing Through the Eye of the Needle: High-Achieving Chicanas. *Hispanic Journal of Behavioral Sciences, 4*(2), 167–179.

Ginorio, A., & Huston, M. (2001). *¡Sí, Se Puede! Yes, We Can: Latinas in School.* Washington, DC: American Association of University of Women.

Gloria, A., Castellanos, G., Lopez, J., & Rosales, R. (2005). An Examination of Academic Nonpersistence Decisions of Latino Undergraduates. *Hispanic Journal of Behavioral Sciences, 27,* 202–223.

Gonzales, P., Blanton, H., & Williams, K. (2002). The Effects of Stereotype Threat and Double-Minority Status on the Test Performance of Latino Women. *Personality and Social Psychology Bulletin, 48*(5), 659–670.

González, K. P., Jovel, J. E., & Stoner, C. (2004, Spring). Latinas: The New Latino Majority in College. In A. M. Ortiz (Ed.), *New Directions for Student Services.* San Francisco: Jossey-Bass.

Gregory, S. T. (2001). Black Faculty Women in the Academy: History, Status, and Future. *Journal of Negro Education, 70*(3), 124–138.

Hernandez, A. (1990). *Puerto Rican, Chicano, Cuban, and White Non-Latino High School Students Educational Expectations: A Longitudinal Analysis.* Unpublished doctoral dissertation, University of California, Los Angeles, CA.

Hill-Collins, P. (2000). *Black Feminist Thought: Knowledge, Consciousness, and the Politics of Empowerment.* New York: Routledge Press, 1990; 2nd edition 2000.

Higginbotham, E. (2001). *Too Much to Ask: Black Women in the Era of Integration.* Chapel Hill: University of North Carolina Press.

Holahan, C. K. (1979). Need for Support and Occupational Sex Typing. *Sex Roles, 5,* 425–436.

Howard-Vital, M. R. (1987). *Black Women in Higher Education: Struggling to Gain Visibility.* Information Analyses (ED 291 270).

Jackson, L. R. (1998). The Influence of Both Race and Gender on the Experiences of African American College Women. *The Review of Higher Education, 21*(4), 359–375.

Jacobs, L. (1981). Problems Encountered by Women and Minority Students at Indiana University. *Indiana Studies in Higher Education, 46.* Bloomington: Bureau of Evaluative Studies and Testing, Division of Research and Development, Indiana University.

Johnson, D. G. (1986). Predicting Academic Performance at a Predominantly Black Medical School. *Journal of Medical Education, 61*(8), 629–639.

King, J. (2007, February 19). University of Maryland, College Park. Speaker, Department of Curriculum and Instruction.

Kutner, N. G., & Brogan, D. (1976). Sources of Sex Discrimination in Educational Systems: A Conceptual Model. *Psychology of Women Quarterly, 1,* 50–68.

Lee, V. (1985). *Access to Higher Education: The Experience of Blacks, Hispanics, and Low Socioeconomic Status Whites.* Washington, DC: American Council on Education.

Lee, V. (1988). Achievement and Educational Aspirations among Hispanic Female High School Students: Comparison between Public and Catholic Schools. In T. McKenna & F.I. Ortiz (Eds.), *The Broken Web.* Claremont, CA: The Tomas Rivera Center: A National Institute for Policy Studies.

Loza, P. P. (2003). A System at Risk: College Outreach Programs and the Educational Neglect of Underachieving Latino High School Students. *The Urban Review, 35,* 43–57.

MacDonald, V. M. (2004). *Latino Education in the United States, 1513–2000: A Narrated History.* New York: Palgrave/Macmillan.

MacDonald, V. M., Botti, J., & Hoffman Clark, L. (2007). From Visibility to Autonomy: Latinos and Higher Education, 1965–2005. *Harvard Educational Review, 77*(4), 474–504.

MacDonald, V. M., & Garcia, T. (2003). Latino Higher Education: Historical Pathways to Access. In L. Jones & J. Castellanos (Eds.), *The Majority in the Minority: Retaining Latina/o Faculty, Administrators, and Students in the 21st Century* (pp. 15–43). Sterling, VA: Stylus Press.

McCandless, A. T. (1999). *The Past in the Present: Women's Higher Education in the Twentieth-Century American South.* Tuscaloosa: University of Alabama Press.

Mercomes, B. W. (1998). African American Sororities. In L. Eisenmann (Ed.), *Historical Dictionary of Women's Education in the United States* (pp. 13–14). Westport, CT: Greenwood Press.

Mendoza, P. (1981). Responding to Stress: Ethnic and Sex Differences in Coping Behavior. In A. Baron (Ed.), *Explorations in Chicano Psychology* (pp. 187–211). New York: Praeger.

Mortenson, T. G. (1991). *Equality of Higher Educational Opportunity for Women, Black, Hispanic and Low Income Students.* Iowa City, IA: American College Testing Educational and Social Research.

Moses, Y. T. (1989). *Black Women in Academe: Issue and Strategies.* Washington, DC: Association of American Colleges.

Munoz, D., & Garcia-Bahne, B. (1978). *A Study of the Chicano Experience in Higher Education.* Final Report for the Center for Minority Group Mental Health Programs, National Institute of Mental Health. Grant No. NN24597–01, University of California, San Diego.

Nash, M. (2005). *Women's Education in the United States, 1780–1840.* New York: Palgrave/Macmillan.

National Center for Education Statistics. (2003) Digest of Education Statistics. 2004 National Study of Postsecondary Faculty Background Characteristics, Work Activities, and Compensations of Instructional Faculty and Staff: Report (NSOPF:04). Retrieved from http://nces.ed.gov/pubs2006/2006176.pdf.

National Center for Education Statistics. (2001) Digest of Education Statistics. 2001 Integrated Postsecondary Education Data System (IPEDS), Winter 2000–2001. Retrieved from http://nces.ed.gov/programs/digest/d05/tables/dt05_227.asp.

National Commission on Secondary Education for Hispanics (1984). Make Something Happen. *Hispanics and Urban High School Reform, 1,* Washington, DC: Hispanic Policy Development Project.

Nielsen, F., & Fernandez, R. M. (1982). *Achievement of Hispanic Students in American High Schools.* Washington, DC: National Center for Education Statistics.

O'Donnell, J. A., & Anderson, D. G. (1978). Factors Influencing Choice of Major and Career of Capable Women. *Vocational Guidance Quarterly, 26,* 214–221.

Ogren, C. (2005). *The American State Normal School: "An Instrument of Great Good."* New York: Palgrave/Macmillan.

Orfield, G., & Eaton, S. E. (1996). *Dismantling Desegregation: The Quiet Reversal of* Brown v. Board of Education. New York: The New Press.

Orfield, G., Marin, P., & Horn, C. L. (Eds.). (2005). *Higher Education and the Color Line: College Access, Racial Equity, and Social Change.* Cambridge, MA: Harvard Education Press.

Padilla, F. M. (1997). *The Struggle of Latino/Latina University Students: In Search of a Liberating Education.* New York: Routledge.

Perkins, L. (1998). The African American Female Elite: The Early History of African American Women in the Seven Sister Colleges, 1880–1960. In C. Woyshner & H. S. Gelfond (Eds.), *Minding Women: Reshaping the Educational Realm* (pp. 291–329). Cambridge, MA: Harvard Education Press.

Perkins, L. (1983). The Impact of the "Cult of True Womanhood" on the Education of Black Women. *Journal of Social Issues, 39*(3), 17–28.

Pizarro, M. (2005). *Chicanas and Chicanos in School: Racial Profiling, Identity Battles, and Empowerment.* Austin: University of Texas Press.

Price, P. V., & Wohlford, J. K. (2005). Equity in Educational Attainment: Racial, Ethnic, and Gender Inequality in the 50 States. In G. Orfield, P. Marin, & C. L. Horn (Eds.), *Higher Education and the Color Line: College Access, Racial Equity, and Social Change* (pp. 59–81). Cambridge, MA: Harvard Education Press.

Reyes, M. (2001, Spring). Tortured Victory or Joyful Accomplishment? Successful Eskimo and Latina College Students. *Race, Gender, & Class in Education (Part II), 7*(4), 82–106.

Roebuck, J. B., & Murty, K. S. (1993). *Historically Black Colleges and Universities: Their Place in American Higher Education.* Westport, CT: Praeger.

Roby, P. (1975). Structural and Internalized Barriers to Women in Higher Education. In J. Freemen (Ed.), *Women: A Feminist Perspective* (1st ed.). Palo Alto, CA: Mayfield.

Rodriguez, A. L., Guido-DiBrito, F., Torres, V., & Talbot, D. (2000). Latina College Students: Issues and Challenges for the 21st Century. *NASPA Journal, 37*(3), 511–527.

Rumberger, W. R. (1988). High School Dropouts: A Review of Issues and Evidence. *Review of Educational Resources, 57,* 101–121.

Samuels, A. (2004). *Is Separate Unequal?: Black Colleges and the Challenge to Desegregation.* Lawrence: University of Kansas Press.

Segura, D. (1984). Labor Market Stratification: The Chicana Experience. *Berkeley Journal of Sociology, 29,* 57–91.

Segura, D. (1990). Chicanas and Triple Oppression in the Labor Force. In T. Córdova, N. Cantu, G. Cardenas, J. Garcia, & C. M. Sierra (Eds.), *Chicana Voices: Intersections of Class, Race, and Gender.* Albuquerque: University of New Mexico Press.

Segura, D. (2003). Navigating between Two Worlds: The Labyrinth of Chicana Intellectual Production in the Academy. *Journal of Black Studies, 34*(1), 28–51.

Sandler, B. R. (1986). *Campus Climate Visited: Chilly for Women Faculty, Administrators, and Graduate Students.* Washington, DC: Association of American Colleges, Project on the Status and Education of Women (mimeograph).

Smith, W. A. (1991). Personal Traits, Institutional Prestige, Racial Attitudes, and Black Student Academic Performance in College. In W. R. Allen, E. G. Epps, & N. Z. Haniff (Eds.), *College in Black and White.* Albany, NY: State University of New York Press.

Smith, W. A., & Allen, W. R. (1984). Modeling Black Student Academic Performance in Higher Education. *Research in Higher Education, 21,* 210–225.

Solomon, B. M. (1985). *In the Company of Educated Women.* New Haven, CT: Yale University Press.

Solomon, L.C., & Wingard, T. L. (1991). The Changing Demographics: Problems and Opportunities. In P. G. Altback & K. Lomotey (Eds.), *The Racial Crisis in American Higher Education.* Albany, NY: State University of New York Press.

Solomon, R. P. (1992). *Black Resistance in High School: Forging a Separatist Culture.* Albany, NY: State University of New York Press.

Squires-Nieves, S. (1991). *Hispanic Women Making Their Presence on Campus Less Tenuous.* Washington, DC: Association of American Colleges.

Suro, R., & Fry, R. (2005). Leaving the newcomers behind. In R. H. Hersch & J. Merrow (Eds.), *Declining by Degrees: Higher Education at Risk* (pp. 169–183). New York: Palgrave/Macmillan.

Swail, W. S., Cabrera, A. F., & Lee, C. (2004). *Latino Youth and the Pathway to College.* Washington, DC: Educational Policy Institute, Inc.

Teranishi, R., Allen, W. & Solorzano, D. G. (2004). Opportunity at the Crossroads: Racial Inequality, School Segregation, and Higher Education in California. *Teachers College Record*, *106*(11), 2224–2245.

Tienda, M., & Mitchell, F. (Eds.). (2006). *Hispanics and the Future of America*. Washington, DC: The National Academies Press.

Tinto, V. (1987). *Leaving College: Rethinking the Causes and Cures of Student Attrition*. Chicago: University of Chicago Press.

Tinto, V. (1988). Stages of Student Departure: Reflections on the Longitudinal Character of Student Leaving. *Journal of Higher Education*, *59*(4), 438–455.

Thomas, G. E. (1980). Race and Sex Group Inequality in Higher Education: Institutional and Major Field Enrollment Status. *American Educational Research Journal*, *17*, 171–181.

Tidball, M. E. (1980). Women's Colleges and Women Achievers Revisited. *Signs*, *5*, 504–517.

Trent, W. T. (1991). Focus on Equality: Race and Gender Differences in Degree Attainment, 1975–76; 1980–81. In W. R. Allen, E. G. Epps, & N. Z. Haniff (Eds.), *College in Black and White*. Albany, NY: State University of New York Press.

Tyack, D., & Hansot, E. (1990). *Learning Together: A History of Coeducation in American Public Schools*. New Haven, CT: Yale University Press.

Watford, T., Rivas, M. A., Burciaga, R., & Solorzano, D. G. (2006). Latinas and the Doctorate: The "Status" of Attainment and Experiences from the Margin. In J. Castellanos, A. M. Gloria, & M. Kamimura (Eds.), *The Latina/o Pathway to the Ph.D.: Abriendo Caminos* (pp. 113–133). Sterling, VA: Stylus Press.

Weber, L., Higginbotham, E., & Leung, M.L.A. (1999). Race and Class Bias in Qualitative Research on Women. In S. Peplau, C. DeBro, R. C. Veniegas, & P. L. Taylor (Eds.), *Gender, Culture, and Ethnicity: Current Research about Women and Men* (pp. 449–462). L. A. Mountain View, CA: Mayfield.

Williams, H. (2005). *Self-Taught: African American Education in Slavery and Freedom*. Chapel Hill: University of North Carolina Press.

Wolf-Wendel, L. E. (1998). Models of Excellence: The Baccalaureate Origins of Successful European American Women, African American Women, and Latinas. *Journal of Higher Education*, *69*, 141–186.

Zambrana, R. E. (1988). Toward Understanding the Educational Trajectory and Socialization of Latina Women. *The Broken Web: The Educational Experience of Hispanic American Women* (pp. 61–77). Encino, CA: Thomas Rivera Center and Floricanto Press.

Zambrana, R. E., Dorrington, C., & Alonzo Bell, S. (1997). Mexican American Women in Higher Education: A Comparative Study. *Race, Gender & Class*, *4*(2), 127–149.

Zambrana, R. E., & Zoppi, I. M. (2002). Latina Students: Translating Cultural Wealth into Social Capital to Improve Academic Success. *Journal of Ethnic & Cultural Diversity in Social Work*, *11*(1/2), 33–53.

Zoppi, I. M., MacDonald, V. M., & Munoz, O. (2007). *Latino Parental Involvement in a New Latino Community*. Working Paper, University of Maryland, College Park.

5

Developing Policy to Address the
Lived Experiences of
Working Mothers

MARY GATTA

Employment in the U.S. labor market does not always translate into economic self-sufficiency especially for marginalized groups.[1] This chapter explores the importance of an intersectional approach to workforce development by addressing three broad research questions:

1. What are the challenges single mothers confront in attaining education and training via public sector initiatives? Specifically how do race, class, and marital status intersect with gender to limit the access of women to public sector education and training?
2. How has the Workforce Investment Act (WIA) conceptualized single working poor mothers and addressed their employment and training needs?
3. Using a case study from New Jersey, how can job training policy be reconceptualized by attending to the intersectionality of women's identities in order to provide real access to education and training to low-wage working women?

While many policymakers have celebrated the success of welfare reform for "ending welfare as we know it" many single working poor mothers could not join the festivities. Instead the end of welfare served to exacerbate their already difficult time of trying to make ends meet. A significant contributor to this was that the "workfirst" policies that were implemented during welfare reform of 1996 primarily used "job placement" as the performance measure of success. In that the goal was to place clients in paid employment, any job was often considered a "good" job, regardless of wages earned, benefits provided, opportunities for advancement, or control over one's hours. As a result many welfare recipients, among them single mothers, flooded into low-wage jobs during the late 1990s.[2] Yet employment in the U.S. labor market does not always translate into economic self-sufficiency especially for marginalized groups. In fact in some cases employment can actually intensify poverty as the increased economic and social costs associated with securing and retaining employment, including childcare, eldercare, transportation, and clothing/uniforms (Boushey, Gundersen, & Bernstein, 2001), typically cost more than one is earning. Moreover, as women tend to bear the brunt of the responsibility for much of this caring labor (Folbe, 2001), employment in low-wage work, without economic and social supports, continues to trap them in poverty.

Policy then must attend to the life experiences of women as workers and mothers in order to help improve their chances of reaching self-sufficiency. To do so, I suggest that job-training policy address the issues of low-wage women using an intersectional approach in order to assess the impacts of public policy. In regard to workforce development policy such an analysis would allow us to examine (among other things) the characteristics of the occupations that women are located in (including the opportunities for advancement, the gender pay gap along race, ethnicity, and irregular work schedules) to determine how they contribute to women's poverty and make it difficult for them to attain the education and skills training to advance; and factors such as transportation, family demands (including childcare and eldercare), and geographic location, which inhibit women's access to education. Critical to this approach is understanding the matrix of domination (Collins, 1999)—how differences among low-wage women workers along variables such as race, marital status, and class, shape and reinforce their ability to access public support for education. Further the intersectional approach is not only important in understanding the experiences of single working poor mothers and the effects of job training policy, but also in formulating strategies to address the inequities of these policies.

Incorporating an intersectional approach to public employment and training policy has significant positive effects on improving single working poor mothers access to education and training, and in turn, their economic self-sufficiency. The New Jersey Department of Labor and Workforce Development (NJDLWD) piloted a successful training program that, from the outset, used an intersectional approach to determine the best way to deliver education and skills training to single working poor mothers. The pilot program was conceptualized and implemented attending to the life experiences of women and incorporated within the department's employment and training system. To accomplish this, the NJDLWD collaborated with gender equity experts to ensure that the program was crafted to accommodate the needs of this population. In doing so, the key players developed and used an intersectional perspective to conceptualize and implement a public policy program. By learning from the New Jersey case study, we can highlight ways to make public policy more effective in meeting the needs of diverse groups.

In this chapter I explore the importance of an intersectional approach to workforce development. To accomplish this I focus on aforementioned broad research questions.

Why Does an Intersectional Approach Matter in Workforce Development?

I contend that workforce policies need to be implemented with a lens that takes into account the impact and intersections of gender, race, class, and other variables on individuals' lives. That is, workforce policy must be formulated and evaluated using an intersectional lens. Such an approach emphasizes the "contemporary outcomes of historical structural patterns of inequality that have resulted in the overrepresentation of people of color and women, especially women of color, among the poor (Dill, Jones-DeWeever, & Schram, 2004, 1). Central to this understanding is that gender and race are not independent analytical categories that can be added together (Browne & Misra, 2003, 487) but instead are socially constructed categories that influence individual identities, organizations, and social systems. Patricia Hill Collins (1999) introduced the matrix of domination to illustrate this interlocking aspect of inequality. Imagine that an individual's arms and legs were tied down. Simply removing the ropes from his/her arm will not free him/her. Instead the ropes of the legs would continue to constrain him/her. One would need to devise a strategy that addressed all the constraints on the individual and how those ropes intertwine.

This metaphor can easily be translated into the social world. Not everyone has an equal chance to be in poverty. Race and gender, and, more aptly, the intersections of these identities, influence one's life chances. Moreover the impacts of welfare and workforce development policies are not equally experienced by all members of society. Instead relations of race, class, and gender shape these experiences. For example, the image of the Black welfare mother as the public face of poverty has allowed sociological concepts—namely, differential access to economic opportunities such as high-wage, high-demand jobs, education, skills training, and healthcare—to be viewed as personal failings as opposed to the results of intersecting systems of inequality. Such conceptualizations gained fuel throughout the past five decades, commencing with Aid to Dependent Children (ADC) and continuing through Temporary Aid to Needy Families (TANF).[3] A glaring example of this is that President George W. Bush recently praised the 1965 report on Black families by Daniel Patrick Moynihan. In that report, Moynihan contended that Black economic progress has not been successful because of the high numbers of weak single mother households among Black families (Stafford, Salas, & Mendez, 2003, 3). Such racialized conceptualizations of single mothers have allowed policymakers and others to mask the real causes of poverty: a lack of access to good paying jobs for single mothers. As women rolled off welfare and typically into low-wage work, they had little opportunity to gain the skills and education to move out of these jobs and instead have remained in poverty.

As such, policy dominated by employing individuals is not enough to ensure economic survival; instead single mothers need access to a multitude of supports that will allow them to raise themselves and their children out of poverty. In particular, much research has documented the positive relationship between education and economic self-sufficiency. Yet the major federal employment and training legislation, the Workforce Investment Act (WIA) of 1998,[4] does not fully take into account the needs of single working poor mothers[5] and their ability to access education and job training, while juggling their work and family demands. Moreover the concept of universal access, which is central to WIA, has the effect of ignoring differences between workers, particularly along variables of gender, race, and marital status. This makes it difficult to provide education and training to single working poor mothers in ways that are congruent with their life demands.

The absence of such inclusive policy frameworks in U.S. employment and training policy is problematic on many levels. WIA's mandate is to provide training for *all workers* through One-Stop Career Centers,[6] yet, as WIA does not effectively attend to sociological variables, incumbent workers are typically lumped together into one group, and the differences among them are not taken into account. In what should be considered an ironic twist WIA was heralded a significant piece of legislation because of its concept of universal access: it brought into the public-sector workforce investment system[7] the educational and employment needs of low-wage workers that for decades were ignored or minimized in the government job-training initiatives. However, simply allowing for universal access in language, does not equate to equity of services. For example, while the goal of One-Stop Career system, under WIA, is that all employment and training services are located in one local area providing easy access for all individuals, in practice this access is not so universal. Several factors including that often One-Stop Career Centers are not open beyond traditional business hours, and a lack of access to childcare and transportation make it challenging for low-wage single mothers to attain services to which they are entitled. Indeed it is precisely the lack of attention to women as mothers, workers, and caregivers, along with a denial of gendered and racial impacts of public policy and labor market opportunities within WIA, which has contributed to single mothers' difficulty in attaining education and skills training to improve their chances of economic self-sufficiency.

Postwelfare Reform and Single Working Mothers

To best understand how policy affects single working poor mothers it is helpful to briefly review the policy context of the late 1990s. In 1996 President Clinton signed the Personal Responsibility and Work Opportunity Reconciliation Act (PRWORA)—a significant piece of legislation that overhauled the U.S. welfare system by replacing Aid to Families with Dependent Children (AFDC) with Temporary Aid to Needy Families (TANF). Unlike its predecessor, TANF is a time-limited,[8] work-based[9] system that requires recipients to participate in work or work-based activities in order to receive cash assistance. This 1996 law was publicized as "welfare reform" and Clinton promised to "end welfare as we know it."

By the beginning of the twenty-first century Clinton's welfare reform was heralded as a success in many circles. Success was gauged by the precarious indicator that PRWORA had moved women, and, in particular, single mothers of color, into paid work. O'Neill and Hill (2002) reported that women had actually "gained ground" as a result of welfare reform in 1996, noting great employment gains for single mothers. They found that by 2000 there was a 40 percent increase in work participation of single mothers who were high school dropouts; an 83 percent increase in work participation among African American single mothers; and among Hispanic single mothers employment rose from 47 percent in 1992 to 63 percent in 2000.

Yet conspicuously missing from O'Neill and Hill's analysis and many others who tout the success of welfare reform is that although employment rates have indeed risen, simultaneously women comprise a large and growing portion of the working poor—individuals who work in the paid labor force, yet do not earn enough money to economically survive. Specifically in 2002, the poverty rate for working men was 4.4, while the comparable rate for working women was 5.5. Yet not all women share an equal probability of being among the ranks of the working poor. The poverty rate of working African American women was 11.8 and the poverty rate of working Hispanic women was 10.0, compared to a poverty rate of 4.4 of working White women.[10] Moreover when we look at family composition, families maintained by women with children under eighteen years old have the highest probability of living in poverty—a rate of 21.9. This is more than double the rate of families maintained by men with children under eighteen years old (rate of 10.1) and four times greater than the rate of married couple families with children (rate of 4.9).[11] How then does one reconcile the notion that despite such employment gains women, in particular single working mothers, continue to comprise a significant portion of the working poor?

The answer is actually quite simple. Welfare reform has served to create a large pool of women who are working, often full-time, in both the paid and unpaid labor force, and still do not earn enough to support themselves and their children. And perhaps even more important is that the situation does not improve on its own after leaving the welfare rolls. Fifty-five percent of single mothers remain in poverty one year after leaving welfare; 49 percent three years later and 42 percent five years later (Cancian & Meyer, 2000). This is related, in large part, to the lack of preparation that single mothers on welfare have to help them gain high-wage, high-demand jobs. Single mothers, in particular, are disadvantaged when it comes to possessing the educational characteristics typically associated with success in the labor market. In the United States, married mothers are twice as likely as single mothers to have a four-year college degree. In addition, 50 percent of single mothers are women of color, as compared to only about 28 percent of married mothers (Levitan & Gluck, 2002). Looking specifically at the population of single mothers who collected welfare during welfare reform, it is evident that "Workfirst" policies did not benefit them in terms of increasing their education and skills training via TANF. An Institute for Women's Policy Research (IWPR) (2002) study confirms that while the employment of single mothers rose during TANF implementation, with its "workfirst" mentality, the share of single mothers with some college education decreased during TANF implementation (6). This is directly related to the fact that in order to secure their benefits they needed to be employed and their chances of gaining an education was drastically reduced.

In additional to educational disparities single mothers tend to be younger than married mothers, indicating that they have less years in the paid workforce (Levitan & Gluck, 2002, 11–13) and are typically employed in low-wage industries and occupations. Just under half of single mothers work in service industries and almost 20 percent of single mothers work in retail trade industries (29–30). Within the service sector the major employers include healthcare, educational, business, and social services. In fact service occupations account for nearly 25 percent of single mothers' employment (as opposed to only 15 percent of married mothers' jobs). Coupling the industry distribution with an occupational distribution confirms that single mothers are overrepresented in traditionally female jobs. In the service sector single mothers often labor as janitors, cafeteria workers, security guards, home healthcare aides, private household workers, orderlies, and childcare workers (Levitan & Gluck, 2002). In addition to service occupations single mothers are also highly represented in administrative occupations, as 23 percent of single mothers are employed in these jobs. These jobs are low-paying and often do not offer employer sponsored pensions, health insurance, or education and job training. In contrast only 13 percent of single mothers are employed in managerial and executive occupations and 16 percent are employed in professional and technical occupations (29–30).

Further, when examining the racial composition of single mother headed households in poverty several important trends emerge. IWPR (2002) research has found that although White single parent headed households comprise the largest share of low-income single parent homes, the relative proportion of White welfare recipients declined significantly postwelfare reform (from 34 percent to 24 percent). During the same time period the proportion of Hispanic households receiving welfare dramatically increased from 20 percent to 29 percent. In addition while the proportion of Black families receiving welfare remained consistent during the time period, the percentage of Black non-welfare recipients who were low-income—the working poor—rose from 29 to 34 percent during welfare reform. Indeed Blacks were the only racial-ethnic group to experience an increase in the proportion of low-income single parent homes. IWPR researchers aptly suggest that these numbers indicate that White single mother headed households are able to move out of the low-income population with slightly more success than other groups because of the racial-ethnic impacts of welfare policy and inequities that exist in the labor market. Indeed one does not have to look further than the gender pay gap to see the impact race plays in labor market rewards. Reskin and Padavic (2002), among others, have found that while all women earn less then men in comparable positions, Black and Hispanic women face additional costs. Specifically Black women earn approximately 87 percent of White women's wages, while Hispanic women earn about 70 percent of White women's wages (124–126).

In addition to the economic impacts of low-wage work and discrimination in the labor market, women, and, in particular, single mothers, face a significant barrier to their ability to reach self-sufficiency—they bear the brunt of the unpaid caring labor in the home. Indeed women's care-giving responsibilities have significant impacts on their participation in both paid work and educational programs. As Albeda and Tilly (1997) note because women perform the bulk of the unpaid household labor themselves, single mothers need jobs that offer them flexibility to take care of their childcare needs, and will often sacrifice pay and job variety for even the smallest degree of flexibility. Further, because the United States does not have paid family leave,[12] mothers are extremely vulnerable when their child, parent, or other dependent requires specific care.

So to a large extent what "ground women gained" from welfare reform was space among the working poor. Central to this is that because benefits were tied to work activities mothers collecting TANF did not have real opportunities to attain job training and education during welfare reform. This fact is particularly detrimental to their present and future economic self-sufficiency. Labor market trends indicate that there will be significant growth in jobs that require advanced skills, with slower growth in jobs that require basic or minimal skills throughout the early part of the twenty-first century (Carnevale & Desrochers, 1999). Further advanced skills are required in all industries, including industries that are not typically associated with high-level skill demands. For example, 60 percent of sales related jobs in the service sector require skills beyond those of a high school graduate (Levenson, Reardon, & Schmidt, 1999). In order to successfully compete in the labor market one needs high-level skills.

Not surprisingly then education and skills training have positive labor market rewards.[13] As summarized in the Institute for Women's Policy Research (IWPR) report, *Working First but Working Poor: The Need for Education and Training Following Welfare Reform* (2001), Thomas Karier's (1998) research found that welfare recipients who earned a bachelor's degree experienced a $2.00 hourly increase in earnings relative to welfare recipients who earned only a high school diploma.[14] Moreover the Center for Law and Social Policy (CLASP) found that TANF recipients in California who completed educational programs experienced significant earnings gains. For example, TANF recipients employed year-round increased their annual earnings by 42 percent during their last year of college. Even more striking is that three years after completing college former TANF recipients experienced annual earnings increases of 88 percent (Mathur, et al., 2002). It is important to note that earnings increases are not just experienced by welfare recipients who completed college. Similarly placed individuals who completed vocational programs and certificate programs also experienced wage gains (Mathur, et al., 2004) continuing to demonstrate the positive correlation between education and earnings for welfare recipients.

Based on studies such as these, state policies have been advanced to provide low-wage workers with access to college education. For example, the Maine Department of Labor instituted the Parents as Scholars program that allows welfare recipients to attend college while still receiving access to all welfare supports.[15] This program has clearly demonstrated how providing education and skills training will raise income levels. Graduates of the program earned a median income of $11.71 an hour, as compared to the $7.15 national median income of former welfare recipients (Maine Equal Justice Partners, 2001; Gault, 2002). In addition to the wage gains Sandra Butler, Luisa Deprez, and Rebekah Smith (2002) found that graduates of Maine's program were significantly more likely to have jobs that provided health benefits than did nongraduates. In addition, they found that graduates of Maine's Parents as Scholars program also reported higher levels of self-esteem as a result of completing their education. Timothy Bartik (2001) has also demonstrated that formal education is critical to their economic success. He found, using data from the Current Population Survey, that finishing high school raises wages more than 40 percent, cuts unemployment in half, and cuts the poverty rate by one-third. Completing a college education continues to improve wages more than 50 percent, and also cuts both the unemployment and the poverty rate each by another half (88–90).

So while the evidence is clear that education and skills training provide routes out of poverty, public policy often falls short of effectively meeting the needs of this population. The result is that single working poor mothers must often forgo opportunities to attain education and job training, and instead remain trapped in low-wage work. This suggests that the fact single mothers

are working for a living yet remaining in poverty must force government policy to not only recognize them as a group in poverty, but also address the question of what to do about their poverty in new and innovative ways.

What is the Workforce Investment Act (WIA)?

The piece of legislation that is charged with providing public-sector education
and skills training is the Workforce Investment Act (WIA). In 1998 WIA, with
the institutionalization of One-Stop Career Centers, organized delivery of the
workforce development system into state and local Workforce Investment
Boards (WIB), which would coordinate and oversee education and job training. WIA includes five titles that prescribe individual programs or goals.[16] WIA
Title I is, the *Workforce Investment System*, with the goal:

> to provide workforce investment activities that increase the employment,
> retention, and earnings of participants, and increase occupational skill
> attainment by participants, which will improve the quality of the work-
> force, reduce welfare dependency, and enhance productivity and compet-
> itiveness of the Nation's economy. The goals are achieved through the
> workforce investment system. (Chicago Jobs Council, 2003, 4)[17]

To achieve these goals, One-Stop Career Centers were established within local
neighborhoods where individuals could access core services and be directly
referred to job training, education, and/or other services.

Significant in WIA is that unlike its predecessor, the Job Training Partnership Act (JTPA), all individuals (eighteen years and older) have access to WIA
services. JTPA participation was limited to those individuals who met a strin-
gent eligibility requirement, as at least 65 percent of clients had to be "hard to
serve."[18] This made it difficult to provide resources for upgrading low-wage
workers' skills, as most resources had to be directed to placing unemployed
individuals in a job. In contrast, WIA is predicated on the concept of universal
access, so that all adults can use WIA services without regard to income eligibility or employment status. To accomplish this there is a three-tiered system
of core, intensive, and training services. Core services, the most basic form,
include informational resources, self-services, job search, and job research
assistance. These services are available to all workers, regardless of income,
job, or educational level. The next level, intensive services, include short-term
assistance to provide individuals job opportunities given their existing skills.
This level is reserved for unemployed or underemployed individuals as long as
the One-Stop operator determines that they need more services to obtain or
retain employment that would lead to self-sufficiency. The highest level, training services, include on-the-job training and classroom skills development
that lead to a credential and/or occupational specific skills. In order to access

training, participants are supplied with an Individualized Training Account (ITA) that serves as a voucher that the individual can use to "purchase" training from an eligible provider. Similar to intensive services, eligibility for training services is determined by the One-Stop operator. In order to advance through the tiers it must be demonstrated that one's employment objectives cannot be met at the lower tier. This provides a venue, at least in theory, for the public workforce system to meet a diverse set of workers' needs.

Is Universal Access a Reality for Single Mothers?

Despite its mandate for full universal access, WIA often falls short of this charge and cannot attend to the needs of single working poor mothers effectively. First it is important to note that there is a history of a general exclusion of workers in all employment and training public policy for decades. A report of the National Governor's Association (2004) notes that very few agencies or institutions focus on low-wage workers as part of their core mission, and do not market postemployment services. In regard to WIA, which in language recognized the need to direct services to this group, the funding is actually tied to performance measures that make directing resources to any low-wage workers seem unproductive. "Some of these measures—namely, newly entered employment levels and earnings gains—provide disincentives to serving individuals who are already working and instead favor the unemployed or other groups" (Miller, et al., 2004). This is perhaps most vividly demonstrated in that fewer individuals have received skills training through the One-Stop system under WIA, than under its predecessor JTPA. According to the U.S. Department of Labor in Program Year 2000 approximately 50,000 adults received training under WIA, as compared to 150,000 annually in the final years of JTPA (Chicago Jobs Council, 2003).[19]

One of the most sustained criticisms of WIA is that the three tiered system often hinders the ability of certain clients to access job training. As noted individuals must pass through core and intensive services before they can access new training on occupational specific skills. While noble in its goal of ensuring that the populations hardest to serve get resources (especially when resources are scarce), this policy has the indirect effect of serving as a barrier to skills training for many members of the working poor. Congressional testimony organized by Wider Opportunities for Women (2003) graphically illustrates this point as they suggest:

> Consider the example of a Vermont woman who sought the help of the One-Stop Center after a long history of employment as a housekeeper. Recently divorced and unable to support her family on her housekeeper wages, she wanted to participate in a skilled trades training program to improve her earnings potential. She was turned away because she had

success in the housekeeping field and therefore was not eligible to participate in the training program, which she was told, was for people with no skills and with a long history of unemployment. (5)

As evident from this description the concept of "universal" access is questionable. Within the sequential series of services, eligibility in training program often is subjective, with education and job training being seen as the last resort, not a core need of all workers.

Further compounding this is that a universal approach does not exist in how states "choose" who can progress through the sequential tiered service. Indeed a "patchwork of policies has resulted; some workforce boards consider education and training a last resort for those unable to secure a job at the core or intensive levels, while others move through the sequence quickly so they may enroll in training programs. In the same way, some local agencies make intensive and training services available only to unemployed persons seeking employment, while others allow such services to be utilized by employed workers seeking higher paying jobs" (Michigan League of Human Services, 2003, 3).

Tied to this is that a universal approach does not take into account true measures of economic self-sufficiency, and more importantly, how they differ by geographic location and family composition. Wider Opportunities for Women (WOW) developed self-sufficiency standards for all fifty states, showing the differences between what is needed to survive.[20] For example, while the self-sufficiency level for a single mother with two children in Prairie County, Montana, was calculated at $20,128 in 2002, the same woman would have to earn $47,881 in suburban Monmouth County in New Jersey. Moreover a single mother with three children in Wilcox County, Alabama, would have had to earn $28,360 in 2003 to economically be self-sufficient, while her counterpart in San Diego County, California, would have to earn more than double that: $65,190. When we compare this to the Federal Poverty line we see a large disparity. In 2002 a family of one adult and two children would be considered poor if they earned $15,020 a year regardless of where they lived or the age of their children.

WIA defines self-sufficiency as the Lower Living Standard Income Level (LLSIL), although it does encourage states to set higher levels. The LLSIL minimally takes geographic location into account by calculating the standard across four broad geographic regions (Northeast, Midwest, South, and West), and by metropolitan and nonmetropolitan area. Unlike the self sufficiency standard, the LLISL calculates cost based on the basic family budget approach (based on the prices of a market basket of goods), and does not take into account childcare costs, or the changing consumption patterns within the family budget such as housing, food, and transportation, along with their share of expenses over time (Working for America Institute, 2003). As such, this measure is really a rough tool to measure poverty, and many individuals are denied access to second- and third-level WIA services.

Moreover it is hard to know exactly who is being served by WIA because many Workforce Investment Boards do not collect data on the individuals they serve. Findings from Wider Opportunities for Women/National Association of Workforce Investment Boards (2003) report found that 35 percent of WIBs do not analyze demographic data including race, sex, ethnicity, and age of program participants. In addition, 58 percent of WIBs did not know if women were placed in nontraditional occupations or if they even analyzed this information.[21] This is particularly problematic because nontraditional occupations offer women opportunities for high-wages, health benefits, and pensions not typically available in traditionally female fields. In addition there is little attention paid to gender in implementing policies. Seventy-three percent of WIBs did not collect data on how displaced homemakers are served disaggregated from information on dislocated workers. About half of the WIBs surveyed did not have representation from organizations that primarily focus on low-income women, making it hard to ensure that women's programs are developed with a gendered lens.

Even more disconcerting is the research that demonstrates racialized differences in the treatment of women by caseworkers and job coaches. Mimi Abramovitz (2001), building on existing research notes that as opposed to their White counterparts, Black women on welfare receive far less support with job search education and training. Moreover research has found that when referred to possible jobs via the public sector, employers treat low-income women differentially based on race. According to Susan Gooden (1999) Black women received shorter interviews; more preemployment drug tests; criminal background and other checks; greater differences between the job offered and the tasks actually performed; more evening hour work; and a negative relationship with supervisors. Differential access to support services along race and ethnicity are further supported by the National Urban League Institute for Opportunity and Equality (2002). They found that more than 70 percent of Hispanic and African American women did not receive any subsidies (including childcare, transportation assistance, and college degree assistance) for work-related activities. In contrast, 62 percent of White women did not receive any subsidies. Findings such as these seriously question how the educational and career needs of single working poor mothers, and in particular single working poor mothers of color, are met by the current Federal employment and training legislation.

Specific Barriers to Skills Training for Single Working Poor Mothers

In addition to the problems associated with WIA legislation, the workforce system faces significant obstacles in regard to how to deliver skills training directly to single working poor mothers. This population faces many barriers that prevent them from attaining skills training via traditional modes of delivery. Foremost childcare needs place a burden on single mothers that often precludes them from attending traditional education programs (Edin & Lein, 1997; Johnson, 2002). Locating affordable childcare and "off-hours" childcare (such as on nights and weekends when many classes are offered) often proves to be a daunting task. In addition, a large percentage of single working mothers are employed in jobs with irregular schedules, such as those characteristic of the service sector, making it difficult to attend classes that are inflexible in their scheduling. This is further complicated because most organizations that provide training typically are not open after traditional work hours or on weekends (Miller, et al., 2004).

In addition to childcare needs and irregular schedules, transportation also proves to be a significant barrier for many single mothers, making it difficult for them to attend classes. Nationally one-third of households earning less than $15,000 a year do not own a car (Van Horn & Schaffner, 2003). This is especially relevant in suburban and rural areas where there are not extensive public transportation systems. Furthermore noncollege educated workers often find very little access to employer-sponsored training. Lisa Lynch and Sandra Black (1995) found that employers' investment decisions in regard to employee training are influenced by the characteristics of the workers that they employ. Overall they found that employees who are perceived as having a high turnover rate and/or possess lower levels of formal education are less likely to receive employer provided training. As such single mothers either forego training opportunities, or spend years attempting to complete credentials or degrees by taking one to two classes every few months.

Developing Policy with an Intersectional Lens: An Example from New Jersey

In order to address the barriers that single working poor mothers face in attaining skills training and education, the New Jersey Department of Labor and Workforce Development (NJDLWD) piloted an innovative workforce development program in 2002 in which single working poor mothers received skills training via online learning in their homes. One hundred twenty-eight single working poor mothers in New Jersey received computers, printers, Internet access, and courses for a year. The preliminary results of this program have been impressive. There was a very high retention rate in the program, with only eleven of the 128 participants not completing the program. In addition, the participants in the program experienced an average wage increase of 14 percent. This is especially significant as the typical cost of living wage increases for the state hover around 3 to 4 percent. It is also important to note that fifteen of the participants enrolled in other educational programs (such as community college and college program). Perhaps most importantly, all the women emphatically reported that they would not have been able to complete their training if it was not available in their homes.

There is much that is unique about this project—single mothers receiving computers from the State Department of Labor and Workforce Development; the high success rate of a public sector training initiative; and using the Internet to deliver training to a group that is often excluded from both Internet access and educational opportunities.[22] In addition to these factors, it is equally important to note that this project was unique because for the first time the NJDLWD developed and implemented a program that was crafted using an intersectional approach—specifically taking gender, class, and marital status into account.

In doing so this project brought the issues and challenges that working poor women face in their daily lives to the forefront of policy discussions. It vividly illustrated a point made by feminist scholars and activists for years—women face a distinct set of demands from men, due in large part to the unpaid labor they perform. Simply put, women bear the brunt of the domestic responsibilities of the home. As a result of this "second shift" (Hochschild, 1989, 2003) women, no matter what type of education they possess or work they perform, face barriers that are different than those of men, and are differentially impacted by state and federal policies.[23] Taking those differences into account at the outset of policy formation helped to better tailor policies to individual women's needs. As the program unfolded, the lives of working poor women, which often are ignored or marginalized at the policy table discussion, took center stage. The relevant question became how could we fit education and skills training into women's lives; *not* how could women fit into education and skills training programs.

Program Overview

The New Jersey program was administered through New Jersey's WIA mandated One-Stop Career Centers' using federal and state training dollars. To participate in the program one had to be a working single mother earning 250 percent or less of the poverty line. Each participant received a computer, Internet access, and courses for a year. The training was tied to high-wage, high-demand jobs in the local area, and the bulk of the women received IT based training, in addition to literary skills and soft skills.

The women in the New Jersey pilot program represented a diverse population of working poor single mothers. For the many of them this was the first time they accessed any public-sector supports. They arrived at this program from a variety of sources—flyers strategically placed throughout town, newspaper articles and advertisements, word of mouth from friends and employers, and referrals from individuals associated with the local employment and training system. As is evident from the following demographic composite they represent a growing slice of the American pie that is working, but "getting by on the minimum" (Johnson, 2001).

The average age of the women was thirty-two years old; with the youngest women aged twenty years old, and the oldest women aged fifty-four. These low-wage workers were thus not teenagers working for "spending" money, but adults working for life's necessities. The women also represented diversity in regard to race/ethnicity, which closely mirrors the distribution of the working poor. Fifty-six women were Black, twenty-four were Hispanic, forty-seven were White and one was Native American. In regard to educational attainment, the majority of women (sixty-eight of them) were high school graduates or earned a GED. Further eighteen women held associates degrees; twenty-four women attended college; six women had a college degree; fifteen women had some type of technical certification; and two women had graduate degrees from universities outside of the United States.[24] In fact only seven women did not graduate high school.

While all women in the pilot program had incomes of 250 percent or less of the poverty line, the average annual income of the women was $16,900. The income data clearly show that the women were for the most part working in minimum wage (or close to minimum wage) jobs. This is the point that cannot be understated. It does not matter that they were earning an income because it was not enough of an income for them to support themselves and their children. Once one takes into account the costs associated with their employment—childcare, transportation, healthcare—along with the daily costs of living (food, housing, etc.), they were as poor as the unemployed.

The income data is clearly related to the women's occupational distribution. As demonstrated the women are employed in a variety of industries and occupations, most of which characterize the low-wage labor market. Many women (fifty-eight of them) worked in administrative office positions such as secretaries, receptionists, and office assistants. Women in the sample were also employed in the growing service sector. Twenty-seven of the women worked in retail sales/restaurants/housecleaning; and fifteen women worked in childcare and daycare. Sixteen women in the program worked in the healthcare industry in such jobs as certified nursing assistants, dietary aides, and medical assistants. There were also three women who worked in factories, two women were employed as bus drivers, five women who were bank tellers, and one mail carrier. This occupational distribution closely mirrors IWPR's (2002) findings of low-income single mothers. As they note, 78 percent of single parent headed households in their study were employed in four typically low-wage occupations: service; administrative support and clerical; operators, fabricators, and laborers; and sales and related.

With the women's lives complicated by work and family demands, providing job training in ways that acknowledged those demands proved critical to the women's successful completion of educational programs. Certain barriers were eliminated by providing training in the home—chiefly transportation inequities. Women did not need access to a car or public transportation to "go" to a classroom. In addition, training in the home helps to democratize access to education and other training. Regardless of where a woman lives she can have access to the same classes and training as someone thousands of miles away. This is especially relevant in rural areas as there are fewer classes available in these areas. Online learning in the home also served to eliminate barriers women faced as they typically work in jobs with irregular schedules. Given that the learning was asynchronous, the women were able to take their classes around their work schedules.

Most significant were the childcare needs of the mothers. While online learning helps alleviate some of the pressures of combining childcare demands and education, it is not a substitution for childcare. Women still "squeeze in" their coursework when their children are sleeping, in school or out of the house. Clearly having the computer in the home makes it easier for women to find time for their education and training, but it does not entirely solve childcare needs. Further the childcare effects on online learning differ depending on the age of children. NJDLWD participants report that the greatest challenges in integrating home and education demands are for older children rather than infant children. Whereas mothers of infants and young toddlers typically report that they take their online classes when their children are asleep, mothers of older children tend to find time only when their children are out of the house and do not need their intense supervision. Some of the mothers of older children spent a great deal of time attending to the extracurricular activities of their children, thereby decreasing the available time to take courses. Further mothers of older children also had to set up boundaries with their children on sharing computer usage.[25]

An Important Note on Race

It is important to state that the intersectional approach that NJDLWD employed focused primarily on gender, class, and marital status. In taking this approach it was clear that while this was a gender-based intervention, women were not treated as an undifferentiated group. Instead the state acknowledged differences among women based on class, educational level, and marital status. However, race, in contrast, was treated more as a "given" in this project. Policy officials did acknowledge the economic inequities associated with race and ethnicity, but did not actively develop interventions to address racism and/or the intersections with racial identities. While the state did ensure a racially diverse group of women were represented in the pilot program, they did not specifically focus the program on how race intersects with and impacts women's poverty. Instead race was treated more generally as an economic disadvantage. So while race was not completely ignored, it was also not fully incorporated into the program. Indeed a full incorporation of understanding the racial impacts of poverty for women and how technology can address them should inform future projects. For example, it would be important to understand how online learning can help eliminate face-to-face racism in job training and educational programs. Such possibilities exist by taking into account the impacts of race and ethnicity on single mothers' poverty.

The Key to Workforce Policy:
Gender, Intersectionality, and Flexibility

The success of the program was due, in large part, because the program was crafted around the lives of the women, and in particular single working poor mothers. Central to this was that a concept of flexibility organized the conceptualization and implementation of this program. Indeed the technology—the Internet and personal computer—allowed policymakers to promote flexible training alternatives to single mothers so that they could gain education in ways that were congruent with their family and work needs. The vast majority of the women reported that the greatest advantage of the pilot program was the flexibility that online learning offers them. They were able to work on their courses around their and their children's schedules. Emphatically all women reported that they could not complete these courses if they were not online.[26] Yet while the concept seems simple enough: provide flexible alternatives to single working poor mothers as states deliver education and skills training, the practice of doing so is not quite so straightforward. Instead to be successful government officials must make a commitment to the full inclusion of an approach that takes into account gender, race, class, and marital status in policy formation and implementation.

What is important to note is that to do so NJDLWD official did not simply allocate training dollars to this training program and then give single mothers computers to use. Instead NJDLWD officials partnered with gender equity researchers at the Center for Women and Work (CWW) at Rutgers University to determine ways to best implement the program and to conduct a formative evaluation of it that would allow officials to quickly respond to any problems that arose. As such, in formulating this program it was designed to eliminate or significantly minimize key obstacles that single mothers faced in traditional educational settings. In conjunction with researchers at CWW, NJDLWD officials spent time identifying the barriers that single mothers face. As noted earlier, childcare, transportation, irregular work schedules, and simply not having classes locally available makes it hard for women to continue their education. In addition, NJDLWD officials asked CWW to identify barriers women face in online learning programs to ensure that the state project has strategies to address them. These barriers include isolation, lack of facility with computers and the Internet, technological problems, and simply finding the time in one's day to take classes.

Working in collaboration gender policy researchers and state policy officials designed mechanisms within the program to help alleviate problems. Most notably, the state set up monthly in-person support groups at the local One-Stop Center for the women to connect in person with other participants and instructors. These support groups were held outside of normal business hours—at nights and on weekends—around the women's schedules. Perhaps even more importantly is that the state provided on-site childcare at these groups. In addition to the support groups the state program also helped to bridge the knowledge gap between the help desk and participants by centralizing technological help at the One-Stop Centers with staff accustomed to working with this population. Finally job coaches at the One-Stop Centers worked with the women to help them find the time in their day to complete the work. Being able to have an active role in the policy and program allowed gender equity experts informed policy decisions around the project to better serve single mothers' educational and job training needs.

In doing so the partnership helped policy officials to acknowledge that the workforce system has faced significant difficulties in delivering training to single working-poor mothers, and in particular single working-poor mothers of color. In turn, this has lead to large numbers of women stuck in low-wage jobs without the education to advance. Poverty is not gender or race neutral nor is the way that workforce development and welfare policy is implemented. As such, a perspective that acknowledges the barriers that single mothers face is necessary to help them achieve economic self-sufficiency. Moreover NJDLWD had acknowledged that employment is not enough to raise women out of poverty. Instead education and training needs to be a lifelong process and the public sector must provide the venues to achieve this. With the lifetime limits on TANF it is even more urgent that single working poor mothers do not get stuck in entry-level low-wage jobs. Research has found that ways out of low-wage work necessitate that women have education and skills to advance to high-wage jobs. As such, state and federal policymakers must craft ways to provide access to education and training. Yet they cannot be expected to do it alone. Instead gender and diversity experts must be integrated into policy formation, implementation, and evaluation. Central to this approach is that gender and diversity experts can help to ensure that programs and policy must be flexible to women's needs as workers and caregivers. That is, one of the greatest accomplishments of the partnership between NJDLWD and CWW was that policy officials not only were aware of the dual roles of women in the public and private spheres, but they were willing to develop programs that were attendant to women's needs. In doing so, partnerships between policymakers and equity experts play a key role in advancing policy that acknowledges the facets of women's lives and the interlocking systems of inequality that prevent them from achieving economic self-sufficiency.

NOTES

1. The Consortium on Race, Gender, and Ethnicity provided support for this chapter at the University of Maryland.

2. Specifically the numbers of single mothers entering paid work rose by 25 percent between 1993 and 1999. Within this group there was a 50 percent increase in the employment of never married single mothers (Jones-DeWeever, Petersen, & Song, 2003, 3).

3. For a sociohistorical review of the impacts of race, class, and gender on these policies, see chapter 3 in Gatta & McCabe, 2005.

4. WIA is currently under congressional reauthorization. This discussion of WIA in this chapter will be focused on the pre-reauthorized law.

5. Although the focus of this chapter is on single working poor mothers, they are not the only group whose educational needs are not fully met by WIA.

6. One-Stop Career Centers are mandated by the Federal Workforce Investment Act to be a local office where individuals can receive information and resources on employment and training opportunities, along with federal and state benefit information.

7. At its most general sense the workforce investment system "refers to a broad range of employment and training services whose purpose is to enable job seekers, students and employers to access a wide range of information about jobs, the labor market, careers, education and training organizations, financing options, skill standards or certification requirements" (Martinson, 1999, 1).

8. Under TANF states may not provide assistance to a family that includes an adult who has received federally funded TANF for five years.

9. States must require recipients to participate in work activities after they receive no more than two years of TANF funding. All recipients must participate in work activities except those with a child under twelve months old, if the state chooses to exempt them.

10. See Bureau of Labor Statistics, 2004, *Women in the Labor force: A Databook.*

11. US DOL, 2002, Report 957.

12. It is important to note that FMLA guarantees up to twelve weeks of job protected, unpaid leave only for public-sector employees as well as private-sector workers who work for organizations with fifty or more employees. This translates into covering less than half of all workers and less then one-fifth of new mothers (Milkman & Appelbaum, 2004, 4).

13. For a full discussion of the effects of higher education on welfare recipients, along with model state legislation see Charles Price and Tracy Steffy, with Tracy McFarlane 2003.

14. The National Center for Education Statistics (2000) provided further evidence for the "education premium" as women with a college education continued to outpace their high school counterparts.

15. Because the program is funded by state dollars, the time spent in the program does not count against the recipients Federal five-year lifetime limit on receiving support that was instituted under 1996 welfare reform.

16. The titles include: Title I-Workforce Investment Systems; Title II-Adult Education and Family Literacy; Title III-Workforce Investment Related Activities; Title IV-Vocational Rehabilitation; Title V-General Provisions. In this chapter, I will focus my discussion on WIA Title I.

17. The law is available at http://www.doleta.gov.

18. "Hard to serve" refers to individuals who possess at least one barrier to employment, such as physical, mental health, or substance abuse problems; domestic violence, language barriers, and/or lack of education, work experience, or skills.

19. Many reasons account for this including: a "workfirst" approach to WIA implementation, restrictive eligibility requirements for use of ITAs, and too little funding appropriated to infrastructure support.

20. The self-sufficiency standard (conservatively) calculates the minimum cost of living and takes into account costs relating to basic housing, childcare, food, transportation, healthcare, and taxes. In addition, the standard also takes into account any benefits accrued via the Earned Income Tax Credit, the Childcare Tax Credit, and the Child Tax Credit (Pierce & Brooks, 2002).

21. Nontraditional occupations refer to occupations that are less than 25 percent female.

22. For a full discussion of this project and its impact on workforce development policy see Gatta and McCabe (2005).

23. Hochschild's (1989) "second shift" refers to the notions that employed women work two shifts—one in the paid labor force and a second shift in the unpaid labor force of the home.

24. The two women who possessed graduate education both held law degrees from other countries. When they came to the United States they found themselves divorced and unable to practice law.

25. The New Jersey Department of Labor and Workforce Development did include children's software on the computers to encourage the participation of the family.

26. For a full discussion of the results see Gatta and McCabe 2005.

References

Abramovitz, M. (2001). Race, Class, and Welfare Reform. Presentation at National Association of Social Workers Welfare Reform Task Force.

Albeda, R., & Tilly, C. (1997). *Glass Ceilings and Bottomless Pits: Women's Work, Women's Poverty*. Boston, MA: South End Press.

Bartik, T. (2001). *Jobs for the Poor: Can Labor Demand Policies Help?* New York: Russell Sage Foundation.

Boushey, H., Brocht, C., Gundersen, B., & Bernstein, J. (2001). *Hardships in America: The Real Story of Working Families*. Washington, DC: Economic Polity Institute.

Browne, I., & Misra, J. (2003). The Intersection of Gender and Race in the Labor Market. *Annual Review of Sociology, 29*, 487–513.

Butler, S., Deprez, L., & Smith, R. (2002). Parents as Scholars: A Model Post—Secondary Educational Program for Low-Income Women in the New Welfare Landscape. *Presentation at the IWPR 7th International Women's Policy Research Conference.*

Cancian, M., & Meyer, D. (2000, June). Work after Welfare: Women's Work Effort, Occupation, and Economic Well-Being. *Social Work Research, 24*(2), 69–86.

Carnevale, A., & Desrochers, D. (1999). *Getting Down to Business: Matching Welfare Recipients Skills to Jobs That Train*. Princeton, NJ: *Educational Testing Service.*

Chicago Jobs Council. (2003). Improving our Response to Work Needs: Recommendations for Reauthorization of the Workforce Investment Act of 1998. Chicago:
Chicago Jobs Council.

Collins, P. H. (1999). *Black Feminist Thought: Knowledge, Consciousness and the Politics of
Empowerment 2nd Edition.* London: Harper Collins.

Dill, B. T., Jones-DeWeever, A., & Schram, S. (2004). *Racial, Ethnic and Gender Disparities
in Access to Jobs, Education and Training under Welfare Reform.* College Park, MD: Consortium on Race, Gender and Ethnicity.

Edin, K., & Lein, L. (1997). *Making Ends Meet: How Single Mothers Survive Welfare and Low-
Wage Work.* New York: Russell Sage Foundation.

Gatta, M., & McCabe, K. P. (2005). *Not Just Getting By: The New Era of Flexible Workforce
Development.* Lanham, MA: Lexington Books.

Gault, B. (2002). Utilizing the Workforce Investment Act Programs and TANF to Provide
Education and Training Opportunities to Reduce Poverty among Low-Income
Women. *Testimony before the United States House Education and Workforce Committee.*

Gooden, S. (1999). The Hidden Third Party: Welfare Recipients' Experiences with
Employers. *Virginia Tech. Journal of Public Management and Social Policy, 5*(1).

Folbe, N. (2001). *The Invisible Heart: Economics and Family Values.* New York: The New
Press.

Hochschild, A. R. (1989). *The Second Shift: Working Parents and the Revolution at Home.* New
York: Viking Penguin.

Hochschild, A. R. (2003). *The Second Shift.* New York: Penguin Books.

Institute for Women's Policy Research. (2001). *Working First, but Working Poor: The Need
for Education and Skills Training Following Welfare.* Washington, DC: IWPR.

Institute for Women's Policy Research. (2002). Life After Welfare Reform: Low-Income
Single Parent Families, Pre- and Post-TANF. *Research-in-Brief.* Washington DC: IWPR.

Johnson, J. (2002). *Getting by on the Minimum: The Lives of Working-Class Women.* New
York: Routledge Press.

Jones-DeWeever, A., Petersen, J., & Song, X. (2003). *Before and After Welfare Reform: The Life
and Well-Being of Low-Income Single Parent Families.* Washington, DC: IWPR.

Karier, T. (1998). *Welfare Graduates: College and Financial Independence.* New York: The
Levy Economics Institute.

Levenson, A., Reardon, E., & Schmidt, S. (1999). Welfare, Jobs and Basic Skills: The
Employment Prospects of Welfare Recipients in the Most Populous U.S. Counties.
NCSALL Reports #10B. National Center for the Study of Adult Learning and Literacy,
Boston, MA.

Levitan, M., & Gluck, R. (2002). *Mother's Work: Single Mothers Employment, Earnings, and
Poverty in the Age of Welfare Reform.* New York: Community Service Society.

Lynch, L., & Black, S. (1995). Beyond the Incidence of Training: Evidence from the National
Employer Survey. *Working Paper No. 5231, National Bureau of Economic Research.*

Maine Equal Justice Partners. (2001). Parents as Scholars Program. Augusta, ME.

Martinson, Karin. (1999). Literature Review on Service Coordination and Integration in
the Welfare and Workforce Development Systems. *Publication of the Urban Institute.*
Washington, DC: Urban Institute Press.

Mathur, A., Reichle, J., Strawn, J., & Wiseley, C. (2004). *From Jobs to Careers: How California's
Community College Credentials Pay Off for Welfare Participants.* Washington, DC:
CLASP.

Mathur, A., Reichle, J., Wiseley, C., & Strawn, J. (2002). *Credentials Count: How California's
Community Colleges Help Parents Move from Welfare to Self—Sufficiency.* Washington,
DC: CLASP.

Michigan League of Human Services. (2003). *Education and Training for Low-Income Workers: Critical Issues for Workforce Investment Act and Perkins Reauthorization.* Lansing, MI: MLHS.

Miller, J., Molina, F., Grossman, L., & Golonka, S. (2004). *Building Bridges to Self Sufficiency: Improving Services for Low-Income Working Families.* New York: MDRC.

Milkman, R., & Appelbaum, E. (2004). Paid Family Leave in California: New Research Findings. *Forthcoming in The State of California Labor.* Berkley: University of California Press.

National Governor's Association. (2004*). A Governor's Guide to Creating a 21st Century Workforce.* Washington, DC: National Governor's Association.

National Urban League, Institute for Opportunity and Equality. (2002). *Differences in TANF Support Services Utilization: Is There Adequate Monitoring to Ensure Program Quality.* New York: National Urban League.

O'Neill, J., & Hill, M. A. (2002). *Gaining Ground: Women, Welfare Reform and Work.* Dallas: NCPA Policy Report.

Peterson, J., Song, X., & Jones-DeWeever, A. (2002). *Life After Welfare Reform: The Characteristics, Work, and Well Being of Low-Income Single Parent Families, Pre- and Post-PRWORA.* IWPR: Washington, DC.

Pierce, D., & Brooks, J. (2002). *The Real Cost of Living: The Self-Sufficiency Standard for New Jersey.* Edison, NJ: Legal Services of New Jersey Poverty Research Institute.

Price, C., Steff, Y., & McFarlene, T. (2003). *Continuing a Commitment to the Higher Education Option: Model State Legislation, College Programs, and Advocacy Organizations that Support Access to Post-Secondary Education for Public Assistance Recipients.* New York: Howard Samuels State Management and Policy Center.

Reskin, B., & Padavic. I. (2002). *Women and Men at Work,* 2nd Edition. Thousand Oaks, CA: Pine Forge Press.

Stafford, W., Salas, D., & Mendez, M. (2003). Gender, Race, Class, and Welfare Reform. In *State of Black America.* New York: National Urban League.

United States Department of Labor, Bureau of Labor Statistics. (2004). *A Profile of the Working Poor.* Washington, DC.

United States Department of Labor, Bureau of Labor Statistics. (2004). *Women in the Labor Force: A Databook.* Washington, DC.

Van Horn, C., & Schaffner, H. (2003). *Winning the Workforce Challenge: A Report on New Jersey's Knowledge Economy.* New Brunswick, NJ: John J. Heldrich Center for Workforce Development.

Wider Opportunities for Women. (2003). *WIA Reauthorization: What Local Workforce Boards Say About Services For Women.* A report of Wider Opportunities for Women and the National Association of Workforce Investment Boards.

Working for America Institute. (2003). Raising the Bar: A Report on Policies and Practices Related to Self-Sufficiency Standards in the Nation's Public Workforce Development System. *AFL-CIO Working for America Institute: Washington DC.*

6

Exploring the Intersections of Race, Ethnicity, and Class on Maternity Leave Decisions

Implications for Public Policy

TIFFANY MANUEL AND RUTH ENID ZAMBRANA

Policymakers in the United States have struggled for decades to devise policies that encourage the labor force attachment of low-income mothers, particularly those receiving public assistance. These efforts culminated in the 1996 passage of the Personal Responsibility and Work Opportunity Reconciliation Act (PRWORA), which imposed substantial work requirements on mothers receiving aid, time limits on the receipt of cash assistance, and other heightened program eligibility requirements (i.e., providing proof of children's immunization, etc.). The PRWORA (also referred to as "welfare reform") was buttressed by the enactment of other federal policies such as the 1993 Family and Medical Leave Act (FMLA), which now provides a critical work support for working mothers and other working caregivers during periods when their families experience heightened care needs.

For low-income mothers who participate in the labor force, work supports play a critical role in enabling the continuous employment now required by government agencies. In response, many states have made investments in a variety of work supports such as childcare subsidies and transportation assistance.[1] These investments have led both to better labor market outcomes for low-income mothers struggling to "transition" from welfare-to-work as well as to a reduction in the labor market disparities between low-income mothers and mothers in other socioeconomic groups (Relave, 2005; Gennetian & Smith, 2005; Boushey, 2005; Paulsell, 2005; Fishman, 2004; McNichol & Springer, 2004; Lee, 2004). While these supports have been helpful, critics note that the work supports offered: (1) have not been universally provided to low-income mothers mostly because of wide variations across states in terms of program eligibility, services, and the costs of providing such support; (2) are often provided in ways that are not readily useful to these mothers (for example, finding childcare facilities that accept childcare vouchers provided by state agencies is difficult); and (3) address only a small portion of the enormous challenges low-income mothers face in juggling the often rigid demands of low-wage jobs alongside the complex care needs of their families—all on poverty wages (Jones-DeWeever, Dill, & Schram, chapter 7; Dodson, Bravo, & Manuel, 2002).

One of the unique contributions of this chapter is the use of an analytic strategy that captures maternity leave decisions as the product of the intersection of many different individual, family, employment, and policy variables by race, ethnicity, and class. The intersectional approach specifically addresses the limitations of the single-explanation approaches that have failed to capture the complexity of disparities across similarly situated groups. While scholarly efforts have partitioned off individual, family, and organizational level factors into fairly discrete explanations of the variation across mothers, in practice it is much more difficult to tease these explanations apart. Illustrative of this complexity is one woman's own discussion about how she managed the birth of her child:

> They say you can take as much time off as you want; I mean six months, you know. I couldn't afford to take that much time. I would have loved to, but you know, I got to work. So, I took a month off with pay. [My husband] took off the next month, and my mother-in-law took a month off from her work, and my mother had him for two weeks. Then after that I finally got him into the day care across the street.
>
> Fried, 1998, 132

In this example, it would be disingenuous to say that the length of childbirth leave taken by this mother was solely due to individual, family, or organizational levels factors—in fact, factors at all levels played some role in the family-care decisions that were made. The fact that low-income mothers have access to fewer financial resources to resolve work and family conflicts around childbirth means that most use an even wider array of survival strategies that defy easy categorization.

The importance of investing in a wider range of work supports that explicitly address the multiple conflicts mothers confront in managing the demands of work and family serves as the catalyst for this research.[2] The lack of work supports that address conflicts that emerge during intense family-care periods (such as the birth of a child) is directly related to an increased likelihood of being poor and of needing public assistance. For example, "one quarter of all poverty spells in the United States begin with the birth of a new child" because low-income parents simply cannot forego their wages while on leave, at the very same time that they are "buying all the gear that babies need, plus food, diapers, and so on" (Waldfogel, 2001, 100). Manuel (2004) found that one such type of work support—family leave benefits (or job protection during a short-term absence from a job especially following a mother's first birth)—positively affected the long-term wage-stream of mothers and dramatically decreased the likelihood of long-term poverty in the years immediately following the birth.

Although the existing scholarship on this issue documents the relationship between poverty and the lack of access to work supports, little research has been conducted on the variations in access to these kinds of work supports and the factors that determine whether (and to what extent) mothers actually utilize them when they are made available. Moreover it is unclear from existing scholarship what the relative importance of individual, family, employment, and governmental policy factors are, in terms of shaping how families respond to work and family conflicts and how those factors (both separately and in tandem) shape employment outcomes. Analyzing National Longitudinal Survey of Youth (NLSY) data with an intersectional framework, this paper examines how race, ethnicity, and class affect the amount of time new mothers take away from their jobs following childbirth and analyzes how factors at the individual, family, employment, and government policy levels affect these decisions.

Background and Maternity Leave Policy Context

A little more than a century ago, only a handful of industrializing nation-states were crafting policies that gave working mothers the right and the financial means to take time away from paid work to care for their children. Today, just beyond the threshold of the twenty-first century, all industrialized nations provide some form of maternity leave; almost all do so at fairly high levels of wage replacement; and most have provisions for paternity leave as well. In this context, the United States is an outlier among other industrialized nations in that it offers families very little in the way of job protection and direct financial support to working caregivers while they are needed to provide direct care for their families. Rather, U.S. policymakers have created institutional arrangements for family leave that are primarily privately financed (mostly through employer fringe benefit programs and employee earnings), cover a small percentage of firms, and disproportionately benefit workers in the shrinking primary labor market rather than universally cover American families (Garrett, Wenk, & Lubeck, 1990). Moreover these programs operate with virtually no coordination across federal, state, and local levels nor do they provide a coherent set of policies to help families address work and family conflicts (Vogel, 1993).

Most family leave policies in the United States were passed in the last three decades, raising the question: why is the United States only now experiencing a "big boom" with regard to the creation of such policies? The primary catalyst for the dramatic turnaround seems to be the significant shift in the gender composition of the U.S. workforce. Women in prime working years moved from just under 40 percent employment in 1950, to nearly 80 percent by the turn of the last century. For the first time in the nation's history, women represent nearly half of the U.S. workforce and women's employment trajectories now closely follow that of men in the same age categories. Interestingly enough, the widest variation in labor force participation today is not between men and women (or the gender disparity) but rather between workers with and without substantial care responsibilities for young children. This is an important trend as 72 percent of all mothers are employed in the United States and 90 percent of all American parents with children under the age of eighteen (more than sixty-nine million Americans) are employed (Fredriksen-Goldsen & Scharlach, 2001).

Recent legislative attempts to extend work supports to working caregivers, in conjunction with the emergence of family-leave policies represent the opening of an important policy window. Generally family-leave policies guarantee the ability of workers to return to their jobs following short-term absences related to their family care-giving responsibilities. The term "maternity leave" (used interchangeably with family leave in this chapter), is one form of family-leave policy and can be defined simply as a family leave taken by a mother to care for her newborn. Some leave policies provide wage replacement while leave-takers are away from their jobs and others simply include job protection provisions. These policies have been passed at all levels of government (particularly at the state level), as well as by private employers, although there is great diversity across the workforce in terms of eligibility, access, and usage of such benefits.

Maternity leave policies are more established forms of family leave policies and have been offered in the United States for about three decades (Hattiangadi, 2000). Just before the passage of the FMLA, an estimated 40 to 60 percent of women workers were covered by maternity leave policies—mostly as a consequence of the federal Pregnancy Disability Act, state maternity leave laws, union contracts, and employer efforts (Waldfogel, 1997; Waldfogel, Higuchi, & Abe, 1999). Most employers did not, however, continue health insurance coverage for women on maternity leave—an oversight later addressed by the FMLA (Gruber, 1994; Trzcinski & Alpert, 2000).[3]

The specific policy origins of maternity leave policies in the workplace were largely the result of the Equal Pay Act of 1963 and the Civil Rights Act of 1964 (predecessors to the FMLA and the Pregnancy Disability Act). These civil rights laws outlawed discrimination with respect to "compensation, terms, condition, or privileges of employment" (Title VII of the Civil Rights Act). Although neither piece of legislation specifically mentioned pregnancy, these laws opened the door for later court battles that challenged a multitude of sex discriminating employment practices. After several court battles and pressure from coalition groups, the Pregnancy Discrimination Act (PDA) was passed in 1978 as an amendment to the Civil Rights Act of 1964. Essentially the PDA made it unlawful for employers to terminate women because they were pregnant or to otherwise force them out of their jobs and mandated that, when a woman was "disabled" because of a pregnancy, she receive the same sick pay, insurance coverage, and job protection as an employer's other employees with short-term disabilities.

This early legislation paved the way for more aggressive leave policies later—first at the state and local levels and eventually in 1993, the Family and Medical Leave Act passed becoming the most sweeping federal family leave law in the United States (albeit more than one hundred years after the first maternity leave law was enacted in Europe).[4] The FMLA covers about half of the U.S. workforce (about 6 percent of the nation's firms) and requires that employers with fifty or more employees allow eligible employees up to twelve weeks of unpaid, job protected leave to care for newborn or newly adopted children, for seriously ill spouses, children, parents, or to take care of their own illnesses, including pregnancy.[5] Although the FMLA was the first piece of federal legislation to specifically address working caregivers, other federal policies, such as public assistance programs, help some mothers defray the cost of taking family leave.

In addition to the federal FMLA policy, there are other sources of family leave assistance in the United States. Although only half of the nation's workers are covered by the FMLA, more workers are covered by state and employer leave policies. Most states have maternity leave policies that actually predate the FMLA and thirty-five states have legislation that is more generous than the federal family-leave provisions. Additionally five states and Puerto Rico have Temporary Disability Insurance programs (TDI) that provide financial assistance to mothers on disability due to pregnancy related illnesses. Finally employers also provide maternity leave benefits and many allow their employees to use sick and vacation time to replace lost wages during the leave.

Although maternity leave policies predate the FMLA, most analysts agree that the FMLA has been an important catalyst for increasing maternity leave coverage and dramatically changing maternal employment behavior around childbirth. For example, the majority of American women no longer routinely quit their jobs when they become pregnant. Between 1961 and 1965, more than 60 percent of all new mothers quit their jobs when they became pregnant with their first child, whereas during 1991–1995, less than 30 percent of new mothers did.[6] Generally women with family leave benefits are more likely to return to jobs and to return faster than those without such benefits (Baum, 2003; Hofferth, 1996). Taken together, these trends have contributed to the formulation of a wide variety of work and family policies implemented by government agencies and private employers.

Theoretical Background

Three major theoretical explanations have been advanced to explain variations in the length of time mothers take away from work following childbirth and other periods of intense family care. The first explanation operates at the individual level and argues that variations are due to the characteristics of the mothers themselves (i.e., their attitudes, motivation to work, and forms of human capital). A second set of explanations operate at the family level. Family-level explanations propose that the size and structure of the family, household financial resources, and/or cultural dynamics are particularly important in explaining variations because families have different social, cultural, and economic resources at their disposal. For example, Black women are much more likely than White or Asian women to have a first birth before marriage, which may reduce the extent to which they are able to depend on children's fathers for care giving and financial support (Burr & Bean, 1996). They may, however, depend on larger extended family networks (McAdoo, 1997; Taylor, Jackson, & Chatters, 1997). Additionally there is considerable variation in fertility rates across racial and ethnic groups. Racial and ethnic differences in the number of children women have and how those births are sequenced with education and early work experiences is likely related to variations in how mothers assess their employment choices after giving birth.

Explaining why some mothers choose to return to work earlier than their counterparts is directly associated with their ability to depend on financial resources that operate partly at the family level but also at the organizational level. Differences in wage rates (partly a function of the firms where women work and the jobs that mothers are able to obtain given their human capital skills) account for variations by race and ethnicity. Access to economic assets or higher wage rates enable some women to transition back into the labor market faster after a first birth by buying the labor of third parties (such as nannies, childcare supports, etc.). White women generally have higher wage rates compared to other minority women and are more likely to have spouses who earn higher wages as well (U.S. Census Bureau, 2004).

Other institutional explanations that account for variations in the length of time mothers take following childbirth are related to both employment and government policy factors. In particular, employer family-leave benefits, other fringe benefits and overall work supports vary sharply across jobs and firms. In terms of employment, some jobs may have greater flexibility in terms of work hours while others may restrict mothers to more rigid schedules (perhaps requiring work on weekends or during evening hours). Like factors at the individual and family levels, governmental policies at the state and federal levels have also been found to affect leave length differences (Waldfogel, 1999). For example, the availability of childcare vouchers or direct cash assistance from government agencies can structure additional opportunities for some mothers to take a leave. As a result, organizational variables are important considerations as well.

We argue that the interrelationships among these factors support the use of an intersectional framework because such an approach addresses the complexity of mothers' experiences around childbirth, revealing new insights and knowledge about the choices and constraints they face. More explicitly, the intersectional lens acknowledges that what "many women experience is often shaped by other dimensions of their identities, such as race and class" (Williams Crenshaw, 1995, 357). George (2001) defines intersectionality and its analytical contribution in this way, "intersectionality goes beyond just looking at the gender aspects of racial discrimination. It seeks to provide a tool for analyzing the ways in which gender, race, class, and all other forms of identity and distinction, in different contexts, produce situations in which men and women become vulnerable to abuse and discrimination" (2). Increasingly, however, intersectional scholarship emphasizes both the benefits of personal characteristics in shaping life experiences as well as the more traditional focus on the challenges (like the increased likelihood of facing discrimination) associated with those characteristics.

Intersectionality theory argues that the socially constructed ways of identifying and categorizing individuals that arise in societies are transformed by and transform history themselves, and that those categories must be studied as interconnected rather than as separate systems (Amott & Matthaei, 1991). In recent years, there has been a growing interest in the notion of intersectionality for many reasons; not the least of which has been scholarly attempts to better conceptualize policy outcomes. There are enormous possibilities for how an intersectional research approach might offer important policy directions that have been largely ignored. While the explicit theory of intersectionality and how it might be used across all policy areas remains underdeveloped, many scholars are employing the basic notion of intersectionality as an organizing framework in their applied policy and academic research. For example, Hum and Simpson (2003), Williams Crenshaw (1989), Browne and Misra (2003), among others, examine intersectionality from the standpoint of labor market inequalities. Wilson (2000) examines intersectionality as it relates to government support for programs and services.[7] In this chapter, the intersectional framework illuminates the mismatch between patchwork policies and the realities of poor women's lives.

Family Leave and Low-Income Mothers

Policymakers have recently given much attention to the role of leave policies in shaping the employment decisions of low-income workers. For example, the U.S. Congress and most state legislatures have introduced family leave legislation that would substantially expand access to low-income families either by covering more firms or replacing worker's wages while they are on leave. While several states have passed legislation covering more firms (and thus more low-income workers), so far only California has passed a measure to replace the lost wages of leave-takers (a provision that is expected to help thousands of low-income mothers during times when their families need them most).

Three particular trends in access to family leave benefits have emerged as important catalysts in the legislative debate of leave policies as a work support for low-income mothers. First, low-income mothers are substantially less likely to have access to work supports and particularly lack those that address work and family conflicts. One reason is that the eligibility requirements associated with leave policies and other work supports target full-time workers in the primary labor market excluding low-income mothers who are more likely to be part-time, seasonal, or intermittent workers. Furthermore low-income mothers are more likely to work in jobs like those in the retail industry that do not typically offer fringe benefits or job-protected time off (such as sick or vacation leave). For example, Heyman (2000) found that 76 percent of working poor adults lacked paid sick leave; 63 percent lacked access to paid vacation leave at some point between 1990 and 1996; 45 percent of working poor adults never had sick leave; and 28 percent never had access to vacation leave over that period. In 2000, only 26 percent of low-wage workers received pay during leave compared to 80 percent of high-income employees (Cantor, et al., 2001). Fringe benefits (which often include additional forms of paid time off) are generally less available to women, minority, and less senior workers (Grosswald & Scharlach, 1999). As such, a study conducted by the Families and Work Institute found that workers with longer job tenure and higher incomes were generally offered more flexibility and fringe benefits by their employers. In particular, "the greater labor force experience and job security enjoyed by older women translates into better benefits when interrupting their job to have a baby" (Smith, Downs, & O'Connell, 2001, 12). Those additional benefits during critical family-care periods are likely to translate into better economic outcomes and also exacerbate the existing economic inequality across racial and ethnic groups.

Second, low-income mothers are more likely to be the sole financial support of their families and without some form of wage-replacement are unable to fully take advantage of leave benefits when they are offered. The case of low-income mothers with access to paid leave (likely obtained because of sick or vacation leave) is not much better; most do not have enough accrued time off to cover an entire maternity leave and as a result, they go without any income from their jobs for some portion of their leave.[8] Moreover the use of paid time off for sick and vacation days is still at the discretion of supervisors and is mediated by informal institutional practices that make it difficult for many workers (especially low-wage workers, men, and upper-level managers) to take advantage of it when they need to do so (Fried, 1998).

In response, low-income mothers have devised a mix of strategies to ease the financial burdens of caring for their children.[9] If they have sick and vacation benefits, the vast majority simply try to save up as much sick and vacation time as they can, work as far into their pregnancies as possible and use whatever paid time off they have. Thereafter they exercise one of three options: (1) use up whatever financial savings/resources they have at their disposal to stay home; (2) return immediately to work because they cannot afford to stay home without pay; or (3) turn to their social networks (such as family, friends) and/or public assistance programs to help defray the costs of leave-taking.

Overall financial considerations weigh heavily on the ability of all workers to take family leave when they need to do so for their families. A significant proportion of leave-takers shorten the duration of their leaves specifically because they cannot afford to lose wages or they simply do not take a leave at all and struggle to handle the care needs of their families from work (Cantor, et al., 2001; Commission on Family and Medical Leave, 1996).[10] About 29 percent of family leave-takers borrow substantial amounts of money during family leave; 39 percent put off paying their bills; 35.6 percent use savings earmarked for other things; and 70.1 percent dramatically limit family spending. Others (approximately 300,000 working families) file bankruptcy each year because they have no access to wage-replacement during a short-term medically necessitated leave from their jobs (Warren & Warren Tyagi, 2003). Manuel (2004) found that having access to job protection under federal leave laws or employer sponsored leave benefit programs helped both to shield mothers against long-term earnings losses in years after the birth as well as avoid poverty. Still other leave-takers turn quickly to their social networks (including community-based resources such as churches, food pantries, etc.) and about 10 percent resort to public assistance programs for some form of financial support while on leave.

The turn to public assistance by low-income mothers is related to a third trend: the shift in the racial/ethnic composition of public assistance recipients. Beginning in the late 1960s, the racial and ethnic composition of public assistance programs began to change such that by the early 1990s, minority women were overrepresented among recipients. As this shift occurred, welfare became socially constructed in the public consciousness as a "Black program" (Neuback & Cazenave, 2001). It was the political currency of the association between race (actually, with being Black) and welfare that helped enact the PRWORA.

> The ease with which political elites abolished the Aid to Families with Dependent Children Program—the primary safety net protecting poverty-stricken mothers and children—would have been impossible had not many politicians along with policy analysts and the mass media, spent decades framing and morphing welfare into a supposed Black problem. Political elites relied upon often subtle racist stereotypes about welfare and its recipients to escalate antipathy toward public assistance.
>
> Neuback & Cazenave, 2001, vii

As a result, employment behavior—seeking, getting, and keeping jobs—became the goal of social welfare policymaking operationalized in the case of the PRWORA as promoting "self-sufficiency" by encouraging the "transition" to work, limiting reproduction among low-income mothers, and, consequently, reducing public financial support.

Although very little data on the racial dynamics of welfare programs in the Untied States following the passage of the PRWORA exist, initial data on welfare reform has not been particularly encouraging for African American and Latino women as they have had much more difficulty finding employment and leaving the rolls compared to White women. "As the welfare rolls continue to plunge, White recipients are leaving the system much faster than Black and Hispanic recipients, pushing the minority share of the caseload to the highest level on record" (DeParle, 1998, A1). Racial imbalances in welfare rolls characterize at least half of the states[11] and welfare rolls continue to "darken," leaving the stereotypical images of women of color and of welfare programs largely intact.[12]

Existing literature clearly links the period around childbirth with increased economic vulnerability, likelihood of being in poverty, and public assistance use. This chapter extends existing scholarship by focusing on women's first birth and the variations in the length of their maternity leaves for three primary reasons: (1) in the United States, the birth and care of a new child is the second most reported reason workers take a family leave (second only to a personal medical emergency); (2) maternity leave following a first birth has been empirically shown to be shaped by a wider variety of factors than subsequent leaves or births; and (3) there is a substantial literature on maternal employment around a first birth that can serve as a benchmark or comparison for these analyses.

Sample and Estimation Methods

Data are derived from a subset of the National Longitudinal Surveys of Youth (NLSY). These surveys were initiated in the mid-1960s under the sponsorship of the Employment and Training Administration and, since 1986, have been administered by Bureau of Labor Statistics (BLS), an agency of the U.S. Department of Labor with assistance from the Center for Human Resource Research at Ohio State University. The NLSY was originally intended to chronicle the long-term labor market and life changes of a nationally representative set of Americans and, as such, it provides the opportunity to examine the longitudinal experiences of a wide range of U.S. workers. The NLSY includes a nationally representative sample of 12,686 young men and women between the ages of 14 to 21 when they were first surveyed in 1979. Subjects were interviewed annually until 1994 after which they were interviewed every other year. Respondent attrition rates have been fairly low with about 90 percent of the original 1979 panel continuing to participate in the survey (Center for Human Resource Research, 2000).

The sampling criteria included all women who met the following conditions: (1) had a first birth between 1987 and 2000 (years in the survey when questions about the availability of wage-replaced or paid maternity leave were asked);[13] (2) were not in the military; and (3) reported earnings the year before the first birth. These selection criteria are employed to ensure that we are in the best possible position to understand the work and family options available to mothers (i.e., the availability of specific types of leave options); and that the sample consists of women who are working at the time of pregnancy and have some attachment to the labor force. Women in the military are excluded because the military makes special arrangements around pregnancy that are likely to be very different from the choices available to other women in the sample.

The sample size consists of 907 women. About 80 percent of the women in the sample had their first child before thirty years of age. Most were married (74 percent), although 10 percent had never been married and 16 percent were either separated or divorced at the time of their first birth. About 74 percent had at least a high school education and about half of the women with at least a high school diploma had some education beyond high school. Work-related characteristics show that half of the women had been with their employers for three or more years at the time of their first birth; half worked for firms with less than fifty employees; and a majority (72 percent) worked for private-sector employers. Most women had access to vacation (83 percent), sick (91 percent), and maternity leave (87 percent) but only about half of the respondents had access to flexible hour benefits (52 percent).

Race, ethnicity, class, and length of leave are all key variables of interest in the study. Women in the sample are divided into four racial and ethnic categories: Non-Hispanic Whites (NHW) (36 percent), non-Hispanic Blacks (NHB) (15 percent), Hispanics (37 percent), and Asian, Native American, and others (37 percent).[14] Similarly socioeconomic status was coded into five categories that correspond to the federal poverty line in the year in which the woman had her first child: "Poor or Near Poor" (7 percent); "Working-Class" (16 percent), "Low-to-Moderate Middle Class" (27 percent); "High-Middle Class" (18 percent); and "High Income" (30 percent).[15] Finally women who were able to take a paid leave from work took about eighty-one days of leave while unpaid leavers took about one hundred days of leave.

An estimation technique that recognizes the hierarchical relationship of the associated characteristics is used to estimate the length of family leave taken. Generally researchers have increasingly used fixed effects models to estimate maternal employment dynamics because ordinary least squares models have tended to produce biased and inconsistent results (James-Burdumy, 2005). The use of traditional linear models may lead to correlations between the error terms among firms (for example, firms in the same state) and biased coefficient estimates (Raudenbush & Bryk, 2002). Additionally unobserved characteristics between factors that are correlated with demographic characteristics of the mothers, the jobs they hold, and firm-level factors may yield biased coefficient estimates. For example, due to discrimination or professional choices, Black women may be more likely to work in certain types of jobs or in particular industries that are (by their very nature) less accommodating around work and family conflicts like childbirth. Further, types of jobs and employers who employ low-income mothers in those jobs may not represent independent observations.

Multilevel linear regression is used to model both the fixed and random effects discretely to ascertain the predictors of maternity-leave length (measured in days) and to address other confounding relationships in the data. The linear regression specification explicitly models mothers' decisions about employment after childbirth nested within jobs and jobs nested within firms, thus accounting for the dependence of observations. Most factors are statistically estimated as fixed effects variables first and subsequently, random effects (across the second and third levels of the model) are tested. In addition, several covariates are tested in the model (including AFQT percentile scores, birth rate in the county and state unemployment rate). The model is estimated using a reduced estimated maximum likelihood method.

Data Limitations

There are some important data limitations that constrain our analysis. First, the sample size (although adequate for the statistical models estimated here) is still fairly small. A slightly larger sample would likely have increased the effect sizes found and several marginally insignificant variables would likely become significant. Second, the selection criteria used in building the sample truncates data on both ends of the spectrum. So women who had their children very early (in their early or late teens) or fairly late in their lives (generally after age forty) are not included in the data set. The rationale for excluding these women was made solely on the basis of the availability of data. Finally the state- and federal-policy variables included in the model were perhaps not specific enough to demonstrate significant findings. Future attempts to model this phenomenon will likely include more discrete maternity policy variables as well as additional variables at all levels of the analysis.

Findings

Three empirical questions are examined in this chapter: How do race, ethnicity, and class affect the length of maternity leave taken by new mothers? How do other individual, family, and employment characteristics evaluated separately and as interrelated phenomenon relate to this outcome? What effect have federal and state policies had on these outcomes? Using one-way Analysis of Variance tests (ANOVAs), table 6.1 presents the statistically significant variables that capture the separate impact of individual, family (including race, ethnicity, and class), employment, and government policy characteristics. The data show that socioeconomic status independently and significantly affects the length of maternity leave taken by new mothers (p = .05), although race and ethnicity do not. Other statistically significant variables at the individual and family level are: age at first birth (p < .001), education (p < .05), attitudes about family roles (p < .05), family background (as the work history of the respondent's parent, p < .001); and marital status (p < .10). At the employment level, both the size of the employer (p < .001) and the level of benefits provided by the employer are shown to affect maternity-leave length. In particular, maternity leave is significant at the p < .001 level while sick leave is significant at the p < .05 level. All of the regional and public policy variables are found to be significantly related to maternity-leave length. Specifically women who had their first births after 1993 (the passage of the FMLA) and/or lived in states with Temporary Disability Insurance programs (TDI) took slightly longer leaves (variables significant at the p < .05 and p < .10 levels respectively). Also the region of residence was significantly related to leave length such that women living in the Northeast or in the West took longer leaves than all other women (p < .05)

Main Effects of Maternity Benefits and Race/Ethnicity on Length of Leave

Figure 6.1 shows that for all women paid and unpaid maternity leave has increased significantly and quitting their job has decreased dramatically over the last three decades. The intersection of race/ethnicity and access to maternity leave benefits show significant differences in the length of time new mothers take for maternity leave in the multilevel model. As indicated by figure 6.2, maternity leave length was almost identical between White and Black (non-Hispanic) women. Both of the latter groups of women took a little more than two months of maternity leave if they had employer provided maternity leave benefits (on average), but only about two months of leave if they had no access to such benefits. Hispanic women (whether they had access to maternity benefits or not) took longer maternity leaves after a first birth than any other group. Moreover Hispanic women were the only group for which maternity benefits seemed to have no effect on the length of leave, such that even Hispanic women with no leave benefits took longer leaves than all other women. Finally, maternity-leave benefits seem to have the biggest impact (in terms of lengthening leave length) on the leave-taking of Asian and Native American women.

TABLE 6.1

Maternity Leave Length by Selected Characteristics

Characteristics	N	Mean	Sig.	Std. Dev.
Individual and Household Level Characteristics				
Age at First Birth				
Ages 22–25	121	38.98	***	59.67125
Ages 26–29	350	55.06		66.38847
Ages 30–32	250	66.97		74.78974
Ages 32+	186	70.72		80.25136
Education				
<12 years of education no high school diploma)	225	59.88	**	62.83855
12 years of education (high school diploma)	250	59.28		72.70303
13–15 years of education (some college)	250	54.72		70.03582
16+ years (college degree)	128	78.47		82.26498
Attitudinal				
Strongly disagree with traditional family roles	224	61.17	**	66.70967
Disagree with traditional family roles	479	61.91		72.50988
Agree with traditional family roles	151	53.22		78.01834
Strongly agree with traditional family roles	18	60.06		71.21258
Race/Ethnicity				
Black, Non-Hispanic	150	54.67		73.79870
Asian, Native American, and Others	300	61.5		73.14577
Hispanic	117	67.09		83.57845
White, Non-Hispanic	333	57.68		64.92067
Parental Status				
Father Worked in a Professional Occupation	286	58.26	**	72.10897
Father Worked in a Labor Position	621	59.93		71.41959
Mother Worked When the Respondent was an Adolescent	134	74.51		77.32382
Mother Worked was a Stay-at-Home Mom	773	56.79		70.28695
Socioeconomic Status (Family Income)				
Poor or Near Poor (1–2 x the poverty line)	51	33.90	**	63.42594
Working class (2–4 x the poverty line)	108	46.32		53.47524

TABLE 6.1

Maternity Leave Length by Selected Characteristics (*continued*)

Characteristics		N	Mean	Sig.	Std. Dev.
Low-to-Moderate Middle-Class (4–5 x poverty line)		178	55.22		69.04991
High Middle Class (6–7 x poverty line)		122	59.21		55.66234
High Income (8 x poverty line)		201	68.73		73.23988
Marital Status					
Never Married		83	45.5422	*	50.89691
Married		590	60.2542		71.24839
Separated		100	42.1200		56.86477
Divorced		31	61.6774		
Employer/Firm Level Characteristics					
Size of the Firm					
Less than 50 Employees		368	48.58	***	61.78935
51 to 250 Employees		164	60.89		74.88691
More than 250 Employees		187	79.69		69.15162
Benefits					
Sick Leave—	No	104	47.15	**	75.86905
	Yes	505	68.47		68.68694
Vacation Leave—	No	56	50.00		83.50177
	Yes	579	64.96		67.47880
Flexible Hours—	No	248	60.3185		62.97914
	Yes	275	68.9018		77.1372
Maternity Leave—	No	89	35.82	***	63.34870
	Yes	592	66.24		68.62188
State and Public Policy Level Characteristics					
Timing of the Birth					
First Birth before Implementation of the FMLA		681	56.33	**	69.50200
First Birth after Implementation of the FMLA		226	68.67		77.00885
TDI State					
Non-TDI State Resident		679	56.84	*	67.29936
TDI State Resident		227	67.34		82.86504
Region					
Northeast		182	70.38	**	71.68566
North Center		233	58.49		72.52979
South		319	52.09		68.70096
West		167	63.58		74.53990

Note: * p ≤ .10; ** p ≤ .05; *** p ≤ .001

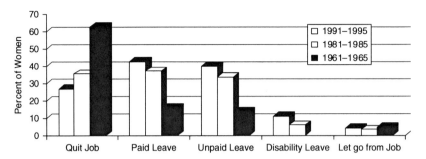

FIGURE 6.1 Leave Arrangements Used by Women Who Worked during Pregnancy with First Child, 1961–1995

Smith et al., 2001; 11

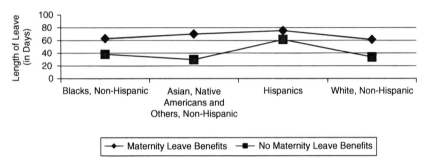

FIGURE 6.2 Length of Maternity Leave Following First Birth by Race/Ethnicity and Access to Employer's Maternity Leave Policies

Main Effects of Marital Status, Level of Education, and Firm Size on Length of Leave

The multilevel model also reveals that there are significant intersectional differences in the mean leave length taken by respondents by marital status, level of education, and size of the employer. In terms of marital status, married and divorced women took substantially longer leaves than those who had never been married or were separated from their spouses. This may reflect more social support and economic resources (married and divorced women may be more likely to receive social and financial support from spouses or former spouses whereas never married or newly separated women may have a limited ability to garner these resources from children's fathers).

With regard to the size of the employer, women in all racial and ethnic groups took more time away from work when they worked in larger firms. They took slightly less time when they were in mid-sized firms and returned to work much sooner when they worked in small firms. Firm size is a primary employment characteristic because larger employers are: (1) generally more likely to provide fringe benefits like family leave, flexible hours, childcare subsidies, and other work-support policies for women; and (2) because of their size, larger employers can more readily handle longer or extended leaves by women employees—whereas smaller firms may have a harder time accommodating longer leaves.

Finally women with college degrees and maternity leave benefits took substantially longer leaves than all other groups. The gap in terms of the length of maternity leave taken is widest between college educated women with maternity leave benefits and those without such benefits; women with college degrees but no maternity leave benefits took the shortest maternity leaves of all mothers in the sample. Notably women with a high school diploma and maternity leave benefits took an average of fifty more days of maternity leave than those with a high school diploma but no access to maternity leave benefits. Alternatively the smallest gap among women with similar levels of education is found between women with less than a high school education. In particular, women with less than a high school education, but who work in jobs with maternity leave benefits, took an average sixty-five days of leave while women with the same education background but no maternity leave benefits took about fifty-five days.

Examining the Intersectional Relationships in More Depth: Interaction Effects

Overall socioeconomic status is significantly related to maternal employment behavior following a first birth—particularly as it relates to race/ethnicity, the work history of the mothers' parents, the number of weeks on the job, and access to employer provided benefits (maternity and flex-leave in particular). Although the direction of the effects varies across these significant variables, two of these variables operate primarily at the family level (race and work history of the mothers' parents) while the latter three variables are employment characteristics of the mothers. Noticeably variables at the individual and government policy level did not produce significant differences across the groups.

More specifically, figure 6.3 shows that, regardless of race and ethnicity, length of leave is strongly associated with socioeconomic status—that is, women from higher socioeconomic groups took significantly longer leaves than women in lower socioeconomic groups. The one exception appears to be higher income middle-class Black women who took shorter leaves. In this income category, Black women took an average of almost two months away from work while White, Asian, and Hispanic women in the same income category took 2 to 3 times more leave time. Although multiple reasons may account for this finding, it is highly likely that higher income Black women are much less likely to be married when they have their first child and thus contribute a

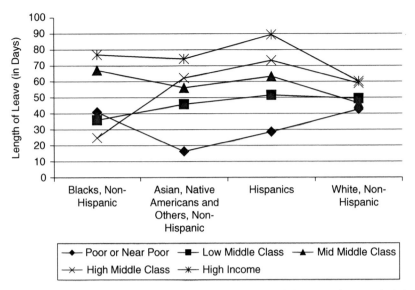

FIGURE 6.3 Length of Maternity Leave Following First Birth by SES and Race/Ethnicity

much higher portion of their earned income to household income than women in all other racial/ethnic groups (Mishel, Bernstein, & Allegretto, 2005).

While Hispanic women tended to take longer maternity leaves regardless of access to maternity-leave benefits (as discussed earlier), figure 6.3 shows that once socioeconomic status is accounted for, Hispanic women are similar to other racial/ethnic groups in the same economic class. That is, the leave-taking behavior of Hispanic women is no longer an outlier once they are compared with women with similar income profiles. Furthermore the wide distribution within each racial/ethnic group in figure 6.3 shows that class mattered more for Hispanic, Black, Asian, and Native American women in terms of leave-taking than for White women. Compared to racial/ethnic minority women, White women tended to have more similar lengths of leave irrespective of their socioeconomic class.

Even so, access to maternity leave benefits significantly affects the length of leave women take. Figure 6.4 illustrates that access to maternity leave benefits significantly increases variation across socioeconomic groups. Although a strong relationship is shown by race and class in mean length of maternity leave days taken by new mothers, having access to maternity leave benefits increases the length of leave for women in all socioeconomic groups. Moreover the most dramatic increases in leave length occur for women in the two highest income categories, such that women with more financial resources took much more leave when employers offer maternity leave benefits and lack of wage-replacement is not a deterrent from taking advantage of full job protection provisions of the policies.

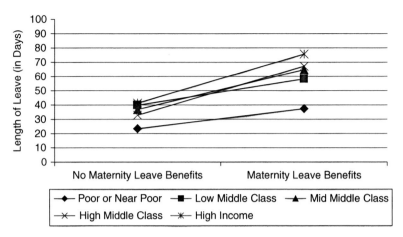

FIGURE 6.4 Length of Maternity Leave Following First Birth by SES and Maternity Leave Benefits

Women's access to flexible work hours as an employment benefit shows substantial increases in leave length among women at opposite ends of the wage scale: among poor and high-income mothers. That is, poor and high-income mothers tend to increase the length of their maternity leave when they work in jobs that offer flexible work hours. For example the data show that poor women take an average of twenty additional days and high-income mothers take almost forty additional days. In contrast, access to flexible leave benefits reduces the length of leave taken by all middle-income groups (albeit only slightly).

Figure 6.5 shows that across all socioeconomic groups, women with fewer weeks on the job take shorter leaves while women with substantially longer job tenure take longer leaves. One major exception across the socioeconomic groups appears to be poor women with one to two years of experience with their employers. The latter group tends to take fairly longer leaves compared not only to other poor women, but across all other socioeconomic groups of women with the same level of education. This may occur because many maternity-leave benefit programs have a one-year waiting period before women become eligible. For example, the FMLA requires that women have worked the equivalent of one year before they can take a job-projected maternity leave. This waiting period may also be related to another finding from figure 6.5; that is, the widest disparities across women with similar levels of job tenure occur for women with less than one year on the job. With the exception of high-income mothers, most women with less than one year on the job take almost no maternity leave at all.

Another important set of findings occurs around the issue of the mother's family history. In particular, having had a mother who worked outside the

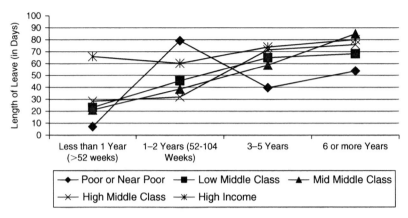

FIGURE 6.5 Length of Maternity Leave Following First Birth by SES and Mother's Job Tenure

home seems to dramatically reduce the overall variation across socioeconomic groups. That is, the length of maternity leave taken by women who had mothers who worked outside of home when they were young was longer for both poor and high-income women. Women whose mothers were at home during their childhoods, took fewer days, regardless of their socioeconomic status.

Finally, given our particular interest in the leave-taking behavior of low-income mothers, we summarize the findings that are noteworthy for this group of mothers:

1. Low-income mothers take shorter periods of maternity leave than mothers in all other socioeconomic groups.
2. Low-income mothers are most dramatically affected by the experience and work histories of their parents and the work history of their own mothers is shown to be particularly important.
3. Low-income mothers with less than one year on the job (a likely circumstance for many low-income women "transitioning" off of public assistance programs) take the shortest maternity leave of all socioeconomic groups.
4. Low-income mothers with one to two years tenure with their current employers take longer maternity leaves when compared with low-income mothers who have been with their current employers for longer periods.
5. Flexible hour benefits have a more dramatic impact in terms of increasing the length of leave taken by low-income mothers than maternity-leave benefits.

Discussion

Each year in the United States about four million families welcome the birth of a new child and make critical decisions to balance the care needs and financial responsibilities of their growing families. Our findings show that race, ethnicity, and class characteristics significantly affect those decisions; that a variety of additional factors at the individual, family, employment, and government policy levels evaluated separately and intersectionally also affect those decisions. When these variables are tested (intersectionally), as nested phenomenon, dramatically different outcomes for different groups of mothers are observed. Finally, we find that leave length is determined most powerfully by variables that operate at the family and employment levels.

These findings represent an important contribution to the scholarly literature on maternity leave in several ways. First, limitations of the traditional linear model have made it difficult for researchers to specifically examine the interrelated nature of maternal employment decisions such as those involving the return to work after childbirth. Existing empirical research has tended to test only the separate impacts of individual, family, employment, and government policy variables as they relate to maternal employment decisions. These analyses clarify the relative importance of individual, family, employment, and governmental policy factors in shaping how families respond to work and family conflicts and, how those factors (both separately and in tandem) shape one type of employment outcome across and within socioeconomic groups.

Second, striking differences were observed in leave length by race, ethnicity, and class. For example, higher income Black women with maternity leave benefits from their employers seem to make very different maternal employment decisions than similarly situated Hispanic women, and we argue that those decisions are directly related to the unique social location of each woman. Understanding maternity leave outcomes as a function of social location provides an alternative analytical discourse for researchers interested in these issues. Future research can use a genealogical "mapping" approach of leave outcomes both within and between different contextual levels of variables including: (1) racial and ethnic identity groupings that capture the impact of different cultural expectations about work and family; (2) socioeconomic categories that capture the ways in which financial resources facilitate, constrain, or otherwise shape the ability of new mothers to mitigate work and family conflicts; and (3) access to jobs that capture the relative value of employment related work supports like maternity and flexible hour benefits—particularly to workers in jobs that traditionally have more rigid work demands.

Finally the social location of low-income mothers with regard to maternity leave represents a particularly important consideration. Low-income mothers are generally assumed to have the strongest economic incentive to return to work quickly both because they do not earn enough to forego wages in the labor market for extended periods and also because of recent changes in public assistance programs that require employment as a condition for financial assistance. Additionally the weight of these work "incentives" are likely to be felt more deeply and experienced differently by low-income women of color, who are already disproportionately affected by reductions in public assistance programs. With little capacity to purchase their own work supports (such as the labor of third parties like nannies, babysitters, etc.) nor to replace lost wages when their labor is needed at home and away from work, the increased work demands for low-income mothers can conflict powerfully with their roles and responsibilities as family and community members.

In the midst of these already difficult transitions, low-income mothers have critical choices to make about how to respond to periods of heightened family-care needs (such as the birth of a new child, a short-term illness, etc.). Low-income mothers use multiple survival strategies to cope with these circumstances and our findings suggest that the strategies they use do not follow neat or consistent patterns across economic categories. Furthermore, although more scholarly research now documents the relationship between poverty and work supports like family leave (Cantor, et al., 2001; Waldfogel, 2001), this research thus far has not yet begun to explore the enormous disparities that exist among low-income mothers. Our research begins to explain why such disparities exist and what factors are likely to be most useful in identifying the conditions under which those disparities may be mitigated.

Our findings also have enormous implications for public policymakers and are especially germane given the level of recent policy attention aimed at shaping the fertility and employment decisions of low-income women. The implications of these data are that: race, ethnicity, and class matter a great deal in terms of how women sort out their employment options and that social policies that do not address the centrality of family and employment variables may very well miss what seems to be key resources women use to make employment decisions. Most importantly, these findings give more credence to the notion that "one-size" policies do not "fit all." That is, policies that seek to help mothers maintain employment by embracing only one set of policy tools are likely to have the intended effect for some but are likely to engender a host of unintended and/or deleterious effects for others. Flexible leave benefits are a good example of how one policy tool used to help employees manage work and family conflicts results in very different outcomes for different groups of new mothers.

Conclusions

Neither marriage nor wages will end women's "welfare dependency" if relations of gender inequality remain inscribed socially and politically in the family, in work, and in the state. . . . If welfare is a problem, it is not that women use it but *why* they do.

Mink, 1995, 189

The primary thrust of public policy efforts to address the problem of "welfare dependency" has focused squarely on increasing employment and earnings from paid work among low-income mothers. More recent attempts to address these issues have added a focus on marriage promotion and work supports. While there are mixed results and opinions about the efficacy of marriage promotion programs, there is more consistent evidence about the impact that work supports have on the ability of low-income mothers to get and maintain earnings that keep their families solvent. Work supports like family leave benefits can help low-income mothers to manage the often conflicting demands of low-wage jobs and family responsibilities—thereby decreasing the likelihood of being poor and of needing public assistance.

As policymakers now debate the efficacy of expanding work supports, scholarly efforts to underscore the value of work supports—particularly in light of welfare reform efforts—are critically important to the debate of these issues. In particular, scholarship that focuses on understanding how families sort themselves out as a result of conflicting demands on their time and resources, seem especially relevant. Several findings (for example, the finding that Hispanic women are likely to take longer leaves whether or not leave benefits are given) warrant substantial future research to help guide policymaker's efforts.

As Mink (1995) argues above, the intersectional approach used in this study recognizes that welfare usage (and in turn, the use of work supports to transition from welfare) is "inscribed socially and politically in the family, in work, and in the state" as interrelated issues (Mink, 1995, 189). As a result, the intersectional approach is not only more applicable and relevant in terms of understanding the experiences of low-income mothers as they confront life choices regarding work and family, but may be particularly valuable in revealing the conditions under which working mothers more effectively utilize work supports (and other public benefits).

In conducting this kind of research, there is an enormous opportunity to raise new questions about policies that affect maternal employment and how women respond to such policies. Researchers have also been able to raise questions about the allocation of societal resources around care giving and, in particular, resources to support working caregivers.

> The problem, the enormous problem for Americans in the 1990s, is that we have not devised any equality-respecting system to replace the full-time caretaking labor force of women at home. We have patchwork systems, but we have come nowhere near replacing the hours or the quality of care that the at-home women of previous generations provided for the country. And the social ills that follow from this incalculable loss of care are all too familiar.
>
> Harrington, 2000, 17

The resource allocation questions raised by these scholars (and by inter-sectionality theorists) will engender considerable policy debate about the efficacy of expanding work and family policies as our understanding of how work supports such as family leave translate into policy outcomes and potentially resolve a wide range of work and family conflicts that today serve to limit maternal employment.

NOTES

1. Work supports can also include other forms of income support such as food stamps and nutrition programs, housing assistance, health insurance for low-income children and adults, transportation assistance, as well as income supplements like tax credits.

2. The focus of this research (and much of the research literature on work and family issues) focuses on the experiences of women as mothers. This is largely because surveys demonstrate that women still shoulder the bulk of care work in most U.S. households, and are more likely to say that they experience serious work and family conflicts. Women are also more likely to say that work and family conflicts greatly affect their employment outcomes (Duxberry, Higgins, & Lee, 1994).

3. Trzcinski and Alpert (2000) found that "the incidence of all forms of leave with health insurance continuation and job and seniority guarantees increases" as firm size increases (Trzcinski & Alpert, 2000, 140). Moreover Gruber (1994) finds that approximately half of all women workers had differential coverage with regard to health insurance for pregnancy versus other covered circumstances. Additionally about 20 percent of women had no health insurance coverage for childbirth when they had health insurance for other comparable illnesses that received "hospital room and board" and other "outpatient services" (624).

4. In fact, by the early 1990s when the FMLA was passed, more than a dozen states had already passed some form of leave legislation granting new parents (some laws even included fathers) leave from work following a childbirth or adoption.

5. To be eligible, employees must have worked at least 1,250 hours in the previous year (equivalent to about thirty weeks of full-time or a full year of part-time work) and work within seventy-five miles of their specific worksite. The leave may be taken all at once or on an intermittent basis. Also the illness must require at least one night in the hospital or continuing treatment by a healthcare provider to be considered a "serious illness or health condition."

6. Of the 26.9 percent of women who quit their jobs as their primary leave arrangement between 1991 and 1995, most did so before the birth of the child (23 percent) rather than after the child was born (4 percent).

7. See also a collection of articles using intersectionality theory edited by Landry (2007).

8. Another concern is that once women use all of their sick and vacation time for maternity leave, they have no time left to handle postmaternity illnesses, illness of their newborn children, or other medically necessary absences.

9. Specifically 6 percent of women use more than one form of leave arrangement before giving birth and 11 percent combine leave arrangements after the birth of the child (Smith, Downs, & O'Connell, 2001).

10. More specifically, about a fifth of all workers in the labor market said that they needed a leave for reasons covered by the FMLA in the survey, yet only a fourth of those who

needed it (83 percent) actually took leave (Gerstel & McGonagle, 1999). More than 87.8 percent of leave-needers say that they would have taken a leave if they had received some pay during the leave (Cantor, et al., 2001).

11. See discussion by Neuback and Cazenave (2001) on pages 181–183 as well as Savner (2000).

12. African Americans have long experienced economic disadvantage in employment through racial discrimination and job segregation (Tomaskovic-Devey, 1993; Reskin, 1999).

13. This period also reflects a key time period in which federal policies changed the options available to mothers in different socioeconomic groups.

14. This category combines Asian, Native American, and women who identified themselves as "other" on the survey solely because of sample size considerations. It is not meant to suggest that these groups have no distinguishable characteristics worth evaluating separately.

15. All data are indexed using the Consumer Price Index in 1988 dollars (the first year for which data are collected) and the federal poverty line is used to compare family income by family size. Note the federal poverty line for a family of four in 1988 was $13,140.

References

Amott, T, & Matthaei, J. (1991). *Race, Gender & Work: A Multicultural Economic History of Women in the United States*. Boston: South End Press.

Baum, C. (2003). The Effects of Maternity Leave Legislation on Mothers' Labor Supply after Childbirth. *Southern Economic Journal, 69*(4), 772–799.

Boushey, H. (2005). *When Done Right, Work Supports Work: Medicaid and Mothers' Employment and Wages*. Washington, DC: Center for Economic and Policy Research.

Browne, I., & Misra, J. (2003). The Intersection of Gender and Race in the Labor Market. *Annual Review of Sociology, 29*, 487–514.

Burr, J. A., & Bean, F. D. (1996, Fall/Winter). Racial Fertility Differences: The Role of Female Employment and Education in Wanted and Unwanted Childbearing. *Social Biology, 43*(3/4), 218–241.

Cantor, D., Waldfogel, J., Kerwin, J., McKinley Wright, M., Levin, K., Rauch, J., Hagerty, T., & Stapleton Kudela, M. (2001). *Balancing the Needs of Families and Employers: Family and Medical Leave Surveys, 2000 Update*. Rockville, MD: Westat.

Center for Human Resource Research. (2000). *NLSY79 User's Guide 1979–2000*. Columbus, OH: CHRR.

Commission on Family and Medical Leave. (1996). *A Workable Balance: Report to the Congress on Family and Medical Leave Policies*. Washington, DC: Women's Bureau, U.S. Department of Labor.

DeParle, J. (1998, July 27). Shrinking Welfare Rolls Leave Record High Share of Minorities. *New York Times*, p. A1.

Dodson, L., Bravo, E., & Manuel, T. (2002). *Keeping Jobs and Raising Families in Low-Income America: It Just Doesn't Work*. Cambridge, MA: Radcliffe Institute for Advanced Study, Harvard University.

Duxberry, L., Higgins, C., & Lee, C. (1994). Work-family Conflict: A Comparison by Gender, Family Type, and Perceived Control. *Journal of Family Issues, 15*, 449–468.

Fishman, M. (2004). *Multiple Work Supports and Services May Help Low-Wage Workers Climb the Economic Ladder*. Washington, DC: National Center for Children in Poverty.

Fredriksen-Goldsen, K., & Scharlach, A. (2001). *Families and Work: New Directions in the Twenty-First Century*. New York: Oxford Press.

Fried, M. (1998). *Taking Time*. Philadelphia: Temple University Press.

Garrett, P., Wenk, D., & Lubeck, S. (1990). Working around Childbirth: Comparative and Empirical Perspectives on Parental-Leave Policy. *Child Welfare*, *69*(5), 401–413.

Gennetian, L., Miller, C., & Smith, J. (2005). *Turning Welfare into a Work Support: Six-Year Impacts on Parents and Children from the Minnesota Family Investment Program*. MDRC.

George, S. (2001). *Why Intersectionality Works*. Retrieved from http://www.isiswomen.org/pub/wia/wiawcar/intersectionality.htm.

Gerstel, N., & McGonagle, K. (1999). Job Leaves and the Limits of the Family and Medical Leave Act: The Effects of Gender, Race, and Family. *Work & Occupations*, *26*(4), 510–534.

Grosswald, B., & Scharlach, A. (1999). Employee Experiences with Family and Medical Leave: A Case Study. *Community, Work & Family*, *2*(2), 187–203.

Gruber, J. (1994). The Incidence of Mandated Maternity Benefits. *American Economic Review*, *84*, 622–641.

Harrington, M. (2000). The Care Equation. *The American Prospect*, *61*, 61–67.

Hattiangadi, A. (2000). *Paid Family Leave: At What Cost?* Washington, DC: Employment Policy Foundation.

Heyman, J. (2000). *The Widening Gap: Why America's Working Families Are in Jeopardy and What Can Be Done about It*. New York: Basic Books.

Hum, D., & Simpson, W. (2003). Labour Market Training of New Canadians and Limitations to the Intersectionality Framework. *Canadian Ethic Studies*, (35), 56, 57–73.

Hofferth, S. (1996). The Effects of Public and Private Policies on Working after Childbirth. *Work and Occupations*, *23*(4), 378–404.

James-Burdumy, S. (2005). The Effect of Maternal Labor Force Participation on Child Development. *Journal of Labor Economics*, *23*(1), 177–211.

Landry, B. (2007). *Race, Gender, and Class: Theory and Methods of Analysis*. Upper Saddle River, NJ: Pearson Prentice Hall Publishers.

Lee, S. (2004). *Women's Work Supports, Job Retention, and Job Mobility: Child Care and Employer-Provided Health Insurance Help Women Stay on Jobs*. Washington, DC: Institute for Women's Policy Research.

Manuel, T. (2004). *Giving Mercenaries a Chance to be Missionaries: Making the Case for Universal Paid Family Leave in the United States*. Dissertation, University of Massachusetts Boston.

McAdoo, H. P. (1997). *Black families*. Third edition. Thousand Oaks: Sage Publications, Inc.

McNichol, L., & Springer, J. (2004). *State Policies to Assist Working-Poor Families*. Washington, DC: Center on Budget and Policy Priorities.

Mink, G. (1995). *The Wages of Motherhood: Inequality in the Welfare State, 1917–1942*. Ithaca, NY: Cornell University Press.

Mishel, L., Bernstein, J., & Allegretto, S. (2005). *The State of Working America*. Washington, DC: Economic Policy Institute.

Neuback, K., & Cazenave, N. (2001). *Welfare Racism: Playing the Race Card against America's Poor*. New York: Routledge Press.

Paulsell, D. (2005). *Promoting Access to Work Supports in Rural Areas: Lessons from Virginia*. Princeton, NJ: Mathematica Policy Research, Inc.

Raudenbush, S., & Bryk, A. (2002). *Hierarchical Linear Models: Applications and Data Analysis Methods*. Thousand Oaks, CA: Sage Publications

Relave, N. (2005). *Work Supports and Low-Wage Workers: The Promise of Employer Involvement*. Washington, DC: The Finance Project Working.

Reskin, B. (1999). Occupational Segregation by Race and Ethnicity among Women Workers. In I. Brown (Ed.), *Latina and African American Women at Work* (pp. 183–204). New York: Russell Sage Foundation.

Savner, S. (2000, July/August). Welfare Reform and Racial/Ethnic Minorities: The Questions to Ask. *Poverty & Race, 9*(4), 3–5.

Smith, K., Downs, B., & O'Connell, M. (2001). *Maternity Leave and Employment Patterns: 1961–1995.* Current Population Reports. Washington, DC: Census Bureau. 70-79.

Taylor, R. J., Jackson, J. S., & Chatters, L. M. (1997). *Family Life in Black America.* Thousand Oaks, CA: Sage Publications, Inc.

Tomaskovic-Devey, D. (1993). *Gender and Race Inequality at Work: The Sources and Consequences of Job Segregation.* Ithaca, NY: ILR Press.

Trzcinski, E., & Alpert, W. (2000). The Economics of Family and Medical Leave in Canada and in the United States. In W. Alpert & S. Woodbury (Eds.), *Employee Benefits and Labor Markets in Canada and the United States* (pp. 129–180). Kalamazoo, MI: W. E. Upjohn Institute for Employment Research.

U.S. Census Bureau. (2004). *Statistical Abstract.* Washington, DC: GPO.

Vogel, L. (1993). *Mothers on the Job: Maternity Policy in the U.S. Workplace.* New Brunswick, NJ: Rutgers University Press.

Waldfogel, J. (1997). The Effect of Children on Women's Wages. *American Sociological Review, 62,* 209–217.

Waldfogel, J. (1999). The Impact of the Family and Medical Leave Act. *Journal of Policy Analysis and Management, 18*(2), 281–302.

Waldfogel, J. (2001, Spring/Summer). International Policies toward Parental Leave and Child Care. *The Future of Children, 11*(1), 99–111.

Waldfogel, J., Higuchi, Y., & Abe, M. (1999). Family Leave Policies and Women's Retention after Childbirth: Evidence from the United States, Britain, and Japan. *Journal of Population Economics, 12,* 523–545.

Warren, E., & Warren Tyagi, A. (2003). *The Two Income Trap.* New York, NY: Basic Books.

Williams Crenshaw, K. (1989). Demarginalizing the Intersection of Race and Sex: A Black Feminist Critique of Antidiscrimination Doctrine, Feminist Theory, and Antiracist Politics. *The University of Chicago Legal Forum,* (139), 141–150.

Williams Crenshaw, K. (1995). Mapping the Margins; Intersectionality, Identity Politics and Violence against Women of Color. In K. W. Crenshaw, N. Gotanda, G. Peller, & K. Thomas (Eds.), *Critical Race Theory: The Key Writings that Formed the Movement* (pp. 357–383). 1st ed. New York: The New Press.

Wilson, George. (2000). Race, Class and Support for Egalitarian Statism among the African American Middle Class. *Journal of Sociology and Social Welfare, 27*(3).

7

Racial, Ethnic, and Gender Disparities in the Workforce, Education, and Training under Welfare Reform

AVIS JONES-DEWEEVER, BONNIE THORNTON DILL, AND
SANFORD SCHRAM

Why have people of color become a larger proportion of the welfare case-load since the implementation of TANF in 1996?[1] What kinds of opportunities enhance women's successful transition from welfare to self-sufficiency? This chapter has three purposes:

- to shed some light on these and other questions by examining the relationship between racial, ethnic, and gender disparities and access to jobs and education for welfare recipients;
- to propose a set of explanations that reveal how historical patterns of racial, ethnic, and gender discrimination result in disparities that have restructured the relationship of the welfare population to the rest of the poor and influenced the implementation and outcomes of the TANF program;
- and to examine the impact of racial, ethnic, and gender disparities in the implementation of TANF specifically in five areas: changes in the composition of the welfare rolls; patterns of leaving and returning to welfare; opportunities for employment; access to education and job training; and the design and administration of state policies and programs.

The chapter then provides examples of promising practices that address these discriminatory barriers and concludes with a set of policy recommendations.

Synthesis of Conclusive Research Findings

Terms such as "responsibility," "self-sufficiency," and "dependency" are all too often hurled like weapons in discussions surrounding the issue of welfare. One thing is certain—poverty is not a life-choice, it is an unfortunate condition. Who would choose to be poor when all around the trinkets of wealth are revered, desired, and associated with personal worth?

Examining the plight of the poor through an intersectional lens emphasizes the contemporary outcomes of historic structural patterns of inequality that have resulted in the overrepresentation of people of color and women, especially women of color among the poor. These patterns include that of a two-tiered welfare state, which, in treating men as workers and women as mothers, has denied women full access to social benefits. Additionally people of color have consistently been denied full access to this social safety net through both policy—such as the exclusion of domestic and agricultural workers from social security benefits—and implementation. These problems are exacerbated in today's global economy when, "economic restructuring and neo-liberal policy 'reforms' have caused increased social inequality and economic polarization in the U.S." (Goode & Maskovsky, 2001). The gap between rich and poor is wider today than ever.

Understanding these broad social, economic, and historical patterns reveals the true needs of genuine welfare reform—not merely shrinking welfare rolls, but rather, creating opportunities for economic self-sufficiency and improved overall family well-being. It is from this perspective that poverty is seen as a societal failure, not merely a personal one.

Welfare reforms of recent years have had an uneven impact on the U.S. population. The Personal Responsibility and Work Opportunity Reconciliation Act (PRWORA) of 1996 abolished the longstanding Aid to Families with Dependent Children (AFDC) program and replaced it with the Temporary Assistance for Needy Families (TANF) block grant. The TANF program has emphasized time limits and work requirements. It has allowed states to use sanctions to reduce benefits and terminate families from assistance. It has given birth to a "workfirst" welfare reform system that puts in place a series of "get-tough" practices designed to reduce the alleged problem of "welfare dependency" by moving women into the workforce. As a result, the welfare rolls declined 69 percent from 1996 to 2007, falling from 12,644,915 to 3,901,890.[2] This approach to social assistance has spurred some families that relied on welfare to achieve a modicum of self-sufficiency through paid employment. For others, it has meant the denial of much needed assistance. For still others, the reforms have meant increased hassles and complications in access to benefits. These effects have not been distributed evenly across the poverty population. Findings indicate that welfare reform has spawned its own forms of discrimination.

Who Is Poor? The Changing Composition of the Welfare Rolls

Poverty is not neutral. Race and gender are significant factors affecting the probability of having an income below the poverty line, with both women and people of color disproportionately overrepresented in the poverty population. In 2001, the poverty rate was 11.7 percent, representing 32.9 million people living below the poverty threshold. Over nine percent, or 6.8 million families were poor; and children, with a poverty rate of 16.3 percent, experienced the highest rates of poverty of any age group (U.S. Census Current Population Survey, 2001).

Among the poor, historic differences in the incidence of poverty in the U.S. population continue. In 2001, the poverty rate for non-Hispanic Whites was 7.8 percent, compared to 22.7 percent for African Americans, 21.4 percent for Hispanics, and 10.2 percent for Asians and Pacific Islanders, all historic lows. Yet, even at historically low levels, people of color—particularly African Americans and Hispanics—experience a much higher incidence of poverty than do Whites (U.S. Census Current Population Survey, 2001).

Gender disparities, especially as apparent in family and household arrangements, are part of the picture as well and women continue to experience greater rates of poverty and predominate among welfare clients and workers (Abramovitz, 2000). Slightly more than one-quarter (28.6 percent) of female-headed households were poor in 2001, compared with 13.6 percent of single male headed households (U.S. Census Current Population Survey, 2001). These rates are two-and-a-half times the rate for the U.S. population overall and five times that for married couples (4.9 percent in 2001). For Black women and Latinas, who experience the multiple and intersecting effects of race, gender, and class, the poverty rates for female headed households in 2001 are even higher: 35.2 percent for Blacks and 37 percent for Latinas compared to 19 percent for non-Hispanic Whites (Proctor & Dalaker, 2002).

A critical byproduct of women's poverty is the poverty of children. In fact, child poverty is higher than poverty for the population overall. While 16.3 percent of all children were poor in 2001, 30.2 percent of Black children and 28 percent of Hispanic children were poor. Although this figure represents a decline in poverty for Black children from a high of 41.5 percent in 1995, the Children's Defense Fund (CDF) has determined that during welfare reform the number of Black children living in extreme poverty (below 50 percent of the poverty line) rose dramatically to its highest level since 1980 when the government first produced the data (Dillon, 2003). The CDF explains this development arguing that as the economy has stagnated, the poorest families have not been able to rely on welfare benefits as much as before due to welfare reform. As a result, they contend, the number of children in extreme poverty has increased. For example, the rate of extreme poverty for Black children rose sharply between 2000 and 2001, from 5.9 percent to 8.7 percent.

Only about 23 percent of the poverty population received welfare or other cash assistance from the government in 2001.[3] The poor who are currently receiving welfare, especially as a result of the implementation of TANF, have become increasingly different from the poor in general, especially with regard to race, ethnicity, and gender. One of the results of the workfirst approach of TANF was to move the most employable recipients off the rolls, leaving those with the greatest barriers to employment behind. As a result, the distinctions between those poor who receive welfare and those who do not have increased. TANF recipients, when compared to the entire poverty population, are more likely to be people of color, to be younger and less educated, to be female, to live in metropolitan areas, to receive food stamps and Medicaid, and are only slightly more likely to live in subsidized public housing. They are less likely to be married or to be working. Although the population of welfare recipients has always consisted predominantly of single women (either divorced, separated, or never married or widowed) the differences in racial composition, age, and geographic location have become more marked, broadening the gap between the poor who receive welfare and those who do not (U.S. Census Current Population Survey, 2001; USDHHS, 2003). Why do the characteristics of those on welfare differ so much from those of the poverty population in general? What is it about the design and implementation of the program, the overall treatment of poverty, and the characteristics of individuals that result in this distinctive profile of TANF recipients? This chapter attempts to explain how race, ethnicity, and gender disparities interact with TANF program policies and procedures to produce some of these differences.

Much has been made of the apparent successes of welfare reform. Plummeting welfare caseloads, rising work participation rates, and declining poverty have all seemingly pointed to resounding policy success. What is not so widely acknowledged however, is the extent to which these apparent successes have been "colored" by the specter of race.

Prior to the implementation of welfare reform it was not unusual for Whites to make up the majority of welfare recipients, despite the stereotypical image of the lazy, sexually loose, and criminally fraudulent Black welfare queen. With the implementation of welfare reform in 1996, however, there has been a dramatic shift in the racial composition of the welfare caseload, which seemingly implies differing levels of success regarding job attainment. As table 7.1 illustrates, non-Hispanic White representation among welfare recipients dropped dramatically over the years, from roughly 36 percent in 1996 to 30 percent in 2001. Conversely Hispanic representation increased by similar proportions, from roughly 21 percent in 1996 to 26 percent in 2001. All the while, Black representation remained comparatively steady over the years, having experienced only a 2 percent increase in caseload representation since TANF implementation (from roughly 37 percent in 1996 to 39 percent in 2001). Notably Blacks were the only racial cohort to experience an increase in the percentage of nonwelfare recipients who are low-income following welfare reform, thus indicating that many Black welfare leavers found themselves worse off after leaving the rolls (Peterson, Song, & Jones-DeWeever, 2002).

TABLE 7.1

Racial Composition of the National Welfare Caseload (Percent of
All AFDC/TANF Families)

	FY 1992	FY 1996	FY 2001
White	38.9	35.9	30.1
Black	37.2	36.9	39.0
Hispanic*	17.8	20.8	26.0
Asian	2.8	3.0	2.1
Native American	1.4	1.4	1.3
Other	–	–	.8
Unknown	2.0	2.0	.7

Source: Department of Heath and Human Services, "2002 TANF Annual Report
to Congress."
Note: *Can be of Any Race

Racial Disparities in Leaving and Returning to Welfare

Analyses of the causes for racial and other demographic changes in the rolls have
often focused on studying "leavers"—i.e., families who have left welfare. Studying
leavers helps assess how those who have left welfare are faring economically and
identifies the significant racial disparities that exist among leavers and
returnees. Although Whites have left the rolls more rapidly than other groups
(Lower-Basch, 2000), Blacks are more likely to be forced off welfare due to sanctions (Finegold & Staveteig, 2002; Kalil, Seefeldt, & Wang, 2002). Families forced
off welfare due to sanctions fare relatively poorly compared to families who leave
for other reasons and are more likely to have overall rates of recidivism (Moffitt
& Roff, 2000). Using the data from the National Survey of American Families
(NSAF), Loprest (2002) found that Blacks and Latinos are far more likely to return
to welfare than Whites, with 32.2 percent of Black and 24.1 percent of Latino
leavers returning to welfare within a year, compared with only 12.7 percent of
non-Hispanic White leavers. Some data suggest that this is, in part, a result of
sanction policies forcing people of color off the rolls who, as a group, may be
least employable due to limited work experience and skills, low levels of education, personal problems, and a need to tend to young children (Kalil, Seefeldt, &
Wang, 2002). Additionally similar disparities exist regarding time limit restrictions imposed by states under welfare reform. Blacks are more likely to be forced
off welfare due to exhausting their time allowed to receive TANF benefits, thus
placing them in serious economic jeopardy (Duncan, Harris, & Boisjoly, 2000).

While studying leavers is important, it ignores an important, yet under-studied population: the "diverted." Under welfare reform, states can establish "diversion" programs that work to discourage new entrants from receiving TANF assistance even when they need it and are eligible to receive it (Diller, 2000). This population actually may be a very important one for understanding disparate treatment under welfare reform. For instance, it is questionable to what extent the massive declines in the rolls from the mid-1990s through 2001 were due strictly to people leaving welfare (Schram & Soss, 2002). In fact, the rolls may have gone down in good part because large numbers of people did not come onto the rolls. For years, the number of recipients was largely static, as new entrants largely replaced leavers. Therefore the rolls could have declined because the numbers of new entrants declined faster than those leaving, contributing to the dramatic change in the rolls in the 1990s (Schram & Soss, 2002). An important issue that remains understudied is whether there is systematic racial discrimination in the application of diversion programs.

Most of the research on the effects of welfare reform on leavers was done while the economy was strong. The economy has recently turned downward and the welfare rolls may begin to inch back up after years of massive declines. Further research is needed to assess whether the racial disparities in leaving and returning to welfare are exacerbated during the current economic downturn and to determine if some people by virtue of their race or ethnicity are more likely to be diverted from receiving needed assistance.

Racial and Gender Barriers to Job Access

To a large extent, the differences in leaving reflect differing levels of success regarding job attainment. Two well-documented explanations of the effects of race and ethnic discrimination on welfare recipients' access to jobs are: employment discrimination and geographic location.

Employment Discrimination

Continuing racial discrimination in the labor market makes the transition off welfare more difficult for people of color than our supposedly "color-blind" welfare policies would assume. Bernstein and Hartmann (2000) in a study of the structure of the contemporary low-wage labor market find that: "Discrimination (still) negatively affects employment rates of African Americans, even when differences in skills have been taken into account." Additionally Holzer and Stoll (2002), in their study of the determinants of employer demand for welfare recipients in four large metropolitan areas, found that Black women and Latinas are less likely to be hired than White women relative to their percentages in the population. This appears to be due primarily to employer preferences, not the women's qualifications. They note that: "Establishments located in the central city, those that are minority-owned, and those that have worked with local agencies appear to be more accessible to welfare recipients, and therefore hire more recipients than do others." On the other hand, Mullings[4] and her colleagues, in their study of Harlem in New York City, found that fast food restaurants did not want to hire neighborhood residents as employees allegedly for fear that they would give food away to relatives and friends. These findings highlight the importance of the social capital that comes from participating in local social networks that can refer former welfare recipients to employers who are likely to hire them, but they also point out that low-income workers seeking employment in urban communities face multiple and complex barriers.

Urban-Suburban Differences

Among the factors that account for widely varying outcomes across race and ethnicity with regard to the welfare caseload is geographic location. America's distinct residential segregation patterns demonstrate the confluence of both race and place on job opportunities. For example, following the implementation of welfare reform, caseloads not only underwent an initial decline, but also experienced a fundamental shift from broader statewide dispersion, to an increasing concentration in America's urban areas (Allen, 1999; Allen & Kirby, 2000; Meyers, 2001). Although urban rolls experienced a decline during the era of economic expansion, the rate of decline was far less than that experienced in suburban areas. This is largely due to the fact that urban communities face a variety of complex problems largely foreign to their suburban counterparts. Cities are home to vast areas of concentrated poverty, failing public school systems, poor job information networks, and scarce employment opportunities. As more and more employers continue to choose suburban locations over urban ones, opportunities for employment will remain substantially reduced for inner-city residents.

The physical disconnect from jobs that inner-city residents face is even more problematic when one considers that most welfare recipients do not have access to private vehicles and, thus, are dependent on public transportation that largely fails to provide access to suburban job opportunities. For example, although Cleveland is home to 4 out of 5 of the state's welfare recipients, 80 percent of Ohio's entry-level job growth occurred in the state's suburban communities. Only a quarter to a third of those jobs were accessible within an hour, one-way, via public transportation. Likewise, in the District of Columbia, between 1995–2000, the city's surrounding suburban communities (located in Maryland and Virginia) experienced job growth at a rate of 19.2 percent, compared to only 2 percent job growth in the District (Allen & Kirby, 2000; Meyers, 2001).

These examples are not unique. According to a study by the Department of Housing and Urban Development (2000), the rate of suburban job expansion was twice that experienced in urban areas in all sectors except wholesale trade that grew at a rate six times faster. Additionally the job growth cities did in fact experience, was largely relegated to opportunities requiring high levels of educational attainment, therefore largely out-of-reach to welfare recipients (U.S. Department of Transportation, 1998).

Given that cities are typically dominated by people of color and suburban communities are most commonly home to non-Hispanic Whites, the significant declines among White welfare recipients following the implementation of welfare reform seems to at least in part be due to the greater likelihood of non-Hispanic Whites to live in areas that experienced the greatest levels of job growth. The Brookings Institution's Center on Urban and Metropolitan Policy reports that since the passage of welfare reform, Black and Hispanic urban welfare recipients left the rolls at roughly the same rates as their White urban counterparts. Such a finding indicates that place and race are intricately linked.

Two recent reviews provide strong evidence of this relationship. Bernstein and Hartmann (2000) conclude: "While there has been disagreement as to whether there is a spatial mismatch of jobs and workers, the majority of evidence does support the conclusions that the disadvantaged workers from central cities do have trouble getting to jobs located in the suburbs." They add that this central city disadvantage is a significant factor contributing to racial disparities in accessing jobs. Considering that job growth is greater in suburbs than in urban areas, this places urban welfare recipients at a particular disadvantage.

But to what extent are place effects themselves, race neutral? The latest National Housing Discrimination Study (Turner, et al., 2002) finds that housing discrimination persists in both sales and rental markets in large metropolitan areas nationwide, thus constricting opportunities for persons of color to have broad choices when making housing decisions. Not only do limitations in housing choice affect job opportunities, we cannot rule out the possibility that the racial composition of an area also influences business location decisions, particularly within the low-skilled employment sector.

The Rural Context

Aside from the contrasting opportunities available to urban and suburban welfare users, recipients residing in rural areas face an entirely different set of challenges. In general, rural areas have higher poverty rates than metropolitan areas, but experience less concentrations of poverty than central cities. Hirschl and Rank (1999) describe this geographical poverty pattern as an "inverse doughnut," where poverty is highest in the middle (central cities), "low in the suburban ring, and high in the outside [rural] ring" (155–156).

Rural areas offer even fewer and lower paying job opportunities than are commonly available in urban markets. Work is more likely to be seasonal, thus leading to greater cycling on and off welfare in rural communities, and rural residents themselves tend to have lower levels of formal education, making acquiring quality jobs in perhaps neighboring metropolitan areas, even more difficult. The rural population is much more dispersed, thus critical supports such as transportation, childcare, access to education, training, and proximity to employment opportunities become even more important in rural areas where public transportation is nonexistent and childcare services are few and far between (Weber & Duncan, 2000).

As to the impact of race on job acquisition success in rural communities, the results are mixed. While some imply that race perhaps has little to do with job acquisition success in rural areas as most of the rural poor are White (Findeis, et al., 2001), nationally rural communities are quite different and those with large concentrations of African American, Latino, and Native American residents have an historical legacy of racial discrimination in employment that influences contemporary patterns of job acquisition (Dill, 2001). One indicator of this is that people of color who live in these areas have higher rates of poverty than their White counterparts (Weber & Duncan, 2000 and Findeis, et al., 2001). However, data show differing levels of job attainment success across communities of color residing in rural areas. For example, McKernan et al. (2000) found that while African American mothers in both rural and urban locations increased job participation rates following welfare reform, Latinas in rural settings were less successful in job attainment than their counterparts in urban settings. The sparse availability of resources for teaching English-as-a-second-language increased the disadvantage of Latinas in rural areas. Without having access to those supports that could help rural-based Latinas become fluent in English, their job prospects were severely limited. Among the Native American population, welfare reform has led to a significant out-migration of Native Americans from reservations, thus in some ways, adding to the destabilization of these communities (Pickering, 2000; Antell, et al., 1999).

Notably not all areas benefited equally from the economic growth of the 1990s (Whitener, Duncan, & Weber, 2002). Rural areas in Appalachia, the Mississippi Delta, and the Rio Grande Valley experienced persistently high levels of poverty and unemployment throughout that period. Welfare recipients in these areas may now be more likely to reach their time limits. Rural residents may need greater flexibility on time limits and work requirements, and increased efforts to create additional job opportunities in persistently poor rural areas could ease the welfare-to-work transition of rural welfare recipients.

It is generally acknowledged that rural workers may face greater barriers to employment than urban workers (Lewin Group, 2001). However, the only significant difference that distinguishes welfare reform in rural areas from urban areas is leavers in rural areas find work and increase their earnings at lower rates than leavers in urban areas (Whitener, Duncan, & Weber, 2002). Special problems associated with rural areas, including less access to transportation, lower levels of available supportive services, fewer jobs, and other factors endemic to rural areas are associated with these differences.

The persistence of discrimination in a variety of forms in current labor markets suggests that welfare reform will likely continue to have disparate race and ethnic outcomes, with regard to employment. Were it not for access to a small number of informal hiring networks in urban communities, Blacks would lag even further behind Whites in accessing jobs when leaving welfare (Holzer & Stoll, 2002). This is a priority issue that must be addressed directly. The success of welfare reform in the future will increasingly depend upon ensuring people of color access to jobs at rates comparable to Whites, helping recipients of color negotiate labor markets that have systematically favored Whites, and ensuring both Whites and non-Whites access to better paying jobs than the ones they tend to get now.

A Note on Health as a Barrier to Work

It is beyond the scope of this chapter to provide a full discussion of the impact of racial and gender disparities and health. Disparities in access to health services and the high rates of debilitating conditions among low-income Black, Latino, and Native American populations have been well documented. An intersectional lens, however, requires that we pay special attention to the ways that race, gender, poverty, and health intersect in the lives of TANF recipients to affect their ability either to leave the rolls or to stay on the path toward achieving self-sufficiency.

Three important findings with regard to women who are or have been on welfare and make up the TANF population are:[5]

- They are more likely than nonrecipients to have health problems and have higher rates of physical and mental health problems. Between one-quarter to one-third of TANF participants have reported that health problems prevented them from working.
- They are more likely than nonrecipients to have children with chronic illnesses or disabilities between 10 to 41 percent of women with welfare have been found to have children who are chronically ill or disabled.
- They experience higher rates of domestic violence.

Through its work requirements, TANF may indirectly influence the health of women and children when family health is compromised due to the difficulties of meeting the demands of managing both work and family health problems.

Women with sick children face multiple barriers due the sporadic needs of children and the high costs and scarcity of care for chronically ill and disabled children. Additionally low-wage jobs frequently lack health insurance and other fringe benefits such as sick leave and vacation days. When these factors are coupled with the higher concentrations of illness among populations of color, it becomes apparent how health problems become a major factor contributing to higher rates of women of color remaining on TANF.

Education and Training: The Key to Quality Jobs

As the national economy has deteriorated and caseload trends have begun to reverse, the economic vulnerability of welfare leavers becomes more apparent. Nearly two-thirds of welfare leavers nationwide were unable to remain consistently employed during their first year after leaving welfare, and in some parts of the country, between 25 and 40 percent did not work at all (Moffit, 2001). Yet, in tough economic times, education can buffer the chance of job loss, such that those with the least education are disproportionately harmed (Deprez & Butler, 2001; Gruber, 1998). In the context of a weak economy, higher education provides a particularly crucial opportunity for welfare recipients to truly leave poverty behind. While a narrow focus on job acquisition may have been possible in the midst of an economic boom, research has now decisively established that even in the best of economic times, the acquisition of any job is simply not equivalent to the acquisition of a good job (Boushey, 2002). The best pathways to long-term economic security, particularly for disadvantaged women, can be found through the acquisition of postsecondary education and effective occupational skills training, including training for nontraditional work.

There is perhaps no greater predictor of long-term employment tenure than initial job quality (as measured by high wages and access to health insurance). Women who initially acquired high-wage jobs were more than twice as likely to remain employed after two years than women gaining employment in low-wage settings (73.4 vs. 35.5 percent). Similarly over three-quarters (78 percent) of single women who had access to employer-provided health insurance remained employed after two years compared with only 40 percent of single women whose job lacked this benefit (Boushey, 2002). Starting out in the right job is crucial to the long-term stability, security, and success of women.

In the current economic downturn, many welfare leavers may have been forced back onto the welfare rolls. Recent caseload data indicates that in the past year, three-fourths of states experienced caseload increases (Richer, Rahmmanou, & Greenberg, 2003). Finding an initial "good" job then, is critical, not only to increasing one's likelihood of staying employed, but also for initiating a cycle of success that includes greater wage growth potential and more opportunities for career advancement. Stability and progress on the job is particularly important in the context of welfare policy that places lifetime limits on cash assistance.

In the context of the current welfare reform system, with its focus on "rapid attachment" to low-skilled jobs, much of the education and training that has been made available to TANF recipients does not result in access to quality jobs. According to Marie Cohen (1998), the education and training programs for welfare recipients have not always evaluated well, especially in comparison to welfare-to-work programs that emphasize immediate job placement. Cohen suggests two reasons for this: education and training for adults is not effectively geared to the labor market; and the impact on earnings of the education and training programs that do exist is minimal because the programs do not overcome welfare recipients' early educational deficits. In contrast, community college education, when subsidized, has been found to lead to both increased employment and higher wage rates among welfare recipients (Cohen, 1998). One study found that with as little as one semester of full-time postsecondary education, recipients with basic skills could improve their yearly earnings by approximately $10,000 (Carnevale & Desrochers, 1999).

Racial Barriers

Differential treatment of welfare recipients across race and ethnicity in terms of access to education and training severely impacts opportunities for welfare-transitioning success. Several state-level studies have found, for example, that White welfare recipients are more likely to be referred to educational programs, given transportation assistance and in various other ways, treated more favorably by employers and caseworkers alike (Gooden, 1998, 1999; Pittz & Delgado, 2002). Women of color are more likely to be subjected to sexually invasive questioning by welfare caseworkers; and, for those whose first language is not English, the likelihood of suffering a severe impediment to receiving assistance increases dramatically, despite federal protections to the contrary (Gorden, 2001). According to one multicity survey, 53 percent of Native American women and 47 percent of African American women were sent to "Dress for Success" classes in lieu of more formalized education and training opportunities, in comparison to only 26 percent of White women (Pittz & Delgado, 2002).

Data from these small studies has been confirmed in the Urban League's Institute for Opportunity and Equality study utilizing two major nationally representative datasets to investigate issues of discrimination in the administration of welfare reform. Their research uncovered startling findings regarding the differential treatment given welfare recipients across race and ethnicity:

- White recipients were more likely than their Black counterparts to receive subsidized childcare, transportation assistance, and assistance to pursue postsecondary education.

- The biggest gap in assistance was found in the area of transportation where only 5.4 percent of Blacks received assistance as compared to 12.4 percent of Whites.[6]
- Over two-thirds (62 percent) of Black recipients and nearly three-fourths (72 percent) of Hispanic recipients were forced to work at unpaid jobs in order to receive their TANF benefits, as compared to less than half of non-Hispanic White recipients (46 percent).
- Among recipients that were able to make that transition from welfare to paid employment, non-Hispanic Whites were most likely to receive critical supports such as healthcare, housing, and transportation assistance.

While this study finds that most recipients (roughly 60 percent) do not receive *any* work supports whatsoever, assistance for Hispanic and Black recipients is particularly rare as roughly 71 percent of each group failed to receive work supports all together (Rockeymoore & Cox, 2002).

Gender Barriers

While making the transition from welfare to work is universally important despite the physical location of the welfare recipient, making the transition to a quality job can make all the difference in terms of access to livable wages and access to benefits, such as sick leave, healthcare coverage, employer-provided pensions, and so on. While many assume that successful workforce integration has taken place among those able to make the transition from welfare to work, a deeper analysis uncovers a more realistic view of the lives of those impacted by welfare reform. While it is true that more women are working after the passage of welfare reform, few have acquired the types of jobs that lead to successful long-term workforce integration. Analyzing data from the U.S. Census Bureau's Survey of Income and Program Participation (SIPP), Peterson, Song, and Jones-DeWeever (2002) conclude that over three-quarters (78 percent) of employed low-income single parents are concentrated in four typically low-wage occupations with single mothers further concentrated into low-wage traditionally female work (characterized by low wages, instability, and limited access to benefits). Increased work participation rates have not translated into increased access to health insurance, a key barometer of job quality. In fact, welfare recipients actually experienced a decline in access to employment-based health insurance following the implementation of TANF, from 21 to 14 percent (Peterson, Song, & Jones-DeWeever, 2002). Thus findings demonstrate that although many women were successful in gaining employment, the acquisition of quality jobs remained elusive.

An important factor in accessing education and training involves the issue of gender and occupational segregation in the workplace. Welfare recipients are largely single mothers with children. Many have limited work experience and their primary identity is as a mother. Welfare reform is requiring these women to go to work, many for the first time. They need to earn enough money so they can support their families as breadwinners even as they continue in their roles as homemakers, and cover the additional costs of having their children cared for when they are at work. Yet most of the studies on women leaving welfare show they are hired in primarily "women's jobs," earning approximately only $7.50/hour (Loprest, 1999). Even with income supplements from the Earned Income Tax Credit (EITC) these low wages are not enough to support a family. The large gender wage gap, one of the consequences of job segregation, has an enormous impact on poverty rates. Poverty rates for single mothers would fall by half if they received wages equal to that of men with similar qualifications (Hartmann, Aleen, & Owens, 1999).

Women who obtain employment in primarily male occupations have enhanced their earnings and job quality. Women in these nontraditional fields typically earn salaries 20 to 30 percent above those received by women in traditionally female occupations. Along with increased earnings, nontraditional occupations generally have established career ladders in place that help promote stability and continual career growth. These jobs typically offer greater access to union membership, leading to a wide variety of benefits including health insurance, sick leave, and retirement plans as well as union protection from arbitrary dismissal. Taken together, these benefits open up a world of opportunity, stability, and earnings growth potential that is simply not widely accessible in traditional woman's work (Negrey, et al., 2000).

The research on occupational segregation has generally concluded that jobs typically performed by women carry several distinct, largely disadvantageous characteristics, such as low wage rates, high levels of instability, and restricted access to employee benefits and opportunities for career growth. Clearly reducing gender segregation in employment should be a key component of any strategy aimed at improving the earning potential of women, and particularly single mothers who have but one income to support herself and her family.

Special Challenges Faced by Black and Latino Males

Race and gender intersect to create special circumstances not only for women of color but also for men of color. During the 1990s, a booming economy, expansions to the Earned Income Tax Credit, and the strong workfirst emphasis associated with welfare reform increased significantly the employment rate of low-income women, especially less educated Black females whose employment rates eventually outpaced that of Latinas. In contrast, Black male employment rates continued their long-term downward spiral, while similarly economically situated Latinos increased their level of job participation. Over the past twenty years, the employment rate of less-educated, young Black men consistently lagged some 10 to 25 percentage points below that of similarly situated White and Hispanic males (Offner & Holzer, 2002). In fact, as of 2000, this cohort of Black men managed an employment rate of only 52 percent. This contrasts sharply with the experiences of less-educated, young Hispanic men, who were able to reach parity with their White counterparts over this period to attain roughly 80 percent employment rates.[7]

While Latinos have fared significantly better in obtaining employment, both Latinos and Black men are much more likely to experience bouts of unemployment during the year than their White counterparts. For example, young male Latinos without a high school diploma face a 38 percent chance of unemployment and young Black men with similar characteristics experience a nearly 99 percent chance of unemployment. These periods of unemployment have a serious impact on earning power as both Black and Latino males tend to have more difficulty becoming reemployed than do their non-Hispanic White counterparts (Stoll, 1998).

Much of the employment problem that Black men face seems to be concentrated in the inner-cities as the employment rates in these areas are some four times lower than that associated with similarly situated Black men who live in suburban areas. Increased law-enforcement activities that disproportionately impact Black men have also contributed to this problem not only due to the substantial number of imprisoned Black men, but also due to the reluctance of employers to hire exoffenders. Blacks in particular are arrested and imprisoned for drug crimes in numbers far out of line with their proportions of the general population, of drug users, and of drug traffickers. Even the bulk of Black men who are not engaged in criminal activity may be the victims of the perceptions of employers who refuse to hire them due to stereotypical notions of Black criminality (Holzer & Stoll, 2001). The effects of this level of incarceration on women and children are staggering. In addition to women having to raise children without assistance from men, law professor Dorothy Roberts (2001) argues that "the prison system supplies children to the child welfare system when it incarcerates their parents [and] . . . the child welfare system supplies young adults to the prison system when it abandons them after languishing in foster care." Efforts to reverse this trend are necessary to not only improve the plight of Black men, but by extension, to potentially improve the overall well-being of Black families.

Variations in State Policies

It is not just policy implementation that is colored by race, so is policy adoption. Just as caseworkers may well allow race to influence their provision of services, state policymakers have allowed race to influence the extent to which they adopt "get-tough" welfare reforms.

A strong statistical relationship between the racial composition of the welfare population and whether a state adopts an aggressive approach to imposing sanctions, time limits, and family cap policies has been observed (Soss, et al., 2001).[8] Of relevance to our discussion of disparities is the tendency of states with relatively large non-White populations to adopt tougher welfare policies that have a disproportionate effect on people of color. Soss et al. note:

> From 1997 through 1999, approximately 540,000 families lost their entire TANF check due to a full-family sanction, and these families tended to fare worse (socially and economically) than families that left for other reasons. Among TANF recipients in 1999, 63.7 percent of Black families were participating under the threat of a full family sanction, while the same was true for only 53.7 percent of White families. If somehow one could have waved a magic wand of racial justice and made the Black percentage (63.7 percent) equal to the White percentage (53.7 percent), the number of African-American families at risk for full-family sanctions in 1999 would have been reduced by about 102,000 families. Not surprisingly, state-level studies from this period indicated that TANF exits due to sanctions (rather than income increases) were higher among Black families than among White families.

Blacks, therefore, are more likely to be sanctioned because they live in states with tougher sanction policies. However, even within a single state with a uniform policy, Blacks are more likely to be sanctioned off welfare (Lower-Basch, 2000; Kalil, Seefeldt, & Wang, 2002). In effect, states are allowing the racial composition of the rolls to affect the extent to which they will get tough with welfare recipients. This disparate application of get-tough welfare policies along racial lines may be an important source of greater economic difficulties for low-income families of color.

Racial and ethnic disparities in the implementation of welfare reform begin with policy adoption and continue through implementation. Thus addressing these disparities requires examining the relationship between policy and practice. The following section addresses current promising practices that demonstrate that these findings can be translated into effective action.

Promising Practices in the Areas of Education, Training, and Access to Quality Jobs

Advocacy groups and grassroots organizations at the state and community level are engaged in developing alternative and creative approaches to eliminating welfare racism and poverty.[9] Skills, abilities, experience, and location in the labor market are factors that intersect with race and gender in ways that result in disparate outcomes for women and people of color, especially women of color. Most programs address these issues of racial and gender disparities indirectly with a focus on human capital and occupational sex segregation. Grassroots advocacy groups, however, have sought to address these racial and gender disparities directly by reframing antipoverty and welfare rights struggles in terms of global human rights. This section looks at some of these practices as they relate to the issues of education and training, access to quality employment and meeting basic human needs.

Access to Education and Training

Although national studies have found that education and training programs show no advantage over workfirst programs, it is important to keep in mind two factors that greatly impact education and training success. First, not all education and training efforts are quality programs. Efforts that focus on soft skills, such as job etiquette, wardrobe, and so on, may be classified as "training," but in practice, do very little in terms of adequately preparing individuals with the skills that they need to obtain quality jobs. Second, due to an intergenerational failure of our nation to provide quality education for all of its children, many welfare recipients lack the basic skills to be prepared for meaningful employment. In fact, 76 percent of TANF recipients score in the lowest two literacy levels, with 35 percent bottoming out at the lowest level (Levinson, 1999). Allowing time for remediation is critical, so that those individuals who have been failed once by public education, are not failed twice by policies that push them into low-wage work without addressing the skill inadequacies that will continue to be a barrier to their long-term earning potential.

Occupational Skills Training

Overall, research on programs across the nation have found that the best welfare-to-work strategies are those that emphasize a mixed strategy, providing education and training opportunities for those who need it, and initial job search assistance for those who come to welfare with an adequate skills base to obtain quality employment (Bloom & Micalopoulos, 2001).

Portland's Job Opportunities and Basic Skills (JOBS) program and Minnesota's Family Initiative Program (MFIP) are examples of programs that have been successful in moving individuals from welfare into quality jobs with an emphasis on basic education and training. Participants in Portland's Job Opportunities and Basic Skills (JOBS) program earned on average, $5,000 more over five years, and were more consistently employed as they experienced a 21 percent increase in employment length than those who did not have access to the program (Hamilton, 2002).

Similarly Minnesota's Family Initiative Program (MFIP) was successful in providing access to quality education and training to participants, helping individuals obtain employment, and supporting those employment efforts by providing earned income disregards. These supports allowed participants to keep both their paychecks and some of the welfare assistance so that they could ultimately earn above poverty-level wages, and provided direct childcare subsidies to childcare providers, so that participants never had to be burdened by the high out-of-pocket expenses associated with childcare. As a result, MFIP participants increased their employment by 35 percent, and their earnings by 23 percent. They were also more likely to obtain employment in stable, full-time jobs and were 13 percent more likely to have continuous healthcare coverage over three years than were their nonparticipant counterparts (Auspos, Miller, & Hunter, 2000).

Training that focuses on occupational skills represents a particularly encouraging avenue to economic self-sufficiency for low-income women. Occupational skills or "sectoral" training is a distinct form of job training that emphasizes technical skills and is matched to specific labor needs in local markets. It often involves working with employers to encourage them to make the most productive use of better skilled workers. This approach to job training is particularly effective in significantly increasing earnings and access to benefits for low-income adults (Boushey, 2002; Rademacher, 2002; Okagaki, Palmer, & Mayer, 1998; Kellner, 2001; Elliot et al. 2001). A national study of several sectoral training programs,[10] found that even two years after completion, over two-thirds (68 percent) of participants reported working year-round and over four-fifths (82 percent) believed that their participation in training significantly improved their career prospects (Conway & Zandniapour, 2002).

Even more striking is the impact skills training had on earning power and access to health insurance. Prior to training, participants averaged earnings of only $4,669 per year. One year following training, average earnings increased to $12,350 and after the second year rose to $19,601, a 320 percent increase in earnings over entry levels. Access to employer-provided health insurance also significantly improved as 73 percent reported health insurance acquisition two-years following training completion, while only 15 percent enjoyed this benefit prior to program participation (Conway & Zandniapour, 2002).

Training Women for Nontraditional Jobs

Effective occupational skills training opens the door to earnings growth potential, increased job stability, and improved access to benefits. Perhaps not so coincidentally, many of the occupations that are emphasized through these training programs are in fields that are nontraditional for women. If replicated on a large scale, these programs could significantly reduce occupational segregation and thereby increase women's access to high-wage, good quality employment.

Nontraditional Employment for Women (NEW) is a nonprofit organization that trains women in New York City for nontraditional jobs in skilled blue-collar trades. NEW provides occupational skills and fitness training as well as job placement services for participants in its program. Women are trained in basic carpentry, electricity, and plumbing; job safety; trades math; health and physical fitness; blueprint reading; interview strategies; employment rights and responsibilities; and life skills. According to NEW's Web site, the organization has helped thousands of unemployed and underemployed women in New York City area achieve economic self-sufficiency through employment in skilled blue-collar trades.[11]

Accessing Higher Education

Along with expanding access to quality basic education and training programs for those who need that extra assistance, there is perhaps no better antipoverty program than accessing the ivory towers of higher education. Programs in Maine and California are examples of programs that provide both job training and access to postsecondary education.

Maine's Parents as Scholars (PAS) program has been widely regarded as a national model of a welfare program that effectively provides access to higher education. Funded through Maine's Maintenance of Effort dollars, this program allows up to 2,000 TANF-eligible Maine residents to enroll in two- or four-year undergraduate degree programs and receive the amount of cash assistance that they would have received under TANF. Furthermore PAS students receive critical support services such as childcare, transportation reimbursement, car repair assistance, eye and dental care, and books and supplies. After twenty-four months toward degree completion, participants must engage in work for at least twenty hours per week, in addition to their coursework, and students must make "satisfactory academic progress" to remain eligible for the program (Center for Women Policy Studies, 2002).

Preliminary examinations of this program have found encouraging results. PAS participants out-perform the typical college student, with a median grade point average of 3.4. Furthermore PAS graduates reported significantly increased earnings over their pre-PAS earnings levels ($11.71 per hour vs. $8.00 per hour). Finally over four-fifths of PAS graduates (82 percent) acquired jobs that provided access to critical benefits, including employer-sponsored health insurance, paid sick and vacation leave, life insurance, disability insurance, and compensatory time off (Smith, et al., 2002).

California's CalWORKs program has opened the doors of postsecondary education to thousands of the state's residents. CalWORKS, California's state-level TANF program, allows welfare recipients to work toward an Associate's degree within the California Community College system if the degree is deemed likely to lead to unsubsidized employment and if the student makes satisfactory academic progress. CalWORKS students must participate in thirty-two hours of educational activities per week, or engage in work activities and education activities totaling thirty-two hours (Mathur, et al., 2002).

Preliminary examinations of the CalWORKS program have found that participants significantly increase their earnings with each additional year of postsecondary education. Students who completed their Associate's degree experienced an 85 percent median annual earnings increase after only one year following school completion. Furthermore, upon graduation, CalWORKS graduates were able to acquire steady employment, a significant first step toward long-term economic self-sufficiency (Mathur, et al., 2002).

Recognizing the importance of higher education, several activist groups have organized to support efforts of recipients to obtain postsecondary degrees, and to fight TANF policies that have reduced access to higher education. The Welfare Rights Initiative, a student organization at Hunter College, composed mostly of welfare recipients is such a group. Responding to the fact that enrollment for welfare recipients at CUNY had dropped from 27,000 in 1995 to 5,000 today, these advocates have challenged limited educational opportunities and proposed state legislation to give welfare recipients broader access to education. Recently similar legislation to expand educational and training opportunities for welfare recipients was passed by the New York City Council. Although the mayor vetoed the legislation, the city council overrode his veto. The mayor is now suing (Arenson, 2003).

LIFETIME, Low-Income Families' Empowerment through Education, is another advocacy group composed of students on welfare and is headquartered in Oakland, CA. LIFETIME's goal is to aid low-income parents to enroll in, continue, and successfully complete higher education and training in order to obtain long-term economic self-sufficiency. The program educates student parents on rights to education under the California welfare system, and works with students to organize for public policies that provide education and training for poor families.[12]

Reframing Welfare Reform and Poverty as a Human Rights Issue

In an effort to directly address the issues of the racial and gender disparities in welfare reform specifically and in the treatment of poverty in the United States generally, social advocacy groups are reframing the antipoverty and welfare reform debate as a human rights issue.

The Kensington Welfare Rights Union (KWRU) has been at the forefront in fighting for the economic human rights of the poor. KWRU is a Philadelphia-based, multiracial organization of, by, and for poor and homeless people.[13] In 1997, KWRU spearheaded a national campaign to document violations of human rights in the United States. KWRU has presented testimonies of violations of human rights collected from poor people across the United States and presented them to the United Nations, requesting an investigation of U.S. welfare policy. "KWRU has also filed a petition against the U.S. government with the Inter-American Commission on Human Rights, detailing human rights violations flowing from PRWORA. Their work has revealed the disproportionately adverse effects of PRWORA on people of color and immigrants" (Neubeck, 2001).

The Women of Color Resource Center (WCRC) also reframes the welfare rights struggles into a human rights issue, and focuses on the disproportionate effect of welfare reform on people of color.[14] The WCRC, headquartered in the San Francisco Bay Area, promotes the political, economic, social, and cultural well being of women and girls of color in the United States. WCRC has also worked to define women's rights as human rights and was involved in writing the Beijing Platform for Action that calls for aid to impoverished women around the world. Combining those two sets of concerns, Linda Burnham, director of WCRC casts PRWORA's elimination of the social safety net for women and children as a human rights issue, arguing that it violates both the Beijing Platform for Action and the U.N. Convention on the Elimination of All Forms of Discrimination against Women.

The programs described above seek to provide stepping-stones to genuine economic self-sufficiency for poor women in two key areas: employment related education and training and access to higher education. These programs were selected because they provide ways to overcome prevailing racial, ethnic, and gender disparities produced by PRWORA. Framing these disparities and their consequences in relation to human rights underscores how imperative it is to design good policies. Effective as these individual programs are, changes in national and state policies are also required to ensure broader implementation of such initiatives.

Policy Recommendations

Up to the present, states have spent most of their efforts on designing programs aimed at transitioning individuals from welfare to work and it is those efforts that are the focus of this brief. In order to live up to the goal of creating healthy, self-sufficient families, a number of specific policy recommendations are put forth. These recommendations are seen as a baseline for expanding skills and job preparedness, along with job availability, particularly in disadvantaged geographic spaces such as central cities and rural localities. Additionally these recommendations seek to increase oversight to both minimize the negative impact of discriminatory actions and ensure the broad and fair distribution of these opportunities across race and gender lines.

Expand access to education and quality skills training. In order to move people from welfare to good jobs, welfare recipients need to be equipped with the necessary skills and credentials that will allow them to obtain quality employment.

A good job offers full-time employment with health benefits, vacation and sick leave at a pay level that is sufficient to bring a household's income sufficiently above the poverty line. Thus expanding access to education and training, particularly higher education and skills training matched to local employment needs, is critical to the long-term success of today's low-income and struggling women and families.

Expand women's access to high quality nontraditional jobs. Despite research that demonstrates that women who move into nontraditional jobs enhance their earnings, job stability, and earnings growth potential, not enough is being done to prepare and support women in obtaining such employment. Local and national organizations need to be enlisted in the efforts to develop effective occupational skills training and placement programs for women in nontraditional jobs. Additionally all jobs programs must work to eliminate both gender and racial segregation in the workplace, ensuring that people of color have access to jobs at rates comparable to those of Whites.

Protect and expand the Earned Income Tax Credit. No current antipoverty program lifts more people out of the ranks of the working poor than the Earned Income Tax Credit (EITC). In 1999, over 4.7 million people, including 2.5 million children, escaped poverty due to EITC (Berube, 2003). Unfortunately the Bush administration is currently seeking to tighten EITC eligibility standards, which threatens the ability of countless poor families to utilize this vital antipoverty weapon in the future. Not only should this attempt be thwarted, but the program should in fact, be expanded, so as to benefit more working families, including welfare leavers and other members of the working poor so that they may finally have a real chance to not only work, but to ultimately, work their way out of poverty.

Provide broad and fair access to critical work supports. Working one's way out of welfare is a challenging endeavor. But this struggle is made even more challenging when one does not have access to the critical supports that could mean the difference between success and failure. In order to facilitate the transition from welfare to work, recipients need broad and fair access to quality childcare so they can go to work confident in the safety and security of their children; transportation assistance, particularly in areas that have experienced limited job growth; healthcare, especially as few low-wage jobs include employer-provided health insurance; and access to affordable housing, which, in urban areas, is pivotal to making ends meet (Edin & Lein, 1997). Unless these vital supports are provided equally to recipients without regard for race or ethnicity, a successful long-term transition to employment may not be realistically attainable and racial disparities will continue unabated.

Strengthen employment prospects in urban and rural areas. As the welfare caseload have shifted to an urban concentration, and as many rural recipients continue to find it difficult to make a transition to long-term quality jobs, welfare policy should also be mindful of not only the actions of individuals, but the impact of "place" on the opportunities of individuals to become economically self-sufficient. Access to education and training should be greatly expanded, particularly in rural areas, where such opportunities are sparse. Also important is the need to address the special employment needs of exoffenders, so that true opportunities exist for those attempting to make a way for themselves and their families without resorting to crime. Finally stopping the clock for recipients who live in geographic areas that have experienced stagnant job growth is critical in that it makes sense to take into consideration the contextual limitations on job opportunities. These issues are key to addressing the needs of those struggling to make the transition from welfare to work, and to responding to some of the specific employment needs of those trapped in geographic spaces that offer limited opportunities for true economic well-being.

Collect and disseminate program data by race and ethnicity. In order to combat the apparent disparate treatment received by welfare recipients across the color lines, it is critical that states collect data on program outcomes by race and ethnicity. This will allow discriminatory behavior to be identified and addressed immediately. In preparing this brief, there were several points where our ability to analyze trends and examine the effects of racial disparities was limited by the lack of readily available data organized by race and ethnicity. Given the documented pattern of disparities in welfare policy and programs the need for these kinds of data to document equitable treatment is imperative.

Support and develop grassroots advocacy groups on welfare reform. Advocacy groups, with agendas generated primarily by women who are themselves welfare recipients are playing an important and dynamic role in securing rights and opportunities for low-income men, women, and children in their local communities. They are also proposing new ways to think about welfare and to address social inequality. Programs that seek to disseminate information about human rights and the concept of full employment represent strategies, which are currently empowering low-income people to develop and push for new solutions to structural inequality in the United States.

Using the UN Universal Declaration of Human Rights (UDHR), they stress the inalienable economic, social, civil, political, and cultural human rights all citizens should be granted. By fighting poverty in an international court, social advocacy groups hope to spur the U.S. government to recognize the economic and social human rights of impoverished people, and provide legislation to remedy the problems. Additionally these groups are also seeking to change the way the U.S. public thinks and speaks about welfare. By drawing attention to economic and social human rights violations experienced by poor people, advocacy groups are highlighting the disproportionate impact of welfare reform on communities of color.

A Note on the Promotion of Marriage

One much-discussed current policy initiative that we feel is misguided, is the promotion of marriage. We do not discuss that policy at length in this chapter because it is our contention that while the goal of seeking to promote marriage sounds laudable, using limited TANF funding for programs that have no proven poverty reduction impacts is unwise, particularly within the current economic downturn. Such a policy focus ignores research that suggests that only 1 in 10 disadvantaged women will marry spouses with enough education or earnings to adequately provide for a family (Lichter, Graefe, & Brown, 2001). Even if married, and both husband and wife are working, many low-income families' mothers would still be poor or near poor (Single-Rushton & McClanahan, 2001). Finally this policy fails to address international data, which show that households headed by single women are increasing throughout the world, among all ethnic and class groups, and in both developed and underdeveloped countries (Goldberg & Kremen, 1990). The problem that bears policy consideration here is not that of nonmarriage, but poverty—poverty that is devastating to the married and nonmarried alike. A much better policy goal would be not merely the creation of healthy marriages but rather, the creation of economic stability and family support for all families, be they married, single, divorced, or cohabiting.

Conclusion

This chapter has applied an intersectional method to interpret racial, ethnic, and gender disparities in access to jobs, education, and training under welfare reform. In particular, our analysis has centered on the experiences of people of color and examined the interconnections between the various kinds of inequality faced by welfare recipients so that previously unexplored avenues of social change can be identified in the pursuit of justice. Our findings illuminate some important relationships between race/ethnicity, gender, poverty, and TANF that identify continuing and worsening patterns of inequality unless these disparities are addressed. In particular, welfare programs need to broaden their scope and aim to alleviate systemic poverty as the means to reduce the numbers of people receiving welfare benefits.

The intersectional interpretive lens used reveals that even as welfare rolls have declined, there remain proportionately more women of color on the rolls with little chance of accessing high quality jobs. This is particularly alarming as the economy worsens and the total number of people accessing TANF begins to increase.

Finally, addressing these problems takes concerted effort and an understanding of their true causes. This brief illuminates these causes in the hopes of providing sufficient documentation to fuel the resistance efforts of communities of color, foundations, and educational institutions to extend their involvement in ameliorating these disparities. We believe that framing these efforts as a struggle for human rights is an important strategy for changing the way we think about and discuss these issues and begin, collaboratively, to work toward their eradication.

NOTES

1. The principal authors for this chapter are Avis Jones-DeWeever, PhD, Study Director at the Institute for Women's Policy Research; Bonnie Thornton Dill, founding director of CRGE and professor and chair of Women's Studies at the University of Maryland; and Sanford F. Schram, Ph.D., professor of Social Work and Social Research at Bryn Mawr College. They and their contributors, Ruth E. Zambrana, Ph.D., Tallese Johnson, Ph.D., Amy McLaughlin, Ph.D., and Ryan Shanahan would like to thank Leith Mullings, Ph.D., Presidential Professor of Anthropology at the Graduate Center of the City University of New York for her thoughtful review and comments.

2. Data on recipients are from U.S. Department of Health and Human Services, Administration on Children. Retrieved April 7, 2008, from http://www.acf.hhs.gov/programs/ofa/caseload.

3. Although the receipt of cash assistance in the form of TANF is the factor that we focus on in this report, it is also important to note that when one takes into account other forms of assistance designed specifically for low income people, 68 percent of the poor have at least one family member who received some form of government assistance, from free and reduced school lunches to Medicaid, food stamps, and subsidized public housing.

4. Leith Mullings, Presidential Professor of Anthropology, The Graduate Center, personal communication.

5. The Henry J. Kaiser Family Foundation in "Welfare, Women and Health: The Role of Temporary Assistance for Needy Families," (April 2003) presented findings from seven key studies on women's health and welfare. See table 1 in the report.

6. This disparity is particularly critical given the overall greater likelihood of Blacks to be residentially segregated from areas experiencing the greatest job growth.

7. One explanation for this disparity between Black and Hispanic male labor participation rates points out that the category "Hispanic" includes immigrant workers and argues that immigrant workers may be preferred because Black workers are unwilling to accept low-wage work on the same terms as those extended to their parents and grandparents and expect the wages and benefits of native workers.

8. The family cap denies aid for any child born to a family already receiving welfare—thereby "capping" the family benefit at its current level.

9. Welfare racism refers to the organization of racialized public assistance, policymaking, and administrative practices. See K. Neubeck. (2002). Attacking Welfare Racism/Honoring Poor People's Human Rights. In R. Albelda & A. Withorn (Eds.), *Lost Ground: Welfare Reform, Poverty and Beyond.* Cambridge, MA: South End Press.

10. Asian Neighborhood Design in San Francisco; Garment Industry Development Corporation in New York City; Focus: HOPE in Detroit; Jane Addams Resource Corporation in Chicago; Paraprofessional Healthcare Institute in Bronx; and Project Quest in San Antonio.

11. NEW's Web site can be found at: www.new-nyc.org.

12. For more information about LIFETIME, see their Web site: www.geds-to-phds.org.

13. For more information about the Kensington Welfare Rights Union, see www.kwru.org.

14. For more information about the Women of Color Resource Center, see www. coloredgirls.org.

References

Abramovitz, M. (2000). *Under Attack: Fighting Back: Women and Welfare in the United States.* New York: Monthly Review Press.

Allen, K. (1999). *The State of Welfare Caseloads in America's Cities.* Washington, DC: The Brookings Institution Center on Urban & Metropolitan Policy.

Allen, K., & Kirby, M. (2000, July). *Unfinished Business: Why Cities Matter to Welfare Reform.* Washington, DC: The Brookings Institution Center on Urban and Metropolitan Policy.

Antell, J., Blevins, A., Jenson, K., & Massey, G. (1999). *Residential and Household Poverty of American Indians on the Wind River Indian Reservation.* Paper presented at the ASPE/ Census Bureau Conference sponsored by the Joint Center for Poverty Research. Retrieved from http://www.jcpr.org/wpfiles/antell_blevins_jensen_massey.PDF.

Arenson, K. W. (2003, June 10). From Welfare to (Course) Work: Students on Benefits Help Write Their Own Rights. *New York Times*, p. B1.

Auspos, P., Miller, C., & Hunter, J. A. (2000). *Final Report on the Implementation and Impacts of the Minnesota Family Investment Program in Ramsey County.* New York: Manpower Demonstration Research Corporation.

Bernstein, J., & Hartmann, H. (2000). Defining and Characterizing the Low-Wage Labor Market. In K. Kaye & D. Smith Nightingale (Eds.), *The Low-Wage Labor Market: Challenges and Opportunities for Economic Self-Sufficiency.* Washington, DC: U.S. Department of Health and Human Services, Office of the Secretary Assistant Secretary for Planning and Evaluation. Retrieved from http://www.urban.org/welfare/lowwage_labor_FR.pdf.

Berube, A. (2003). *Rewarding Work through the Tax Code: The Power and Potential of the Earned Income Tax Credit in 27 Cities and Rural Areas.* Washington, DC: The Brookings Institution Center on Urban and Metropolitan Policy.

Bloom, D., & Michalopoulos, C. (2001). *How Welfare and Work Policies Affect Employment and Income: A Synthesis of Research.* New York: Manpower Demonstration Research Corporation.

Boushey, H. (2002). *Staying Employed after Welfare: Work Supports and Job Quality Vital to Employment Tenure and Wage Growth.* Washington, DC: Economic Policy Institute.

Burnham, L. (2002a). Working Reform, Family Hardship, and Women of Color. In R. Albelda & A. Withorn (Eds.), *Lost Ground: Welfare Reform, Poverty and Beyond.* Cambridge, MA: South End Press.

Burnham, L. (2002b). Working Paper Series, No 2. *Racism in U.S. Welfare Policy: A Human Rights Issue.* Oakland, CA: Women of Color Resource Center.

Carnevale, A. P., & Desrochers, D.M. (1999). *Getting Down to Business: Matching Welfare Recipients' Skills to Jobs That Train.* Princeton, NJ: Educational Testing Service.

Center for Women Policy Studies. (2002). From Poverty to Self-sufficiency: The Role of Postsecondary Education in Welfare Reform. Washington, DC.

Cohen, M. (1998). *Education and Training under Welfare Reform.* Washington, DC: Welfare. Welfare Information Network. Retrieved from http://www.financeprojectinfo.org/ Publications/edissue.htm.

Conway, M., & Zandniapour, L. (2002). *Industry-Based Employment Programs: Implications for Welfare Reauthorization and Key Survey Findings.* Washington, DC: The Aspen Institute.

Deprez, L., & Butler, S. (2001, Fall). *Higher Education: A Route Out of Poverty for Women: On Campus with Women.* Washington, DC: Association of American Colleges and Universities.

Dill, B. T. (2001). Poverty in the Rural U.S.: Implications for Children, Families and Communities. In J. Blau (Ed.), *Blackwell Companion to Sociology.* Malden, MA: Blackwell Publishers.

Diller, M. (2000). The Revolution in Welfare Administration: Rules, Discretion, and Entrepreneurial Government. *New York University Law Review, 75*(5), 1121–1220.

Dillon, S. (2003, April 30). Report Finds Number of Black Children in Deep Poverty Rising. *New York Times,* p. A18.

Duncan, G. J., Harris, K. M., & Boisjoly, J. (2000). Time Limits and Welfare Reform: New Estimates of the Number and Characteristics of Affected Families. *Social Service Review, 74,* 55–75.

Edin, K., & Lein, L. (1997). *Making Ends Meet: How Single Mothers Survive Welfare and Low-Wage Work.* New York: Russell Sage Foundation.

Elliott, M., Roder, A., King, E., & Stillman, J. (2001, September). *Gearing Up: An Interim Report on the Sectoral Employment Initiative.* New York: Public/Private Ventures.

Findeis, J. L., Henry, M., Hirschl, T. A., Lewis, W., Ortega-Sanchez, I., Peine, E., & Zimmerman, J. N. (2001, February 21). *Welfare Reform in Rural America: A Review of Current Research.* Columbia, MO: Rural Policy Research Institute. Retrieved from http://www.rupri.org/pubs/archive/reports/P2001-5/index.html.

Finegold, K., & Staveteig, S. (2002). Race, Ethnicity, and Welfare Reform. In A. Weil & K. Finegold (Eds.), *Welfare Reform: The Next Act.* Washington, DC: Urban Institute Press.

Goldberg, G. S., & Kremen E. (1990). *The Feminization of Poverty: Only in America?* New York: Greenwood Press.

Goode, J., & Maskovsky J. (2001). *The New Poverty Studies. The Ethnography of Power, Politics and Impoverished People in the US.* New York, NY: New York.

Gooden, S. (1998). All Things Not Being Equal: Differences in Caseworker Support toward Black and White Welfare Clients. *Harvard Journal of African American Public Policy, 4,* 23–33.

Gooden, S. (1999). The Hidden Third Party: Welfare Recipients' Experiences with Employers. *Journal of Public Management and Social Policy, 5*(1), 69–83.

Gorden, R. (2001). *Cruel and Usual: How Welfare "Reform" Punishes Poor People.* Oakland, CA: Applied Research Center.

Gruber, A. (1998). Promoting Long-Term Self-Sufficiency for Welfare Recipients; Postsecondary Education and the Welfare Work Requirement. *Northwestern University Law Review, 93,* 247, 280.

Hamilton, G. (2002). *Moving People from Welfare to Work: Lessons from the National Evaluation of Welfare-to-Work Strategies.* Washington, DC: Manpower Demonstration Research Corporation for the U.S. Department of Health and Human Services and the U. S. Department of Education.

Hartmann, H., Aleen, K., & Owens, C. (1999). *Equal Pay for Working Families.* Washington, DC: Institute for Women's Policy Research.

Hirschl, T. A., & Rank, M. R. (1999). *The Likelihood of Poverty Across the American Adult Life Span.* Social Work, *44*(3), 201–216.

Holzer, H., & Stol, M. (2001). *Employers and Welfare Recipients: The Effects of Welfare Reform in the Workplace*. San Francisco: Public Policy Institute of California.

Holzer, H., & Stoll, M. (2002). Employer Demand for Welfare Recipients by Race. Washington, DC: Urban Institute.

Kalil, A., Seefeldt, K. S., & Wang, H. (2002, December). Sanctions and Material Hardship under TANF. *Social Service Review, 76,* 642–662.

Kellner, S. (2001). *Scanning the Field: A Profile of Sector Practitioners Nationwide.* Oakland, CA: National Network of Sector Practitioners.

Levin-Epstein, J. (2003). *Welfare, Women, and Health: The Role of Temporary Assistance for Needy Families, Issue Brief: An Update On Women's Health Policy.* The Henry J. Kaiser Family Foundation. Retrieved from http://www.kff.org/content/2003/3337/Welfare _and_Women_FINAL.pdf.

Levinson, M. (1999). Who's in Charge Here? *Dissent, 46*(4), 21–23.

Lewin Group (M. Farrell, S. Opcin, & M. Fishman, Consultant: D. Stapleton). (2001, April). *How Well Have Rural and Small Metropolitan Labor Markets Absorbed Welfare Recipients?* Washington, DC: Assistant Secretary for Planning and Evaluation U.S. Department of Health and Human Services.

Lichter, D., Graefe, D. R., & Brown, J. B. (2001). *Is Marriage a Panacea? Union Formation among Economically Disadvantaged Unwed Mothers.* Paper presented at the 2001 Annual Meeting of the Population Association of America, Washington, DC.

Loprest, P. J. (1999). *How Families That Left Welfare Are Doing: A National Picture.* Washington, DC: Urban Institute, Assessing the New Federalism, B-01. Retrieved from http://www.urban.org/UploadedPDF/anf_b1.pdf.

Loprest, P. J. (2002). *Who Returns to Welfare?* Washington, DC: Urban Institute, Assessing the New Federalism. Retrieved from http://www.urban.org/url.cfm?ID=310548.

Lower-Basch, E. (2000). *"Leavers" and Diversion Studies: Preliminary Analysis of Racial Differences in Caseload Trends and Leaver Outcomes.* Washington, DC: U.S. Department of Health and Human Services. Retrieved from http://aspe.hhs.gov/hsp/leavers99/race.htm.

Mathur, A., with Reichle, J., Wiseley, C., & Strawn, J. (2002). *Credentials Count: How California's Community Colleges Help Parents Move from Welfare to Self-Sufficiency.* Washington, DC: Center for Law and Social Policy.

McKernan, S.-M., Lerman, R., Pindus, N., & Valente, J. (2000, June 23). *The Relationship between Metropolitan and Non-Metropolitan Locations, Changing Welfare Policies and the Employment of Single Mothers.* Washington, DC: The Urban Institute.

Meyers, C. (2001). *The District and Baltimore Face Double Whammy in Welfare Reform: Greater Challenges and Less Funding for Needed Services.* Washington, DC: The Brookings Institution.

Moffit, R. (2001). From Welfare to Work: What the Evidence Shows. The Welfare Reform and Beyond Project. Washington, DC: Brookings Institution.

Moffitt, R., & Roff. J. (2000). *The Diversity of Welfare Leavers. Welfare, Children, and Families: A Three-City Study.* Working Paper no. 00–01. Johns Hopkins University, Baltimore.

Negrey, C., Um'rani, A., Golin, S., & Gault, B. (2000). Job Training under Welfare Reform: Opportunities for and Obstacles to Economic Self-Sufficiency among Low-Income Women. *Georgetown Journal on Poverty Law & Policy, 7,* 347–362.

Neubeck, K. J. (2001). Attacking Welfare Racism/Honoring Poor People's Human Rights. In R. Albelda & A. Withorn (Eds.), *Lost Ground: Welfare Reform, Poverty and Beyond.* Cambridge, MA: South End Press.

Offner, P., & Holzer, H. (2002). *Left Behind in the Labor Market: Recent Employment Trends among Young Black Men.* Washington, DC: The Brookings Institution Center on Urban & Metropolitan Policy.

Okagaki, A., Palmer, K., & Mayer, N. S. (1998). *Strengthening Rural Economies: Programs That Target Promising Sectors of a Local Economy.* Washington, DC: Center for Community Change.

Peterson, J., Song, X., & Jones-DeWeever, A. (2002). *Life After Welfare Reform: Low-Income Single Parent Families, Pre- and Post-TANF.* Washington, DC: Institute for Women's Policy Research.

Pickering, K. (2000). Alternative Economic Strategies in Low-Income Rural Communities: TANF, Labor Migration, and the Case of the Pine Ridge Indian Reservation. *Rural Sociology, 65*(1), 148–167.

Pittz, W., & Delgado, G. (2002). *Race and Recession.* Oakland, CA: Applied Research Center.

Proctor, B. D., & Dalaker, J. (2002, September 24). *Poverty in the United States: 2001.* Series pp. 60–219. Washington, DC: U.S. Bureau of the Census. Retrieved from http://www.census.gov/hhes/poverty/poverty01/table1.pdf.

Rademacher, I. (2002, February). *Working with Value: Industry-Specific Approaches to Workforce Development.* Washington, DC: The Aspen Institute.

Raphael, S., Stoll, M. A., & Holzer, H. J. (1998). *Are Suburban Firms More Likely to Discriminate against African Americans?* University of Wisconsin-Madison, Institute for Research on Poverty.

Richer, E., Rahmanour, H., & Greenberg, M. (2003). *Welfare Caseloads Increase in Most States in Fourth Quarter.* Washington, DC: Center for Law and Social Policy.

Roberts, D. (2001). *Shattered Bonds: The Color of Child Welfare.* New York: Basic Books

Rockeymoore, M., & Cox, K. (2002). *Differences in TANF Support Service Utilization: Is There Adequate Monitoring to Insure Program Quality?* Washington, DC: National Urban League.

Schram, S. F., & Soss, J. (2002). Success Stories: Welfare Reform, Policy Discourse, and the Politics of Research. In R. Albelda & A. Withorn (Eds.), *Lost Ground: Welfare Reform, Poverty and Beyond.* Cambridge, MA: South End Press.

Single-Rushton, W., & McClanahan, S. (2001). *For Richer or Poorer?* Princeton, NJ: Center for Research on Child Well-Being.

Smith, R., Smith, J., Deprez, L. S., & Butler, S. (2002). *Parents as Scholars: Education Works, Outcomes for Maine Families and Implications for TANF Reauthorization.* Augusta, ME: Maine Equal Justice Partners

Soss, J., Schram, S. F., Vartanian, T. F., & O'Brien, E. (2001). Setting the Terms of Relief: Explaining State Policy Choices in the Devolution Revolution. *American Journal of Political Science, 45,* 378–403.

Statistical Abstract of the United States. (2002). Washington, DC: U.S. Bureau of the Census.

Stoll, M. A. (1998). When Jobs Move, Do Black and Latino Men Lose? The Effect of Growth in Job Decentralisation on Young Men's Jobless Incidence and Duration. *Urban Studies, 35*(12), 2221–2239.

Turner, M., Ross, S., Galster, G., & Yinger, J. (2002). *Discrimination in Metropolitan Housing Markets: National Results from Phase I HDS 2000.* Washington, DC: The Urban Institute. Retrieved from http://www.huduser.org/publications/pdf/Phase1_Report.pdf.

U.S. Census Current Population Survey. (2001). *Annual Demographic Supplement: Poverty Section.* Washington, DC: A Joint Project Between the Bureau of Labor Statistics and the Bureau of the Census.

U.S. Department of Health and Human Services (USDHHS). (2003). *Temporary Assistance for Needy Families: Fifth Annual Report to Congress.* Washington, DC: U.S. Department of Health and Human Services, Office of Family Assistance.

U.S. Department of Housing and Urban Development. (2000). *The State of the Cities 2000: Megaforces Shaping the Future of the Nation's Cities.* Washington, DC: U.S. Department of Housing and Urban Development, Office of Policy Development and Research.

U.S. Department of Transportation, Bureau of Transportation Statistics. (1998). *Welfare Reform and Access to Jobs in Boston.* Washington, DC: U.S. Department of Housing and Urban Development, Office of Policy Development and Research.

Weber, B., & Duncan, G. (2000, June 21). Welfare Reform and Food Assistance in Rural America. Prepared for the Congressional Research Briefing on Welfare Reform and Rural Poverty. Retrieved from http://www.jcpr.org/conferences/rural-summary.pdf.

Whitener, L. A., Duncan, G. J., & Weber, B. A. (2002, June). Reforming Welfare: What Does It Mean for Rural Areas? Food Assistance and Nutrition Research Report, Number 26-4. Washington, DC: U.S. Department of Agriculture, Economic Research Service.

8

Racial, Ethnic, and Gender Disparities in Early School Leaving (Dropping Out)

L. JANELLE DANCE

In contrast to traditional approaches to framing early school leaving, this chapter utilizes an intersectional approach.[1] An intersectional approach will not illuminate race or ethnicity or class or gender or geographical/spatial location as a social location that singularly correlates with high school dropout. Instead, given the discriminatory practices that disproportionately affect ethnic minorities in the United States, an intersectional approach reveals how these categories converge and thereby place students, for example American Indians, Latinos/as, and Blacks, in particularly disadvantageous situations. Class-based measures of dropout rates do, indeed, reveal that regardless of race or ethnicity, students from low-income backgrounds are more likely to dropout of school than their more affluent counterparts. But dropout scenarios may become graver still when race, ethnicity, gender, or other social locations intersect with class. The intersections of multiple social locations render students from ethnic minority and low-income backgrounds vulnerable to early school leaving.

For instance, a researcher may take an intersectional approach to understanding the relationships between "high-stakes" testing and dropout rates. Such an analysis reveals that these tests, implemented in school districts across the United States, cause disproportionately more negative consequences for African Americans and Mexican Americans—especially those students who are poor and from inner-city communities—than their White, affluent, suburban counterparts (Valencia & Bernal, 2000). High-stakes testing refers to the mandated use of achievement tests in order to assess the performance of schools and students. Districts may offer financial awards or sanctions based on school-wide averages. Student scores can be used to promote, hold back, or even deny a diploma (American Educational Research Association [AERA], 2004). Although touted as objective, high-stakes testing is actually based on a limited model of learning: the rote mastery of a series of skills that lead to good grades and high scores without enhancing critical and creative thinking capacities (Nieto, 1999). Consequently other aspects of learning that influence children's educational experiences are not taken into consideration. Because these tests do not influence or alter structural or systemic problems related to schooling (e.g., school segregation, history of racial/ethnic discrimination, inequitable levels of school finance, high teacher turnover, fewer credentialed teachers, and high quality curricular offerings), African Americans, Latinos, and schools with high percentages of these students are more likely to suffer its negative consequences (Valencia, 2000). In the aftermath of the widespread use of high-stakes testing in several states, Blacks and Latinos consistently score lower than their White peers (Lomax, et al., 1995). Subsequently these students are placed at greater risk for school failure and/or dropping out (AERA, 2004). An intersectional analysis of high-stakes testing facilitates a more sophisticated understanding of how race, gender, class, geographic location, and other dimensions of inequality mutually influence and reinforce one another.

Synthesis of Conclusive Research Findings

Clarifications (and Conceptualizations) of "Dropouts"

At first glance, the term "dropout" seems simple and clear; it implies that some students simply drop out of school. Upon closer inspection, it belies the definitions of "simple" and "clear"; the term "dropout" is not "uncomplicated," "plain or evident to the mind, unmistakable, or apparent" (American Heritage College Dictionary, 2002). Instead of being "evident to the mind" the concept "dropout" is loaded with conventional and scholarly meanings, is not always clearly defined and is often open to interpretation. This concept is measured in "percentages" and "rates" beyond which real students are rarely seen. These percentages and rates, although quantitatively useful, reveal little about the lived experience and personal perspectives of students who "drop out." This chapter addresses these and other complications surrounding school dropout in order to promote a clearer understanding of this loaded concept. The subject(s) of this chapter on "dropouts" are not mere trends, rates, and percentages but rather the lived, schooling realities of Latino and Black youths in particular, and all students who "drop out" in general.

To capture the phenomenon of early school leaving (leaving school before achieving a high school diploma or "dropping out"), educators, researchers, and policymakers have used a variety of concepts largely derived from quantitative assessments of educational attainment. In addition to the oft-used concept of "dropout" (event dropout rate, status dropout rate, cohort dropout rate),[2] are the concepts "high school completion rates," "stop-out," "push-out," and "school holding power" (Natriello, 1987). Given these numerous conceptualizations, we often see statistics, trends, and patterns instead of complexly human students who are Latino, or Black, or American Indian, or working-class, and so on. To borrow the words of Theodore Sizer (1992, [1983]), when findings about early school leaving "are largely judged on the basis of data which happens to be easy to collect and to manipulate statistically," these findings "can produce strikingly misleading assessments."

One of the most misleading assessments produced from quantitative data is the implication of the term "dropout." Generally speaking, "a dropout is a person who is not currently enrolled in school and does not have a high school diploma or equivalent certificate." (Rumberger & Rodriquez, 2002). Immediately the term "dropout" places negative action upon the student. Dropout connotes a general sense of deviance, dysfunction, cultural deprivation, and individual deficiency. This term was influenced by early work on dropping out of school, which examined family background, personal traits, and social group characteristics (Natriello, McDill, & Pallas, 1990; Fine, 1991). From among this clutter of misleading assessments, multiple ways of measuring dropout rates, and scholarly definitions there is, however, a growing consensus that the term dropout is anachronistic, pernicious, and indicative of "deficit thinking." As argued by Richard R. Valencia (1997), those who engage in deficit thinking have failed to examine external causes of school failure that exist beyond the control of individual students who dropout.

This chapter will not offer a definitive definition that encompasses the numerous conceptualizations and measurements of early school leaving. As observed by Russell Rumberger and Gloria M. Rodriquez (2002), "[A]vailable data on dropouts are potentially inaccurate and incomparable because they are collected by different agencies, using different definitions, and different sources of data." Having unloaded the concept dropout, one thing is clear: we do not blame the characteristics of individual students as the root cause of early school leaving. We believe that the concept "push-out" is central to a clearer understanding of why some students leave school without achieving a high school diploma. For example, students who come from nonmainstream backgrounds have little to no access to the forms of social and cultural capital (for example, caring teacher-student relationships, mainstream social networks, and exposure to dominant group cultural codes) that can be exchanged for social goods like a high school diploma. Schools proactively sustain inequality by failing to provide equal access to these valuable forms of capital and, therefore, push students out of school (Gambetta, 1987; Croninger & Lee, 2001). This and other notions of push-out are important because they place the onus on schools instead of blaming the students. Moreover we prefer the term push-out because we are convinced that students who are ethnic minorities (for example, American Indian, Latino, or Black) and/or from low-income communities (for example, urban or rural) do not simply drop out of school. As explained by Susan Roberta Katz (1999):

> "Drop out" implies a conscious choice on the part of the students as if all options were open to them. However, students of color leave school largely because they feel discriminated against, stereotyped, or excluded. . . . The term "push out" puts the responsibility on where it should appropriately fall: schools and schooling in the U.S.

As observed by Dale Mann (1987), the difference implied by the concept dropout compared to that implied by the concept push-out is a difference of perspective. The concept dropout implies that children fail to learn whereas the concept push-out implies that schools fail to teach (Mann, 1987). Michelle Fine (1991) has appropriately conveyed why the term push-out is far more appropriate than the term dropout:

> [At the dawn of the 21st century] every child may enjoy access to a public education. But. . .the bodies of some are exported out prior to graduation. These bodies are disproportionately bodies of color and of low-income students. These are the bodies that constitute the group euphemistically called "high school dropouts," as if they freely decided to go.

Who is "Pushed Out"?

Since the middle of the twentieth century, there have been substantial declines in rates of early school leaving. Whereas over 60 percent of all persons 25 to 29 years of age had not finished high school in 1940, by 1980, 16 percent of all persons from that age range had not finished high school (Rumberger, 1987). Despite the long-term declines going into the twenty-first century, there are some persistent trends in rates of early school leaving.

CLASS CHARACTERISTICS OF PUSH OUTS. It is well established that affluent students, especially those who attend private schools, not only have the highest rates of high school completion, they also have the highest rates of college attendance (Jencks, 1979; Hodges Persell & Cookson, 1985; Cookson & Hodges Persell, 1985; Orfield, 1996). Even more, privileged parents choose to place their children in smaller schools because these schools have higher degrees of teacher efficacy, higher rates of achievement, greater attendance rates, and lower dropout rates (Powell, 1996). In fact, research shows that smaller schools improve teaching, bring about a greater sense of community, and heighten student achievement (Bank Street College of Education, 2000).

In contrast to privileged students who attend smaller schools, students from low-income backgrounds, regardless of race/ethnicity, have the lowest rates of high school completion and attend the largest schools. This is especially true of students who reside in areas of high and severe poverty (Kasarda, 1993). Furthermore event dropout rates reported in 2000 reveal that for fifteen to twenty-four year olds who dropped out of high school, students in the bottom 20 percent of all family incomes were six times more likely to drop out than students in the top 20 percent (National Center for Education Statistics, 2000). Many researchers argue that social class location is one of the most powerful predictors of early school leaving. An intersectional approach adds complexity and dimension to this finding about the predictive power of social class. Ethnic minorities are disproportionately represented in working and lower class locations, women and children are disproportionately located in working- and lower-class locations. Hence, without diminishing the influence of class, it is important to keep in mind that class is always spliced with other social locations.

RACE/ETHNIC CHARACTERISTICS OF PUSH OUTS. Although event, cohort, and status dropout rates provide different percentages, these rates provide a consistent picture. American Indian students have the highest dropout rates, followed by Latino students, and then Black students.[3] For example, for the last ten years, the national dropout rate for Blacks has hovered between 12 percent and 14 percent and the rate for Latinos has hovered between 25 percent and 30 percent (see table 8.1 and figure 8.1). And it is important to note that though dropout rates for American Indians are not as well documented as those for Latinos and Blacks, "in 1992, the U.S. Department of Education's Indian Nations at Risk Task Force reported the Native American dropout rate to be twice the national average" (U.S. Department of Education, 2003). A review of census data reveals that "[a]t virtually every age group, dropout rates are higher for Latinos than any other ethnic or racial group except for [Native Americans]" (Rumberger & Rodriguez, 2002). More specifically, census data on Latinos, disaggregated by national origin, reveal that Mexicans have the lowest rates of educational attainment and Cubans have the highest rates of educational attainment (see table 8.1).

GENDER CHARACTERISTICS OF PUSH OUTS. Males, especially Black and Latino males, are more likely than females to drop out of high school, yet they are also more likely to return and achieve a high school diploma or equivalency degree. In a study done of urban areas, 42 percent of males returned to school and graduated, but only 25 percent of females did so. Further Black and Latino males return at a rate of about 10 percent higher than females in these racial/ethnic groups (The Mid-Atlantic Equity Center, 1993). In regard to the educational attainment of Latinas, there is a growing concern that dropout rates for Latinas are poised to increase: Latinas lag behind other ethnic minority girls

TABLE 8.1

Percent of High School Dropouts among Persons 16 to 24 Years Old by Race/Ethnicity: April 1960 to October 1998

Year	White	Black	Hispanic
1960[*]	–	–	–
1970[**]	13.2	27.9	–
1980	11.4	19.1	35.2
1985	10.4	15.2	27.6
1990	9.0	13.2	32.4
1992[***]	7.7	13.7	29.4
1993[***]	7.9	13.6	27.5
1994[***]	7.7	12.6	30.0
1995[***]	8.6	12.1	30.0
1996[***]	7.3	13.0	29.4
1997[***]	7.6	13.4	25.3
1998[***]	7.7	13.8	29.5
1999[***]	7.3	12.6	28.6

Source: U.S. Department of Education, National Center for Education Statistics, Digest of Education Statistics, 2000, table 106.
Note: [*] Based on the April 1960 decennial census.
[**] White and black include persons of Hispanic origin.
[***] Because of changes in data collection procedures, data may not be comparable with figures for earlier years.
– Data not available.

in several important measures of academic achievement, and benefit less from gender equity programs and policies (Zambrana & Zoppi, 2002).

SPATIAL (GEOGRAPHIC) LOCATION OF PUSH OUTS. Students who reside in urban settings have higher dropout rates than students in either suburban or rural areas.[4] The dropout rates for large, urban school systems are the highest (Croninger & Lee, 2001). As mentioned earlier, children who live in neighborhoods with high crime and poverty do not achieve academically as those who live in safer, cleaner, and more affluent neighborhoods (Center for the Study of School Organization, Johns Hopkins University, 2001). Sixty percent of youth living in public housing who enter the eighth grade never graduate from high school. Students who live in urban settings have higher dropout rates than

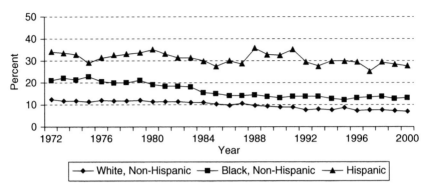

FIGURE 8.1 Percent of 16- to 24-Year-Olds Who Were High School Dropouts by Race/Ethnicity, 1972–2000.

The data presented here represent status dropout rates, which is the percentage of persons ages 16–24 who are out of school and who have not earned a high school credential. Another way of calculating dropout rates is the event dropout rate, the percentage of 15- to 24-year olds who dropped out of grades 10 through 12 in the 12 months preceding the fall of each data collection year. Event dropout rates are not presented here

Source: "Highlights from the Status and Trends in the Education of Hispanics," National Center for Education Statistics. http://www.nces.ed.gov/Pubs2003/Hispanics/figures.asp?FigureNumber=3_3

students in either suburban or rural areas: dropout rates for urban areas are approximately 24.5 percent, suburban areas are approximately 15.1 percent, and rural areas are 15.6 percent (Roderick, 1993). Further, according to the Center for the Social Organization of Schools at Johns Hopkins University, much of the nation's dropout problem is concentrated in a few hundred high schools in poor communities of the nation's largest cities.

Depending upon how you measure "dropouts" the rates vary, but one thing remains the same. With respect to the intersections of class, race/ethnicity and geographic location, studies on school completion and occupational mobility reveal two extremes: (1) affluent, White, suburban students have high levels of the educational attainment and, (2) low-income, Latino, and Black, urban students, as well as American Indian students, have low levels of educational attainment.

Review of Relevant Literature

In *The Path to Dropping Out: Evidence for Intervention*, Melissa Roderick (1993) provides an extensive review of quantitative and qualitative literature on school dropouts. We both borrow and build upon Roderick's review. Roderick summarizes survey-based findings of the reasons dropouts themselves provide for leaving school, quantitative studies on the influence of family background as well as school organization and policy, and qualitative research on why students withdraw from school. When supplemented with studies conducted by other scholars such as Nilda Flores-Gonzales (2002), Russell Rumberger (1983; 1987), Russell Rumberger and Gloria Rodriguez (2002), Angela Valenzuela (1999), Anne Arnett Ferguson (2000), Michelle Fine (1991; 1994), and Jean Anyon (1997), the ensuing characterization of school dropout yields both breadth and depth.

Students report in surveys that they "dropout" due to problems with school performance and engagement, early pregnancy and marriage, and discipline. In addition to these self-reported "problems," students also report that they drop out due to economic responsibilities (Roderick, 1993). For girls, especially Black girls, pregnancy or marriage play a large role in a student's decision to drop out. For boys, especially Black boys, discipline problems and conflicts with school personnel play a large role. For Latino youths (both boys and girls), economic responsibilities play a large role in educational decisions (Roderick, 1993, 23).

In addition to student surveys, other quantitative studies link family background characteristics to early school leaving. While some scholars implicate the differential learning between Black and White children that occurs over the summer months, others implicate the educational involvement of parents in a student's home, and still others paint a more complex picture that links school dropout to "insufficient education" in home, school, and community contexts (Roderick, 1993; Entwistle & Alexander, 1992; Rumberger, 1983; Natriello, McDill, & Pallas, 1990). We argue that this last point is extremely important. Otherwise claims about family background may regress to "culture of poverty" explanations that blame poor families for structural conditions that are beyond the control of these families. "Blaming the victim" approaches have never been useful, ideologically or practically, as effective interventions for preventing early school leaving. A lasting influence of these cultural deprivation models is that they blame the experiential deficits of students as the root cause of the early school leaving.

Quantitative studies also link school organization and policy to dropout rates. For example, dropout rates are noticeably higher in larger schools than in smaller schools, in public schools than in Catholic schools, and higher in schools that lack effective schooling characteristics (such as a safe school climate, high school staff commitment, and low degrees of tracking) than in schools that have these characteristics (Roderick, 1993, 34–35). There is growing evidence that low-income minority students attend schools where the overall climate, quality of and relationship with teachers, as well as the curriculum, tracking, disciplinary, and other policies, conspire to push them out. For example, because Black and other minority students continue to be disproportionately enrolled in schools in central cities, they tend to be overrepresented in large, comprehensive or "zoned" schools that are in racially isolated and high-poverty areas. Academic achievement and graduation rates in these schools are often very low (Jordon, 2002). The 1996 report of the National Commission on Teaching and America's Future stated that students enrolled in such schools are unlikely to have classroom teachers with certification or college degrees in their teaching fields. These students have less than a 50 percent chance of taking a course with a math or science teacher who has a license and or undergraduate degree in the field he or she teaches (National Commission on Teaching and America's Future, 1996).

In contrast to the breadth of information from quantitative studies, qualitative studies provide a deeper understanding of the actual interactions within schools that are linked to early school leaving. Many of these studies illuminate the incongruence or dissonance between what students need and what schools provide (Roderick, 1993, 37–39). For example, with regard to Latino students, there is discord between how students define education or "educación" as a process that involves a caring relationship between teacher and students, and schools that provide noncaring environments (Valenzuela, 1999). And, given the extracurricular activities that exist, schools are also deficient in the types of extracurricular activities that Latino students need to secure both a niche for engagement and positive school identity (Flores-Gonzales, 2002).

Qualitative studies on Black students reveal, among other things, an incongruence between the humanistic and nonstereotypical views that these students have of themselves and the stereotypical views and harsh disciplinary systems enacted by teachers and other school officials. Black male students, in particular experience incongruence between the realities of navigating street culture and the realities of navigating mainstream school settings (Luttrell, 1997; Arnett Ferguson, 2000). These recent studies of incongruence corroborate a wealth of earlier studies and findings about the discordance between Black American cultural settings and the cultural settings of schools that value mainstream, White American culture. For example, in recent years, scholars have documented the incongruence between the indirect statements/commands of middle-class teachers and the direct statements/commands of working-class parents and students (Delpit, 1995). Scholars have also documented the incongruence between the mainstream cultural assumptions of teachers and the hip-hop, street cultural realities of inner-city students (Dance, 2002; Arnett Ferguson, 2000).

It should come as no surprise that American Indian students also experience cultural dissonance; they often struggle against cultural misrepresentations. For example, there has been a long-standing tendency to judge American Indian students by Eurocentric cultural norms. One of the stereotypes born of this tendency is the "silent Indian" with low self-esteem. Instead of interpreting this so-called silence from the standpoints of American Indian students, and instead of implicating Eurocentric practices within schools that facilitate silence, school officials misrepresent American Indian students as deficient. The Eurocentric practices that teachers employ with impunity include low expectations of American Indian students, blatant misinterpretations of American Indian cultural expressions, and the tendency to devalue American Indian cultural capital, just to name a few (Foley, 1996; Delpit, 1995).

In addition to these findings on incongruence between schools and students, Michelle Fine documents school policies and practices of exclusion that target Latino and Black students. These practices include the school officials' disrespectful interactions with the parents of Latino and Black students, school officials' uncaring, low expectations of Latino and Black students, and textbooks that praise "Whiteness" and "maleness" at the expense of the contributions of people of color. These exclusionary practices insure that the voices of students of color are silenced. And, as elaborated by Fine (1991):

> The silenced voices are disproportionately those who speak neither English nor standard English, the voices of the critics, and the voices which give away secrets that everyone knows and feverishly denies. Their secrets tell of racism; of an economy of substandard (or no) housing; and ideology of education as the Great Equalizer when there's little evidence; and of the secrets of sexism that claim the bodies and minds of their mothers, sisters, aunts, and themselves.

With regard to the "secrets of sexism," Peggy Orenstein (1994) corroborates Fine's observations. In her qualitative study that specifically focuses upon gender inequality and schooling, Orenstein offers the following findings in regard to low-income females who are ethnic minorities:

> [D]evaluation by race or class does not preclude devaluation by gender. . . . [G]irls are far more likely than boys to attend school on a regular basis . . . and tend to earn higher grades than boys. But on those occasions when boys are equally represented [in the classroom] . . . boys grab the questions, . . . are rewarded for aggressiveness, [and] get whatever limited attention the teachers may offer. . . . [Hence,] although underclass girls outshine and outscore boys scholastically through middle school, by high school they lose that edge and the boys begin to make disproportional gains.

Finally school tracking, testing, and other policies can lessen the academic motivation of low-income and minority youth, and even encourage them to leave school. Tracking, the practice of placing students in different classes based on perceived differences, can begin as early as second or third grade, and determine a students' entire academic career. Black and Latino students are underrepresented in gifted and college-preparatory tracks, and overrepresented in remedial and vocational tracks. Exit exams are another barrier erected between students of color and a high school diploma. In some states, like Texas and Florida, students of color tend to have a high rate of failure and many, who have completed all graduation criteria, are still denied a diploma (The Applied Research Center, 2000, 16–22).

According to the Hispanic Dropout Project, many Latino students say they were encouraged by teachers and school administrators to stop coming to school. The report concluded that schools often make an effort to keep Latino students on the rolls until they have been counted in the year's census. However, once schools receive state monies for the year and there are no sanctions for dropouts, schools can decrease their enrollments and get relief from overcrowding. The report also noted that district and state policies could provide schools with incentives for dropping low-performing students. The students targeted are generally those with limited English proficiency, and have a need for special education or other academic support (Hispanic Dropout Project, 1998).

Hence quantitative and qualitative studies combine to reveal a complexity of factors that render students from ethnic minority backgrounds more vulnerable than their affluent, White counterparts to early school leaving. Disproportionately high numbers of Latino and Black students reside in urban and inner-city communities and experience what Jean Anyon (1997) refers to as "ghetto schooling." Given this urban context, we must understand that in the final analysis, high dropout rates among Black and Latino youths reveal little about the innate abilities of these students and more about the deterioration of urban communities. Jean Anyon asserts, "[U]ntil the economic and political systems in which [central cities] are enmeshed are themselves transformed so they may be more democratic and productive for urban residents, educational reformers have little chance of effecting long-lasting educational changes in city schools" (1997, 13).

Promising Practices

Scholarly Perspectives on Promising Practices

There are numerous innovations and school reform initiatives occurring in school districts across the United States, hundreds in the New York and Chicago school districts alone (Fullan & Stiegelbauer, 1991; Lee, 2002). It would be impossible to catalogue this virtual plethora of policies and practices. But when the focus is narrowed to those reforms and innovations with staying power, there are promising practices worth noting. These practices exist on, at least, three different levels: (1) Teacher-to-student practices in the classroom; (2) Structural changes at the school level; and (3) Community and organizational practices that exist beyond the walls of the school at the neigborhood-level.

TEACHER TO STUDENT PRACTICES IN THE CLASSROOM. Jaime Escalante and Marva Collins are two teachers renowned for their ability to inspire "unteachable" students to academic success. Due in large part to his culturally sensitive teaching at Garfield High School in East Los Angeles, Escalante motivated Latino students from low-income, gang and drug-infested communities to excel in Advanced Placement (AP) calculus. Collins founded her own school that addressed the needs of inner-city students in Chicago. Given the statistical projections regarding Collins' first class of thirty-three students, several of these students would have been shot, arrested, or placed on welfare. But thanks to Collins's culturally sensitive approach to teaching, all thirty-three students completed school and now lead successful adult lives. Escalante and Collins are well-known, but many other teachers have similar success stories.

In *Promising Lives: The Promise of Public Education*, Mike Rose (1995) provides examples of other successful teachers who work with "at-risk" students. Rose visits schools and classrooms across the United States from Los Angeles to Baltimore, schools with students from communities that are low-income and urban as well as rural, schools with students who are Latino, American Indian, and/or Black. Rose finds many of the challenges and problems facing schools today, but he focuses on examples of success, places where there was good teaching and learning going on. At the helm of these successful classrooms are teachers who created learning environments that students experienced as havens, places of respect; learning environments where teacher authority was never abusive, but derived from knowledge, care, and "solidarity with students' background" (Rose, 1995). Three things Escalante, Collins, and the teachers documented in *Possible Lives* have in common are cultural sensitivity, high expectations, and empathetic regard for the students they teach. High expectations, cultural sensitivity, and empathy are key ingredients that pull students into school (Noddings, 1992; Nieto, 1999). Without these characteristics, students from ethnic minority and low-income backgrounds would likely be pushed out of school.

STRUCTURAL CHANGES AT THE SCHOOL LEVEL. Many school systems across the country have undergone structural changes at the school level: these changes range from school based management to radical decentralization; from the creation of small learning communities to the restructuring and reconstitution of entire public school sites (Fine, 1994; Sanders, 2000; Lee, 2002; Legters, et al., 2002). Although these reforms have had varying degrees of success and failure, there is one reform that has had incredible success and staying power: the Comer School Development Model (Comer, 1980; Comer, et al., 1999). This model, founded in 1968 to meet the educational needs of low-income, Black students, promotes the cooperation and collaboration of parents, teachers, academic researchers, and community representatives to facilitate positive educational outcomes for children from low-income communities. Key components of this model include a Mental Health Team, Pupil Personnel Team, Parent Program, and Parent-Teacher Workshops that are organized and orchestrated to restore power to students, school officials, parents, and community leaders. The ultimate goal of these teams is the improvement of teaching and learning for all students, especially students of color from low-income neighborhoods. The Comer Model has been employed successfully in over five hundred elementary and secondary schools across the United States.[5] This model turns failing schools into effective schools and reorganizes chaotic schooling climates into safe, academically productive havens. Because this model includes parents and community leaders in its team-based approach, it is a promising practice for school-based communities whether these communities are ethnic minorities and/or lower-income (Comer, et al., 1999). In addition to the Comer Model, the Career Academies approach to dropout prevention has been widely established in high schools for more than thirty years and has been implemented in over 1,500 schools around the country. Its core features offer direct responses to problems that have been identified in the large comprehensive high schools that many low-income, minority youth attend. Career Academies create a more supportive and personalized environment through a school-within-a-school structure. The curricula combine both academic and occupation-related course requirements that promote career awareness and college preparation. An impact study of Career Academies, published by Manpower Demonstration Research Corporation in 2001, showed the Academies' model to be an effective approach for reducing dropout rates and improving attendance and school engagement among students at most risk of dropping out of school (Kemple & Snipes, 2001).

Community and Organizational Practices at the Neighborhood Level

Milbrey McLaughlin and her coauthors (McLaughlin, Irby, & Langman, 1994) provide examples of neighborhood-based organizations that are also safe havens. These organizations include youth groups, sports teams, art programs, and civic organizations. These organizations, deemed successful by the youths involved in them, provide inner-city youths with an atmosphere in which they thrive. Characteristics these organizations possess, which the public schools lack, include accessible support, adequate guidance, a safe environment, and opportunities for growth and learning. These organizations coexist with schools in inner-city communities yet do something that inner-city schools often fail to do: attract and retain youths. More importantly, some of these organizations promote educational success and thereby provide examples of promising practices. For example, Building Educational Strategies for Teens (BEST) is an agency that provides students with tutors, mentors, and the promise of a college scholarship. BEST students "meet after school, often on Saturdays, and throughout the summer in study, work, and performance programs that require specific academic, social, and cultural development. . . . Educational activities [are designed] to be relevant to the lives of BEST youth." (McLaughlin, Irby, & Langman, 1994). Like the other organizations documented by McLaughlin and her coauthors, BEST provides teens with accessible support, adequate guidance, a safe environment, and opportunities for growth and learning.

Though it was not featured in *Urban Sanctuaries*, the Omega Boys Club, located in San Francisco, California, is an organizational safe haven, renown for its ability to facilitate the academic success of students from inner-city communities. Among other things, this club offers tutoring, positive recreational activities, academic preparation, violence prevention, and conflict resolution. The Llano Grande Center for Research and Development, located in Elsa, Texas, helps to build leadership skills in Latino youths. One, among many, of this center's noteworthy accomplishments is the placement of fifty-one students from the local community into Ivy League schools (Llano Grande Center for Research and Development, 2006). The Omega Boys Club and the Llano Grande Center, like the organizations documented in *Urban Sanctuaries*, meets youths where they are—even if this means meeting students on tough, urban streets—in order to guide students to academic success.

Whether occurring within classrooms, broader school environments, or community contexts, the key ingredient for promising practices include culturally sensitive academic support and instruction, mentoring and providing students with accessible guidance into adulthood, and safe, encouragement-filled environments in which students may aspire to academic achievement and leadership positions. These practices, like those exemplified by the Omega Boys Clubs and Llano Grande Center, attend to the political and economic structural challenges presented by deteriorating cities and those local realities that may differ from city to city. These practices strive toward broader, structural changes, yet encompass community-based efforts as well as maverick and pioneering teachers within schools that are otherwise failing their students. In short, the most promising practices aim to remove the structural barriers that facilitate early school leaving and increase those instances and situations of caring, cultural sensitivity, and other qualitatively powerful characteristics of schools that inspire students to complete high school.

Policy Implications

There is more debate and disagreement than consensus about the policy implications that ensue from research findings on early school leaving. However, some researchers argue that to prevent early school leaving, the four Cs—cash, care, computers, and coalitions—make a difference (Mann, 1987). Given the contents of this chapter, at least three of these Cs, namely cash, care, and coalitions, figure prominently as policy implications.

Cash

Jonathan Kozol (1991) has documented the vast inequalities that exist within school districts. Within the same school district, students who are White and affluent are more likely to attend schools with higher per pupil expenditures than students who are ethnic minorities and poor. Although equitable funding of America's school is no panacea, it is a necessary step to facilitating positive schooling experiences. Kozol (1991) discusses how some powerful government officials deny that funding will solve educational problems yet these very same government officials place their children in well-funded, well-resourced private schools. By including cash (or equitable funding) as a policy recommendation, we simply argue that what's good for affluent students in private and suburban public schools, is good for impoverished students who attend public schools. Whether through a redistribution of the tax-base of schools or through other measures, state and local governments must equitably allocate educational funds to alleviate the "savage inequalities" that exists within and among public school districts.

Instead of "throwing money" at public schools, the equitable distribution of funds must involve thoughtful attention to important details. Many funding reform movements focus on economic disparities caused by the U.S. system of using property taxes to support public schools (Okpala, Okpala, & Smith, 2001). These movements help fill important gaps, but they fail to address broader resource disparities overlooked by the oft-cited per pupil expenditure statistic.[6] For example, revenue generated by property taxes in 1999–2000 was lower for school districts with highest levels of poverty (Wirt, et al., 2003). Districts with the lowest levels of poverty (less than 5 percent of students) received three times more in local revenue per student than districts with the highest level of poverty (35 percent or more of students). However, high poverty districts received significantly more funding from state and federal funding sources. High poverty schools also received more categorical revenue (revenues for specific educational purposes, including compensatory programs where resources to school districts are targeted for the needs of economically and educationally disadvantaged students) (Wirt, et al., 2003). Even though state, federal, and categorical sources make up much of the discrepancy produced by property tax revenue, they do not offset the entire differential. The total per student expenditures at high-poverty districts were 6 percent lower than in the low-poverty districts. Still these statistics tell only part of the resource disparity story.

Commonly reported per pupil spending statistics should take into account Hanushek's notion of economic efficiency (1986). Economic efficiency involves whether (or not) resource expenditures are related to student performance. This is particularly important given findings that suggest that expenditures such as instructional supplies are not statistically correlated with academic achievement (Okpala, Okpala, & Smith, 2001). Studies like this presume the presence of more relevant factors on student achievement. Factors such as the disparities in teacher turnover rates, quantity of credentialed teachers, and percentages of students receiving free and reduced lunch create different needs and, consequently, different expenses. By not accounting for costs, which are common to schools with high percentages of Blacks and Latinos, districts may inefficiently allocate funds or not assign funds to issues pertinent to achievement. This illustrates the need to distinguish equal funding from equitable funding. Hence examining per pupil expenditure is a start but is by no means an end to analyzing financial inequities.

Given the ongoing debate over school expenditures, a debate in which Hanushek's findings are frequently cited, it is important to elaborate how Hanushek's own research obscures his very important point about economic efficiency. In a variety of publications, Hanushek has stated and reiterated that "[t]here is no strong or systematic relationship between school expenditures and student performance" (1989; 1994; 1995; 1997). Hanushek often goes on to clarify his point about economic efficiency: there are conditions under which expenditures do, indeed count and that "some schools [use] funds effectively whereas others do not"(1989; 1994; 1995). He provides several other caveats and disclaimers. Yet it is Hanushek's mantra that increased school expenditures do not improve student performance and not his clarifications about effective or efficient funding that resounds throughout his writings. It is, therefore, easy to ignore his clarifications, when, in fact, Hanushek's clarifications are extremely important. For example, as Hanushek, himself, points out:

> The evidence from statistical analyses] does not indicate that money could not matter. In fact, the major focus of *Making Schools Work* (Hanushek, et al., 1994) is on ways to improve the chance that resources will be used effectively. The results here indicate that money is not used well within the current organization of schools or in the way schools use incentives. Change those and money could become a potent policy instrument. (1995)

Thus it would be more appropriate for Hanushek to assert that there is no systematic relationship between inefficient spending and student performance. That is, when schools, like other bureaucratically run institutions, use resources and funds inefficiently, this inefficient use of funds does not translate into improved student performance.

Receptiveness to Hanushek's unclarified mantra that there is no relationship between expenditure and performance reveals both a lack of vision and a propensity to give up on public schools. This lack of vision does not apply to elite schools. Imagine the disagreement that would ensue if Hanushek claimed and reiterated that for elite private schools like Phillips Exeter and Phillips

(Andover) Academy, there is no strong or systematic relationship between school expenditures and student performance. Or, if a researcher claimed that the academic performance of Harvard University students was not linked to Harvard's $30 billion endowment. For such claims to have even a sliver of a chance to be taken seriously, clarifications, disclaimers, and caveats would have to be stated and reiterated. The caveats and clarifications would become the mantra, not the claim that performance was not linked to expenditure.

But of course there is a strong or systematic relationship between elite school expenditures and the performance of private school students. This is largely due to the fact that the economic capital of elite schools intersects with symbolic, social, and cultural capital elements, as well as other qualitative factors. These complex intersections are difficult to capture with quantitative analyses. Likewise the story about resources and public schools is a story in which economic capital and efficient funding are key ingredients that intersect with a complexity of factors. And, as stated above, by including economic capital and efficient funding as a policy recommendation, we simply argue that what's good for affluent students in elite private schools is good for impoverished students who attend public schools.

Care

In the wake of reforms like the Comer Model and other promising practices like those listed above, there is a growing body of evidence that caring and culturally sensitive teaching goes a long way to facilitate the educational success of students by drawing these students into the school community instead of pushing these students out. Caring is one form of social capital that benefits students in their relationships with teachers. Teachers and other school officials must be trained and encouraged to employ culturally sensitive pedagogies that meet the needs of students who are ethnic minorities and/or come from low-income communities. Caring, empathy, and sensitivity must be structured into the relationships between teachers and those students with the highest risk of being pushed out of school.

In addition to teacher caring, study after study reveals that trust is another form of social capital in the relationship between teachers and students that facilitates positive school outcomes. Robert Croninger and Valerie Lee (2001) find that "When adolescents trust their teachers and informally receive guidance from teachers, they are more likely to persist through graduation. Although teacher-based forms of social capital are generally beneficial for all students, those who benefit most are students most at risk of dropping out of high school." A key outcome of promising practices like those listed above, is that these practices engender trust between youths and adult role models. In essence, caring adults inspire trusting students who persist through the completion of their high school years.

Coalitions

Although maverick, pioneering teachers like Jaime Escalante, Marva Collins, and others are inspirations to be applauded and supported, early school leaving may also be prevented through coalition building. The Comer Model, the Omega Boys Club, and the Llano Grande Center may have started as the dream of an innovative and dedicated individual. But these organizations endure due to collaborations and alliances among a variety of individuals and groups that may include community members, community leaders, nonprofit organizations, private organizations, government agencies, educators, and researchers. Like those scholars who study beneficial relationships between teachers and students to better understand the importance of teachers as a source of social capital, there are those who study the social capital inherent in broader relationships, networks, and coalitions. Those who study the benefits that accrue from coalition building among schools and other important social institutions, refer to this type of networking as synergistic social capital (Warren, et al., 2001).

For example, Pedro Noguera (1995; 2003) finds that when school officials lack meaningful knowledge of and connection to the communities of their students, these school officials are likely to serve their students poorly, exclude parents from meaningful involvement in the school community, and fail to utilize parents as resources. To acquire knowledge of and connection to the communities they teach, school officials should build coalitions by facilitating parental involvement. A vivid example of parental involvement is documented in *Child by Child* edited by James Comer, et al. (1999):

> If you walk around the school, you'll see parents from the Family Interactive Center helping out throughout the school community. As you enter classrooms, it's going to be difficult for you to tell who's the teacher, who's the parent, and who's the teacher's aide. You'll find children here who are limited in the English language interacting with English-dominant students. (English-dominant students use Spanish as a foreign language when engaging with other students because over 80 percent of the students are Hispanic and 65 percent of these students have limited English proficiency.) Students will tell you about their vision of a better world and how they see themselves as a stakeholder group that can make a difference because they already have made a difference in the school community.

School officials should also build coalitions with community-based organizations and other public, nonprofit, and private institutions that can support schools in the quest to better serve at-risk populations (Warren, et al., 2001). Like equitable funding (cash) and culturally sensitive teaching (care), the creation of social networks (coalitions) is instrumental to preventing early school leaving.

Conclusion

As quoted above, Jean Anyon (1997) asserts that "[U]ntil the economic and political systems in which [central cities] are enmeshed are themselves transformed so they may be more democratic and productive for urban residents, educational reformers have little chance of effecting long-lasting educational changes in city schools." Although we heed Anyon's assertion, in the meantime we recommend policies that facilitate these three Cs of cash, care, and coalitions. Like Mike Rose (1995), we believe that "[l]ife in the classroom is vulnerable not only to political and economic forces, but also to the inhumane and anti-egalitarian beliefs and biases in the culture at large. Schools are open systems, permeable institutions: beliefs about race and gender, about class and language, about intelligence, ability, and achievement emerge in the classroom." Therefore changing beliefs systems is a prerequisite to transforming the economic and political systems in which schools are enmeshed.

The economic and social realities of the twenty-first century demand high school completion at a bare minimum. For instance, the unemployment rate is highest among people without a high school degree (U.S. Census Bureau, 2002). Moreover jobs that do not require a minimum of a high school diploma are diminishing nationally. Those who do not complete high school are denied access to the essential goods that can be exchanged for a quality life. Conversely the lack of a degree grants access to impoverished and oppressed lifestyles. Often those who cannot earn a degree or enter the workforce turn to crime. In general, former prisoners report lower levels of income and education than nonprison populations (U.S. Census Bureau, 2002). The correlation between education and incarceration may explain the swell of imprisoned Blacks and Latinos across the country. Given the rapid growth of Latinos in the United States, as well as the increase in other ethnic minority populations, the failure of the public school system to provide adequate schooling environments for all U.S. students will leave generations of ethnic minorities trapped in poverty. Solving problems that facilitate early school leaving is an essential step to ensuring lively and economically viable communities. Although early school leaving has followed us into this century, we must employ those promising practices and policies that will make both the loaded concept "dropout" and the more appropriate notion of "push-out" obsolete.

NOTES

1. L. Janelle Dance is Associate Professor of Sociology at the University of Nebraska. She and her contributors Andre Perry, Ph.D., Amy McLaughlin, Ph.D., and Ruth E. Zambrana, Ph.D., wish to acknowledge with great appreciation the comments and suggestions received from Michelle Fine, Ph.D., Richard Valencia, Ph.D., and Charles Payne, Ph.D.

2. Event rates reflect the actual "event" of dropping out, more specifically the percentage of students who drop out of high school within a single year. Status rates reflect the status of "a given group in the populations at large (not just students)," or more specifically the percentage of a population within a given age range who have either not finished or are not enrolled in high school. Cohort rates reflect the changes that affect a given group over a given period of time, for example, what happens to a single group of students, currently sixteen years of age, over time (Howley & Huang, 1991).

3. According to "School Completion Rates: Dropout Rates and Their Implications for Meeting the National Goal," by Craig Howley and Gary Huang (1991, ERIC Identifier 335177), during the period of 1987–1989, event dropout rates reveal that 8 percent of Hispanic students and 7 percent of Black students dropped out each year, compared to 4 percent of White students. Status rates are numerically different, but still present the highest rates for Hispanic students. For example, in October of 1989, for the population within the age range of 16 to 24, 33 percent of Hispanics, 14 percent of Blacks, and 12 percent of Whites had not completed high school. According to "Latinos in School: Some Facts and Findings," (2001, ERIC Identifier 449288), for that same age range in 1998, 30 percent of Latinos, 14 percent of Blacks, and 8 percent of Whites had not completed high school.

4. According to calculations of dropouts from the High School and Beyond data set, dropout rates for urban areas are approximately 24.5 percent, for suburban areas are approximately 15.1 percent, and 15.6 percent for rural areas (see Roderick, 1993).

5. See the Comer School Development Program Web site: http://info.med.yale.edu/comer/.

6. Average amount of federal, state, and local dollars spent on each pupil. The statistic also includes special compensatory programs.

References

American Educational Research Association (AERA). (2004; Adopted July 2000). *AERA Position Statement Concerning High-Stakes Testing in PreK-12 Education.* Retrieved June 23, 2003, from http://www.aera.net/policyandprograms/?id=378&terms=Position+Statement+Concerning+High-Stakes+Testing&searchtype=1&fragment=False.

American Heritage College Dictionary. (2002). Boston: Houghton Mifflin Company.

Anyon, J. (1997). *Ghetto Schooling: A Political Economy of Urban Educational Reform.* New York: Teachers College Press.

The Applied Research Center. (2000).

Arnett Ferguson, A. (2000). *Bad Boys: Public School in the Making of Black Masculinity.* Ann Arbor: University of Michigan Press.

Balfantz, R., & Letgers, N. (2003, March 1). *How Many Central City High Schools Have a Severe Dropout Problem, Where Are They Located, and Who Attends Them? A Multiple Cohort Analysis of the 1990s Using the Common Core of Data.* Research Paper prepared for The Eastern Sociological Society Annual Conference in Philadelphia.

Bank Street College of Education. (2000). *Small Schools: Great Strides.* New York: Bank Street College of Education.

Center for the Study of School Organization, Johns Hopkins University. (2001). *Neighborhood and School Influences on Family Life and Mathematics Performance of Eighth-Grade Students.* Report 54. Retrieved from http://www.csos.jhu.edu/crespar/tech-Reports/Report54.pdf.

Comer, J. (1980). *School Power: Implications of an Intervention Project.* New York: The Free Press.

Comer, J. P., Ben-Avie, M., Haynes, N. M., & Joyner, E. T. (Eds.). (1999). *Child by Child: The Comer Process for Change in Education*. New York: Teachers College Press.

Comer School Development Program Web site: http://info.med.yale.edu/comer/.

Cookson, P. W., & Hodges Persell, C. (1985). *Preparing for Power: America's Elite Boarding Schools*. New York: Basic Books.

Croninger, R. G., & Lee, V. E. (2001, August). Social Capital and Dropping Out of High School: Benefits to At-Risk Students of Teachers' Support and Guidance. *Teachers College Record, 103*(4).

Dance, L. J. (2002). *Tough Fronts: The Impact of Street Culture on Schooling*. New York: RoutledgeFalmer.

Delpit, L. (1995). *Other People's Children: Cultural Conflict in the Classroom*. New York: The New Press.

Entwistle, D., & Alexander, K. (1992, Summer). Summer Setback: Race, Poverty, School Composition, and Mathematics Achievement in the First Two Years of School. *American Sociological Review, 57*, 72–84.

Fine, M. (1991). *Framing Dropouts: Notes on the Politics of an Urban Public High School*. Albany: State University of New York Press.

Fine, M. (Ed.). (1994). *Chartering Urban School Reform: Reflections on Public High Schools in the Midst of Change*. New York: Teachers College Press.

Foley, D. E. (1996). The Silent Indian as a Cultural Production. In B. A. Levinson, D. E. Foley, & D. C. Holland (Eds.), *The Cultural Production of the Educated Person: Critical Ethnographies of Schooling and Local Practice*. Albany: State University of New York Press.

Flores-Gonzales, N. (2002). *School Kids/Street Kids: Identity Development in Latino Students*. New York: Teachers College Press.

Fullan, M., & Stiegelbauer, S. (1991). *The New Meaning of Educational Change*. New York: Teachers College Press.

Gambetta, D. (1987). *Were They Pushed or Did They Jump: Individual Decision Mechanisms in Education*. New York: Cambridge University Press.

Hanushek, E. A. (1986). Educational Production Function. In G. Psacharopoulos (Ed.), *Economics of Education Research and Studies*. New York: Pergamon.

Hanushek, E. A. (1989, May). The Impact of Differential Expenditures on School Performance. *Educational Researcher, 47*.

Hanushek, E. A. (1994, May). Money Might Matter Somewhere: A Response to Hedges, Laine, and Greenwald. *Educational Researcher, 6*.

Hanushek, E. A. (1995, November). Moving beyond Spending Fetishes. *Educational Leadership, 61*.

Hanushek, E. A. (1997, Summer). Assessing the Effects of School Resources on Student Performance: An Update. *Educational Evaluation and Policy Analysis, 19*(2).

Hanushek, E. A., & Raymond, M. E. (2001). The Confusing World of Educational Accountability. *National Tax Journal, 54*(2), 365–384.

Hispanic Dropout Project. (1998). Retrieved from http://www.ncela.gwu.edu/pubs/hdp/

Hodges Persell, C., & Cookson, P. W. (1985, December). Chartering and Bartering: Elite Education and Social Reproduction. *Social Problems, 33*(2).

Howley, C., & Huang, G. (1991). School Completion 2000: Dropout Rates and Their Implications for Meeting the National Goal. *ERIC Clearinghouse on Rural Education and Small Schools*, 1991-05-00, ED335177.

Jencks, C. (1979). *Who Gets Ahead?* New York: Basic Books.

Jordon, W. J. (2002, December). CAN Corporation and Robert Cooper. *Cultural Issues Related to High School Reform: Deciphering the Case of Black Males*. Report No. 60. Los Angeles: University of California.

Kasarda, J. (1993). Cities as Places Where People Live and Work: Urban Change and Neighborhood Distress. In H. G. Cisneros (Ed.), *Interwoven Destinies: Cities and the Nation.* New York: W. W. Norton.

Katz, S. R. (1999, Summer). Teaching in Tensions: Latino Immigrant Youth, Their Teachers and Structures of Schooling. *Teachers College Record, 100*(4), 812.

Kemple, J. J., & Snipes, J. C. (2001). Career Academies: Impacts on Students' Engagement and Performance in High School, *Executive Summary.* New York: Manpower Demonstration Research Corporation.

Kozol, J. (1991). *Savage Inequalities: Children in America's Schools.* New York: Crown Publishers.

Latinos in School: Some Facts and Findings. (2001). ERIC Identifier 449288.

Lee, V. E. (Ed.). (2002). *Reforming Chicago's High Schools: Research Perspectives on School and System Level Change*, Chicago: Consortium on Chicago School Research.

Lomax, R. G., West, M. M., Harmon, M. C., Viator, K. A., & Madaus, G. F. (1995). The Impact of Mandated Standardized Testing on Minority Students. *Journal of Negro Education, 64*(2), 171–185.

Legters, N. E., Balfanz, R., Jordan, W. J., & McPartland, J. M. (2002). *Comprehensive Reform for Urban High Schools: A Talent Development Approach.* New York: Teachers College Press.

Llano Grande Center for Research and Development. (2006). Youth Voice and the Llano Grande Center. *International Journal of Leadership in Education, 9*(4), 1360–3124.

Llano Grande Center for Research and Development Web site: www.llanogrande.org.

Luttrell, W. (1997). *Schoolsmart and Motherwise: Working-Class Women's Identity and Schooling.* New York: Routledge Press.

Mann, D. (1987). Can We Help Dropouts? Thinking about the Undoable. In G. Natriello (Ed.), *School Dropouts: Patterns and Policies.* New York: Teachers College Press.

McLaughlin, M. W., Irby, M. A., & Langman, J. (1994). *Urban Sanctuaries: Neighborhood Organizations in the Lives and Futures of Inner-City Youths.* San Francisco: Jossey-Bass.

The Mid-Atlantic Equity Center. (1993). *Beyond Title IX: Gender Equity Issues in Schools.*

National Center for Education Statistics. (2000). *Dropout Rates in the United States: 2000.* Retrieved from http://nces.ed.gov/pubs2002/droppub_2001/.

National Commission on Teaching and America's Future. (1996). What Matters Most: Teaching for America's Future. New York, NY.

Natriello, G. (1987). *School Dropouts: Patterns and Policies.* New York: Teachers College Press.

Natriello, G., McDill, E., & Pallas, A. (1990). *Schooling Disadvantaged Children: Racing against Catastrophe.* New York: Teachers College Press.

Nieto, S. (1999). *The Light in Their Eyes: Creating Multicultural Learning Communities.* New York: Teachers College Press.

Noddings, N. (1992). *The Challenge to Care in Schools: An Alternative Approach to Education.* New York: Teachers College Press.

Noguera, P. A. (1995). Preventing and Producing Violence: A Critical Analysis of Responses to School Violence. *Harvard Educational Review, 65*(2), 189–212.

Noguera, P. A. (2003). *City Schools and the American Dream: Reclaiming the Promise of Public Education.* New York: Teachers College Press.

Okpala, C., Okpala, A., & Smith, F. (2001). Parental Involvement, Instructional Expenditures, Family Socioeconomic Attributes, and Student Achievement. *Journal of Educational Research, 95*(2).

Orenstein, P. (1994). *Schoolgirls: Young Women, Self-Esteem, and the Confidence Gap.* New York: Anchor Books.

Orfield, G. (1996). The Growth of Segregation: African Americans, Latinos, and Unequal Education. In G. Orfield & S. E. Eaton (Eds.), *Dismantling Desegregation: The Quiet Reversal of Brown v. Board of Education.* New York: The New Press.

Powell, A. G. (1996). *Lessons from Privilege: The American Prep School Tradition.* Cambridge, MA: Harvard University Press.

Roderick, M. (1993). *The Path to Dropping Out: Evidence for Intervention.* Westport, CT: Auburn House.

Rose, M. (1995). *Possible Lives: The Promise of Public Education in America.* New York: Penguin Books.

Rumberger, R. W. (1983). Dropping Out of High School: The Influence of Race, Sex and Family Background. *American Educational Research Journal, 20*(2), 199–220.

Rumberger, R. W. (1987) High School Dropouts: A Review of Issues and Evidence. *Review of Educational Research, 57*(2), 101–121.

Rumberger, R. W., & Rodriquez, G. M. (2002). Chicano Dropouts: An Update of Research and Policy Issues. In R. Valencia (Ed.), *Chicano School Failure and Success: Past, Present, and Future.* New York: RoutledgeFalmer.

Sanders, M. G. (Ed.). (2000). *Schooling Students Placed at Risk: Research, Policy, and Practice in the Education of Poor and Minority Adolescents,* Mahwah, NJ: Lawrence Erlbaum Associates, Publishers.

Sizer, T. (1992 [1983]). Essential Schools: A First Look. In J. M. Rich (Ed.), *Innovations in Education: Reformers and Their Critics.* Boston: Allyn and Bacon.

U.S. Department of Education, Publications and Resources, Information and Research on Dropout and Dropout Prevention Strategies. (2003). Retrieved from http:/www.ed.gov/offices/OESE/DropoutProgram/dropoutprogram.html.

U.S. Census Bureau (2002). *The Big Payoff: Education Attainment and Synthetic Estimates of Work-Life Earnings.* Washington, D.C.

Valencia, R. (1997). Conceptualizing the Notion of Deficit Thinking. In R. Valencia (Ed.), *The Evolution of Deficit Thinking: Educational Thought and Practice.* Washington, DC: The Falmer Press.

Valenzuela, A. (1999). *Subtractive Schooling: U.S.-Mexican Youth and the Politics of Caring.* Albany: State University of New York Press.

Valencia, R. (2000a). Inequalities and The Schooling of Minority Students in Texas: Historical and Contemporary Conditions. *Hispanic Journal of Behavioral Sciences, 22,* 445–459.

Valencia, R. (2000b). *Legislated School Reform Via High-Stakes Testing: The Case of Pending Anti-Social Promotion Legislation in Texas and Its Likely Adverse Impact on Racial/Ethnic Minority Students.* Washington, DC: Paper presented at the workshop on School Completion in Standards-Based Reform: Facts and Strategies.

Valencia, R., & Bernal E. (2000). An Overview of Conflicting Opinions in the TAAS Case. *Hispanic Journal of Behavioral Sciences, 22*(4), 423–444.

Warren, M. R., Thompson, J. P., & Saegert, S. (2001). The Role of Social Capital in Combating Poverty. In S. Saegert, J. P. Thompson, & M. R. Warren (Eds.), *Social Capital and Poor Communities.* New York: Russell Sage.

Wirt, J., Choy, S., Provasnik, S., Rooney, P., Sen, A., & Tobin, R. (2003). *The Condition of Education.* Washington, DC: National Center for Education Statistics.

Zambrana, R. E., & Zoppi, I. M. (2002) Latina Students: Translating Cultural Wealth into Social Capital to Improve Academic Success. *Journal of Ethnic and Cultural Diversity in Social Work, 11*(1/2), 33–53.

9

Racial, Ethnic, and Gender Disparities in Political Participation and Civic Engagement

LORRIE ANN FRASURE AND LINDA FAYE WILLIAMS

In the closing decade of the twentieth century, a veritable cottage industry of research bemoaning the decline of civic engagement and political participation in the United States sprang up (Putnam, 2000; Skocpol & Fiorina, 1999). The focus of most studies was on social trust, social capital, and other individual-level factors. The political system was treated as open and even encouraging everyone to participate. Racial and economic inequalities and their structural origins were virtually ignored as factors linked to participation, and thus the search was to find out what was happening in the lives of individuals or in their personal ties or associations that influenced civic engagement and political participation rates.

An intersectional lens reveals the concern over the level of participation in the United States and the overreliance on personal characteristics are ironic, as, for most of U.S. history, the emphasis has been on limiting participation through exclusion of a considerable number of people from the U.S. political community on a group, not individual, basis. Thus property-less, non-Protestant, White men were initially barred from voter participation in many places during the colonial period in the United States (Kernell & Jacobson, 2000; Neuborne & Eisenberg, 1976). The battle to extend political rights to all White men, however, took minuscule effort compared to the battle for rights for other groups. Inclusion of the pan-European population of White men did not require constitutional and statutory change as it did for women, youth, and African Americans (DeSipio, 1996). In contrast, women of all races were forced to struggle a century for suffrage; they (mostly White women) did not get the vote until the Nineteenth Amendment in 1920 (Flexner, 1973). U.S. youth who were challenging the Vietnam War and supporting civil rights during the 1960s and 1970s were provided the vote almost as a consolation prize in the Twenty-Sixth Amendment, ratified in 1971 (Kernell & Jacobson, 2000).

The struggle for people of color was different. Not only were enslaved Africans not provided the right to assemble and organize, it took a civil war to provide African American men the right to vote—a right soon nullified in the South where most Blacks still lived after the short-lived Reconstruction era. For more than fifty years after Reconstruction, African Americans faced poll taxes, literacy requirements, gerrymandering, at-large elections, White primaries, violence, and other devices which denied them the most basic of democratic rights (Grofman, Handley, & Niemi, 1992).

American Indians faced relocations and reservations, Americanization campaigns that sought to destroy their cultures, and a host of other indignities and brutalities. Given assimilationist campaigns forced on the native peoples, it is ironic that the franchise was first denied and then forced upon American Indians. In 1924, they were made citizens in their own land. In actuality, however, American Indians continued to face antidemocratic contrivances to keep them from voting. For example, states with large populations of American Indians, such as Idaho, New Mexico, and Washington, denied them the vote because of specific provisions such as "Indians not taxed." As late as 1937, Colorado claimed American Indians were not yet citizens. Until 1948, Arizona denied American Indians the right to vote on the specious grounds that they were "under guardianship." North Carolina required American Indians to pass literacy tests (Wilkins, 2002, 191).

Asians, also, were barred from participation in democratic life. Indeed, after the infamous decision in *People v. Hall*, handed down by the California Supreme Court in 1854, "Asiatics" were not only prohibited from serving on juries but their participation in politics was viewed as "an actual and present danger." Whether Chinese, Japanese, Filipino, Indian, Korean, or any of the other nationality groups now lumped under the Asian-Pacific Islander (API) category by the U.S. Census Bureau, Asian Americans were subjected to deep suspicion about their political loyalties; this suspicion led to attempts to exclude Asians, not only from citizenship rights, but from immigration through laws such as the Chinese Exclusion Act in 1882, the Asiatic Barred Zone in 1917, and the Immigration Act of 1924 (Chang, 2001).

Latinos stand out among people of color in regards to their social construction as an *ethnic*, not *racial*, group. For example, Mexicans were legally defined as "White" at the conclusion of the War of 1848. To an extent, then, Latinos are framed as an extension of the conceptualization of European immigrants to the United States, "Yet the pattern of relations that established the initial set of parameters that defined the 'place' of Mexicans in the transformed landscape of the southwest was clearly racially encoded," (Almaguer, 1994, 27) and in turn shaped their modes of access and incorporation into the political sphere. As a result, and although there are national and regional differences among Latinos, the vast majority of Latinos in the United States were both part of a racialized labor force and part of the population excluded from politics through disingenuous schemes such as literacy tests, English-only ballots, and at-large elections seeking to dilute the influence of their voting power. Moreover the differences in the economic plight of many Latinos (especially Mexican Americans) and other immigrants (including many Asian ones) have been ignored.

In sum, throughout most of U.S. history, the concepts of common vision and inclusive democracy were contradicted by policies of exclusion based on race, gender, and ethnicity. For most people of color, the turning point was recent: 1965. In that year, the Voting Rights Act was passed. It prohibited tests or other devices intended to disenfranchise citizens and it required the provision of bilingual ballots; it also sought to protect people of color against schemes such as at-large elections and other measures intended to dilute the voting power of people of color. This (1965) was also the year federal immigration law was changed to allow entry of significantly more immigrants. As a result, millions more Asians immigrated. In 1965, there were approximately one million Asian Americans in the United States; by the year 2000, that number had increased to more than eleven million (Chang, 2001, 2). In short, the U.S. political experience, viewed historically, has been far more concerned with finding means to exclude and discourage many groups from civic engagement and political participation than with promoting inclusion and encouraging engagement and participation. At every level of U.S. government, groups have had unequal access to participation and power within civil society itself. Throughout U.S. history the concept of democracy as an inclusive process has been contradicted by policies of racial exclusion (Gerstle, 2001).

This chapter uses an intersectional approach to examine how well the United States has overcome its dismal exclusionary past. We begin by clarifying our key concepts and synthesizing what is known about current levels of civic and political disparities and their causes. By centering the experiences of people of color, we identify innovations and promising practices for eradicating civic and political disparities among the nation's racial and ethnic groups. Finally we focus on the policy implications that flow from research findings on civic and political disparities.

A Note on Data Limitations

How do rates of political participation and civic engagement vary across racial and ethnic groups? Given the growing diversity of the population, this question is ever more important. Yet the first point to be made is that existing knowledge remains very limited for answering this question (Leighley, 2001). Studies of engagement and participation depend disproportionately on the national mass survey. However, the small samples of people of color often prohibit subgroup analysis, contributing to the tendency to see all people of color as homogenous. Thus, if mobilizing working-class Black Americans, for example, requires a different set of actions than mobilizing middle-class Blacks, or if mobilizing Latinos requires different strategies than mobilizing Blacks, we can learn little or nothing given the sample size of these groups in most surveys. To be sure, there is a growing number of surveys that oversample people of color, but these remain sporadic and tend to focus on unique issues and/or on one racial or ethnic group at a time, and thereby fail to provide either a means of comparative analysis or a basis for trend studies.

Concomitantly conclusions about factors influencing civic engagement and political participation of people of color have been based primarily on samples of Whites, which are assumed to hold for all individuals in the sample regardless of color. To assume the civic and political behavior of all communities of color are driven by the same factors that drive non-Latino Whites or to assume that the same factors that drive Blacks also drive Latinos, Asian Americans, Native Americans, and other people of color is suspect given different historical experiences, cultures, current economic situations, and political goals (Leighley & Vedlitz, 1999; Walton, 1985).

Indeed, although current data give us some indication of political and civic disparities, they will remain vague until studies of groups such as Latinos and Asian Americans in particular can be disaggregated. For example, Mexican Americans, the most populous of the Latino national origin groups, vote at a far lower rate than Cuban Americans, for example, when one controls for socioeconomic factors. As a result, analyses of Latinos that do not disaggregate by national origin fail to account for the differential political participation of Mexican Americans and other Latinos (Uhlaner, 1991; DeSipio, 1996). Similar conclusions can be reached in regards to differences among groups such as Chinese and Japanese and more recent Asian American immigrant groups such as Koreans, Vietnamese, Cambodians, and others. It is patently ironic that in a country that ideally places such a premium on democracy (and political equality as a guarantor of it) that so little has been invested in providing comprehensive databases to monitor and assess participation trends and attitudes toward democracy.

With these empirical caveats in mind, what do we know about political and civic disparities among racial and ethnic groups in the United States?

Synthesis of Conclusive Research Findings

Clarifications (and Conceptualizations) of Civic Engagement and Political Participation

The following analysis distinguishes between civic engagement and political participation. Civic engagement is defined as informal political and nonpolitical activities engaged in through voluntary organizations such as citizen and community associations and charitable groups. Civic engagement enables individuals, families, and groups to influence issues and factors that affect them and to experience the value of collective action. It should be noted that civic engagement allows people to participate who might otherwise be disconnected or shut out from political participation (for example, noncitizens).

Political participation is defined as formal political activities such as voting, volunteering, working for and contributing to political campaigns, and membership in explicitly political organizations. Political participation falls squarely in the realm of the electoral-representative system and enables individuals, families, and groups as part of an active citizenry to elect public officials and influence formulation and implementation of public policy solutions to societal problems.

Disparities in civic engagement and in political participation are important for two broad reasons. First, for a genuine democracy to function, it must fairly reflect the will of the people. But how do we know the will of the people if some groups' voices are silenced? Those who participate communicate information to public officials about their concerns and preferences and exert pressure on them to respond. Government is far more likely to confer with the participatory privileged and act in their behalf, even if not at their behest; and policies in most critical areas heavily favor their interests. Thus advantaged groups use government power and preference to deepen still further their advantages. In sum, disparities in political participation compromise the fairness of the political process and the political process, thus compromised, produces public policies that protect its advantaged patrons at the expense of the disadvantaged. Equal political involvement is required for the equal protection of interests in public life (Schlozman, Verba, & Brady, 1999, 427).

Second, and relatedly, disparities in civic engagement are especially important in a time when governments at all levels face budget deficits and program cuts. In this context, there is more pressure on communities of color to address socioeconomic problems through their own volunteer activities. Through collective action, groups can begin to recreate their communities and cultivate democratic values. In an age of stark and growing economic inequality, civic engagement, and political action are virtually the only tools disadvantaged groups have for redressing long-standing grievances. To the (substantial) extent that opportunities for individuals are influenced by opportunities for the groups to which they belong, disparities in participation influence disparities among individuals as well as groups.

Political Participation by Race and Ethnicity

For all racial and ethnic groups, voting ranks as the most widespread form of political activity. Yet, despite progress in closing the racial/ethnic participation gap (Frasure & Williams, 2002), voter registration and voter turnout remain unequal by race and Latino origin. Table 9.1 presents the relevant data regarding voter turnout in the 2004 presidential election. According to the U.S. Census Bureau, non-Latino White citizens continued to vote in substantially higher numbers (67 percent) than African Americans (60 percent), Latinos (47 percent), and Asians (44 percent). The bureau reported that turnout rates increased from the 2000 election among Whites (by five percentage points) and Blacks (by three), but held steady for Latinos and Asians. Voter registration rates demonstrate a similar pattern: in 2004, 75.1 percent of non-Latino Whites reported they were registered to vote compared to 68.7 percent of Blacks, 67.9 percent of Latinos, and 51.8 percent of Asians.

As has long been established, three variables (education, age, and residential stability) account for most of the lower aggregate voter turnout of Blacks and Latinos (Verba & Nie, 1972; Wolfinger & Rosenstone, 1980; Leighley & Nagler, 1992; Teixeira, 1992; Rosenstone & Hansen, 1993). For example, for all racial and ethnic groups the higher the education, the higher the voter participation. Similarly older age cohorts and those with greater residential stability among all groups participated at higher rates. Indeed Blacks with lower levels of education actually out-voted their White counterparts and similarly educated Latinos nearly paralleled Whites; the same class/race patterns surfaced in regards to residential stability. In fact, it appears that the Black and Latino middle classes contribute substantially more to the continuing racial/ethnic gap in voter participation than do the Black and Latino working classes. This is demonstrated also in regards to family income and home ownership statistics (U.S. Census Bureau, 2005, tables 9 and 10). Nonetheless it is clear that for all racial/ethnic groups, the higher the family income, the higher the rate of voting; and home owners are significantly more likely to vote than renters among all racial/ethnic groups. In sum, higher socioeconomic status (SES) generally correlates with higher voter participation.

It should be noted, however, that Asian Americans present a complicated picture with regard to the relationship between SES and voting. Asian Americans are not only relatively affluent compared to other people of color and on some dimensions compared to Whites, but also they have the highest level of educational attainment of all racial and ethnic groups; however, in contrast to other groups, Asian Americans have the *lowest* aggregate levels of voter participation. Thus a growing number of scholars conclude that socioeconomic status, the cornerstone of traditional theories of participation, does not adequately explain patterns of participation among Asians. First, some recent studies either find educational achievement and family income to be of no effect or of less effect on Asians than on Whites and other people of color (Lien, 2001; Uhlaner, 1991). Second, most Asian American communities contain large numbers of recent immigrants. Many newer studies (for example,

TABLE 9.1

Reported Voting by Race, Latino Origin, and Selected Characteristics: November 2004 (%)

	Total	White Non-Latino	Black	Asian	Latino (of any race)
Total voting-age citizen population	63.8	67.2	60.0	44.1	47.2
Education					
Less than 9th grade	38.8	39.5	45.6	23.2	37.2
9th to 12th grade, no diploma	39.8	40.6	45.4	24.3	30.5
High school graduate	56.4	58.3	56.3	42.7	42.7
Some college or associate degree	68.9	71.7	66.7	40.7	56.1
Bachelor's degree	77.5	80.7	72.6	47.4	66.5
Advanced degree	84.2	86.6	78.8	58.8	78.1
Age					
18 to 24 years	46.7	49.8	47.0	34.2	33.0
25 to 44 years	60.1	63.5	59.3	40.2	45.2
45 to 64 years	70.4	73.2	65.3	51.1	56.2
65 years and over	71.0	73.1	65.9	47.7	57.0
Residential stability/ Duration of residence					
Less than 1 month	45.4	45.9	54.3	21.9	33.3
1 to 6 months	52.3	55.6	52.6	40.0	33.2
7 to 11 months	56.5	58.4	57.8	45.9	43.7
1 to 2 years	63.5	66.9	62.5	43.0	46.0
3 to 4 years	70.8	73.8	71.9	52.6	54.3
5 years or longer	76.2	78.3	76.1	58.4	68.1

Source: U.S. Census Bureau, Current Population Survey, November 2004, "2004 CPS Microdata File for Voting and Registration in the United States," tables A-1, 6, and 10. Internet Release date: May 25, 2005, http://www.census.gov/voting.

Wong, 2002) find that immigration-related variables such as English-language skills, citizenship status, nativity, immigration generation, and length of stay in the United States may have significant impact on the participation of Asians. Third, the unique status of Asians being simultaneously perceived as non-White, foreign, and affluent may shape their group interactions, heighten their consciousness of group identity, and invite targeted mobilization efforts by community elites and organizations (Kim, 1999; Lien, 2000; Uhlaner, 1991;

Wong, 2002). Finally, "because adult citizens of Asian descent tend to come from an immigrant background and carry a different socialization experience than their U.S.-born counterparts, their education, skills and other personal characteristics, traditionally considered as participation assets among the American electorate, may be accrued outside the U.S. system and cannot be directly translated into participation resources" (Lien, Conway, & Wong, 2004, 220). All of these insights help to shed light on the anomaly posed by Asian Americans to the role of SES in voter participation.

Yet it should be noted that U.S. Census Bureau data, based on a far larger sample size than most surveys, pose a challenge to conclusions with regard to the effects of citizenship status and naturalization. The census found that unlike naturalized non-Latino Whites and Blacks, naturalized Asians, as well as Latinos were actually more likely to report voting in 2004 than native-born Asians and Latinos. Among native Asian citizens, 40.5 percent reported voting while 46.4 percent of naturalized Asian citizens reported voting. Among native Latino citizens, 45.5 percent reported voting while 52.1 percent of naturalized Latino citizens reported voting (U.S. Census Bureau, 2005, table 13). Perhaps the safest conclusion is that consistent with past studies, variables related to SES are independently significant for predicting the voter participation rates within the Asian American population (Lien, Conway, & Wong, 2004). Questions surround how much and through what mediations, not whether, SES factors are closely tied to voting.

There is one group, however, that is clearly, albeit only slightly, more likely to vote than their economically better off counterparts: women compared to men. Since 1976, Black women have voted in presidential elections at a higher rate than their male counterparts; and since 1980, non-Latino White women and Latinas have voted at higher rates than their male counterparts. In 2004, Asian women joined this pattern (U.S. Census Bureau, 2005, table 2). In the November 2004 election, women turned out a higher rate (65 percent) than men (62 percent). Black women voted in proportionately higher numbers (63.4 percent) than Black men (55.8 percent). A higher proportion of non-Latino White women (68.4 percent) voted than White men (65.9 percent). Latinas (49.4 percent) voted at a higher rate than Latino men (44.8 percent); and Asian women (46.3 percent) voted at a higher rate than Asian men (42.0 percent). Gender consciousness appears to heighten women's voter participation across racial and ethnic groups (Githens & Prestage, 1977; Conway, 2000; and Burns, Schlozman, & Verba, 2001).

With the exception of the gender difference, the best available data indicate that those who vote are also those who participate in most other forms of political activity. At this writing, however, one is limited in the evidence that can be mounted to support this conclusion as there has never been a national survey of the political and civic views and activism of all major racial and ethnic groups (Blacks, Latinos, Asian Americans, Native Americans, and Arab Americans as well as Whites) conducted at one point in time; and it has been more than a decade since a survey of a sample of Blacks, Latinos and Whites with sizeable enough numbers to allow subgroup and genuinely comparative analyses was conducted. That survey, the American Citizen Participation Study conducted in 1989–1990, found that with the exception of a slightly higher percentage of Blacks attending community meetings and taking part in protests (a category with few participants of all races and ethnicities), Whites participated in all forms of politics at higher rates than Blacks and Latinos. They were significantly more likely to be affiliated with political organizations, to contact elected officials, to be members of political boards and commissions, and to contribute money to and/or work for political campaigns.

Surveys, however, tend to be snapshots in time and much has changed in the United States in general and among people of color in particular in the last fifteen years. Yet more recent national surveys that sample people of color in large numbers tend to be focused either on just Blacks with a small comparative sample of Whites (for example, annual surveys conducted by the Joint Center for Political and Economic Studies) or samples of single race- and/or ethnic-specific groups (for example, the National Black Election Study, 1996, Tate, 1998; the Latino National Political Survey, 1989–1990, de la Garza, et al., 1998; the Pilot Study of the National Asian American Political Survey, 2000–2001, Lien, 2004; Pew Hispanic Center Survey, 2004a; and the Latino National Survey, 2006, Fraga, et al., 2008). To be sure, these surveys deepen knowledge of differences among people of color and between each group and Whites, but for the most part, all reveal that those who are less likely to vote are also less likely to have attended a public meeting or demonstration in the community where they live, contacted an elected official, contributed money to a candidate running for public office, attended a political party meeting or function, or worked as a volunteer or for pay for a political candidate. Extrapolating from these surveys taken at different points of time in the late 1990s through the early years of the twenty-first century, Whites continue to out-participate each community of color in all these instances. In short, other kinds of political activism do not seem to diminish the kind of demographic inequalities found at the ballot box. In fact, disparities in most dimensions of political activity are even greater than disparities in voter participation. Not surprisingly, given the influence of economic resources, racial and ethnic disparities in political participation are worst of all when it comes to campaign contributions. In the most expensive presidential campaign in U.S. history, a 2004 study found that 89.1 percent of all campaign contributions of $200 or more came from wealthy White zip codes—despite the fact that people of color composed roughly a third of the nation. Only 2.7 percent of such contributions came from predominantly African American zip codes, 2.2 percent from predominantly Latino zip codes, and 0.6 percent from predominantly Asian zip codes (Color of Money, 2005). To the extent that donors are more important than voters in determining who gets elected, to the extent that politicians are more likely to listen to the voices of donors, and to the extent that such voices find their positions more likely to be represented in policy debates and outcomes, people of color and the poor in general remain severely underrepresented because of their inability to keep pace with campaign contributions from wealthier, non-Latino White communities. This disparity may explain in part why legislators expend significantly more time in repealing estate taxes and reforming bankruptcy laws than on job creation and minimum wage reform.

Civic Engagement, by Race and Ethnicity

Data on civic engagement in nonpolitical, informal political, and charitable activities generally follow formal political participation patterns. For instance, recent data from surveys of Blacks, Latinos, and Asians demonstrate that Whites remain substantially more likely to belong to civic associations and to contribute time to charitable work (Pilot Study of the National Asian American Political Survey, 2000–2001, Lien, 2004; Joint Center for Political and Economic Studies, 2002; American National Election Study, 2002, Burns, et al., 2003; and Pew Hispanic Center Survey, 2004a). The racial/ethnic gap in civic engagement is apparent in reports of volunteerism in general and contributing time and money to charities in particular. Whites are more likely to report contributing both more time and more money to charities than do people of color.

In addition to racial and ethnic differences in the rate of civic engagement, there are also notable variations in the kinds of organizations in which volunteers participate. Among Whites who volunteer, religious, child-focused, or education-related organizations get top priority (American National Election Survey, 2002, Burns, et al., 2003), followed by civic associations and health organizations. A similar pattern exists for Latino volunteers, although they are significantly more likely to participate in religious and children and education-related organizations and significantly less likely to participate in civic organizations than their White counterparts (Pew Hispanic Center, 2004a). Asian American volunteers are roughly equally as likely to support religious, civic, and children's and education-related organizations (Lien, Conway, & Wong, 2004). African Americans are a big exception in one regard: those who volunteer are overwhelmingly more likely to participate in religious organizations than other organizations (Joint Center for Political and Economic Studies, 2002; Verba, Schlozman, & Brady, 1995). Given the historic role of the Black church as a sociopolitical institution in African American communities, this result is perhaps not surprising (Harris, 1999).

Some studies show that disparities in volunteerism based on race and ethnicity are even stronger than those found in voting (Ramakrishnan & Baldassare, 2004). In effect, patterns in broad-based civic engagement do not make up for lower political participation rates. They tend, instead, to reinforce the disparities between those who are actively involved and those who are not. In sum, as the size and proportion of the population composed of communities of color grow, there continues to be a disturbing racial and ethnic disjuncture between those who live in the United States and those who shape its civic life.

As with political participation, SES and related variables such as residential stability, place, and home ownership explain most of the racial and ethnic variation in civic engagement (Markus & Walton, 2002; Keeter, et al., 2002; Leighley, 2001; Verba, Schlozman, & Brady, 1995; Bobo & Gilliam, 1990; Guterbock & London, 1983; Olsen, 1972). Succinctly stated: those advantaged in these arenas have greater resources to make their voices heard. People of color tend to be resource-poor. To date, levels of political participation and civic engagement among the nation's racial and ethnic groups reflect and reproduce socioeconomic inequalities, rather than alleviate them.

What Factors Contribute to Racial, Ethnic, and Gender Disparities?

For the most part, civic and political disparities among the nation's racial and ethnic groups have been attributed to economic inequality, constrictive immigration policy, systemic bias, and mobilization bias. Each of these is briefly discussed below.

Socioeconomic and Place Inequality

More than any other single factor predicting participation in the civic and political realms, education disparities have been identified as the key variable. The fact that education plays a central role in determining occupation, which in turn influences income, means that these three resources are correlated and their cumulative and interactive effects are substantial in influencing political participation and civic engagement (Wolfinger & Rosenstone, 1980; Leighley & Nagler, 1992; Teixeira, 1992; Markus & Walton, 2002; Keeter, et al., 2002; Leighley, 2001; Verba, Schlozman, & Brady, 1995, 447; Rosenstone & Hansen, 1993; Bobo & Gilliam, 1990; Guterbock & London, 1983; Olsen, 1972). The longer education disparities by race and ethnicity remain palpable, the longer non-Latino Whites remain advantaged in securing occupations that require skills that are transferable to the civic realm (for example, administration, writing, making presentations, contacting elites, and decision making—i.e., skills people gain in professional and managerial jobs), and the longer that non-Latino Whites have incomes nearly twice that of Latinos and Blacks, the longer political and civic disparities by race and ethnicity are likely.

What has been less studied in regards to participation in the civic and political arenas is wealth. Wealth disparity is far starker than income disparity.

In 2002, for example, the median net worth of non-Latino White households was $88,651 but the net worth of Latino and Black households was only $7,932 and $5,988 respectively—or less than one-tenth the wealth of White households (Pew Hispanic Center, 2004b). Data on home ownership (the principal source of wealth for the average American) and voter participation provide an example of the relationship between wealth and political inequality.

There is a strong relationship between the ownership of a home and the net worth of a household; but as a result of more limited access to financial markets, Blacks and Latinos are substantially less likely than non-Latino Whites to be homeowners. The percentage of non-Latino White households who owned homes in 2002 was 74.3 percent, but the homeownership rates for Latinos and Blacks were 47.3 percent and 47.7 percent respectively (Pew Hispanic Center, 2004b). Home ownership is strongly related to racial disparities in political participation. Those who own homes are significantly more likely than those who rent to participate in various types of political and civic activities. For instance, as discussed above, census data indicate that home owners are more likely than renters to vote in every racial and ethnic group. Other research has shown that if all groups shared the same rates of homeownership, racial inequalities in participation would decline considerably for a wide range of activities such as working for political parties, contributing money to political causes and charities, and belonging to civic associations and community groups (Ramakrishnan & Baldassare, 2004). Thus policies that reduce racial disparities in home ownership should have a salutary effect on racial disparities in civic and political participation. The overall implication is that economic inequality acts as a powerful barrier to political equality (APSA, 2004; Tilly, 2003; Fung & Wright, 2003).

Place inequality (suburban sprawl, concentrated poverty in cities, and segregation) amplifies the effects of income and wealth inequality on civic and political participation (Orfield, 2002; Squires, 2002; 2004; Raphael & Stoll, 2002; O'Connor & Bobo, 2001). As a result of the large and growing amount of place inequality among the poor, middle class, and wealthy (Jargowsky, 2003; Swanstrom, Dreier, & Mollenkopf, 2002), various racial/ethnic groups tend to live in separate and unequal local political jurisdictions (especially municipalities and school districts). Not only does place inequality mean that some have more opportunities and some have fewer opportunities because they live in places that are sharply distinct in terms of tax bases and the quality of public services, but place inequality also makes it easier to isolate people with similar economic and social backgrounds into the same political jurisdictions. The more homogenous political jurisdictions become, the more "safe" districts become, the more predictable elections become, the more levels of political participation decline, especially voting. Concomitantly political parties and activists have fewer incentives to mobilize new groups of voters or develop new issue appeals among people of color. In short, economic segregation has civic effects. Unable to overcome their dire socioeconomic straits or to shape local policies due to fiscal constraints, the poor tend to lose interest in and drop out of politics. Thus place inequality increases economic inequality and decreases civic participation (Oliver, 1999).

Immigration Policy, Naturalization, and Citizenship

As the sizes of the Latino and Asian populations have grown, so has the literature on citizenship and naturalization's effects on participation in the civic and political realms. In particular, some researchers have pointed to the ways in which residency and naturalization requirements tend to alienate immigrant and naturalized citizens—especially from the electoral process. For example, DeSipio concludes that "[n]aturalization of all eligible Latino immigrants and their exercise of the franchise at rates comparable to the current pool of naturalized citizens would add between 50 and 75 percent to the national Latino electorate" (1996, 133). Even just a targeted outreach to naturalize Latinos could add between 400,000 and 1.8 million new Latino citizens and arguably nearly as many voters (DeSipio, 1996). Moreover it should be emphasized that all immigrants are not equal. Latinos in the aggregate often face socioeconomic and concomitantly naturalization hurdles not faced by Asians in the aggregate or Western and Eastern European White immigrants (Hero, 1992; Jones-Correa, 2001; and de la Garza & DeSipio, 1998). There are also considerable differences among immigrants from particular Latin American and Asian countries (de la Garza & DeSipio, 1998). In sum, contemporary immigrants are a very diverse group and current disparities in a wide range of civic and political activities are linked to this diversity as well as to differences in citizenship status (Lien, Conway, & Wong, 2001; Uhlaner, 1991; de la Garza & DeSipio, 1998).

Biases in the Electoral System and Its Practices

Another body of research concentrates on structural features of the U.S. political system that continue to serve as barriers to equalizing participation rates across races and ethnic groups. The most pernicious of these barriers are the loopholes in election laws that permit vote suppression.

Vote suppression results from schemes masquerading as ballot security programs whose actual intent and effect is to discourage or prevent voters in heavily Black, Latino, or American Indian voting precincts from casting a ballot (Hayduk, 2002; Davidson, et al., 2004). Vote suppression programs, facilitated, of course, by place inequality, have several significant characteristics. They focus on minority areas exclusively. There is often only the flimsiest evidence that vote fraud is likely to be perpetrated in such areas. In addition to encouraging the presence of sometimes intimidating poll watchers or challengers, who may slow down voting lines and embarrass potential voters by asking them humiliating questions, these programs have sometimes posted people in official-looking uniforms with badges and side arms who question voters about their citizenship or their registration. "In addition, warning signs may be posted near the polls, or radio ads may be targeted to minority listeners containing dire threats of prison terms for people who are not properly registered—messages that seem designed to put minority voters on the defensive. Sometimes false information about voting qualifications is sent to minority voters through the mail" (Davidson, et al., 2004, 97).

Other barriers related to vote suppression, with significant implications for racial and ethnic disparities in civic and political participation, include exfelon disenfranchisement and wrongful purges. Because people of color make up such a disproportionate number of the exfelon population, the denial of the vote to exfelons has become a subtle method of excluding people of color from the franchise according to some studies. These studies indicate that states with large Black populations are much more likely than states with small Black populations to disenfranchise exfelons (Uggen & Manza, 2002; Harvey, 1994; Shapiro, 1993). The United States now has 1.75 million people disqualified from voting because of criminal convictions—including 1.4 million Black men who have lost their right to vote, almost 15 percent of the Black male population (Uggen & Manza, 2002). Arguably, at least, barring exfelons from voting is a fundamental contradiction of the principle that once a man has served his punishment, he can rejoin society.

Other researchers have focused on the effects of early registration closing dates, limited hours for voting, and the failure to engage in a wide range of postregistration activities to encourage voting on racial and ethnic disparities in voting. A large body of research shows that the effect of state laws prescribing how, when, and where citizens can become eligible to vote influences levels of participation. The greatest aggregate efforts of more difficult registration laws are on those with the least amount of formal education and/or who are younger. By far the most consequential legal provision is the closing date or registration deadline; allowing citizens to register shortly before the election or at the polls on election day has been demonstrated to be an effective way to encourage voting. Where registration requirements are minimal or nonexistent, the effect of education is reduced because less educated citizens vote at higher rates while the turnout of the better educated is nearly unchanged (Highton, 1997). Moreover permissive registration arrangements are especially beneficial to younger citizens (Teixeira, 1992, 119; Highton & Wolfinger, 2001).

Postregistration activities also have a disparate effect upon citizen participation. Wolfinger, Highton, and Mullin, 2004, for example, conclude that postregistration laws (such as extended polling hours, postregistration mailings of sample ballots and polling place location information, and extended polling hours on election day) increase turnout among the registered. Such effects vary widely by education, age, race and ethnicity. A larger impact is observed for Latinos compared to Blacks.

They estimate that universal implementation of longer polling hours and more election mailings would increase turnout of Black registrants by 3.3 percentage points and Latino registrants by 4.3 points. Overall they project that turnout of the registered would increase by 2.8 percentage points if all states adopted "best practices" postregistration procedures. These are substantial gains from adoption of procedures that are neither risky nor expensive and therefore should attract little overt opposition (Wolfinger, Highton, & Mullin, 2004).

Mobilization Bias

Finally many researchers focus on differential mobilization by race and ethnicity. While SES is a primary determinant of civic and political action, high-status individuals are more likely to participate in part because they are more likely to be asked or recruited to participate. On the other hand, individuals of lesser social status are forced to rely on the political mobilization of organized community groups more heavily than do individuals of greater social status (Verba, Schlozman, & Brady, 1995; Leighley, 2001). Surveys confirm that people of color are disproportionately less likely to be asked to participate by politicians and activists (Rosenstone & Hansen, 1993). They are especially less likely to be contacted by Whites. For example, Verba, Schlozman, and Brady (1995) demonstrate how race and ethnicity structure who is asked to participate. Non-Latino Whites are far more likely to be asked (56 percent) than either African Americans (40 percent) or Latinos (25 percent). When asked, African Americans are most likely to report being asked to participate by other African Americans, while Latinos are more likely to report being asked by non-Latino Whites. Even higher income Blacks are only slightly more likely to be asked to participate than lower-income Blacks.

Promising Practices

In general, what helps young and/or less affluent Americans participate will help people of color. From the least to most difficult proposals to achieve, insights drawn from both the literature and praxis can be grouped into six categories: personal contacting, community organizing, youth targeting, structural reform, structural electoral reform, fostering more competitive elections, and policy change.

Personal Contacting

Recently a host of field experiments have examined the effects of personal contacting (for example, Gerber & Green, 1999; Green, Michelson, & Bedolla, 2007;

Michelson, 2003). These field experiments reveal statistically significant support for the effectiveness of personal contacting for people of color (particularly young persons). Door-to-door or face-to-face interactions have demonstrated their effectiveness in encouraging people of color to become both more civically and politically involved. Moreover people of the same racial/ethnic group have been shown to be better at contacting those of their same racial/ethnic group (Michelson, 2003). In sum, asking people to participate and giving them a reason to do so results in higher rates of civic and political participation (DeSipio, 1996).

Community Organizing

Past organizing has demonstrated that meeting people "where they are" (that is, focusing on the local issue they already see as important to their quality of life) is the first step in getting people politically involved. Framing and reframing issues in each community's popular vernacular produces maximum benefit. In short, successful mobilizations begin by finding consensus, not creating it. Successful work around a specific issue can then be used to move on to larger, more complex issues. As issues broaden, diverse ethnicities and races and both genders can be attracted to groups, bridging gaps. Through this process, community rooted activities reconnect citizens to engaged, responsible public life, not just on election day but throughout the year.

Community institutions can play a key role in this process. In fact, it has never been more important that they do—given the decline of political parties as mobilizers and the growth of high-tech politics emphasizing money, not voters. The situation is made still more critical by the membership decline of organizations such as labor unions that also historically "mobilized the un-mobilized." Into this vacuum, community institutions and organizations have moved and played a remarkably vital role. For example, there is a convincing body of evidence that African American churches are conduits for political skills, resources, and mobilization. Research evidence shows that religious institutions such as Catholic dioceses and faith-based organizations are also important to Latino and Asian American civic engagement. Work by groups such as the Industrial Areas Foundation (IAF), one of the most successful community organizing associations, demonstrates that church-based institutions are key resources for developing social capital across racial and ethnic communities.

Other organizations such as community economic development organizations and other community-based nonprofits and ethnoracial civic associations including social service agencies and legal and voter education, registration, and get-out-the-vote organizations are all playing important roles in mobilization efforts in particular and social capital development in general. Indeed activism in community-based institutions with strong leadership is the most common theme in studies aimed at addressing ways to overcome civic and political disparities (Markus & Walton, 2002). It is noteworthy, however, that although community organizations play a strong role in making up the mobilization deficit left in the wake of parties that now disproportionately focus on activating loyal non-Latino White voters rather than mobilizing new minority voters, they are limited in what they can achieve given these organizations' other priorities, narrow constituencies, and limited resources. The most powerful political institutions such as parties and political elites are the ones with the resources, responsibility, and mandate to expand the circle of inclusion to all Americans.

Electoral Reform

Two types of structural reforms have demonstrated significant capacity to promote political involvement. The first type involves eradication of features of the electoral system that constrain people's ability to choose decision makers; and the second involves creation of new structures, particularly at the community level.

Regarding the import of eradicating structural barriers to equalizing participation, one need look no further than the immediate impact of the Voting Rights Act of 1965. African American voter turnout rose dramatically from barely one-third in the 1956 presidential election to nearly two-thirds in the 1968 presidential election (Rosenstone & Hansen, 1993).

Regarding creation of new community governance structures, what is called "empowered participatory governance" structures, have proved effective in a growing number of communities. For example, neighborhood governance councils that develop substantial power over arenas such as policing and public schools; participatory budgeting enabling residents to participate directly in forging city budgets and habitat conservation planning that empowers stakeholders to develop governance arrangements that satisfy the double imperatives of human development and the protection of endangered species have all raised the participation rates of families as well as individuals in public life (Fung & Wright, 2003).

Fostering More Competitive Elections

Even without changes in the electoral system, more competitive elections produce higher voter participation rates. This was perhaps the most obvious lesson of the 2004 presidential election where reported voter turnout rose by 4.3 percentage points (from 59.5 percent to 63.8 percent). Especially when it comes to people of color, candidates on the ballot that produce strong feelings of attachment and/or aversion produce high turnout. This has been demonstrated in national and local elections—for example, when Jesse Jackson was on the ballot for the Democratic presidential nomination; when Harold Washington ran for mayor of Chicago; and, alternatively, when former Ku Klux Klan leader David

Duke ran for governor of Louisiana. In each of these instances, Black voter participation rose significantly (Tate, 1994).

Targeting Youth

Given the disproportionate share of young people in communities of color, efforts specifically targeted to youth have shown promise. Best practices in this area include public policy consultations with youth where youth opinions on decisions that affect them promote involvement. Including youth in organizational decision making as members of governing boards not only provides exposure to the world of politics but also encourages their participation. Other efforts that have promoted youth involvement include strengthening the civic curricula, providing financial assistance to encourage students to apply scientific knowledge to projects addressing community-wide problems, and providing opportunities for youth to work in the electoral politics arena as canvassers, representatives, and spokespersons.

In 2004, one effort targeted at youth that secured considerable media attention was the formation of groups associated with popular entertainers focused not only on college youth, but also school dropouts and, in states where felons can vote, young people who had been to prison and/or succumbed to the allure of gangs (Sullivan, 2004; Smalley, 2004). Building upon the history of Rock the Vote (RTV), a fifteen-year-old organization founded by members of the recording industry that uses popular culture to spur youth participation, political empowerment was held out as a different path to power, focusing on issues such as linking poor neighborhoods with underachieving schools to low participation in deciding who becomes policymakers. Future research evidence is sorely needed to assess the impact of these efforts to mobilize the youth population before conclusions about their effectiveness can be drawn.

Policy Implications

Given the intersections of race, ethnicity, class, age, and gender in influencing participation rates as well as the interaction of economic and political inequalities, there can be no permanent and fully successful effort to end civic and political disparities without strategies directed toward equalizing opportunities among racial and ethnic groups to share in the nation's wealth. Ethnic and racial disparities in civic and political action are not likely to disappear over time unless there is general social and economic progress among today's subjugated groups. There are, however, several policy proposals that could increase civic and political participation rates among people of color. Based on the preceding analysis, seven such recommendations are set forth. Rather than considering the list to be exhaustive, it should be understood as simply a top seven baseline for progress.

Link civic engagement and political participation, and encourage both. Increase and strengthen outreach efforts by civic, community, and political institutions that are targeted toward reducing racial and ethnic disparities in civic engagement and political participation. Create more awareness among low-participating groups about the volunteering opportunities, outreach, and education efforts of community organizations by developing public service announcements (PSAs) for the old (television, radio, and print) and new (Internet and other electronic forms) media. Focus on issue and policy education and advocacy, not just outcomes of electoral campaigns. Identify volunteer opportunities that can be performed with more flexibility (for example, from home or in hours outside of a 9-to-5 workday) and reach out to individuals and families who need flexibility.

To encourage youth participation and send a message that service and politics are not separate and alternative activities, amend AmeriCorps legislation to allow participation in political activities, particularly voter registration, under the same constraints that govern 501(c)3 organizations involved in advocacy work. Facilitate use of federal work-study funding for civic and political service. Develop initiatives and outreach strategies and tactics that capture the diversity among youth, on the basis of both racial and ethnic differences and differences in lifestyle, experiences, and current opportunity structure (for example, programs not just for students but also for dropouts and youth with experiences in the criminal justice system). Begin political education and service courses at an earlier age, for example, in middle schools. Encourage civic courses to become more relevant to community needs and more focused on democratic life. In general, in designing programs to increase political participation and civic engagement, public and nonprofit groups should consider the unique differences among and within racial and ethnic groups.

Expand and enforce voting rights protections. Reauthorize the Voting Rights Act (VRA) in 2007 and continue to reauthorize it until civic and political disparities by race, gender, and ethnicity disappear. Make tougher rules against vote suppression. Through litigation, if necessary, clarify and liberalize the Voting Rights Act, the National Voter Registration Act (Motor Voter), and the Help America Vote Act (HAVA) to make them more applicable to "ballot security" intimidation than they currently are. Establish a network of volunteer lawyers as a component of a campaign to be prepared for ballot intimidation (Swirsky, 2002). Effectively use media and comprehensive voter education so that victims of vote suppression know it when they see it. Encourage the victims of excesses of ballot security programs who have been unlawfully challenged, harassed, denied assistance in voting, or purged from the rolls to bring private damage suits, payable by poll officials. Eliminate or at least alter the ID requirement of HAVA as well as more expansive identification requirements recently passed by some state legislatures, which that have resulted in aggressive poll officials singling out minority voters and interrogating them with humiliating questions. Require all college and universities to set up polling places on campuses and outlaw scare tactics targeting students, such as warnings that voting could affect financial aid, lead to fines or prison sentences, and other voter suppression efforts. Make voter intimidation efforts related to voter identification a felony. Mandate safeguards for accurately counting votes, including requiring all electronic machines used in voting to produce a voter-verified paper trail. Simplify, clarify, and reform laws across the nation barring exfelons from voting rights.

As a first step, reenfranchise citizens with first-time nonviolent felony convictions who have completed their sentences. Also, closely scrutinize state processes to purge felons from voter rolls that wrongfully remove registered, eligible citizens from the rolls. Find election officials who conduct wrongful purges. Improve implementation of the "motor voter law," by monitoring state compliance with the provision of the law requiring that those utilizing public assistance be asked if they would like to vote, and if so, provided with voter registrations forms and assisted in the completion and submission of the forms. In general, enforce Motor Voter, reauthorize the VRA, and strengthen HAVA.

Adequately reform campaign finance laws. Provide full public financing of elections as an antidote to the inequities of the current finance system in order to make sure that candidates who do not have access to wealthy families and rich special interest donors have a chance to compete in political campaigns and that voters have more choice. By equalizing the campaign finance playing field, candidates and officials should be more likely to listen to the voices of those who have no money to contribute.

Reform the presidential election structure. Only one office is filled through an election of "all the people" in the nation; yet that office is the only federal electoral office left that denies the people the right to directly vote to fill it and that openly violates the principle of "one person, one vote." Amend the constitution and allow either for election of the president by popular vote or proportional representation in awarding electoral votes. Given that amending the constitution is always an arduous process, accomplishing this change will require bottom up pressure on both major parties, Congress, the president, and state legislatures. The struggle to achieve this change could be an exercise in recruiting many groups and individuals in collective action in ways that bridge difference.

Reform registration, voting, and postregistration systems in a way that equalizes opportunities for participation. Mandate uniform national voter registration rules and uniform national standards for voting roll purges for all federal elections. Make election day a holiday and/or at least urge the government, the private sector, and the nonprofit sector to encourage people to participate by allowing them time off the job and paid leave to perform their civic duty. Other similar or related reforms include multiday balloting, same-day registration, and keeping the polls open longer. Make polling places more accessible. Provide clear provisional ballot rules that are the same in every state. Develop federal standards to address the removal of physical and cognitive barriers in voting systems. Increase the currently insufficient funding of the Election Assistance Commission (EAC), created by HAVA, whose mandate is to advise states on election standards and distribute federal funding for election reforms to the states. Strengthen the mandate for the EAC to conduct studies focusing on nationwide statistics and methods of identifying, defining, and investigating voter fraud and voter intimidation; recruiting, training, and improving the performance of poll workers; educating voters about registration, voting, operating voting machines, locating polling places, and other aspects of participation. For federal elections, provide funding to the states with federal oversight for effecting postregistration provisions such as mailing sample ballots, information about polling place locations, keeping polls open longer, and other procedures that have demonstrable effects on encouraging participation of subjugated groups.

Reform immigration law. Make naturalization simpler and more accessible. Reinstate noncitizen voting rights as a way of empowering legal residents, increasing their interest in U.S. politics, forging loyalty to the nation, and providing fairness to people who already must submit to all other laws and citizenship requirements.

Fully fund research to improve understanding of racial and ethnic disparities in civic and political participation as well as attitudes toward democratic life. Given the important role government plays in funding research and development and given the paucity of scientific evidence regarding the participation of communities of color, create a new program at the National Science Foundation (NSF) whose mission is to: (1) support research aimed at developing more rigorous databases, indicators, and indices to measure trends and patterns in attitudes toward democracy; (2) study exclusionary barriers as well as civic structures facilitating greater participation; (3) examine levels and types of civic engagement and political participation in diverse communities; and (4) analyze perceptions and realities of what participation produces in terms of national and local results. In a large-scale biennial survey, similar to the Panel Survey of Income Dynamics (PSID), gather data points that identify patterns and trends in civic and political participation. In addition to categories that would be followed across time, continuously reassess about 20 percent of the categories used to study volunteerism and political participation across various groups and new and different ways of engaging diverse populations.

Also provide funding to the U.S. Department of Commerce to provide data on forms of participation in addition to voting in its current population surveys (CPS). Given the large size of the CPS sample (about 50,000 households), it would be possible to do state level analyses as well as subgroup analyses.

Conclusion

The primary focus of this chapter is how to prepare productive, effective citizens among all groups of Americans and thereby strengthen the democratic way of life. The intersectional analysis we have used reveals the persistence of racial, ethnic, and gender disparities, deeply rooted in the very structure of our political systems. This is an immense problem for democracy as government is more likely to confer with those who participate at high rates and act in their behalf. Consequently policies in most critical areas are likely to heavily favor those who participate most rather than serving democracy's egalitarian ideal.

Indeed the very construction of difference and inequality among families, neighborhoods, and races is a concomitant of a range of policy decisions made by public officials and policy-related actions taken in the private and nonprofit sectors. Policies at all levels of government continue to play a fundamental role in creating disadvantaged, resource-poor, or isolated neighborhoods for some individuals, children, families, and communities.

A wide range of changes in social and economic policy arenas that contribute to lower participation rates among people of color are necessary. From the interstate highway system to home mortgage deductions to zoning decisions of local governments to taxation, tax credits, franchises, charters, banking, trade regulation, and research funding, policies at all levels of government have played an important role in fostering place inequalities. Inequalities nurtured by policy can be altered by policy as well. Similarly, as home ownership and residential stability are intimately related to participation rates, policies that encourage home ownership should have salutary results for political participation. The presence or absence of job-creation incentives, wage policies, and labor-market policies in general are implicated in the mix of why some participate less than others. Finally national policies aimed at expediting the process of naturalization should help boost the extent to which first-generation immigrants (who are disproportionately Latino or Asian) participate in civic associations. Governmental and nongovernmental actors at the state and local levels could strengthen the association between citizenship acquisition and volunteerism by incorporating civic skills and civic recruitment efforts into courses that help immigrants to pass the naturalization exam.

Considering that politics and policy have played such an apparent role in determining the distribution of wealth in this country, there can be little change in patterns of inequality without policy change. Yet there is a significant complication in this situation, in that it is unlikely that policy reform will occur without significant and persistent pressure from those most negatively affected, as evidenced by higher levels of civic and political engagement within today's currently underrepresented groups. Thus the authentic work of improving outcomes for these groups will never be accomplished without equalizing opportunities for the collective action that lies at the heart of civic engagement and political participation. With sustained attention to the issue of civic engagement and political participation from researchers, foundations, community organizations, and political leaders, we can hope for reductions in racial and ethnic disparities, increase the influence of those currently disengaged from civic life, and realize the democracy we all deserve.

References

Almaguer, T. (1994). *Racial Fault Lines: The Historical Origins of White Supremacy in California*. Berkeley: University of California Press.

APSA Task Force on Inequality and American Democracy. (2004). *American Democracy in an Age of Rising Inequality*. Washington, DC: American Political Science Association.

Bobo, L., & Gilliam, Jr., F. D. (1990). Race, Sociopolitical Participation, and Black Empowerment. *American Political Science Review, 84*, 377–393.

Burns, N., Kinder, D. R., & The National Election Studies. (2003). American National Election Study, 2002: Pre- and Post-Election Survey (Computer file). ICPSR version. Ann Arbor, MI: University of Michigan, Center for Political Studies (producer), 2003. Ann Arbor, MI: Inter-university Consortium for Political and Social Research (distributor).

Burns, N., Schlozman, L. K., & Verba, S. (2001). *The Private Roots of Public Action: Gender, Equality, and Political Participation* Cambridge, MA: Harvard University Press.

Chang, G. H. (2001). *Asian Americans and Politics: Perspectives, Experiences, Prospects*. Washington, DC: Woodrow Wilson Press.

Color of Money: The 2004 Presidential Race, Campaign Contributions, Race, Ethnicity and Neighborhoods. (2005). *Public Campaign, the Fannie Lou Hamer Project, and the William C. Velasquez Institute*. Retrieved from www.colorofmoney.org.

Conway, M. M. (2000). Gender and Political Participation. In S. Tolleson-Rinehart & J. J. Josephson (Eds.), *Gender and American Politics: Women, Men, and the Political Process*. Armonk, NY: M. E. Sharpe.

Davidson, C., Dunlap, T., Kenny, G., & Wise, B. (2004, September). Republican Ballot Security Programs: Vote Protection or Minority Vote Suppression—Or Both. *A Report to the Center for Voting Rights and Protections*, unpublished.

de la Garza, R., & DeSipio, L. (1998). *Making Americans, Remaking America: Immigration and Immigrant Policy*. Philadelphia: Westview.

de la Garza, R., Falcon, A., Garcia, F. C., & Garcia, J. A. (1998). Latino National Political Survey, 1989–1990 (Computer file). 3rd ICPSR version. Philadelphia, PA: Temple University, Institute for Social Research (producer), 1992. Ann Arbor, MI: Inter-university Consortium for Political and Social Research (distributor).

DeSipio, L. (1996). *Counting on the Latino Vote: Latinos as a New Electorate.* Charlottesville: University Press of Virginia.

Flexner, E. (1973). *Century of Struggle: The Women's Rights Movement in the United States.* New York. Atheneum.

Fraga, L., Garcia, J. A., Hero, R., Jones-Correa, M., Martinez-Ebers, V., & Segura, G. M. (2008). Latino National Survey, 2006 (Computer file). ICPSR version. Ann Arbor, MI: University of Michigan, Center for Political Studies (producer), 2008. Ann Arbor, MI: Inter-university Consortium for Political and Social Research (distributor).

Frasure, L., & Williams L. F. (2002). *Civic Disparities and Civic Differences: Ethno-Racial Civic Engagement in the United States.* Civic Engagement Working Paper #3. College Park: Democracy Collaborative, University of Maryland.

Fung, A., & Wright, E. R. (2003). *Deepening Democracy: Institutional Innovations in Empowered Participatory Governance.* London: Verso.

Gerber, A. S., & Green, D. P. (1999). Does Canvassing Increase Voter Turnout? A Field Experiment. *Proceedings of the National Academy of Sciences of the United States of America, 96*(19), 10939–10942.

Gerstle, G. (2001). *The American Crucible: Race and Nation in the Twentieth Century.* Princeton, NJ: Princeton University Press.

Githens, M., & Prestage, J. (1977). *Portrait of Marginality: The Political Behavior of the American Woman.* New York: C. McKay Co.

Green, D. P., Michelson, M. R., & Bedolla, L. G. (2007). ACORN Experiments in Minority Voter Mobilization. In R. Fisher (Ed.), *The People Shall Rule: ACORN, Community Organizing, and the Struggle for Economic Justice.*

Grofman, B., Handley, L., & Niemi, R. G. (1992). *Minority Representation and the Quest for Voting Equality.* New York, NY: Cambridge University Press.

Guterbock, T., & London, B. (1983, August). Race, Political Orientation, and Participation: An Empirical Test of Four Competing Theories. *American Sociological Review, 48,* 439–453.

Harris, F. (1999). *Something Within: Religion in African-American Political Activism.* New York: Oxford University Press.

Harvey, A. E. (1994). Ex-Felon Disenfranchisement and Its Influence on the Black Vote: The Need for a Second Look. *University of Pennsylvania Law Review, 142,* 1145–1171.

Hayduk, R. (2002). The Weight of History: Election Reform during the Progressive Era and Today. In R. Hayduk & K. Mattson (Eds.), *Democracy's Moment: Reforming the American Political System for the 21st Century.* Lanham, MD: Rowan and Littlefield Publishers.

Hero, R. (1992). *Latinos and the U.S. Political System: Two-Tiered Pluralism.* Philadelphia: Temple University Press.

Highton, B. (1997, May). Easy Registration and Voter Turnout. *Journal of Politics, 59,* 565–575.

Highton, B., &. Wolfinger, R. E. (2001, January). The First Seven Years of the Political Life Cycle. *American Journal of Political Science, 45,* 202–209.

Jargowsky, P. (2003). Stunning Progress, Hidden Problems: The Dramatic Decline of Concentrated Poverty in the 1990s. Washington, DC: The Brookings Institution.

Joint Center for Political and Economic Studies. (2002). Washington, DC, National Opinion Poll–Politics. Data supplied by David Bositis, October 23, 2004.

Jones-Correa, M. (2001, February). Institutional and Contextual Factors in Immigrant Citizenship and Voting. *Citizenship Studies, 5*(1), 41–56.

Keeter, S., Andolina, M., Jenkins, K., & Zukin, C. (2002, August). Schooling and Civic Engagement in the U. S. Presented at the Annual Meeting of the American Political Science Association, Boston.

Kernell, S., & Jacobson, G. C. (2000). *The Logic of American Politics*. Washington, DC: Congressional Quarterly Press.

Kim, C. (1999). *Bitter Fruit: The Politics of Black-Korean Conflict in New York City*. New Haven, CT: Yale University Press.

Leighley, J. E. (2001). *Strength in Numbers? The Political Mobilization of Racial and Ethnic Minorities*. Princeton, NJ: Princeton University Press.

Leighley, J. E., & Nagler, J. (1992, August). Individual and Systemic Influences on Turnout: Who Votes? 1984. *Journal of Politics*, *54*, 718–740.

Leighley, J. E., & Vedlitz, A. (1999). Race, Ethnicity, and Political participation: Competing Models and Contrasting Explanations. *The Journal of Politics*, *61*, 1092–1114.

Lien, P. (2000). Who Votes in Multiracial America: An Analysis of Voting Registration and Turnout by Race and Ethnicity? In Y. Alex-Assensoh & L. Hanks (Eds.), *Black and Multiracial Politics in America* (pp. 199–221). New York: New York University Press.

Lien, P. (2001). Voting Participation: Race, Gender, and the Comparative Status of Asian American Women. In G. H. Chang (Ed.), *Asian Americans and Politics: Perspective. Experiences, Prospects*. Stanford, CA: Stanford University Press.

Lien, P. (2004). Pilot National Asian American Political Survey (PNAAPS), 2000–2001. ICPSR version. Van Nuys, CA: Interviewing Service of America, Inc. (producer), 2001. Ann Arbor, MI: Inter-university Consortium for Political and Social (distributor).

Lien, P., Conway, M. M., & Wong, J. (2004). *The Politics of Asian Americans: Diversity and Community*. New York: Routledge Press.

Markus, G., & Walton, Jr., H. (2002, February). Civic Participation in American Cities. Presented at the Annual Meeting of the American Political Science Association, San Francisco, CA.

Michelson, M. R. (2003). Mobilizing the Latino Youth Vote. *CIRCLE Working Paper #10*, College Park: Maryland.

Neuborne, B., & Eisenberg, A. (1976). *The Rights of Candidates and Voters*. New York: Avon Books.

O'Connor, C. T., & Bobo, L. D. (Eds.). (2001). *Urban Inequality: Evidence from Four Cities*. New York: Russell Sage Foundation.

Oliver, J. E. (1999). The Effects of Metropolitan Economic Segregation on Local Civic Participation. *American Journal of Political Science*, *43*(1), 186–212.

Olsen, M. (1972). Social Participation and Voting Turnout: A Multivariate Analysis. *American Sociological Review*, *37*, 317–333.

Orfield, M. (2002). *American Metropolitics: The New Suburban Reality*. Washington, DC: The Brookings Institution Press.

Pew Hispanic Center. (2004a). July 2004 political survey, Toplines. Retrieved from http://www.pewhispanic.org/site/docs/pdf/2004%20Latino%20Political%20Survey-toplines.pdf.

Pew Hispanic Center. (2004b). Wealth Gap Widens between Whites and Hispanics. Retrieved from http://www.pewhispanic.org.

Putnam, R. (2000). *Bowling Alone: The Collapse and Revival of American Community*. New York: Simon & Schuster.

Ramakrishnan, S. K., & Baldassare, M. (2004). *The Ties That Bind: Changing Demographics and Civic Engagement in California*. San Francisco: Public Policy Institute of California.

Raphael, S., & Stoll, M. A. (2002). Modest Progress: The Narrowing Spatial Mismatch between Blacks and Jobs in the 1990s. Washington, DC: The Brookings Institution.

Rosenstone, S. J., & Hansen, J. M. (1993). *Mobilization, Participation, and Democracy in America*. New York: Macmillan Publishing Company.

Schlozman, K., Verba, S., & Brady, H. (1999). Civic Participation and the Equity Problem. In T. Skocpol & M. Fiorina (Eds.), *Civic Engagement in American Democracy* (pp. 427–459). Washington, DC: Brookings Institution Press.

Shapiro, A. L. (1993). Challenging Criminal Disenfranchisement under the Voting Rights Act: A New Strategy. *Yale Law Journal*, *103*, 537–568.

Skocpol, T., &. Fiorina, M. P. (Eds.). (1999). *Civic Engagement in American Democracy* Washington, DC: Brookings Institution Press.

Smalley, S. (2004, July 26). Voter Drives Reach out to Youths with Records. *Boston Globe*, p. B1.

Squires, G. D. (2002). Organize: The Limits of Public Awareness in Assuring Fair Housing. *Housing Policy Debate*, *13*(3), 505–513.

Squires, G. D. (2004). Privileged Places: Race, Uneven Development and the Geography of Opportunity in Urban America. Unpublished paper.

Sullivan, J. (2004, July 26). Hip-Hop Takes Action, *Boston Globe*, p. A18.

Swanstrom, T., Dreier, P., & Mollenkopf, J. (2002). Economic Inequality and Public Policy: The Power of Place. *City and Community*, *1*(4), 349–372.

Swirsky, S. A. (2002). Minority Voter Intimidation: The Problem That Won't Go Away. *Temple Political and Civil Rights Law Review*, *11*, 359, 361–62.

Tate, K. (1994). *From Protest to Politics: The New Black Voters in American Elections*. Cambridge, MA: Harvard University Press.

Tate, K. (1998.) National Black Election, 1996 (Computer file). ICPSR version. Columbus, OH: Ohio State University (producer), 1997. Ann Arbor, MI: Inter-university Consortium for Political and Social Research (distributor).

Teixeira, R. A. (1992). *The Disappearing American Voter*. Washington, DC: Brookings Institution.

Tilly, C. (2003, January). Inequality, Democratization, and De-Democratization, *Sociological Theory*, *21*(1), 37.

Uggen, C., & Manza, J. (2002). Democratic Contraction? The Political Consequences of Felon Disfranchisement in the United States. *American Sociological Review*, *67*, 777–803.

Uhlaner, C. (1991). The Acquisition of Partisanship by Latinos and Asian-Americans: Immigrants and Native-Born Citizens. *American Journal of Political Science*, *35*(2), 390–422.

U. S. Census Bureau. (2005). *Voting and Registration in the Election of November 2004*, Current Population Survey (CPS). Retrieved from http://www.census.gov/population/www/socdemo/voting.

Verba, S., & Nie, N. H. (1972). *Participation in America: Political Democracy and Social Equality*. New York: Harper and Row.

Verba, S., Schlozman, K. L., & Brady, H. (1995). *Voice and Equality: Civic Voluntarism in American Politics*. Cambridge, MA: Harvard University Press.

Walton, Jr., H. (1985). *Invisible Politics: Black Political Behavior*. Albany: State University of New York Press.

Wilkins, D. E. (2002). *American Indian Political and the American Political System*. Lanham, MD: Rowan & Littlefield Publishers, Inc.

Wolfinger, R. E., & Rosenstone, S. J. (1980). *Who Votes?* New Haven, CT: Yale University Press.

Wolfinger, R., Highton, B., & Mullin, M. (2004, June). *How Postregistration Laws Affect the Turnout of Registrants*, Circle Working Paper 15.

Wong, J. S. (2002, January 11). The Role of Community Organizations in the Political Incorporation of Asian American and Latino Immigrants. *Presented at the Wingspread Conference on Race and Civil Society.*

10

Intersections, Identities, and Inequalities in Higher Education

BONNIE THORNTON DILL

Intersectionality is the intellectual core of diversity work. As Frank Hale points out in the introduction to his book, *What Makes Racial Diversity Work in Higher Education*: "Institutions of higher education are a part of a global culture that maintains the racial divide and highlights the constant clashes between the ideals America espouses and what Americans practice in fact" (2004, 3). Scholars doing intersectional analysis—many of whom are scholars of color—are widely dispersed across their colleges and universities in the arts, humanities, social sciences, health sciences, and in schools of international affairs, law, and business. Many embody the diversity that they seek to understand and explain in their research, writing, and teaching about the ways race, class, gender, and sexuality influence and are influenced by other social factors. Thus they often find themselves struggling both professionally and personally to establish legitimate, accepted, and supported space for the work of intersectionality as a scholarly contribution to diversity and for themselves, as individuals within a predominantly White, male, heteronormative U.S. academy.

Over the last thirty years, the scholarship that laid the groundwork for what has come to be known as intersectional analysis has been pioneering work.[1] It has been done in the face of indifference and hostility. Scholars engaged in building programs in women's studies, ethnic studies, and in lesbian, gay, bisexual, and transgender studies have had their intellect, their scholarship, their professionalism, and even their sanity questioned. In more recent years, they have been attacked as agents in the destabilization of a perceived collegial university based on unitary principles of U.S. cultural literacy. The social and political context that shaped these scholars' experiences in the academy is marked by the post–civil rights struggles to establish ethnic and women's studies programs, efforts to implement affirmative action programs, changes in immigration laws permitting foreign students increased access to U.S. higher education, philanthropic initiatives supporting curricular innovation, and the backlash against these changes most notably the Bakke, Hopwood, Gruter, and Gratz court decisions restricting affirmative action in higher education (Anderson, 2005; Elliott & Ewoh, 2005).

The purpose of this chapter is twofold: (1) to synthesize insights of academics that have been at the forefront of the development and institutionalization of intersectional work as revealed in a series of interviews and conversations focused on the strategies, barriers, and resources they encountered in their efforts to integrate new forms of interdisciplinary knowledge around race, class, and gender into their own academic institutions; and (2) to derive from these a set of lessons for a subsequent generation of scholars who will, hopefully, continue this work and for those administrators in higher education who have the will to assure multiple diverse perspectives in the production and dissemination of knowledge about difference and persistent patterns of inequality in the United States.

The Study

In order to capture the insights and experiences of these scholars to prepare a report for the Ford Foundation, I conducted interviews with approximately seventy faculty and a few graduate students at seventeen universities and colleges in the United States during the spring of 2001.[2] The conversations had two major foci: defining, describing and characterizing intersectional work; and exploring the organizational and leadership structures through which the work is done.

The faculty members selected for interviews are not representative of any clearly identifiable larger population but instead reflect a group of scholars who see themselves or are seen by others as engaged in intersectional scholarship. I generated names from the literature and through referrals among informal networks of scholars in the field. Often these yielded people who were currently or had recently chaired a department or program in which intersectional issues were central. On the four campuses I visited, I invited my initial contacts to identify other colleagues with whom they thought I should speak. This chapter is based on the data collected and findings of that report read in the broader context of the scholarship on diversity in higher education.

Leadership: Intersectional Scholars in Academic Locations

A number of the faculty members with whom I spoke had established long-standing academic careers, while others were relative newcomers. The more experienced people had been among those who had either initiated or institutionalized race or gender based programs and departments on their campus. They were intellectual leaders and institution-builders and had gained considerable knowledge about the workings of their institution. Thus they had profound insights about the skills and abilities needed to direct and sustain these programs and deep feelings about the professional and personal costs and benefits of being engaged in this kind of institution building work.

The qualities and characteristics they identified as essential in advancing and promoting intersectional scholarship and teaching on their campus over the previous decade stressed a willingness to work hard and a desire to be engaged in institutional change. Strategically leaders were required to have knowledge of the institution, an understanding of how power works within it and the ability to demonstrate how one's program adds value to the institutional mission in order to garner support from top administrators. In their view, leaders had to see themselves as change agents, willing to take risks as well as to identify and work cooperatively with allies; have passion for the work and a readiness to be pushy, persistent, and dogged in the pursuit of their objectives. They also had to develop skills in fundraising, knowing how to attract money for special programs. Although many of those interviewed had entered this work early in their careers, they argued that it is now essential that the leaders be tenured, senior faculty with established scholarly reputations, who are powerful, strong, aggressive, and know how to build an infrastructure.

With so much expected and needed in these positions of leadership it is not surprising that respondents saw them as having both high costs and high benefits. Among the benefits mentioned are: personal growth as a scholar and teacher; opportunities to support and mentor students and junior faculty especially people of color and women; experience in dealing with multiple constituencies—a skill that led some to get tapped for deanships and other high-level administrative positions; a chance to build institutions and create programs where intersectional ideas are paramount and the scholarship is nurtured; more occasions to engage in interdisciplinary scholarship and to stretch and grow from those experiences; enhanced learning about university organization and politics; as well as facilitating a fuller understanding of the needs for and benefits of community. Drawbacks were often stated in dramatic terms describing how the demands of the work had: "gutted (my) entire concept of a personal and private life"; devastated work on individual projects; resulted in experiencing years of economic deprivation; taken a toll on personal relationships; been responsible for the failure of numerous talented scholars to move ahead at the institution; and increased personal paranoia. One scholar summarized the advantages and disadvantages by saying that his loss of a personal life had nevertheless been replaced by "the most enriching professional life possible." An African American woman scholar at a large institution on the West Coast shared the following reflections on her own cohort of scholars and in doing so summarizes ideas expressed by many of the respondents:

> We haven't been able to do the scholarship we wanted to do, haven't produced to the potential we could have. We've experienced considerable professional wear and tear, having to reckon with intense feelings of personal and intellectual alienation. We've had to carve out a place to be in the institution, not just for ourselves but for others as well. Many people have paid a high personal price to do this work. I've had five close friends who are colleagues die in five years. I've seen a lot of talented people unable to move up in their institutions. On the other hand, there are many things about the career that have been extremely rewarding—teaching and nurturing students and junior colleagues are at the top of the list.

Who Speaks for People of Color and at What Cost?

The question, "Who speaks for people of color" is at the heart of issues of inclusion, exploitation, authenticity, and representation on every campus because there is a disjuncture between the stated desire to build diverse institutions of higher education and the makeup of the faculty in most U.S. colleges and universities. According to Myra Gordon:

> Most campuses have elaborate mission statements about valuing diversity . . . yet when it comes to faculty demographics, improvements have been painfully slow (Harvey, 2002). Why is this the case? . . . no one can deny that there are supply and demand dynamics in the labor pools from which we are attempting to recruit diverse candidates. However, the work of Daryl Smith and her colleagues (1996) has shown that the majority of minority doctoral recipients of prestigious scholarships and fellowships are neither highly sought after nor exorbitantly paid . . . .The real reason for a general failure to diversify lies in the culture and practices typically associated with faculty hiring. (2004, 183–184)

Faculties and departments in which there is a growing emphasis on scholarly questions related to race and ethnicity, facing what they see as a limited supply of faculty of color, find they are grappling with this tension in hiring, retention, tenure, and promotion decisions. Once hired, faculty of color most often come to realize that they are expected to "represent" people of color in a variety of service capacities, none of which are incorporated fully into their compensation or tenure evaluations. Even departments and institutions with good intentions of making race, ethnicity, and difference central to their work rely heavily on a very small number of scholars of color whose personal commitments to diversity scholarship, diverse students, and institutional change put them at the risk of exploitation and/or self-sacrifice.

These issues are compounded by a secondary tension that occurs within diverse communities about authenticity and representation: who can claim membership in or speak on behalf of the group. Questions of identity, essentialism, and representation occur in the scholarship, in hiring, tenure, and promotion of faculty, and around both national and global concerns. Within intersectional scholarship itself, critiques of speaking for and writing about diverse people as "the other"—an outsider that is deviant from the normative insider—have been central to the discourse. As scholars have sought to reclaim and present the stories and lives of previously silenced groups, and to define new areas of scholarship such as Black feminist studies, Chicana studies, etc., it is not surprising that that this would become a thorny issue.

Both of these tensions were apparent in the example of a women's studies program at a large Southwestern university that decided to make Chicana feminism more central to their program. The search for faculty, preferably Chicanas, engaged in feminist, intersectional scholarship took several years, involved a few unsuccessful efforts to recruit senior scholars from other institutions and had culminated, at the time of my visit, with hiring over a two-year period, two talented Chicana literary scholars who were new PhDs. These young women were the first and only Chicanas in the department. Prior to their arrival, most of the research and teaching about Chicanas was conducted by White scholars. So, although the department had established strong ties to the Mexican American studies program on the campus, the appointments of these scholars carried with it the expectation that they would be the key players in developing a Chicana studies concentration in the Women's Studies Department. This recruitment clearly reflected a departmental commitment to diversifying its faculty in an area that they felt was vital to the future of their program and demonstrated their persistence and determination in accomplishing this goal.

At the same time, however, it was clear that the young women who joined the faculty would find themselves at the center of several hotly contested issues. What, I wondered, would be the effects and experience of being the first and only Chicanas among the women's studies faculty? How would the work involved in developing a new program area shape their scholarly careers, tenure prospects, and personal lives? What kind of institutional and departmental leverage would they have as junior faculty members doing this work? How would they navigate department politics in addressing such questions as whether making Chicana studies central to the curriculum means all women's studies majors would be required to take a course in Chicana feminist thought or whether the feminist theory course should be redesigned to place Chicana feminism at its center? As Chicanas, these young scholars had certain claims of authenticity that their more senior White colleagues lacked, but as junior faculty without tenure, reputation, or established alliances within the institution, they could be particularly vulnerable to exploitation or self-sacrifice in the service of a cause to which they were deeply committed. Strong support and mentoring by the department chair and colleagues across the campus committed to intersectional and Chicana studies would be required to help them overcome these obstacles.

Alliances/Networks/Multiple Affiliations

Intersectional work is dependent upon collaborations, alliances, and networks among scholars with similar intellectual interests, visions, ideas, and values. Overwhelmingly the existence of these collaborations and networks were dependent on particular individuals and the personal and professional relationships they developed with other colleagues. Even in women's studies and ethnic studies departments, the existence of these networks relies heavily upon the particular scholars located in the program. In most institutions where this work is taking place, women of color who hold faculty appointments in either ethnic studies, women's studies, or other academic departments are key participants and often central to developing and maintaining these networks on their campus. Women of color do this work, even though, as women and minorities, they face a number of institutional and professional challenges. Not the least of which is that among a small pool of minority faculty, women of color make up an even smaller group. In 2003, about 15 percent of faculty in U.S. colleges and universities were minorities (based on a total excluding persons whose race/ethnicity was unknown, but including nonresident aliens who were not identified by race/ethnicity). Six percent of the faculty was Black, 5 percent was Asian/Pacific Islanders, 4 percent was Hispanic, and 0.5 percent was American Indian/Alaska Native. Nearly half of college faculty (47 percent) was White males, while 36 percent was White females (U.S. Department of Education, National Center for Education Statistics, 2006). Earlier data for women indicates that in 2000, according to the National Center for Education Statistics: 6.7 percent of PhDs were granted to African American women, and 4.1 percent to Latinas. Among those who enter faculty ranks, only 2.9 percent of all those with tenure was African American or Latina in 2001.[3]

Because their numbers are so small, women of color experience the stress of hypervisibility and isolation among other factors. Studies of women of color faculty members demonstrate that institutional factors have negative effects on their retention and that they face greater demands and expectations for institutional service (Aguirre, Martinez, & Hernandez, 1993; Olsen, Maple, & Stage, 1995; Talbert-Hersi, 1995; Alex-Assensoh, 2003; Dey & Thompson, 1998).

The remarks of one of the women I spoke with reflect these stressors. She stated that she had learned how to insulate herself from institutional insensitivity and lack of support by practicing fighting racism and sexism in her everyday life: "Networking, coalition building and making ties with people who support similar visions, ideas and values (at other institutions) . . . that's what keeps me growing." Thus one of the benefits of intersectional work is that the people who do it, especially women of color, form alliances and networks with others, both on and off their campuses, who are also engaged in this work.

For example, an African American professor of English at a large midwestern university became chair of the English Department after serving as chair of the Women's Studies Department. This woman, in fact, had faculty standing in three departments: English, African and African American studies (AAAS), and women's studies and anticipated that collaborations between women's studies and AAAS would improve because of her ties to both departments and because of AAAS's awareness of her knowledge and perspective on the place of race in women's studies. Indeed most of the women of color I spoke with had either standing or affiliations in several academic units. These usually include both women's studies and an ethnic studies area along with a traditional discipline.

Multiple affiliations are both an asset and a liability. They mirror the complex intersectional nature of the women's personal, political identities and intellectual interests and they enhance the possibilities of finding an intellectual "home" within the university. Nevertheless the affiliations also increase the demands on their time as well as the amount of reading, publishing, teaching, and service they are expected to do to contribute to the reputation of each of these units. These commitments are particularly problematic for junior scholars and for those who engage in the collaborative and interdisciplinary work that results from multiple affiliations without institutional recognition, credit, or support.

One Asian American professor at a private East Coast university for sixteen years spoke quite frankly about the lack of incentives, vision, and resources available to bring scholars with similar interests together on her campus or to support their potential for multiple affiliations. She describes struggling for many years to teach a course on Asian Americans and only being allowed to do so in 2000. She attributes this struggle to a cost-benefit mentality that permeates this private university. "Efforts at collaboration" she argues, "are overwhelmed by a climate where power struggles over scarce resources and the need to protect turf prevail."

Although women of color are still principle players in the conduct of intersectional scholarship, a broad variety of individual scholars located in a diverse array of departments are also engaged in intersectional scholarship. Scholars acknowledged that on most campuses there was no institutional location that fostered interdisciplinary dialogue and exchange on these issues. Thus on most campuses when these exchanges do take place, they were often ad hoc or informal, occurring in people's homes, in reading groups, brown bag seminars, or in campus lecture series. I was told, for example, that at an urban midwestern university, a Black male scholar of race and queer studies and a relative newcomer at the time, began a race, gender, and sexuality discussion group by hosting monthly meetings at his home. The group included people from institutions throughout the community and was seen as a place where discussions of the intersections of race and ethnicity with gender and sexuality were welcomed. Another example occurred at a liberal arts college in the Northeast in a study group focused on gender and social justice. Described by a women's studies faculty member as a loose collection of women's studies faculty engaged in antiracist, cross-cultural work, the group developed and taught courses around these issues, conducted faulty development workshops, and mentored students. However, they never received institutional support.

Resources and Support

It is not surprising, therefore, that a consistent theme in these conversations was the difficulties of obtaining college or university resources and support to build institutional structures that would facilitate and sustain intersectional work. Only two of the institutions represented in this study in 2001 had a unit specifically designated to give campus-wide visibility to intersectional work: the University of California, Berkeley, and the University of Maryland. Other institutions had dedicated some of the time of faculty and administrators toward initiatives that were related to this work and even supportive of it. Nevertheless differing structures and dynamics on campuses generated a range of supports and challenges in building intersectional scholarship and these are illustrated in case examples from four different institutions.

Scholars at a large midwestern university, which they described as a place where disciplinary organization and insularity tends to keep interdisciplinary programs and scholarship somewhat on the margin and even suspect in some circles, described a program of cluster hires that they found helpful in building a community of intersectional scholars. Cluster hires are a strategy in which several faculties with similar specialties are hired at the same time in different departments with an eye toward interdisciplinary teaching and academic programming. Other strategies that had been used to support intersectional and interdisciplinary scholarship were discussion circles, joint appointments, and technology funding for comparative projects. Each of these approaches has both advantages and limitations. Cluster hires, as one professor pointed out, have helped in some departments but they have not been effective in transforming more traditional disciplines which remain insular and unwilling to hire scholars who do intersectional work. And, as an African American professor of English at this same midwestern University pointed out: "You can dream things up in the department but it will not happen without the support of the dean, associate deans, divisional committees, and other administrators."

Gaining the support of senior administrators is difficult for a variety of reasons, not the least of which is because every program and initiative on the campus is also trying to gain their support and good favor. A number of the people with whom I spoke argued that a major barrier is that most administrators do not understand the work and how crucial it is to the larger intellectual life of the campus. The fact that people doing intersectional work are thinking and theorizing about complexities—many of the very complexities that the campus confronts in its efforts to build a more diverse student body—is neither appreciated nor drawn upon in efforts to wrestle with these issues. Additionally collaboration is an important aspect of intersectional work and yet a number of institutions have been slow to encourage and reward these kinds of cross-disciplinary engagements. Because of this, those engaged in multidisciplinary collaborations saw themselves as risking or experiencing devaluation of their work because it could not be readily evaluated within existing disciplinary criteria.

One of the most interesting and creative institutional strategies for building a community of intersectional scholars and supporting interdisciplinary work that I encountered took place at a large university on the West Coast. This particular institution had been engaged in curricular change activities for many years. Those activities, combined with an administrative commitment to invest in building faculty and departmental capacity to pursue scholarship on race, gender, ethnicity, and other dimensions of difference, increased the number of intersectional scholars on the faculty through a planned and systematic approach designed to improve campus diversity.

Rather than leave academic units on their own to hire individual scholars that fit some parochial definition of departmental needs, the divisional dean (a woman who was formerly chair of the Women's Studies Department) initiated a program designed to recruit a group of scholars focused on the work of intersections from a variety of disciplinary and interdisciplinary perspectives. According to her, it took a year and a half of groundwork to prepare departments and administrators to participate in this initiative as a way not just to increase their faculty but also to change their departments.

The result was that thirteen professors were hired in one year. These professors generated new courses, colloquia, and a project to establish connections with HBCUs[4] and new programs linking the campus to nearby ethnic communities. Cohorts of faculty at both the senior and mid-career level who had been engaged in this scholarship for several years supported those who were newly hired in initiating and implementing these programs. Also, departments lent their support to this new work as part of their participation in the initiative and, according to the dean, newly hired faculty, "didn't have to sacrifice their careers in order to do this (work) while others sat around and watched."

The institution then applied for and received external grant support for a project designed to support those newly hired scholars through a program of course development, colloquia, and interdisciplinary seminars designed to increase the impact of their work on the future of the university. Yet even in the face of this kind of support, ethnic studies faculty felt that this new generation of scholars is still battling the devaluation of their scholarship in the academy at large. An African American woman professor of ethnic studies, who had become associate graduate dean not long before our interview, acknowledged that her successful move into administration had helped the Ethnic Studies Department gain additional legitimacy.

At a Historically Black University, a Black woman who chaired a major disciplinary department in the social sciences argued that her position as chair was a key factor facilitating her ability to establish a research center and a graduate certificate in women's studies—both of which focus on intersectional work. Department chairs at her institution have considerable power and authority and she leveraged that to provide resources (money and space) essential to establishing the certificate program. It took ten years to get approval for the program along with the support of a dean eager to have his school reflect current trends in higher education. Even in the face of that support, she had to host the program in her department for the first year to keep debates about money and resources from undermining the idea itself.

While many of these interviews highlight the role of women of color at predominantly White institutions, this particular case illustrates that even at an HBCU, work examining the intersections of race and class with gender is the work of women of color. This woman was one of only two women department chairs in the entire university, having arrived there with a well established commitment to intersectional ideas. She used her position as a catalyst to facilitate and support the work of other faculty who wished to develop courses and programs on these topics on the campus. She was also quite strategic in gaining support from her male colleagues, first accepting their support as a personal favor and waiting as they gradually came to see the intellectual and institutional value of participating in and collaborating with this new initiative. In assessing the factors that were essential ones in bringing this institute about, she acknowledges that her institutional location as a department chair, her willingness to be pushy, and her ability to bring both male and female colleagues on board were the most important.

The cases described above demonstrate some of the institutional supports and hindrances referred to throughout the interviews. In varying degrees, respondents felt that despite institutional rhetoric promoting diversity, research and scholarship that contribute to the intellectual understanding of difference were largely ignored with emphasis, instead, being placed on metrics: numbers of students, faculty, or staff. Additional hindrances frequently cited were the lack of financial support; bureaucratic resistance to new ideas; a failure to understand the work and mission of the newer disciplines; and a lack of a sincere and thorough commitment to diversity. While most of the institutions represented in this study have responded to pressure from faculty engaged in this work to facilitate its growth in some ways, none of them used as well planned and deliberate a recruitment strategy as the institution on the West Coast. In most places, recruitment, hiring, and retention still take place within individual departments that are largely ignorant of race and gender issues (Agathangelou & Ling, 2002) and therefore unable and often unwilling to see this as a priority. As a result, intersectional scholarship becomes an institutional concern only when a critical mass of intersectional scholars emerges serendipitously out of multiple recruitment processes, and after that collection of individuals realize that there is a group of colleagues with whom they can collaborate. Thus support for this work seems to come in one of three ways: individual, senior scholars decide to take responsibility for championing this scholarship and building institutional support; those same individuals move into positions of power and use those resources to invest in the development of this work; or a dean or other high-level administrator responds to the entreaties of senior faculty and provides financial and/or institutional mechanisms to promote this kind of work through approaches such as cluster hires, joint appointments, and targeted hiring; funding for institutes or for faculty development programs that promote this scholarship and help build community. In many cases, however, the tendency to focus on diversity progress in terms of metrics or cocurricular programming misses the opportunity inherent in intersectional scholarship, which links diversity to the research and teaching missions of higher education.

Teaching and Curriculum Transformation

Teaching is at the heart of the enterprise of higher education and curriculum transformation has been a major strategy in the project of diversifying colleges and universities (Banks, 1996; Banks & Banks, 1989; Adams, Niss, & Suarez, 1991). Most of the scholars interviewed, identified teaching as an important tool linking theory and practice both in their own lives and potentially in the lives of their students.

Advances in Teaching

Closely linked to concerns about the creation and production of knowledge are issues of its dissemination. Faculty members were eager to discuss their teaching goals and strategies and identified promising approaches to disseminating this scholarship both in the classroom and in society at large. Several approaches that seek to convey the relationship between power, social change, and social justice in critical social theory stood out. These include teaching about power and privilege, integrating service learning or other forms of community engagement in courses and using technology to share materials that may be less accessible or create international discussions and exchanges. Each of these approaches is used to teach students to think beyond traditional and static conceptions of race, gender, identity, class, nation, and society.

Power and Privilege

As argued in chapter 1, understanding power is at the heart of intersectional thinking. Teaching students to identify and understand the concepts of power and privilege as they are implicated in systems of racial, gender, and class oppression is therefore a shared priority among interviewees. A prominent South Asian scholar described this as "[the] most radical and interesting teaching—keeping up with scholarship but pushing students to ask questions about the choices they make." She uses her classroom examinations of power to encourage students to examine their own thoughts and beliefs about such concepts as race, class, nation, and the influence these constructs have in their lives. A Latina assistant professor, whose concentration is literary studies, described her approach as a turn to theory that inspires a return to liberatory pedagogy. She believes that incorporating discussions of social inequality and coalition politics into literature classes not only gives students more voice in what is discussed, but inspires them to work for social justice.

Students also gain important critical thinking skills when exposed to intersectional scholarship in the classroom. A White male assistant professor of communications described teaching media literacy as "teaching people and creating groups to engage what this stuff means culturally, politically, and historically." By learning how to understand and read the symbols that surround them, he argued, students explore their own assumptions about race, class, and ethnicity. As straightforward as this may seem, however, he and his African American woman colleague took pains to point out that this kind of work is contested within their field and is often not viewed as theoretical. Two senior White women literature professors described how novels are helpful in explaining important concepts in intersectional thinking to undergraduates such as the concept of "othering." Because much of this teaching takes place in interdisciplinary fields, faculty find that incorporating knowledge from a variety of sources fosters the students' ability to change perspectives and learn about inequality by breaking through the veils of privilege that surround many White middle- and upper-class students. Many scholars find fiction and poetry particularly helpful in accomplishing this purpose.[5] A White woman professor and chair of a Women's Studies Department added, "Students get an incredible sense about diversity and exclusionary practices looking at the world through the eyes of those at the bottom."

Over the years, these scholars point out that their access to teaching resources (textbooks, readers, films, etc.) that include material on intersections has increased. A White male historian and professor of gender studies described how his teaching of a course on the history of sexuality changed over the ten-year period. With the materials currently available, he found that he was better able to center the course on the intersections of race and sexuality in a way that was not possible earlier. The growth in this scholarship and in publications, which take this work seriously, brings with it great advantages for those teachers who incorporate its themes into their courses. Indeed two White women literature and women's studies professors suggested that it is becoming almost routine to see the intersections of social identities taught in introductory courses on their campus. Two White women professors at another institution, both of whom had chaired their women's studies departments, discussed requiring the inclusion of multicultural materials in the courses in their program. Indeed another professor pointed to the film "It's Elementary" that illustrates how even elementary school teachers are beginning to incorporate such topics as homophobia into their classrooms (Hackman, 2002).

Several scholars also pointed to ways in which students at many different levels are beginning to benefit from an expanded curriculum. One Black woman professor of women's and Black studies discussed her participation in the work of the New Jersey Project where teachers from kindergarten through twelfth grade are taught to internationalize their curricula with materials drawn from the fields of African and Caribbean studies. The New Jersey Project was the only statewide, state-funded curriculum transformation project in the nation. The project encouraged and supported curriculum and faculty development around issues of gender, race/ethnicity, class, culture, and sexuality at New Jersey's four- and two-year public and private colleges and universities (Rothenberg, et al., 1996). This project and some others designed to promote multicultural education are in the forefront of disseminating theoretical developments of intersectional thinking across different levels of learning, extending exposure to these ideas beyond higher education.

Nevertheless, while the people interviewed for this research are developing exciting ways of disseminating this knowledge in the classroom and through curriculum transformation projects within their own and other institutions, it would be a mistake to convey the impression that the teaching of intersectional ideas and approaches is sweeping any of these campuses. It does represent an important and acknowledged part of the approach in some fields, women's studies and ethnic studies being the primary ones, and among scholars who focus on race, class, gender, ethnicity, and sexuality in other fields.

Innovations in Pedagogy

Scholars acknowledged developing innovative and creative teaching methods as a means of giving students a better grasp of the concepts, nuances, and complexities of this scholarship. These include service learning, a variety of group and individual projects, and an interdisciplinary framework that requires students to expand their knowledge beyond traditional understandings of race, nation, gender, class, sexuality, and ethnicity. The excitement that emerged as they described the ways they taught about intersectionality revealed their passion and commitment to sharing this knowledge with students of every background.

Service learning and community connections are one of the ways that they sought to illuminate the connections between theory and practice. A strong proponent of this approach, one African American woman professor of literature and women's studies used the terminology "theory-practice learning" to describe it. In her approach, students move out of the classroom and away from what is familiar "to gather and assess data . . . experience actual hands on learning and practice. In the process, they revise and recreate theory." She takes her class to work in a battered women's shelter and finds it pays off in terms of students gaining practical knowledge about the issues on which they are theorizing.

In an article that describes a vision of teaching that transforms individuals and promotes justice, Chow et al., describe a teaching strategy that they call, DPE—dialogic, participatory, and experiential. Through the combination of these three approaches, the academic process of teaching and learning in the classroom becomes less rigid and more accessible. An intellectual space is created that opens up the classroom so that a more extensive and diverse group of people can participate in learning. For example, in one course, students went on field trips to visit social service agencies. The goals are to reveal the benefits to the learning process of a diverse environment and to facilitate maximum student engagement in their own learning (Chow, et al., 2003). The teachers use these approaches to also illustrate some of the institutional and structural aspects of the topics the courses are addressing.

A South Asian women's studies professor at a liberal arts college assigns her own institution as the basis for one of her class projects and has students analyze the culture of power within the institution. Her students "read about power and agency in complicated ways and then have to do the work of examining how it actually operates in the place where they . . . live." These active and innovative approaches to learning seek to teach students how to theorize about the interconnections between identity, power, social structures, and inequality.

In addition to classroom strategies, programs and courses that stress interdisciplinary approaches are increasing and many are excellent conduits for promoting work at the intersections. A Latino male professor of ethnic studies explained that ethnic studies majors at his West Coast institution are required to concentrate, not on a particular racial/ethnic group but in two out of three broad areas: histories, languages, or cultures. This approach is designed to insure that students learn to compare groups structurally through a multifaceted lens. The department itself supports this curricular design by hiring faculty whose scholarship focuses comparatively on at least two ethnic groups.

Two women professors, one White and one Black, at a large midwestern university pointed out that the faculty of their women's studies department had willingly engaged in an extensive process of pedagogical review to insure that all of the courses in their program were truly interdisciplinary. Reiterating the importance of intersectionality for women's studies, an African American ethnic studies professor argued that the emphasis on intersections had extended the focus in the field of women's studies beyond that of White middle-class women by ensuring that the interconnections among race, gender, sexuality, and class are central to core courses. Intersectional interdisciplinarity increases teachers' ability to rethink the content of courses and expand the scope of their scholarship. Nevertheless implementing these courses is easier at some institutions than others. On those campuses that are still rigidly organized around disciplines, interdisciplinary work may be seen as less rigorous and more transitional. Thus scholars on those campuses may encounter more difficulties in creating interdisciplinary teaching and learning environments.

Team teaching, encouraged in institutions where there is a growing acceptance of interdisciplinarity, is an important tool in creating courses that can explore the intersections of social statuses from multiple perspectives. An African American professor of history described team teaching as allowing folks with "different reservoirs of knowledge" to bring their specialties to bear in a connected and exploratory way. At a large northeastern university, a team of young faculty successfully redesigned a traditional course on the dynamics of race, sex, and class to place intersectionality into a more global framework emphasizing the concept of nation and its relationship to the other categories. This expansion of scope benefited the students, the faculty, and the institution itself.

Uses of Technology

The increase in technological applications for teaching over the past decade has widened the number of tools that can be used to enhance students' understanding and comprehension of scholarship at the intersections. First and foremost the Internet offers unlimited access to enormous amounts of information previously unavailable to faculty or students. Two Latino law professors have used it to create a cyber-community with reading groups that involve both national and international participants. They also seek to create cyber-classrooms that can "truly overcome the lack of international focus many U.S. law school programs tend to have" (www.LatCrit.org). At my own university within the last two years, one colleague created an extremely useful tool for teaching visual literacy that incorporates intersectional analysis, entitled: *The Visual*

Literacy Toolbox: Learning to Read Images. Another colleague facilitated the development and implementation of a multinational online course on women's health and well-being entitled "Women's Health and Well-Being: Transnational Perspectives and Pedagogies." The course, which focused on intersections of gender, class, nation, and culture in women's health, involved four instructors and students at institutions in four different countries working together through the Internet and culminating with a teleconference in real time where students and faculty exchanged their research findings on the most vital issues affecting women's health and well-being today. Topics covered included reproductive health and sexuality, women and mental health, and women's social well-being and bodily integrity. Scholars and students also discussed how their research contributes to addressing women's health needs at all levels, nationally and transnationally, and how much they had learned through the international, cyber-classrooms that were part of the project.

Concerns

Despite the enthusiasm and commitment expressed by these scholars engaged in teaching intersectional ideas, a number of concerns were identified. Among these is a dearth of opportunities to come together and discuss the challenges and successes of intersectional teaching.

A continuing challenge in the field that is manifested in teaching is how the multiple differences that we acknowledge and discuss are identified, understood, and prioritized. A White woman professor of sociology and women's studies suggested that differences in training, background, and knowledge among students leads to very different understandings of notions of identity and difference in her graduate women's studies classes. "Some students," she said, "want to think that all the categories are equally oppressive. And we often do not have the tools needed to convey to students the nature of the differences between these categories. For example, sexuality has a different effect on people's daily lives than redlining neighborhoods." She attributed this dilemma, in part, to the disparities between poststructuralist theorizing about the nature of difference and the ways oppressed groups theorize difference. Often, she argued, those who come to the concept of difference through poststructuralist theory tend to see all of the categories as abstractions that are empty and interchangeable. In her experience, these students lack knowledge of the cultural and historical factors that have shaped the categories and that provide the basis for understanding difference as an outgrowth of the experiences of oppressed groups.

Additional concerns about teaching turn on the ongoing issue of institutional support. Some institutions are more supportive than others of intersectional, interdisciplinary teaching, and faculty engaged in this work place considerable value on teaching as one of the most important ways of disseminating these ideas. Nevertheless faculty at some of the large universities said that they are not convinced that good teaching is truly valued and adequately rewarded and these value differences are compounded by the small numbers of faculty of color at most of these institutions. This conundrum led one Black woman professor and chair of African American studies to question whether students of color are receiving adequate mentoring. She pointed to the reality that at some institutions, students would not even have the option of taking a course from a person of color to say nothing of having a scholar of color as a mentor.

Inherent in intersectional teaching is a commitment to exploring questions of identity, inequality, and social justice. Faculty and graduate teaching assistants are eager to discuss and explore ways to improve pedagogical practice and to share insights and experiences from teaching these ideas. For many, teaching is an important form of social praxis. It is a way to develop critical thinking and awareness of social issues among their students. The material they present and the ideas they convey are often new to undergraduates and they encounter resistance, enthusiasm, as well as outrage from students when the students' understand that their earlier education had denied them access to this knowledge. Curriculum transformation programs have generally been important in disseminating this scholarship and are still needed not only to introduce this knowledge to faculty outside the field, but to help support faculty engaged in teaching it.

Marginalization and Institutional Identity

Despite successes and inroads, the interviews convey the belief that intersectional work remains at the margins of the academic enterprise. Although scholars acknowledge that strides have been made, that the amount of this scholarship is growing and that various institutions have begun to support some aspects of this work, those engaged in it feel that it continues to be far more peripheral to the central mission and activities of colleges and universities today than is appropriate. The reasons for this are both organizational and intellectual and these perceptions are exacerbated by the culture of power in most institutions of higher education. Paul Kivel (2004), in an essay entitled "The Culture of Power" argues that:

> Whenever one group of people accumulates more power than another group, the more powerful group (the "in" group) are accepted as the norm, so if you are in that group it can be very hard for you to see the benefits you receive (25). [He continues,] Those inside the culture of power rarely notice it, while those excluded are often acutely sensitive to how they and others are being marginalized. Therefore leadership in efforts to eliminate the culture of power needs to come from those in excluded or marginalized groups. Unless they are in leadership positions

with sufficient respect, status, and authority, the organization's efforts
to change will be token, insufficient, and have limited effectiveness . . .
Every institution of higher education has a culture of power. Each
department, division, school, program and office within it has its own
subculture of power. (30–31)

To some extent, those who have achieved leadership positions of "sufficient respect, status and authority" have begun to open spaces for work on
race, class, and gender within a culture of power designed and dominated by
White men. However, as many scholars indicate, much remains to be done.
One of the most striking findings of this study is that, on most campuses, this
work has no institutional identity. There is no unit or office with the specific
mission of bringing this usually widely dispersed work together or promoting
and facilitating it. Most often, these ideas are made visible in the teaching and
programming of women's studies and ethnic studies departments or programs. The University of California, Berkeley, and the University of Maryland
are the only two institutions in this study that had a unit specifically designated to support and promote work on the intersections of race and gender.[6]
Interestingly both were directed by women of color.

The Center for Race and Gender at Berkeley was started in the spring of
2000. It was initiated by the chancellor as a response to student hunger
strikes. Although there had been requests in previous years to establish such a
center, those requests had never been granted. The director, Evelyn Nakano
Glenn, an Asian American sociologist and professor of ethnic and women's
studies saw the announcement of this center as a golden opportunity and
chose to direct it because of the possibilities of developing the work on intersectionality. The university gave them $125,000 for all of the center's expenses
including staffing and programming. Although the funding is small, Glenn
feels that with staff and energy they can accomplish a lot. She used the money
to give small grants, to support one dissertation fellowship, and to bring people from different departments who are engaged in this work together by supporting working groups led by faculty. Glenn acknowledges that promoting
this kind of work at Berkeley will be difficult. She describes UCB as a conservative institution, one in which disciplines seek rankings based on national reputations, which are usually defined by disciplinary cannons. Intersectional
analysis is marginal in all of the mainstream disciplines. In addition, Berkeley
is not particularly supportive of interdisciplinary work. These factors make it
even more challenging to achieve her goals.

The Consortium on Race, Gender, and Ethnicity at the University of Maryland
was established in 1998 with an external grant and limited university resources.
Its focus is intersectional work and its development, mission, and institutional
placement is described in a detailed case study in the following chapter.

Scholars explain the intellectual marginalization of intersectional ideas by pointing out that, fundamentally, this body of scholarship is about connecting ideas across disciplines and interlacing constructs that have customarily been treated as separate and distinct. As an interdisciplinary enterprise within the conventionally structured academy, it occupies a precarious place and is often viewed with skepticism. Thus scholars engaged in this work often find that they have to fight the perception of their work as less rigorous, more transitory, and less prestigious than the work done in traditional disciplines. At the same time, efforts to transform traditional disciplines so that they incorporate intersectional analyses are slow and difficult.[7] Although some fields have made strides, many have not. One African American woman professor referred to the work of a colleague when she said:

> the academy has not done enough with what Deborah McDowell calls the social inflections of scholarly discourse. It has not done enough to interrogate how scholarship gets done and who does it. They (traditional disciplines) assume that what they do is best and most appropriate. New ideas are seen as a result of a lack of knowledge of those standard long-time expectations instead of recognizing that people have deliberately chosen to assume—to use Chandra Mohanty's phrase—"oppositional space" within an institutional space.[8]

A White woman sociology professor and chair of a Department of Women's Studies at a large southern university suggested that part of the explanation for the marginalization of this scholarship is racism. Because work by and about women of color is central to this field, she argued, Whites who control and predominate in the academy do not see the work as something that could be at the center of academic life and scholarship.

Another explanation of the marginality of this scholarship, which combines both organizational and intellectual explanations, was suggested by a South Asian professor at a northeastern liberal arts college who linked the discourse on diversity and intersectionality as an intellectual and teaching enterprise to the impact of the increasing corporatization of the university. She asked, "If the student is constructed as a consumer and multiculturalism is a product to be consumed, who owns the courses?" and what kind of multiculturalism is most marketable? In other words, will the corporatized university be interested in a multiculturalism that unveils and challenges power relationships of inequality or will it endorse a multiculturalism that merely manages diversity?[9] These are important questions because colleges and universities, for a variety of educational, social, economic, and political reasons are increasingly working to develop programming and a public image that highlights diversity. Most often this notion of diversity focuses on increasing numbers and improving human relations throughout the campus by developing awareness, acceptance, understanding, and appreciation of human differences. Rarely does it focus on the inequalities of power and resources embedded in these differences; even more rarely is the expertise of intersectional scholars seen as central to this enterprise. The push for diversity and multiculturalism coincides with a push toward a more corporatized and entrepreneurial academy. What will be the result of these converging trends for scholarship that focuses on intersectionality?

At present it appears that the structure and organization of most large universities is porous enough that the answer to these questions is open. In other words, it is possible—at least in some institutions—for both the power analysis and diversity management strategies to coexist; the former in the scholarly side of the institution and the latter on the administrative and fundraising side. However, in the face of reductions in state budgets and foundation support, many universities, hungry for external support, will seek an approach that manages diversity rather than engage in a thorough analysis of power and inequality that would require major structural and organizational changes.

Conclusions and Recommendations

The insights and experiences of the scholars with whom I spoke as a part of this study reveal several important things about the nature and place of intersectional work in today's academy:

1. Intersectional scholarship is the intellectual and scholarly manifestation of diversity. It is an outgrowth of the struggles of oppressed people to end oppression and achieve social justice.
2. Scholars engaged in this work often embody the differences they write and teach about and are therefore engaged in creating places for themselves and for this scholarship in institutions of higher education where their numbers are few and their ideas represent new knowledge.
3. Leadership on these issues has had both professional and personal benefits and costs. Those who have been successful have been willing to make considerable investments of their time and energies in the work of institutional transformation.
4. The costs have been high and the work hard because institutions seek to represent themselves as diverse but do so at the expense of faculty of color, whose numbers are small, and yet are in great demand to "represent" themselves or their group on behalf of their institutions.
5. Committed individuals, particularly women of color, with the ability to build networks and alliances, develop strategies for institutional change, and strive with persistence toward the goals of establishing a legitimate

and acknowledged place for this work, are the primary force behind the growth and institutionalization of this scholarship.

6. Teaching is one of the primary modes of dissemination of these ideas and people engaged in this work express considerable engagement in finding innovative and creative ways to teach about power, inequality, and social justice.

What lessons for administrators and upcoming scholars do these findings suggest? The obvious ones are that institutions need to train and hire more historically underrepresented women and men of color and support and facilitate their participation in knowledge production so that they can readily promote them through the ranks to be in positions where they can become institutional leaders. They need to invest money in infrastructure and programming to support junior and senior scholars engaged in this work; collaborative research and teaching with intersections as a core and central idea; forums for discussion, debate, and dialogue; and workshops on practice and theory.

Given the costs of leadership, senior scholars made specific recommendations about ways to prepare the next generation—junior faculty, graduate students, and undergraduates—to continue this work. For junior faculty, they proposed mentoring and protecting them so that they could do the work required to get tenure; establishing interdisciplinary working groups to support and enhance their scholarship; and providing good travel budgets, state of the art equipment, and making sure they are not overburdened with teaching. They also identified the need to provide special financial support for scholars of color; some of whom arrive in junior faculty positions with considerable student loan debt and no family resources to help them get established.

In preparing graduate students to be leaders on issues related to intersectional scholarship, issues of training and professional socialization were mentioned. These included suggestions such as helping them to see beyond their disciplines toward humanitarian roles; engaging them in collaborative work; developing cultural competence and sensitivity so that they have some understanding of social, economic, and cultural differences among people; and offering them leadership opportunities in their programs. Introducing intersectional ideas and concepts in courses and exposing students to organizations and agencies involved in this work were seen as important ways to work with undergraduates.

In conclusion, the ability to grow and sustain intersectional scholarship depends on a combination of institutional support and faculty leadership. Over the years, there have been faculty whose personal commitments and intellectual interests have led them to leadership positions where they have—by dint of hard work, sacrifice, and strategic alliances—garnered university support for their programs. They have been pioneers in developing a small but growing and increasingly important area of knowledge in the contemporary academy. These faculty and those who follow in their footsteps, continue to need the support of foundations and other external organizations to facilitate their continuation of this work and to produce young scholars who will engage in the work of transforming higher education into a truly inclusive enterprise.

NOTES

1. In 1978, I, along with four other women of color sociologists, came together to prepare a small grant proposal to be submitted to the American Sociological Association under their "problems of the discipline" competition. The "problem" we identified was that of the intersection of race and gender. We had all been teaching courses on race relations and/or on gender and were struck by the lack of material that tried to conceptualize the distinctive experiences of women of color who interacted with structures of racial oppression and gender exclusion daily. Sociological theory, however, was limited in its ability to help us explain those experiences because it either focused on race without regard for gender or on gender without regard for race. We wanted to try to develop a new theoretical approach and saw this as a "problem of the discipline." The review committee, however, either did not agree or did not see our proposal as meritorious and thus our initial plan to explore the intersections of race, class, and gender in sociology was not funded. Fortunately other opportunities opened up and about a year later we applied for and received a small grant to begin to study these issues. From that project grew a broader vision that developed into the Center for Research on Women at Memphis State University, one of the first women's studies research centers funded by the Ford Foundation with an explicit interest in the intersections of race, class, gender, and ethnicity. See: Thornton Dill's "Sisterhood as Collaboration: Building the Center for Research on Women at the University of Memphis" (with Elizabeth Higginbotham and Lynn Weber), in Barbara Laslett and Barrie Thorne, *Feminist Sociology*. New Brunswick, NJ: Rutgers University Press, 1997.

2. In September 2000, I was invited by Janice Petrovich, director of education, knowledge, and religion—a unit of the Education, Media Arts, and Culture Program of the Ford Foundation to study and prepare a report on university-based programs that conduct research and teaching at the intersections of race, ethnicity, gender, and other categories of identity. The purpose of this consultation was to provide information and insights that might be helpful in the development of a new funding initiative focused on interdisciplinary knowledge building in the areas of gender, ethnicity, and identity, on the use of this knowledge in the transformation of curricula, and on its place in creating a new intercultural, global education suitable for the cultural and technological challenges of the twenty-first century.

3. See table titled, doctoral degrees conferred by degree-granting institutions by racial/ethnic group and sex of student, 1976–1977 through 2003–2004.

4. HBCU refers to Historically Black Colleges and Universities.

5. Some of the texts used at the University of Maryland during the 2007–2008 academic year include: *America's Dream* by Esmeralda Santiago; *Picture Me Rollin'* by Black Artemis; *Transformations* by Anne Sexton; *Imagining Medea: Rhodessa Jones and the Theatre for Incarcerated Women* by Rena Fraden; *This Bridge Called my Back* by Cherrie Moraga and Gloria Anzaldua; and *Blu's Hanging* by Lois-Ann Yamanaka.

6. The University of Colorado at Boulder housed a Center for Studies of Ethnicity & Race in America. Founded in 1987, it was absorbed into the Department of Ethnic Studies as a research unit when the department was established in 1996.

7. Women's Studies & the Transformation of the Curriculum. (1995). (With B. Schmitz, J. Butler, & B. Guy-Sheftall). In J. A. Banks & C. A. McGee Banks (Eds.), *Handbook of Research on Multicultural Education*. New York: Simon & Schuster MacMillan, 708–728.

8. Under Western Eyes: Feminist Scholarship and Colonial Discourses. (1988, Autumn). *Feminist Review, 30*, 61–88.

9. The concept of managing diversity vs. acknowledging and challenging power was attributed to Professor Evelyn Hu-DeHart by Professor Lynn Weber in a personal conversation.

References

Agathangelou, A. M., & Ling, L.H.M. (2002). An Unten(ur)able Position: The Politics of Teaching for Women of Color. *International Feminist Journal of Politics, 4*(3), 368–398.

Adams, J. Q., Niss, J. F., & Suarez, C. (Eds.). (1991). *Multicultural Education: Strategies for Implementation in Colleges and Universities*. Vol. 1. Macomb, IL: Western Illinois University.

Aguirre, Jr., A., Martinez, R., & Hernandez, A. (1993). Majority and Minority Faculty Perceptions in Academe. *Research in Higher Education, 34*(3), 371–384.

Alex-Assensoh, Y. M. (2003). Race in the Academy: Moving beyond Diversity and toward the Incorporation of Faculty. *Journal of Black Studies, 34*, 5–11.

Anderson, G. (2005). The Search for a Critical Mass of Minority Students:

Affirmative Action and Diversity at Highly Selective Universities and Colleges. *The Good Society, 14*(3), 51–57.

Banks, J. A. (Ed.). (1996). *Multicultural Education, Transformative Knowledge, and Action: Historical and Contemporary Perspectives*. New York: Teachers College Press.

Banks, C.A.M., & Banks, J. A. (1989). *Multicultural Education: Issues and Perspectives*. Boston: Allyn & Bacon, Inc.

College of Arts and Humanities, University of Maryland. *The Visual Literacy Toolbox: Learning to Read Images*: Retrieved April 27, 2008, from www.arhu.umd.edu/vislit/index.html.

Chow, E., Fleck, C., Fan, G., Joseph, J., & Deanna, M. L. (2003). Exploring Critical Feminist Pedagogy: Infusing Dialogue, Participation, and Experience in Teaching and Learning. *Teaching Sociology, 31*(3), 259–275.

Dey, E. L., & Thompson, C. (1998). Pushed to the Margins: Sources of Stress for African American College and University Faculty. *Journal of Higher Education, 69*.

Elliott, E. W., & Ewoh, A. I. E. (2005). Beyond Gratz and Grutter: Prospects for Affirmative Action in the Aftermath of the Supreme Court's Michigan Decisions. *Review of Policy Research, 22*(4).

Gordon, M. (2004). Diversifications of the Faculty. In F. W. Hale (Ed.), *What Makes Racial Diversity Work in Higher Education* (pp. 183–198). Sterling, VA: Stylus Publishing, LLC.

Hackman, H. W. (2002). It's Elementary: Talking about Gay Issues in School. *Multicultural Education*.

Hale, F. W. (Ed.). (2004). *What Makes Racial Diversity Work in Higher Education*. Sterling, VA: Stylus Publishing, LLC.

Harvey, W. B. (2002). *Minorities in Higher Education: Nineteenth Annual Status Report*. Washington, DC: American Council of Education.

Kivel, P. (2004). The Culture of Power. In F. W. Hale (Ed.), *What Makes Racial Diversity Work in Higher Education* (pp. 24–32). Sterling, VA: Stylus Publishing, LLC.

Olsen, D., Maple, S. A., & Stage, F. K. (1995). Women and Minority Faculty Job Satisfaction: Professional Role Interests, Professional Satisfactions, and Institutional Fit. *Journal of Higher Education, 66*(3), 267–293.

Rothenberg, P., Friedman, E., Kolmar, W., & Flint, C. (Eds.). (1996). *Creating an Inclusive College Curriculum: A Teaching Sourcebook from the New Jersey Project.* New York: Teachers College Press.

Smith, D. G., Wolf, L. E., & Busenberg, B. E. (1996). *Achieving Faculty Diversity: Debunking the Myths.* Washington, DC: Association of American Colleges and Universities.

Talbert-Hersi, D. E. (1995). The Impact of Chronic Job Stresses and Work Support on Job Satisfaction for Women in Higher Education: A Communication Climate Study (Women Educators). *Dissertation Abstracts International,* 55-10A, 3332.

U.S. Department of Education: National Center for Education Statistics. (2006). *Digest of Education Statistics, 2005* (NCES 2006-030).

11

Transforming the Campus Climate through Institutions, Collaboration, and Mentoring

BONNIE THORNTON DILL, RUTH ENID ZAMBRANA, AND
AMY MCLAUGHLIN

> The university counts among its greatest strengths and a major component of its excellence the diversity of its faculty, students, and staff. It is committed to equal educational opportunity. It strives to hire a diverse faculty and staff of exceptional achievement through affirmative action, to celebrate diversity in all of its programs and activities, and to recruit and retain qualified graduate and undergraduate minority students.
>
> —University of Maryland Mission Statement, 2000

In 2004, a National Academy of Sciences report acknowledged the growing recognition and appreciation of interdisciplinary scholarship that facilitates intellectual collaboration (The National Academies, 2004).[1] Institutional climates are often changed through faculty leadership and collaborative partnerships. This case study of the Consortium on Race, Gender and Ethnicity (CRGE) at the University of Maryland (UM) illustrates the ways faculty engagement in institution building, intellectual collaboration, and mentoring has contributed to transformation in one institution of higher education. The consortium focused its approach to fostering change on faculty-led collaborative intersectional and interdisciplinary scholarship. Nevertheless this process encountered a number of challenges because essential resources were not always readily available. Faculty leaders on other campuses who have pioneered institution building around intersectional scholarship encountered such problems as: university systems' unwillingness to allocate grant dollars to multiple departments and colleges; continuing doubts among faculty colleagues about the rigor of collaborative and interdisciplinary scholarship; disagreements about how to assess individual contributions to coauthored articles or books; and fewer outlets for publication and dissemination of their work (Dill, McLaughlin, & Nieves, 2007).

In spite of these challenges, innovative and under rewarded campus leaders have continued to devote their time and energy to ensuring recognition of this work as valuable and transformative. Faculty leaders at the University of Maryland faced many of the same challenges. Nevertheless CRGE has had a significant impact on the diversity climate at Maryland by promoting the use of an intersectional approach to scholarship that is linked to social change.

Using a case study approach to examine this process, multiple data sources are drawn upon. These include: (1) oral history interviews with the founding director focused on the development of her scholarship and of events that contributed to the creation and support of a transformative organization; (2) interviews with other faculty collaborators and campus organization leaders; (3) annual reports, grant applications and journal articles that were written and outline CRGE's contribution to the growth of intersectional scholarship at UM; and (4) additional interviews conducted with CRGE affiliated faculty.

The third author of this chapter conducted the interviews with the founding director and six well-known campus leaders.[2] Because the work of CRGE is intertwined with several key diversity initiatives on campus, leaders familiar with those initiatives were chosen. Interview questions focused on three major themes: leadership in interdisciplinary scholarship and collaboration; mentoring and training the next generation of scholars; and activism and lessons learned in fostering institutional change.

This chapter explores how and why CRGE was created, the innovative programs that move our work forward and showcase an intersectional approach, and the challenges and strategies learned in this process. The findings illuminate one set of processes of social and institutional change.

Institutional Context: Diversity at the University of Maryland

As the flagship campus of the University System of Maryland, UM, located in College Park, is currently showcased as a model, setting the standard for excellence, innovation, and success. The university's history, however, was shaped by policies and practices of segregation that were law and custom in the state. UM enrolled its first Black undergraduate, Hiram Whittle, in 1951 after the University of Maryland Board of Regents was advised that they could not defeat his racial discrimination lawsuit and voted to admit him. (Mr. Whittle did not finish his degree, leaving at the end of his second year.) In 1954 after the landmark Supreme Court ruling, the board voted to admit qualified African Americans at all campuses. Nevertheless the university system remained segregated in practice, if not in law, for three decades. It was not until 1985 that the university finally presented an acceptable plan to the Office of Civil Rights for compliance with Title VI of the Civil Rights Act of 1964. At that time, Chancellor

John Slaughter, himself African American, made significant progress in recruiting African American faculty and students. His successor, William "Brit" Kirwan, insisted on the connection between excellence and diversity, and continued to build the numbers of Black faculty, staff, and students throughout his tenure. Later the term diversity was broadened to include age, gender, disability, sexual orientation, religion, social class, national origin, and ethnicity.

Transformative change cannot occur without commitment at the very top and the University of Maryland is no exception. Here we briefly review milestones of change at UM that contributed to the creation of CRGE. Kirwan is widely recognized as the leader who, following Slaughter's initiative, transformed the campus climate by devoting significant resources to institutionalizing a commitment to diversity and by expressing his own commitment in public statements. Under his leadership, a campus climate initiative was instituted to study and remediate a documented "chilly climate" for women and for racial ethnic minorities. The women's studies and African American studies departments were strengthened and a Curriculum Transformation Project, focused on integrating material on women and minorities into the curriculum throughout the campus, was initiated with generous university funding. Through these years, Maryland gained national recognition for its leadership around campus diversity issues. A pivotal event was UM's ultimately unsuccessful defense of the Banneker Scholarship Program for African Americans. The program was launched under Slaughter and targeted academically talented incoming African American students. The Supreme Court's 1995 refusal to review a lower court's ruling that the program was unconstitutional effectively terminated it as a university recruitment tool. Yet the act of defending this program by publicly documenting the residual harm of UM's segregationist past to the state's African American population demonstrated the strength of the university's commitment to diversity in higher education. President Kirwan also provided support for an activist Office of Human Relations Programs, which launched several initiatives designed to improve the campus climate and assist in the coordination of diversity efforts across campus. Of note was the collaboration between the Office of Human Relations Programs, the Ford Foundation, and the Association of American Colleges and Universities to create a *Diversity Blueprint: A Planning Manual for Colleges and Universities* (Brown, 1998), which provided guidelines for diversity. The guidelines called for: *accountability* to ensure that programs meet their diversity goals; *inclusiveness* of all dimensions of diversity to be represented campus-wide; *shared responsibility* among all UM faculty, staff, and students to work toward diversity goals; *evaluation* to maintain continuous feedback on the success of the efforts; and *institutionalization* to incorporate diversity efforts into the university structure. Although the *Diversity Blueprint* marked Dr. Kirwan's determination to institutionalize diversity, its usefulness as a resource and a consistent plan for change was limited by his departure.

In 1998, C. D. Mote, Jr., was appointed UM president. A series of initiatives in the 1990s and early 2000s were designed to address the university's legacy, and to make "excellence through diversity" an actual principle governing campus policy. Indeed a 2000 panel on diversity convened by President Mote found that diversity work on campus had become fragmented and was rarely evaluated and that "there is no accountability for lack of progress in implementing diversity on our campus" (UM Report and Recommendations of the President's Diversity Panel, 2000). In the wake of Kirwan's departure, it appears that social change is dependent on the commitment of leaders; support that is not institutionalized into the daily operations of university offices, departments, and programs can shift as leadership changes.

Accordingly President Mote has emphasized broad access to the university's enriched undergraduate curriculum programs and launched the Baltimore Incentive Awards Program to recruit and provide full support to high school students of outstanding potential who have overcome extraordinary adversity during their lives. While the grade point average of entering students, the amount of grant monies secured, and the success of special honors programs are indisputably higher, racial diversity still lags.

The University of Maryland still prides itself on its reputation for having a diverse student population, staff and faculty, and a curriculum that incorporates dimensions of difference. Nevertheless there continue to be both challenges and opportunities at Maryland for expanding this work. Thus one of the diversity goals identified for the university includes achieving a critical mass of 35 percent minority undergraduate students on campus by fall 2009. As of 2006, 33 percent of the undergraduate student body is racial-ethnic minority (down 2 percent from 2000), and the university ranks fifth nationally in the number of African American baccalaureates graduated from predominantly White institutions—figures to be proud of (UM, 2005). UM faculty is more diverse racially at the assistant professor level than at the full professor level. More than fifty years after desegregation, UM's percentage of African American and Hispanic faculty remain disproportionately low compared to their representation nationally and in the state of Maryland (UM, 2005). Similarly the pipeline of graduate students of color also does not reflect our diverse society. Thus there is still a need to improve the recruitment, promotion, and retention of both faculty and graduate students from historically underrepresented minority groups.

Intellectual Collaboration as an Institutional Intervention

Established in 1998, CRGE receives support from the Colleges of Arts and Humanities, Maryland Population and Research Center in the College of Behavioral and Social Sciences, the Graduate School, and the Office of the Provost. CRGE seeks to: support, coordinate, and facilitate the activities of the outstanding faculty, graduate students and academic units at Maryland engaged in scholarship that focuses on intersections of race, gender, and ethnicity; and to build visibility both on and off campus of our exceptional wealth of resources. The consortium is an association of academic units and individual faculty on the University of Maryland campus whose mission is to promote, advance, and conduct research, scholarship, and faculty and student development that examines the intersections of race, gender, and ethnicity with other dimensions of difference. It accomplishes its goals by facilitating intellectual collaboration among units, individual faculty, and graduate students as it seeks to train the next generation of intersectional scholars. Finding this niche was a defining feature of CRGE's development and one that was strategically chosen as a way to unite and strengthen race-gender scholarship at the university and change the intellectual climate to make this scholarship more central to the university's mission.

An intersectional approach to research and scholarship that emerged from the intellectual and professional experiences of the founding director was elemental in the development of the mission of CRGE. The first joint project was developed on the recommendation of a Ford Foundation Program Officer who suggested that a collaborative and coordinated approach of three related projects would be a more effective intervention in the climate and institutional practices of the campus and provide a model more consistent with the foundation's funding preferences.

CRGE in collaboration with two other campus institutions: the Department of African American Studies (AASD) led by Dr. Sharon Harley and the Curriculum Transformation Project (CTP) led by Dr. Deborah Rosenfelt submitted a grant to the Ford Foundation entitled, *Collaborative Transformations in the Academy: Re-Constructing the Study of Gender, Race, Ethnicity and Nation*. The project emphasized the unique expertise of each program but also the shared commitment to scholarship at the intersections of race, gender, ethnicity, and other dimensions of difference.

These three scholars had each been engaged in campus change efforts for many years, sharing a number of similar experiences in their early training as graduate students and as junior faculty and maintaining a strong commitment to diversity throughout that time. Dill had learned early in her career that collaboration could be an important strategy for overcoming intellectual isolation as well as enhancing knowledge production. In the interview, Dill recollected:

> [When I was in graduate school] I started looking for other young scholars who were doing similar kinds of work, who I could really talk to about my work. I really didn't feel that there were people immediately around me who could read it critically; because they didn't know the race literature . . . I wasn't sure I was getting a good critical reading on those aspects of my work.

Dill acknowledges that these early experiences in collaboration developed into an intellectual approach to promoting intersectional scholarship and creating campus change. Dr. Harley, in a separate interview, shared a similar story, "We would go to these conferences and there was almost nothing about Black women's history . . . [After a while] we decided to stop complaining about the errors of the scholarship and presentations on Black women's history, and to do something about it." She and her fellow graduate students collaboratively wrote an anthology entitled: *The Afro-American Woman: Struggles and Images* (Harley & Terborg-Penn, 1978), and after contacting over 100 different presses, managed to finally get it published. It is not surprising therefore that a focus of the CRGE, AASD, CTP collaboration would be the creation of an institutional site to promote new knowledge to transform thinking, teaching, and research in the academy.

The confluence of these personal histories in the context of a university that was actively pursuing a mission of diversity increased Dill's belief that major institutional change was possible at the University of Maryland. She, along with Harley and Rosenfelt, saw an exceptional opportunity and wanted to capitalize on it. Dr. Harley, who arrived on campus in 1981 and had initially found little support for faculty of color, described the impact of Drs. Slaughter and Kirwan's leadership on how she saw herself in relationship to the university: "I think it helped me to shift . . . to College Park as my primary center of academic thinking as these two men developed a strong interest in diversity and academic excellence." Dr. Rosenfelt came to UM in 1989 to direct the Curriculum Transformation Project, which was being funded by the provost's office recognizing that at that time it was rare that a university would commit resources toward diversifying the curriculum. The excitement for her was that "this would be a project that would help faculty [throughout the university] become equipped to incorporate this new scholarship into their classroom." Dr. Dill, arriving in 1993, was impressed to discover a core group of Black women scholars and states, "I had this sense of a community and felt that it represented a unique and historic moment."

Building Alliances and Networks

In a climate where diversity was a stated goal, CRGE had a unique opportunity to establish alliances and networks among a relatively large group of researchers and teachers. Those alliances enhanced UM's reputation for expertise in intersectional scholarship at the same time that CRGE was creating a new kind of intervention into campus culture that placed knowledge at the forefront of understanding inequality based on social difference.

Over the past eight years, CRGE has instituted a number of programs aimed at capitalizing on the presence of the many talented scholars at UM.

Each program is designed to promote and advance exemplary intersectional scholarship, develop collaborative projects that can attract external grant monies, and leverage those resources to gain additional financial commitments from senior administrators within the institution.

One way CRGE facilitates intersectional research is by administering interdisciplinary Research Interest Groups (RIGs).[3] RIGs are collaborative interdisciplinary assemblages of faculty and students that share an interest in a particular topic and use an intersectional focus in their work. These groups examine such issues as race, poverty, material and visual culture, health of low-income women and children of color, and qualitative methodologies. They meet regularly to share research and teaching information, hear and interact with guest speakers, and promote research activity among participants through grant review, seed grant initiatives, conversations with funding agency representatives, and so on. Additionally they help create a sense of community among faculty and graduate students with shared research interests. Research Interest Groups (RIGs) have included over sixty faculty, graduate students, and community members participating.

CRGE appeals to faculty and graduate students from around the campus. It has become uniquely adept at building interdisciplinary collaborative ties with faculty from various departments and colleges including ARHU, BSOS, the School of Architecture, the College of Education (EDUC), and the School of Public Health (SPH). It hosts a monthly colloquium designed to foster and disseminate graduate student and faculty intersectional work across the campus. Over thirty UM faculty members have participated in the sessions, with an average attendance of twenty-five students from approximately fifteen departments. The sessions help graduate students identify peers and faculty from across the campus who are using an intersectional lens to guide their scholarship. Past colloquia have covered such topics as "What is a Public Intellectual?" "Black and Latina Feminist Thought," "Intersectional Methodology," and "Combining Research and Activism."

CRGE uses its Web site (www.crge.umd.edu) not only to inform the campus community and beyond about research products, programs, and symposia but is also building an online community of scholars to help cultivate and increase access to its resources on intersectional scholarship. The centerpiece of these resources is the Intersectional Research Database, a searchable database on intersectional scholarship that includes annotated citations of research by scholars in the social sciences, arts and humanities, law, medicine, and many other fields. Additionally CRGE's Diversity Web-Calendar is the one cyber-location at UM that provides information on all events with an intersectional focus that take place on campus. All of the online initiatives are fueled by a goal to create a distinct space on the Internet for intersectional information. The resources on the site are available to not only members of the University of Maryland community, but to the greater population of scholars interested in work on intersectionality. CRGE stays in touch with our affiliates through a frequently disseminated email listserv of 160 subscribers and a mailing list with approximately 360 contacts, 40 percent of which are off-campus. The homepage receives nearly 12,000 hits per week.

In addition, CRGE has raised the national profile of the University of Maryland in relation to intersectional scholarship through several symposia that have drawn scholars from throughout the nation, and within the UM, academic community. Over the past five years, CRGE has had three campus-wide events that centered on our findings in specific crucial areas: Push-outs In the Schools: A Policy Briefing; Tools for Social Justice: UM at the Intersection of Community and Social Justice; and Tools for Social Justice: Katrina One Year Later. These gatherings impressively identified the University of Maryland as a place that fosters scholarship about race, gender, ethnicity, and their intersections. The symposia drew crowds of over 200 and the policy briefing was attended by approximately fifty faculty, educators, and parents.

CRGE has developed an exceptional record of program development and high name recognition based on innovative programs with strong intellectual content. The nationally distributed newsletter, *Research Connections*, continues to highlight the multiple collaborations CRGE engages in with faculty across campus and beyond.

Mentoring: Developing the Next Generation

Maryland's efforts to improve the recruitment of underrepresented faculty and students, which began in the 1980s, set the stage for the founding of CRGE. Its contribution to continuing that process is to focus on training the next generation of scholars in intersectional theory, methodology, and pedagogy making mentorship a crucial aspect of our mission. The dearth of scholars of color in the pipeline is of particular concern at CRGE because this group of scholars includes those most likely to engage in intersectional interdisciplinary research. New and promising scholars will have the opportunity to influence the future directions and meanings of higher education particularly on issues of diversity. As the current cohort of senior professors begin to retire, the intellectual leadership of these emerging scholars will become increasingly important. Faculty in CRGE have engaged in mentoring junior faculty of color through the Office of Academic Affairs and the Provost, developed a CRGE Faculty Affiliate Program, and engaged in individual mentoring of new junior faculty of color. They also developed a specific program for entering graduate students interested in intersectional approaches to research.

Scholars of color, especially junior scholars, still confront many obstacles including: tenure and promotion; exploitation and self sacrifice; multiple affiliations; and lack of family resources (see chapter 10). In addition, their limited presence in higher education institutions maintains and reinforces their minority status (Fong, 2000; Johnsrud, 1993; Alexander-Snow & Johnson, 1999; Jarmon, 2001; Garza, 1993). In fall 2006 at the University of Maryland, as shown in table 11.1, slightly more than 5 percent of tenure track faculty are African American, 9.7 percent Asian American, 3.3 percent Hispanic, and 0.13 percent Native American. These numbers are better than those at many previously White institutions (PWIs) but are still far lower than one would expect based on the proportion of these groups present in the general population. For graduate students, 7.5 percent are African American, 7.6 percent Asian American, 3.7 percent Hispanic, and 0.2 percent Native American (see table 11.2). The numbers are even more striking when examining Ph.D. degree completion rates for 2007: 6.1 percent African American, 5 percent Asian American, 1.8 percent Hispanic, and 0.15 percent American Indian graduate students received Ph.D.s. At CRGE, we acknowledge that the ultimate success of our leadership depends on preparing and mentoring the next generation of scholars to confront and conquer the many challenges that they will face.

Mentoring includes such support as critical feedback, introductions to senior faculty and administrators, and acting as a resource for up and coming scholars. Literature on mentoring details how in general faculty of color has different experiences than their White colleagues upon entering the academic workforce and therefore requires different strategies to ensure their retention. As observed by Boykin, Zambrana, Williams et al. (2003), "effective mentoring of historically under-represented women includes: a trusting relationship, understanding of the mentoring experience, positive regard/ validation of individuals and availability of time" (15). Most new faculty members experience tremendous anxiety about survival and success in the academy. Levinson et al. (1991), found that women (medical) faculty members with mentors published more, spent more time on research activities, and were more satisfied with their careers. Added stress experienced by faculty of color often hinders their progress toward achieving tenure and reduces their potential to produce excellent scholarship and be effective professors. Faculty of color are more likely to feel undervalued and unwelcomed (Fong, 2000; Johnsrud, 1993; Alexander-Snow & Johnson, 1999, Jarmon, 2001, Garza, 1993). In order to avoid such outcomes, universities must be committed to providing extra support for the retention of ethnic minority faculty. Mentors should be able to bolster motivation, socialize their protégés to their new environment through revealing what Jarmon (2001) calls the "hidden rules," provide emotional support, be aware of extra demands and the need to protect the time of faculty of color, and ensure that additional demands placed on faculty of color are rewarded

TABLE 11.1

University of Maryland Tenure/Tenure-Track (FTE) Faculty by Race/Ethnicity and Rank, Fall 2006

Race/Ethnicity	Professor #	Professor %	Associate Professor #	Associate Professor %	Assistant Professor #	Assistant Professor %	Other Faculty #	Other Faculty %
American Indian (.1%)*	2	0.2	0	0	0	0	2	0.1
Asian/P.I. (9%)* U.S.	49	7	50	11	26	10	116	8
African American (5%)* U.S.	24	4	34	7	19	7	57	4
Hispanic (3%)* U.S.	17	3	16	3	7	3	23	2
White (78%)* U.S.	574	85	363	77	163	61	822	60
Foreign	0	0	6	1	48	18	309	23
Not Known (1%)*	8	1	5	1	5	2	37	3
Total (100%)	674		474		268		1366	

Source: Faculty by Race/Ethnicity 2006, IRPA Web site, accessed 9/07/07.
Note: * The overall percentage of faculty excludes the category "Other Faculty" from the calculation; it is based solely on tenure track faculty.

and considered for promotion and tenure. Another important factor is that the campus culture be conducive to diversity (Thomas, 2001).

One of the most rewarding aspects of mentoring is that it is self-perpetuating; faculty who have been mentored are more likely to mentor (Roche, 1979). Dr. Sharon Harley states, "For those of us who came out of the civil rights, women's rights and women's liberation, or gay rights struggles, the mentoring part is important because we want to produce the next generation of scholars." The drawback with mentoring is that it requires a significant investment of faculty time with little recognition from the university. Dr. Jim Greenberg, founder of the UM's Center for Teaching Excellence (CTE), says that currently "faculty who engage [in it] think it's the right thing [to do] and are personally interested" without receiving adequate compensation.

TABLE II.2

University of Maryland Graduate Students by Race/Ethnicity and Gender, Fall 2006

Race/Ethnicity	Total %	Total #	Female #	Male #
American Indian	0.2%	28	15	13
Asian/P.I.	7.6%	683	323	360
Black/African American	7.5%	735	467	268
Hispanic	3.7%	334	186	148
Caucasian	56.3%	5170	2604	2566
International	20.4%	2451	989	1462
Not Known	4.3%	547	274	273

Source: Graduate Students by Race/Ethnicity 2006, IRPA Web site, http://www.irpa.umd.edu/Profiles, accessed 10/2/2007.

Indeed research bears out that these faculty members, especially faculty of color, often experience an overload of demands on their time. In addition to being highly sought after by students because of their minority status, faculty of color are usually placed on committees more often, taking time away from their research and scholarship commitments (Johnsrud, 1993; Fong, 2000; Garza, 1993; Howard-Vital & Morgan, 1993). Alexander-Snow and Johnson (1999) suggest that faculty of color experience "cultural taxation." "Rather than being allowed—and indeed encouraged—to concentrate on their academic work, many are sucked into a plethora of activities often unrelated to their competence and interests" says Banks (1984, 327). In addition, faculty are rarely rewarded for their mentoring work. As Professor Harley points out, "the campus is more likely to recognize somebody with a major grant who's done nothing in the mentoring area than somebody who does the multiple things that we do." And yet she continues to make plans within her own projects to "expand the mentoring component and bring in younger scholars. I'd like to expand [the program] and replicate it around the country." The challenge is in obtaining the institutional support needed to create these broadened programs and to add them to the already heavy workload.

Mentorship is an area of growing concern at the University of Maryland. Although UM gives a system-wide mentoring award, which in 2006 was awarded to the founding director, Bonnie Thornton Dill, the recognition for these efforts remain minimal. In 2006, the faculty senate passed a set of mentoring program guidelines, which require that all new faculty be assigned mentors within their department and also includes a recommendation to create a network of faculty from underrepresented groups to be available to meet with recruited faculty (UM Senate Task Force Report, 2006). These recommendations disregard prior findings: that underrepresented faculty of color do not feel welcomed in many academic departments as their experiences are not understood or validated, and that underrepresented faculty already experience overload as mentors to graduate students and other faculty of color.

CRGE continues its commitment to mentoring in spite of the many costs involved. Senior faculty in CRGE read grant applications, manuscripts, and other materials and also met with faculty of color interested in intersectionality. Senior CRGE faculty have mentored several junior scholars from across the campus that have since received tenure. If this work receives any recognition at all it is through the mechanism of CRGE. Mentoring junior scholars cannot be accomplished without administrative support and resources and these energies must be directed toward assistant and associate professors as well as among graduate students. To support and extend the mission of collaborative interdisciplinary research, CRGE proposed to formalize and extend a faculty mentoring fellowship program to create a multilevel mentorship program. UM junior faculty, with research interests in dimensions of difference, will be invited to apply for funding that will allow them to pursue their intersectional research in CRGE for a semester. As faculty with these interests tend to be faculty of color, they would be mentored by senior CRGE faculty in research, pedagogy, and in the process learn how to mentor future scholars of color. The CRGE Interdisciplinary Scholars Program (CrISP) will benefit from their participation and the faculty will learn how to train and mentor graduate students without adding permanent students to their advisory load. However, institutional support has not been provided.

Institutionalizing programs that preserve and maintain the ability of faculty of color to continue to produce new knowledge is a key to a vibrant and inclusive academy. If that academic pipeline is diminished, diverse perspectives in knowledge production will be severely curtailed.

Mentoring Graduate Students: Description of the CrISP Program

CRGE's work is aligned with the University of Maryland's mission of achieving excellence and diversity in areas of research, scholarship, teaching, and community service by providing an apparatus to facilitate the university's ability to attract and retain graduate students. In collaboration with academic departments, the Graduate School, and the dean of the College of Arts and Humanities, CRGE implemented a special program to provide intensive training and mentoring for a select group of graduate students with a commitment to intersectional scholarship. Since fall 2002, the Consortium on Race, Gender and Ethnicity has offered fellowships for graduate students interested in the intersections of race, gender, and ethnicity. The goals of this exciting program are to:

- Attract exceptionally talented graduate students who have an interest in interdisciplinary ideas, a desire to study issues of race, gender, and ethnicity, and the ability to creatively utilize the breadth of faculty and research resources available on the campus.
- Increase the visibility and impact of research and scholarship on these issues by enhancing affiliated departments' resources for recruitment and support of highly qualified graduate students.
- Create an innovative training program for the next generation of UM scholars who are helping to reconceptualize epistemological, theoretical, and methodological approaches to the study of the intersections of race, gender, and ethnicity, with other dimensions of difference, identity, and inequality.

CRGE Interdisciplinary Scholars Program (CrISP) provides graduate students with an opportunity to learn firsthand the processes of research, administration, and publication through a mentoring relationship with CRGE faculty. CrISP scholars are first- and second-year incoming graduate students from departments affiliated with CRGE. In spring 2007, the sixth cohort of students for the academic year 2007–2008 was selected, and the first and second cohorts have completed their fellowship years. The CrISP program follows a specific academic course for all the scholars selected. First year students enroll in a training seminar that focuses on intersectionality—examining theoretical and methodological insights into the current work in the field. This seminar has been developed as an interdisciplinary enterprise that will provide the foundation for the scholars to use in their work, regardless of home department. Because the scholars come from different departments (CrISP scholars have been enrolled in MA/PhD programs in the following departments: women's studies, American studies, history, sociology, education policy and leadership, public health, and urban planning), the seminar discussions can truly examine how an intersectional approach provides a flexible and useful tool for understanding the construction of identities, power, privilege, policy, and social institutions across disciplines.

After completing the seminar, the students then meet as a group with the second-year cohort and continue professionalization seminars every three weeks throughout the remainder of the year. The professionalization seminars focus on socializing the students to an academic environment and ensuring they receive adequate information and support about the hurdles and opportunities they will face throughout their careers. At the same time, students continue to work with their assigned faculty advisor, receiving direct feedback about their work.

Evaluation is an important developmental aspect of this training program. Students are evaluated twice during the first semester and at the close of the second semester. The first evaluation is a session where the students receive feedback about their work, their participation and engagement in the training and professionalization seminars, and have an opportunity to provide feedback about their experience. This first evaluation is crucial for assuring that the scholars understand what is expected and are receiving adequate instruction and support. The second evaluation occurs at the end of the semester and is shared with the graduate director in their home department; this is done so that the department is aware of what the student is learning and it helps strengthen the collaborative relationship between CRGE and the participating departments. The third evaluation at the close of the spring semester is also shared with the graduate director in the home department.

Second-year CrISPs are expected to take a leadership role in regard to incoming scholars. They may be asked to lead a session of orientation, and to help the new cohort whenever possible. The staggered design of the program (three incoming, three returning) has helped the students connect across department lines and provided a very useful peer support network.

Although the long-term impact of the program cannot be yet assessed due to its relative newness with students still pursuing their doctoral education, in personal anecdotes students attribute much of their early success in their graduate education to their experiences with CrISP. The fifteen students who have participated in the program through 2007 have come from five different departments and examples of their scholarly interests include: Black women's spirituality and hip-hop; disability, inequality, and identity; race, nation, and gender in public health discourse; Latina feminist thought; and meanings of work among immigrant nurses. Each year students are asked to provide written evaluations of their experiences in the program and they each highlight different aspects of it.

One student wrote, "Through the CrISP program, I have access to formal and informal mentorship, research training, and a foundation in intersectionality that is critical to my present and future work." Another wrote, "CRGE provides me with a rare opportunity to engage in intersectional scholarship. I have benefited greatly from the work that CRGE has produced and events that they have sponsored, such as their colloquia, research seminars, and research interest groups as well as CRGE's research and scholarship day." A third student stated, "I appreciate having the opportunity to meet faculty from different departments all over campus. I don't think the other first-year students in my cohort are able to have that experience so early in their graduate programs."

The CrISP program has enhanced the students' graduate experience by providing both intellectual and emotional support in their adjustment to a new academic environment. Although still engaged in the work of completing their Ph.D., four have obtained the masters degree and six of the students have passed their general exams and are beginning their major field and dissertation work. Four are currently participating as the 2007–2008 cohort.

Although the financial arrangements have changed over the years, due to a reduction in support from the graduate school, CRGE provides one year of fellowship support and enhanced funding for two years in the form of an assistantship. Departments then fund the students for one year of fellowship and two additional years on assistantship.[4] Students receive a full university fellowship and an additional half time assistantship from CRGE that qualifies them for health insurance. In return, students work ten hours a week at the consortium. Although we do not grant degrees, CRGE works with seven different departments[5] from four different colleges providing an interdisciplinary mentorship program to attract and recruit graduate students. The focus of this exceptional program is twofold: rigorous training and dedicated mentoring. CRGE faculty are available to work with the students' departmental advisor to help design a course of study complimentary to the students' interests and departmental expectations.

CRGE has struggled to maintain funding for the CrISP program negotiating with several different deans and a number of departments. Because the program is designed for entering students and has facilitated departmental recruitment by offering enhanced funding, it has been an important tool for building and sustaining departmental alliances.

Achieving Institutional Support: Challenges and Lessons Learned

Institution building in higher education is not easy because one must compete in a constantly changing intellectual and institutional environment. What some may see as "cutting-edge," visionary scholarship poised to change a field; others may label a passing trend and argue against investments in it. These differing intellectual perspectives are compounded by continuous institutional shifts and the need to negotiate and renegotiate agreements as administrators change and seek to implement their individual vision. A second complicating factor is that faculty and graduate students of color are still likely to find themselves in settings where they are isolated and often misunderstood. A program like the CrISP program may provide a safe and supportive environment for a student interested in issues of race, class, gender, and ethnicity, but that same student may not have that level of support or understanding within their home department. This disjuncture makes it difficult to assess the impact of the program and to use those data as leverage for increased funding. As this case study indicates, there are many challenges in continuing this work and the costs, in terms of time and energy of senior faculty are high and inadequately compensated.

The overall methods of the university, and the bureaucracy that supports it, affect this program in other important ways. UM, as is true of higher education, generally does not exist in a vacuum and as the external climate changes, so do the funding priorities of the university, particularly when the majority of funds are state funds. According to Dill:

> [UM has] changed in some ways with the changes in society. I mean the society has become less progressive. This institution is more focused on the bottom line, corporate, managerial metrics you know . . . measuring things in countable ways. . . . Units are all encouraged to get out there and get funding, and you know you have to compete in a really small market.

In a climate where entrepreneurship is encouraged and an increasingly important measure of value is the amount of external grant dollars generated, it is becoming more challenging to secure funding for institutional transformation projects. Because UM is a state institution that is generally acknowledged as under-resourced, internal funds are limited and the drive for external dollars is great. Although collaborations are increasingly recognized as a valuable way to address many research and scholarly questions, collaborative aspirations are vulnerable because the university's system of tracking achievement is through the progress of individuals and units (a department or a college). Thus collaborative activities can get pushed aside or bureaucratically fall through the cracks and languish or be dismissed. The time and energy invested in ensuring that adequate credit is given requires taking time and energy away from the production of research and scholarship. Current director Zambrana observes:

> The scarcity of resources at the University places programs in competition with one another rather than in cooperation. The price of institutional change continues to be paid by the few faculty who invest in pursuing social change often at the cost of their scholarly production, time spent away from their personal lives, and lack of adequate compensation from the University. (2007, 3)

Consistent with this observation, the founding director Dill comments: "We don't want to be in competition [with other units doing intersectional work] we want to be in support, but it becomes challenging to do that when the resources are limited and you're all eating at the same trough." The current funding climate outside the university has changed considerably in the past ten years and there are many indications that it will not improve in the near future (Dill, McLaughlin, & Nieves, 2007; Hollander & Saltmarsh, 2000). If diversity research and scholarship continues to be under supported, it will be increasingly difficult to engage junior faculty in ways that will support their research agendas and advance their progress toward tenure.

Attention to and support of collaborative work is further complicated by institutional location. Because intersectional work takes place across traditional boundaries it may be difficult to coordinate and obtaining resources may require multiple negotiations. According to Dill:

> I think one challenge for the consortium is that we really don't sit squarely anywhere in terms of the bureaucratic and institutional structure of the university and the flow of resources; because resources flow to departments, and we're not a department. So for us the struggle for resources is compounded by an institutional location that is outside that loop and by our desire not to compete for the same resources that women's studies and African American studies are competing for.

Both Dill and Zambrana acknowledge that having the support of senior administrators committed to diversity who understand that this work contributes to the university mission has been pivotal in gaining university resources. They also acknowledge that receiving external grants was an important signal to these administrations that the work was worthy of their support. In addition, Dill says:

> If you have people in places that can be influential, who support what you are doing and who are willing to be your advocates behind the scenes, you won't even know about it necessarily. But you have to be prepared to build from whatever opportunities you have. . . . We have been able to sell this work to the administration in a way that resonates with them, but we have also had people on the inside who keep our efforts on the radar screen, and say positive things about it.

Christine Clark, of the Office of Human Relations, argues that support for this work would be further facilitated by diversifying senior leadership on campus. Andrea Levy, formerly in the Provost's office, adds, "[we must] recognize that diversity has a positive impact on educational outcomes—we cannot separate diversity/inclusiveness from any other part of students' education."

These challenges are formidable and make success stories all the more laudable. And yet they point to significant concerns for the future, namely, how can institutional transformation continue when these data show how change thus far has depended on the leadership of faculty whose own life experiences and scholastic work has motivated them to devote significant portions of their energy and time to improving the campus climate at significant cost to themselves, often without adequate compensation or recognition?

While there are no easy answers, and the lessons from this institution are not applicable to all others, several useful approaches have emerged.

CRGE has carved out a unique niche with intersectional scholarship and has worked to make itself *the* source for expertise in that specifically defined area. This focus helped gain the attention of the president and his Commission on Diversity that charged CRGE with developing a report on diversity research on campus. The report, *Research on Race, Gender and Ethnicity at UM: Perspectives on Diversity* (Consortium on Race, Gender and Ethnicity, 2004) lists all the names and research interests of faculty on campus with an interest in diversity/intersectional issues and is maintained in an active, on-line database. The report served an administrative need and in highlighting UM's expertise brought recognition to CRGE. In addition it helped facilitate one of CRGE's major goals, that of promoting collaboration and exchange around ideas of intersectionality.

Collaboration, despite the challenges, remains an important way that CRGE has generated alliances and support across the campus. Its leadership has worked hard to insure that the university developed ways to acknowledge the primary participants in these projects. CRGE faculty have also worked hard on projects designed to enhance recognition of mentoring and teaching activities, especially the increased workloads of scholars of color and to enhance the inclusion of diversity scholarship in the undergraduate curriculum.

Ultimately, however, units like CRGE, in order to be successful, need a level of financial stability that does not require that the administrative faculty spend a majority of their time each year seeking funding. Long-term funding and inclusion in state budgets and capital campaigns are the primary means to this kind of stability. Zambrana's words cogently summarize the challenges, accomplishments, and lessons learned from the CRGE case study. She writes:

> We acknowledge that our achievements have had an impact at UM; but we continue to struggle with many of the challenges that hinder our ability to expand our efforts to be a truly transformative institution on campus. . . . Diminished funding from external grants in these conservative political times has also seriously challenged our ability to engage in social justice research. . . . Increasing access to higher education has long been one strategy to improve the social capital of [historically] underrepresented groups and improve life chances. Unfortunately, progress has been slow. In the academy itself, we still observe major disparities in the professorate of color at full professor or in high-level administrative positions and in the distribution of resources. Our work continues to provide voice to these disparities and to promote small but significant changes. (2007, 3)

In conclusion, the social changes that have resulted from the work of CRGE are tied to individual leaders at CRGE and within the institution itself. If these interventions are not institutionalized within the university, they are likely to dissipate as senior administrators change. CRGE and other interdisciplinary social justice oriented programs on campus challenge the university structure and make the collaborative process visible through the many accomplishments outlined above. New ways of knowing, the production of new knowledge, their dissemination through pedagogy, and the development of the next generation of scholars, who will continue the struggle for the work of social justice and social change, is a primary motivation for this work in institution building. It is only through the creation and sustaining of these smaller institutions within large institutions that changing the climate of the university and creating a place that can be truly inclusive of and beneficial to scholars committed to intersectional scholarship can occur.

NOTES

1. We are grateful for the financial support received through the "Re-affirming Action: Designs for Diversity in Higher Education" project at the Institute for Women's Leadership at Rutgers University and from the Ford Foundation. Special thanks to Winnifred Brown-Glaude, Mary Hartmann, and Cheryl Wall. Additional thanks go to research assistants Crystal Espinoza, Laura A. Logie, and Anaya McMurray for their help in preparing this chapter.

    The authors have been engaged in the development and direction of CRGE for the past eight years. Amy McLaughlin is former associate director and was the primary researcher on the project that led to this chapter. Bonnie Thornton Dill serves as founding director and Ruth E. Zambrana is the current director.

2. Additional interviews were conducted with Dr. Sharon Harley, chair of African American studies; Dr. Deborah Rosenfelt, director of the Curriculum Transformation Project; Dr. Christine Clark, director of the Office of Human Relations Programs; Ms. Andrea Hill Levy, J.D., associate vice president of Academic Affairs; Dr. James Greenberg, founder of the Center for Teaching Excellence (CTE); and Dr. Angel David Nieves, assistant professor of Historic Preservation, who arrived on campus in 2004 and has engaged extensively with CRGE, CTP, and other avenues of campus diversity work.

3. The term RIG (research interest group) was adapted from the work of the Center for the Study of Women in Society (CSWS) at the University of Oregon.

4. At the University of Maryland, graduate fellowships carry no work requirement while assistantships are tied to a work assignment.

5. The departments are: women's studies, American studies, history, education, policy and leadership, curriculum and instruction, sociology, and family sciences.

References

Alexander-Snow, M., & Johnson, B. (1999). Perspectives from Faculty of Color. In R. J. Menges (Ed.), *Faculty in New Jobs: A Guide to Settling in, Becoming Established, and Building Institutional Support.* San Francisco: Jossey-Bass Publishers.

Banks, W. (1984). Afro-American Scholars in the University: Roles and Conflicts. *American Behavioral Scientist, 27*(3), 325–338.

Boykin, S., Zambrana, R. E., Williams, K. P., Lopes-Salas, D., Sheppard, V., & Headley, A. (2003). Mentoring Under-Represented Minority Female Medical School Faculty: Momentum to Increase Retention and Promotion. *Journal of the Association for Academic Minority Physicians, 14*(1), 15–18.

Brown, G. (Ed.). (1998). *Diversity Blueprint: A Planning Manual for Colleges and Universities.* Created by the Office of Human Relations Programs in collaboration with associates at the University of Maryland, College Park and the Association of American Colleges, and Universities (AACU). Washington, DC: AACU.

Consortium on Race, Gender and Ethnicity. (2004). *Research on Race, Gender and Ethnicity at UM: Perspectives on Diversity.*

Dill, B. T. (Unpublished). The Brown Decision and the University of Maryland: Past, Present and Future.

Dill, B. T., McLaughlin, A., & Nieves A. D. (2007). Future Directions of Feminist Research: Intersectionality. In S. N. Hesse-Biber (Ed.), *Handbook of Feminist Research: Theory and Praxis.* Thousand Oaks, CA: Sage Publications.

Fong, B. (2000). Toto, I Think We're Still in Kansas. *Liberal education, 86*(4).

Frost, S. H., & Jean P. M. (2003). Bridging the Disciplines: Interdisciplinary Discourse and Faculty Scholarship. *Journal of Higher Education, 74*(2), 119–148.

Garza, H. (1993). Second-Class Academics: Chicano/Latino Faculty in U.S. Universities. In J. Gainen & R. Boice (Eds.), *Building a Diverse Faculty: New Directions for Teaching and Learning, 53.* San Francisco: Jossey-Bass.

Gonzalez, K. P., & Padilla, R. V. (1999). *Faculty Commitment and Engagement in Organizational Reform.* Presented at Annual Meeting of the Association for the Study of Higher Education, San Antonio, Texas.

Hollander, E. L., & Saltmarsh, J. (2000, July/August). The Engaged University. *Academe, 86*(4). Retrieved from www.aaup.org/publications/Academe/2000/00ja/JA00Holl.htm.

Harley, S., & Terborg-Penn, R. (Eds.). (1978). *The Afro-American Woman: Struggles and Images.* Port Washington, NY: Kennikat Press.

Howard-Vital, M. R., & Morgan, R. (1993). *African American Women and Mentoring.* Washington, DC: U.S. Department of Education.

Jarmon, B. (2001). Unwritten Rules of the Game. In R. O. Mabokela & A. L. Green (Eds.), *Sisters of the Academy: African American Women Scholars in Higher Education.* Sterling, VA: Stylus.

Johnsrud, L. K. (1993). Women and Minority Faculty Experiences: Defining and Responding to Diverse Realities. In J. Gainen & R. Boice (Eds.), *Building a Diverse Faculty: New Directions for Teaching and Learning* (p. 53). San Francisco: Jossey-Bass.

Levinson, W., Kaufman, K., Clark, B., & Tolle, S. W. (1991). Mentors and Role Models for Women in Academic Medicine. *Western Journal of Medicine, 154,* 423–426.

Monk, J., & Rosenfelt, D. S. (2000). Introduction: Internationalizing the Study of Women and Gender. In J. Monk & D. S. Rosenfelt (Eds.), *In Women in the Curriculum* (pp. 1–53). Baltimore: Uptown Press.

Roche, G. R. (1979). Much Ado about Mentors. *Harvard Business Review, 57,* 14–28.

Rosenfelt, D. S. (2002). Culturally Challenging Practices and Pedagogical Strategies. In M. M. Lay, J. Monk, & D. S. Rosenfelt (Eds.), *Encompassing Gender* (pp. 456–458). New York: The Feminist Press.

The National Academies. (2004, November 19). *Facilitating Interdisciplinary Research.* NEWS. Retrieved from http://www8.nationalacademies.org/onpinews/newsitem.aspx?RecordID=11153.

Thomas, D. A. (2001, April). The Truth about Mentoring Minorities: Race Matters. *Harvard Business Review, 79*(4), 98–107.

UM Senate Task Force Report on Mentoring and Success of Junior Faculty, Executive Summary. (2005, April 6). Retrieved from http://www.provost.umd.edu/MS07/TopicB_November1.pdf.

UM Report and Recommendations of the President's Diversity Panel. (2000, August 15). Retrieved from http://www.inform.umd.edu/CampusInfo/Departments/PRES/divrpt.pdf.

UM Mission Statement. (2000, October 27). Retrieved from http://www.provost.umd.edu/Strategic_Planning/Mission2000.pdf.

Zambrana, R. E. (2007, Spring). Director's Message. *Research Connections*, CRGE, 3.

12

Conclusion

Future Directions in Knowledge Building and Sustaining Institutional Change

RUTH ENID ZAMBRANA AND BONNIE THORNTON DILL

This collection of chapters illustrates the viability and analytical power of intersectional analysis for studying inequality in the U.S. context, for building knowledge, and for creating institutional change. Drawing on empirical research and studies of policies and practices that impact the lives of low-income women and women of color, it reveals the interplay of power, identity, and social location as it affects options and opportunities in employment, access to and use of government and employer benefits, political and civic participation, K–12 schooling, and in the scope and structure of higher education. This concluding chapter summarizes the theoretical conclusions of the articles and discusses the ways they contribute to an understanding of intersectionality. In light of these insights it briefly discusses the numerous critical debates, tensions, and major intellectual challenges about the scope, purpose, place, meaning, and future of intersectional analyses, and describes new frontiers for future inquiry and theoretical development.

The intersectional analytic lens that informs all of these articles acknowledges that social relations involving historically underrepresented and poor people are complex and that much of that complexity is hidden by the way relations of power are embedded in social structures, policies, and practices.[1] Examining the roots of the problems these groups encounter requires unveiling these relations of power. Primary among the social relations that effect these populations are issues of race, racialization, and racial formations. A fundamental theoretical conclusion of the articles in this collection is that racialized constructions of groups are used to maintain systems of inequality. Yet, increasingly, these historical patterns of discrimination and inequality are masked by a new focus on diversity and a new rhetoric of a color-blind society (Bonilla-Silva, 2006; Collins, 2006).

Consistent with other writings using an intersectional frame, the chapters in this book demonstrate that dimensions of inequality are not readily separable but mutually constituted and that social problems, policies, and practices are not singly the result of either race, or class, or gender alone but the product of a particular intermeshing of these and other dimensions of inequality to create varied results for differing groups or individuals in specific locations at distinct historical moments. The second theoretical conclusion challenges a pattern that remains prevalent in too many areas of the social sciences where increased attention to race, ethnicity, gender, and socioeconomic status has yielded simplistic explanations in which these factors are treated separately and used as causal explanations failing to accurately represent or explain the lived experiences of poor and racialized women and men in U.S. society. (For a discussion of this issue as it applies to political science, see Simien, 2007.) Intersectional analyses challenge monocausal explanations of inequalities and differences to make visible power relations and structural arrangements that maintain the oppressions and exclusion of low-income people and people of color and seek to promote interdisciplinary knowledge building to produce understanding of and change in the lives of groups of people who have been and remain in subordinate positions.

Chapters 2 through 4 of the book illustrate the importance of historical and geographic context in shaping domains of inequality. These chapters reveal the ways race, ethnicity, low socioeconomic status, gender, and culture combine in producing discriminatory policy and practices. There are two important theoretical conclusions that we draw from the application of intersectional analysis in these cases. First, historical context is essential in revealing how domains of inequality are intermeshed, how those particular arrangements have been produced, and how they affect contemporary policy such as access to higher education, low representation of women of color in the professional and corporate world, and the design and implementation of programs targeted toward poverty. In these chapters we see that meaningful insights about the similarities and differences among racial and ethnic groups can only be derived from an understanding of historic inequities and the role they play in producing contemporary inequalities. Their findings also demonstrate that historic, economic, and cultural patterns of subordination result in processes of social and emotional disadvantage that are cumulative over generations.

The second conclusion is that intersectionality as a theoretical framework provides tools for examining the relationship of race and power in relationship to other dimensions of inequality and difference. In that process, we gain a deeper understanding of the subtle and often invisible ways that racial formations combine with dimensions of privilege (such as Whiteness) and exclusion (such as poverty) to produce inequities for people in a variety of different social and geographic locations throughout U.S. society. In other words, these chapters demonstrate that the analytical power of intersectionality, although developed in understanding the lived experiences of people of color, are useful in unveiling the ways race, class, gender, and ethnic distinctions are embedded in social institutions, practices, and representations and contribute to patterns of social inequality in U.S. society more broadly.

Chapters 5 through 9 focus on the differential implementation and effects of public policy on poor and historically underrepresented groups. The set of theoretical conclusions derived from these articles are that access to resources in welfare, education, modalities for civic participation, and maternity leave benefits are less likely to be available to those who need them most. Differential treatment in the form of fewer resources and lower quality services permeates public systems such that schools in poor neighborhoods, for example, have fewer monetary as well as computer resources and these shortages disadvantage the educational outcomes and opportunities of the low-income African American and Latino students who attend them. The research syntheses and analyses presented in these chapters emphasize the understanding that adverse outcomes for poor and historically underrepresented groups that are often characterized as individual or group failures are likely the result of inadequate resources in public service systems. This emphasis on the inadequacies of public systems provides a theoretical intervention to unmask the racial, class, and gender constructions that underlie them and that construct public systems to serve as gatekeepers rather than safety nets to help vulnerable individuals and populations. Discriminatory patterns within public systems favor middle income and non-Hispanic Whites over poor African Americans, Latinos, and Native Americans. Evidence of persistent historical and contemporary patterns of exclusionary and inequitable forms of implementation of policy were found in recent reviews of empirical and historical work on major public systems, namely, welfare, education, and reproductive health (Jones-DeWeever, Dill, & Schram, in this volume, chapter 7; Noguera, 2003; Silliman, et al., 2004). Intersectional approaches make visible commonalities of inequalities across public systems.

The last three chapters of the anthology apply intersectional analysis as a tool for social change. The findings are derived from lessons learned from scholars, including the editors themselves, in a variety of higher education institutions throughout the country. The major theoretical conclusion is that social change cannot occur without institutions of higher education allocating resources to those alternative initiatives within their institutions that have an intersectional lens, that seek to promote inclusivity in knowledge production, curriculum transformation, mentoring, and pedagogy, and that actively seek to use knowledge to achieve social justice. This is particularly challenging because institutions of higher education are at once conservative—as transmitters of legacy and gatekeepers for established norms and practices of knowledge production—and creative—as laboratories for innovation. Their claims to legitimacy derive from hegemonic and disciplinary power that shapes the priorities and decision-making practices of institutions regarding the allocation of resources (Collins, 2000; Bonilla-Silva, 2006). Nevertheless these chapters argue that neglecting the intersections of race, ethnicity, gender, and socioeconomic position as a central component in knowledge formulation contributes to reinforcing existing myths of individual or cultural failure of groups and perpetuates continuous misrepresentation and misconceptions of the restricted options and opportunities of historically underrepresented groups in the United States (Young & Braziel, 2006).

Challenges, Tensions, and Emerging Frontiers of Inquiry

This volume also contributes to a larger discussion about the nature and future of intersectional knowledge building that is occurring in multiple disciplines such as sociology, political science, psychology, and literature and discourses including race and ethnic studies, feminist theory, critical race theory, queer theory, literary theory, and cultural studies. Intersectional scholarship, as we know it today, emerged as an amalgamation of aspects of women's studies and race and ethnic studies. Both of these fields were intellectual projects growing out of civil and women's rights activism of the 1960s and 1970s. Women's studies focused on gender and sexism while Black and Latino studies focused on race and racism as experienced within their respective communities. Each field sought to interrogate historical patterns of subordination and domination. Thus categories of race, class, and gender were defined as major markers and signifiers of oppression with limited attention to other markers of oppression such as sexuality, nation, ethnicity, age, bodily ability, religion, and others. The last two decades have witnessed the development and maturation of a number of debates and discourses about intersectionality. Scholars debate whether its contributions are methodological or theoretical. Others seek to expand its analytical frame, while still others seek to incorporate its early emphasis on race and ethnicity into areas that have ignored this aspect of the framework.

The intellectual ferment within and around intersectional theory is yielding new frontiers of knowledge production that include but are not limited to scholarship on identity and the applicability of intersectionality to groups in other social locations and/or in multiple social locations simultaneously (Browne & Misra, 2003; Henderson & Tickamyer, in this volume, chapter 3). Discussions about methodologies, language, and images most accurately convey the complexities of these interrelationships. For example, the development of queer of color critique (Ferguson, 2003; Johnson & Henderson, 2005) as an intervention into sexuality studies establishes race and ethnicity as a critical dimension of queer studies; scholarship on globalization and international human rights moves intersectionality beyond the U.S. context (Mohanty, 2003; Yuval-Davis, 2006); and work that continues to explicitly link theory and practice provides an analytical foundation for social justice and critical resistance. Within each of these topics there are disagreements about approach and perspective, but the debates and discussions contribute to the vibrancy of the topic and thus to advancing this scholarship and producing knowledge that illuminates the many factors that shape processes of experiencing multiple identities and social locations.

Identity remains a contested and much debated category both between and within various groupings of intersectional scholars. Among promising aspects of identity studies has been the growth and expansion of studies of race and ethnicity that examine processes of racialization for groups other than Blacks and Whites in the United States. For example, Salvador Vidal-Ortiz's *On Being a White Person of Color: Using Autoethnography to Understand Puerto Ricans' Racialization* provides an example of the ways identity studies has been productively enhanced through the inclusion of concepts of nation and nationality. The author challenges classical definitions of race, ethnicity, and nationality, while also repositioning debates about identity politics in the United States. Vidal-Ortiz (2004) argues that an alternative racialization process occurs when Puerto Ricans represent themselves while living in the United States, contrasted with living on the island. By studying the impact of more than one racialization system, he shows how categories of analysis like gender, class, and sexuality may be mobilized differently depending on an individual's own geopolitical location.

Further the application of critical race theory in the studies of Asian Americans and Latina/os has been particularly thoughtful in expanding understandings of the concept of race, challenging what some term a Black-White binary, and exploring interrelationships *among* U.S. racial/ethnic groups (Delgado & Stefancic, 2000). In addition, Whiteness studies—when constructed as part of an understanding of the interrelationships and distribution of power among racial groups—have also broadened notions of racial identity (Andersen, 2003).

Postmodernism has also been a major factor in reshaping identity studies—challenging it to move beyond its early "essentialist" tendencies to more complex and nuanced notions of the meaning, nature, and construction of both individual and group identities. Critiques of "identity politics" have come from many sectors: from parts of the political right that perceive it as a form of balkanization of U.S. culture; from sectors of the political left that see it as a way of undermining class solidarity; and from postmodernist theory that sees it as an attempt to codify a continually shifting and contested set of ideological categories among others (Moya, 2002). To some extent, this is a conflict between a conceptualization of identity that focuses on the tension between identity as a personal struggle between the individual and the "groups" in which s/he holds membership on the one hand and identity as part of a system of power and inequality in which certain categories and individuals within them receive unmerited rewards and benefits. These debates also reflect a split between theory and lived experience, between abstract ideas and political realities. As Martin Duberman astutely pointed out in an essay in *In These Times*:

> Many minority intellectuals are troubled about the inability of overarching categories or labels to represent accurately the complexities and sometimes overlapping identities of individual lives. We are also uncomfortable referring to "communities" as if they were homogeneous units rather than the hothouses of contradiction they actually are. We're concerned, too, about the inadequacy of efforts to create bridges between marginalized people. Yet we hold on to a group identity, despite its insufficiencies, because for most non-mainstream people it's the closest we have ever gotten to having a political home—and voice.

The meanings and complexities of language and the images used to capture the insights and knowledge that intersectional analyses have produced is a central concern for intersectional theory. Questions of language are compounded by the multiple intellectual domains in which this work is being generated and discussed. Each field approaches these issues through its own specific lens and specialized vocabulary. This process yields new insights and interdisciplinary ways of viewing the world yet it readily lends itself to misinterpretation and miscommunication. Intersectional scholars must think carefully about whether or not there are ways to negotiate this tension so that it gains greater clarity with regard to some of the most central concerns—for example, what is social justice?—while allowing room for the vibrancy and messiness that interdisciplinary ideas generate. Patricia Hill Collins suggests that we need debates that will clarify what is meant by social justice and at the same time provide a framework broad enough to accommodate people's different locations within these debates.[2] She finds herself wanting to return to language with long historical roots that resonate for people outside the academy. For example, she prefers the notion of racism to that of race because, she argues, racism is a term that people recognize as politicized and in which notions of power and inequality are embedded. It is also a term that is not limited to the U.S. context.

Central to the discussion of language has been debates about the adequacies and limitations of the notion of "intersectionality" itself. Scholars working with these ideas continue to seek ways to overcome an image that suggests that these dimensions of inequality such as race, class, and gender are separable and distinct and that it is only at certain points that they overlap or intersect with one another. Intersectionality is more than a car crash at the nexus of a set of separate roads (Crenshaw, 1989). Instead it is well understood that these systems of power are mutually constituted (Weber, 2001) that there is no point at which race is not simultaneously classed and gendered or gender is not simultaneously raced and classed. How to capture this complexity in a single term or image has been an ongoing conversation. Recent work by Kennelly (2007) provides both a useful overview of a number of the conceptual images in use, analyzing their limitations and suggesting aspects of intersectionality that remain unexplained. The author then goes on to propose an innovative and promising approach to thinking about these ideas using the processes of producing, using, experiencing, and digesting sugar as a metaphor for describing, discussing, and theorizing intersectionality (Kennelly, 2008). For example, she addresses the importance of context-specific relationships in understanding how race, class, and gender oppression is "produced, what people and institutions do with it once they have it in their hands, what it feels like to experience it, and how it then comes to shape us." She argues that the relationships among sources of oppression, like race, class, and gender start with production—every aspect of race, class, and gender has been and is produced under particular social, historical, political, cultural, and economic conditions.

Debates around methodologies center on the concern of remaining grounded in the questions, struggles, and experiences of particular communities that generate an intersectional perspective and at the same time extend this approach to identify common themes and points of connection between specific social locations and broader social patterns. Stated somewhat differently: How do we benefit from comparisons and interrelationships without negating or undermining the complex and particular character of each group, system of oppression, or culture? We argue that finding the answers for many of these questions will require more cross field collaborations, more dialogue about critical assumptions, more critiques of existing work, and more theory development based on what we already know. There is a need to explore and expand the methodologies that we use to address an even broader range of questions that can be generated by this scholarship. These should include applied and theoretical, qualitative and quantitative, and interdisciplinary and transversal modes of inquiry, among others. Interdisciplinary research must embrace multiple methodological approaches to capture the complexities and nuances in the lives of individuals and the experiences of groups of people. As scholars in this field, we seek methodologies that avoid essentializing people's experiences by utilizing isolated analytical categories to identify a person's location such as woman, queer, or Latino.

An intersectional approach that emphasizes multiple dimensions of identity and their relationship to systems of power has been part of lesbian, gay, bisexual, and transgender (LGBT) studies, revealing the heterosexism of institutions and practices, broadening our understandings of gender, exposing the artificiality of presumed sex differences, and expanding knowledge of sexual desire. However, this use of intersectionality primarily as a methodological tool has been criticized by scholars of color, in particular, because LGBT and queer studies have largely ignored race and ethnicity and failed to incorporate the insights of intersectional analysis with regard to race and racialization into its larger theoretical frame. Correctives to this are found in the work of such scholars as historian John D'Emilio (2003), whose book on the life of labor and civil rights activist Bayard Rustin examines the complex ways race, gender, and sexuality intersected in Rustin's life and affected key strategies and actions of the civil rights movement. Roderick Ferguson, in his book *Aberrations in Black: Toward a Queer of Color Critique* (2003), develops what he calls "queer of color analysis" that reveals the interconnections among sexuality, economic inequality, and race not only in the history of U.S. labor, but within various forms of knowledge production. His book lays out the historical role sociology has played in labeling African American culture as deviant and, by carefully highlighting this process, Ferguson reveals how identity is inextricably linked to power, political representation, and the ever-shifting power dynamics of identity politics.

In a recent edited volume, Johnson and Henderson (2005) state that "Black Queer Studies serves as a critical intervention in the discourses of Black Studies and Queer Studies" [with the objective of] building a bridge and negotiating a space of inquiry between these two liberatory and interrogatory discourses (1, 8–9). The introduction to the anthology provides a useful analysis of the limitations of both queer studies and Black studies in incorporating the "multiple subjectivities" within each group. They point out that both fields emerged from political movements and strategies that focused primarily on only one dimension of selfhood and each erased difference and the mutually constituted nature of identity that shapes lived experience. Nevertheless work in the area of queer studies may require some precautions as shifts in language usage and terminology, from "gay" to "queer," is not without controversy. As Rhonda M. Williams (1998) suggested, although queer is seen as a "necessarily expansive impulse, we must understand how it still also reflects and, in some cases, might blur the complexities of sexual orientations and racial politics among Black gays and lesbians." Johnson and Henderson (2005) note that the authors in their collection "question the effectiveness of Queer studies in addressing issues of public policy that have had a direct impact on gays, lesbians, bisexuals and transgendered people of color" (7). The intersectional project of Black queer studies and queer of color critique is to theorize sexuality in a manner that is fully inclusive of the ways race, class, and gender mutually shape and are shaped by each other.

Globalization has emerged as a critical area of inquiry as the United States has assumed a more imperialist and dominant position as a world power. The outsourcing of goods and services and the development of labor markets outside the United States have contributed to a dispersion of labor markets, relocation of U.S. workers, and displacement and replacement of low-wage workers. For example, benefits information on Temporary Assistance for Needy Families (TANF) has been outsourced to workers in India (Hu-DeHart, 2007). Public policy decisions such as these disproportionately impact poor women and women of color in the United States who, if working, are often working in low-wage jobs in competitive industries. For African American and Latino women recipients of TANF, who are the least likely to obtain training or a position that would lead to economic self-sufficiency, as Jones-DeWeever, Dill, and Schram (in this volume, chapter 7) found, such strategies are deeply ironic. The search for cheap labor in global markets both exploit the labor of poor third world/southern women at the same time that they increase economic vulnerability and limit options and opportunities for economic self-sufficiency and social mobility for women of color in the United States. Further for those women who remain TANF recipients, the ability to access information on benefits is decreased by a "provider group" that is unfamiliar with the U.S. social and political context and is less likely to be linguistically appropriate to the recipients of the service.

Theorizing about third world/southern women done in the framework of comparative women's studies has had a similar project of making power and inequality visible and being "attentive to the micropolitics of context, subjectivity and struggle as well as to the macropolitics of global economic and political systems and processes" (Mohanty, 1991). Mohanty has suggested that "comparative women's studies," a cross-national approach to studying the lives of women of color globally and in the United States, is intersectional scholarship. She argues that in addition to conceptualizing identity in multiple categories, it helps foreground ideas of nationhood and citizenship that may in turn be used to elucidate the position of women of color in the United States.[3] The work on third world/southern women has also emphasized the existence and importance of indigenous feminisms further stressing the importance of a global perspective to intersectional scholarship. This scholarship is advancing our knowledge on how political structures, U.S. hegemony, and geographic space and place shape definitions and roles of gender and sexuality.

Knowledge Production and Social Justice

The production of knowledge is an academic enterprise and has been controlled and contained within predominantly White, elite, and middle-class institutional structures. Within this context, research is guided by normative roadmaps, which are presumed to be neutral or objective theoretical frame-works and methodologies but in actuality are built upon assumptions that are subjective and convey particular images of various population groups. The culture of science, which rests upon claims of neutrality, empiricism, and positivist thinking, maintains invisible structural arrangements that perpetuate patterns of inequality. Thus the meaning and interpretation of the numerous studies on race, ethnicity, and poverty, which appear under terms such as disparity and social gradient, must be unveiled with respect to the systems of power and inequality that structure the processes of knowledge production in the sciences and social sciences and works against changes in public policy. The following normative research practices are among those that must be unveiled to facilitate linking knowledge production with social justice and public policy:

- Ignoring the structural arrangements of power leads to assumptions of equity, an overemphasis on the role of individual agency and prevents researchers from identifying the intersections of institutional racism, poverty, gender, and the associations of these factors with the domains of individual well-being, economic and social outcomes, and racial/ethnic disparities.

- Relying on cultural determinism as an explanation for both positive and negative attributes leads to scientific conclusions that outcomes are unchangeable and cannot be modified.

- Resources that support knowledge production are controlled and distributed by those who have successfully engaged in normative, not critical scientific practice. Thus the politics of knowledge production are largely uncontested yet visible in the patterns of who receives coveted research funding; and who is included as both research principals and research subjects; who holds leadership positions in the academy and administrative positions in the federal research and philanthropic world; as well as who determines research priorities and what scholarship shapes that thinking.

Intersectional work emerging predominantly from the social sciences and humanities is an alternative mode of knowledge production that seeks to validate the lives and stories of previously ignored groups of people and is used to help empower communities and the people in them. The production of knowledge to address real-life social issues and problems and to apply and use the knowledge to solve problems of inequality has been fundamental to the intersectional project of promoting social justice.

The links between theory and social justice have been demonstrated quite effectively in the work of critical race theorists (CRT). Arguments in CRT scholarship include analyses of White privilege as structured throughout the legal system and other sociopolitical structures, as well as the examination of civil rights law that operate through "race-neutral" principles to sustain White dominance. Linking theory, policy, and practice is the principal focus of the field of Critical Legal Theory (CLT). Because this knowledge is grounded in the everyday lives of people of diverse backgrounds, it is seen as an important tool linking theory with practice. Two spin-offs are LatCrit Theory and Asian Pacific American Critical Race Theory.

Latina/o critical theory, although largely ignored, has been around for a long time (Stefancic, 1997). LatCrit Theory (www.LatCrit.org) calls attention to the way in which conventional, and even critical, approaches to race and civil rights ignore the problems and special situations of Latina/o people—including bilingualism, immigration reform and laws, the binary Black-White structure of existing race remedies law, and other key social issues (Stefancic, 1997, 1510). The invisibility of Latina/o issues is evident in multiple fields including health (Zambrana & Logie, 2000), education, and child welfare. This oversight is most likely associated with the fact that Latina/os as an ethnic group were classified as White up until 1980, although their historic mistreatment had been documented by Chicano scholars (Almaguer, 1994). An organization that has been particularly active in the application of critical race theory to Latina/os is LatCrit.

LatCrit is a national organization of law professors and students that seek to use critical race theory to develop new conceptions of justice by actively engaging in what they term, "anti-essential community building." Linking theory and practice, especially in work that brings together scholarly analysis with community organizing, is seen as a vital dimension of this scholarship, one that grows out of its roots in lived experience and is directed toward its goal of social justice. Recognizing that knowledge produced in the field of law effects structures of power in society, LatCrit seeks to focus its analytical lens on policies and areas of the law that have previously been overlooked. No single community, they argue, can produce a theory about intergroup justice without connections to other groups, and yet every single social justice movement has had a problem of essentialism, giving primacy to some aspects of their identity while ignoring others that intersect with and reform that primary identity (Delgado Bernal, 2002). As a result, LatCrit seeks quite consciously to consider Latino identity as a multifaceted, intersectional reality. Latina/os, they argue, are Black, White, Asian, gay, straight, and speak many different languages. Thus the term antiessentialism has particular meaning for them because the work of LatCrit is primarily focused on incorporating issues of identity, hybridity, antiessentialism, and liberation into the analysis of law and in legal institutions, discourse, and process.

Asian Pacific American Critical (APACrit) theory focuses on the intersecting formations of race, gender, nation, citizenship, and immigration. APACrit frames analyses of social inequalities and poses possibilities of social justice that take into central account contentious national identity processes. Foregrounding formations of "Asian America" reveal Critical Race Theory's (CRT's) limitations, particularly CRT's constricted focus on the Black-White binary and its lack of attention to issues of immigration and citizenship. Additionally APACrit scholarship approaches formations as simultaneously raced and nationed within the context of border maintenance, national security, immigration laws and policies, racial profiling, sexual harassment laws, hate speech, and the nation-form's identity project. By foregrounding experiences of Asian American women and men and critiquing cultural representations of racial-sexual policing, APACrit also examines identity formations as simultaneously gendered, sexualized, raced, classed, and nationed.

Since the mid-1990s, APACrit has continued to grow and expand as interdisciplinary scholarship committed to social justice. Gotanda (1995) is one of the first CRT scholars to place issues in Asian American studies and CRT in conversation. He challenges legal liberalism's presumption that identity formations rest outside the law, such that the Japanese American internment, for example, is understood in legal liberalism as a result of bad decisions and misunderstandings and certainly not as the result of broader structural inequalities in society and the legal system. Matsuda (1996) proposes "outsider jurisprudence," as a politically productive challenge to legal liberalism that considers the histories and experiences of marginalized groups, including immigrants and those positioned outside the national identity. Chang and Aoki (1997) argue that CRT scholarship center the immigrant in analyses of the social construction of borders, race, and national identity. Cho (1997) analyzes sexual harassment cases involving APA women university faculty members and calls for a change in how the law conceives of harassment. Due to the confluence of race and gender stereotypes shaped by immigration laws and cultural representations, APA women are constructed as the model minority female—as especially vulnerable to "racialized (hetero)sexual harassment." Finally APACrit has moved into the post-9/11 world with Volpp's (2002) examination of the racialization of "Middle Eastern, Arab, or Muslim" as terrorists and disidentification as citizens. The formation of this new identity category is shaped by structures and ideologies of citizenship, nation, and identity. A significant focus of APACrit is the shifting nature and definitions of citizenship, the exclusionary and discriminatory practices of immigration laws, and the standardization of APA groups as foils for real Americans (Jen, 2006).

Other examples that link theory, policy, and practice can be found in the work of Professors Barbara Ransby, Elsa Barkley-Brown, and Deborah King who organized a national response to the Anita Hill/Clarence Thomas controversy. Ransby, Barkley-Brown, and King prepared a public statement that applied an intersectional analysis to the vilification of Anita Hill as well as Clarence

Thomas's distorted use of the concept of lynching. Signed by over sixteen hundred African American women scholars, the statement offered an interpretation of those events that went beyond the singular focus on sexual harassment that had become the overriding concern of many White feminists and the racial victimization evoked by Clarence Thomas's "high-tech lynching" claim. Their statement argued that constructs of race and gender intersected in the treatment of Anita Hill to demean and discredit her in a way that was consistent with the historical pattern of treatment of Black women who speak out on sexual matters or publicly criticize Black men. The statement, published in the *New York Times* and six African American newspapers, offered a perspective on the case that had been totally omitted from the public discourse.

On the global front, intersectionality has been applied in discussions of international human rights. Yuval-Davis (2006) critiques the debate among three "different approaches" used in discussions of intersectionality in UN and international human rights discourse. The first she describes as *additive*, based on the image of a traffic intersection. The second Yuval-Davis terms *identity* as used in Australian human rights documents that emphasizes the indivisible aspects of identity. The third she labels *structural*, which builds on the work of the Center for Women's Global Leadership at Rutgers University that emphasizes *structural* subordination and multiple forms of oppression. Yuval-Davis argues that "what is at the heart of the debate is conflation or separation of the different analytic levels in which intersectionality is located, rather than just a debate on the relationship of the divisions themselves" (2006, 194). She concludes her essay with a call for "theory formation and research which accounts for the diverse conditions which gave rise to the constitution of differences as well as their historical interconnectedness'—or, using the terminology presented here, the ways different social divisions are constructed by, and intermeshed with, each other in specific historical conditions" (202). Although the articles in this collection focus on intersectionality in the U.S. context, both U.S. and other international scholars and human rights advocates are discussing, debating, and applying its approach to unveiling the interwoven relationships of power and inequality both to produce new knowledge about women and excluded groups in other countries and to design global struggles for social justice around these understandings.

Conclusions

This book exemplifies the need for and importance of an intersectional framework because it expands the narrow boundaries of traditional research approaches; emphasizes the connection between research, public policy, and social justice; and challenges higher education to support intersectional research and expand curriculum content to provide an education that links, knowledge, policy, and social justice.

Traditional research, particularly in the social sciences, public health, and education among others is largely reactive, seldom identifying root causes of social problems and rarely providing appropriate solutions to complex issues (Zambrana and Holton, 2007). Over the last decade, we have witnessed the distortion and obfuscation of language through conservative appropriations of such words and phrases as equity, equal opportunity, and, even, civil rights. This twenty-first-century version of Orwellian "new-speak" further hampers support for research that seeks to interrogate the historical and contemporary meanings of inequity, poverty, racism, and sexism in the United States. For the United States to gain intellectual and social clarity around the multiple structural factors associated with inequities such as school failure, poor health, and the unprecedented growth of a prison industrial complex, would represent a radical commitment to social change and social justice.

True equity and equal opportunity for historically underrepresented and low-income people in the United States requires honoring our ideals as a democratic nation. It is a powerful process that the society is increasingly unwilling to implement because it requires structural changes including the redistribution of society's goods and services. It also requires ideological changes that would begin with dismantling notions of White supremacy in all of its manifestations not the least of which is the negative representations of other-than-White groups of people. For example, the persistent notion that low-income Latinos and African Americans do not value education is based on narrow research approaches that focus on individual parents and children often misinterpreting their goals and aspirations rather than taking a broader frame of reference that would examine children and families within the resource-poor school and community environments in which they reside. Thus conclusions around school failure and success often engage in a victim blaming approach relying on individual or cultural deterministic explanations, failing to address issues of equity or reveal the intersections of race, ethnicity, class, and power relations.

The debates occurring within intersectional scholarship today reflect the growth and maturation of approach and provide us the opportunity to begin, as Lynn Weber says, to "harvest lessons learned." Among the lessons learned and knowledge produced is a broader and more in depth understanding of the notion of race, racial formation, and racial projects. Another is a broader understanding of the concept of nation and of notions of citizenship both in the United States and globally. Concepts such as situated knowledge's, oppositional consciousness, and strategic essentialism offer ways to theorize about difference and diversity. A third lesson is the knowledge that there is no single category (race, class, ethnicity, gender, nation, or sexuality) that can explain human experience without reference to other categories. Thus we have and will need to continue to develop more nuanced and complex understandings of identity and more fluid notions of gender, race, sexuality, and class. The work relies heavily on a more expanded sense of the concept of social construction and rests much of its analyses on the principle of the social construction of difference. Organista (2007) contests dominant culture's imperialism and resistance to discussion of human differences within and across cultures and calls for a discussion of difference "beyond the kind of defensive and superficial hyperbole that leaves social oppression unchallenged" (101). And, while the scholarship still struggles with the pull either to establish a hierarchy of difference or a list that includes all forms of social differentiation, a body of knowledge is being produced that provides a basis for understanding the various histories and organizations of these categories of inequality, which is helping us better understand what difference makes.

NOTES

1. Underrepresented is first used to include the underserved (African Americans/Black, Asian, Hispanic, American Indian, and multiracial) plus low-income people, in the Higher Education Act of 1965 Title III first enacted by President Lyndon B. Johnson. These are people who have been traditionally excluded from full participation in our society and its institutions. The basis of exclusion has primarily been race and color including African Americans/Black, Asian, Hispanic, American Indian, and multiracial.

2. Personal Conversation, 2001.

3. Personal Conversation, 2001.

References

Almaguer, T. (1994). *Racial Fault Lines: The Historical Origins of White Supremacy in California*. Los Angeles: University of California Press.

Andersen, M. (2003). Whitewashing Race: A Critical Review. In E. Bonilla-Silva & W. Doane (Eds.), *Whiteout: The Continuing Significance of Race* (pp. 21–34). New York: Routledge Press.

Bonilla-Silva, E. (2006). *Racism without Racists: Color-Blind Racism and the Persistence of Racial Inequality in the US*. Second edition. Lanham, MD: Rowman & Littlefield Publishers, Inc.

Browne, I., & Misra, J. (2003). The Intersection of Gender and Race in the Labor Market. *Annual Review of Sociology, 29*, 487–513.

Chang, R. S., & Aoki, K. (1997). Centering the Immigrant in the International Imagination. *California Law Review*, (85), 1395.

Cho, S. K. (1997). Converging Stereotypes in Racialized Sexual Harassment: Where the Model Minority Meets Suzie Wong. *Journal of Gender, Race & Justice, 1*, 177–211.

Collins, P. H. (2000). *Black Feminist Thought: Knowledge, Consciousness, and the Politics of Empowerment*. New York: Routledge Press.

Collins, P. H. (2006). *From Black Power to Hip Hop*. Philadelphia: Temple University Press.

Crenshaw, K. W. (1989). Demarginalizing the Intersection of Race and Sex: A Black Feminist Critique of Antidiscrimination Doctrine, Feminist Theory, and Antiracist Politics. In D. K. Weisberg (Ed.), *Feminist Legal Theory: Foundations*. Philadelphia: Temple

University Press, 1993. Reprinted in J. James & T. D. Sharpley-Whiting (Eds.), *The Black Feminist Reader*. Malden, MA: Blackwell, 2000. Reprinted in A. Wing (Ed.), *Critical Race Feminism: A Reader*. New York: New York University Press, 2003.

Delgado, R., & Stefancic, J. (2000). *Critical Race Theory: The Cutting Edge*. Philadelphia: Temple University Press.

Delgado Bernal, D. (2002). Critical Race Theory, Latino Critical Theory, and Critical Raced-Gendered Epistemologies: Recognizing Students of Color as Holders and Creators of Knowledge. *Qualitative Inquiry, 8*(1), 105–126.

D'Emilio, J. (2003). *Lost Prophet: The Life and Times of Bayard Rustin*. New York: Free Press.

Duberman, M. (1991). In Defense of Identity Politics. *In These Times*. Retrieved July 2001 from http://www.alternet.org/story/11160.

Ferguson, R. (2003). *Aberrations in Black: Toward a Queer of Color Critique*. Minneapolis: University of Minnesota Press.

Gotanda, N. (1995). Critical Legal Studies, Critical Race Theory and Asian American Studies. *Amerasia Journal, 21*, 127–135.

Hu-DeHart, E. (2007). Surviving Globalization: Immigrant Women Workers in Late Capitalist America. In S. Harley (Ed.), *Women's Labor in the Global Economy* (pp. 85–103). New Brunswick, NJ: Rutgers University Press.

Jen, C. (2006). Technoscientific Race-Nation-Gender Formations in Public Health Discourses. Unpublished paper, University of Maryland-College Park.

Johnson, E. P., & Henderson, M. G. (2005). *Black Queer Studies: A Critical Anthology*. Durham, NC: Duke University Press.

Kennelly, I. (2007) Race-Class-Gender Theory: An Image(ry) Problem. *Gender Issues, 24*(2), 1–20.

Kennelly, I. (2008). Beyond the Intersection: A New Culinary Metaphor for Race, Class, and Gender Studies. *Sociological Theory, 26*(2), 100–110.

LatCrit. (2006). Retrieved from www.LatCrit.org.

Matsuda, M. J. (1996). Where Is Your Body?: And Other Essays on Race, Gender, and the Law. Boston: Beacon Press.

Mohanty, C. T. (1991). Under Western Eyes: Feminist Scholarship and Colonial Discourses. In C. T. Mohanty, A. Russo, & L. Torres (Eds.), *Third World Women and the Politics of Feminism*. Indianapolis: Indiana University Press.

Mohanty, C. T. (2003). "Under Western Eyes" Revisited: Feminist Solidarity through Anticapitalist Struggles. *Signs, 28*(2), 499–535.

Moya, P. (2002). *Learning from Experience: Minority Identities, Multicultural Struggles*. Berkeley: University of California Press.

Noguera, P. A. (2003). *City Schools and the American Dream: Reclaiming the Promise of Public Education*. New York: Teachers College Press.

Omi, M., & Winant, H. (1994). *Racial Formation in the United States: From the 1960s to the 1990s*. Second Edition. New York: Routledge.

Organista, C. K. (2007). *Solving Latino Psychosocial and Health Problems: Theory, Practice, and Populations*. Hoboken, NJ: John Wiley & Sons, Inc.

Sillman, J., Fried, G., Ross, L., & Gutierrez, R. (Eds.). (2004). *Undivided Rights: Women of Color Organize for Reproductive Justice*. Cambridge, MA: South End Press.

Simien, E. (2007, June). Doing Intersectionality Research: From Conceptual Issues to Practical Examples. *Politics and Gender, 3*(2), 264–271.

Stefanic, J. (1997). Latino and Latina Critical Theory: An Annotated Bibliography. *California Law Review, 85*, 1509–1584.

Vidal-Ortiz, S. (2004). On Being a White Person of Color: Using Autoethnography to Understand Puerto Ricans' Racialization. *Qualitative Sociology, 27* (2), 179–110.

Volpp, L. (2001). Critical Race Studies: The Citizen and the Terrorist. *UCLA Law Review, 49,* 1575.

Weber, L. (2001). *Understanding Race, Class, Gender and Sexuality: A Conceptual Framework.* New York: McGraw-Hill.

Williams, R. M. (1998). Living at the Crossroads: Explorations in Race, Nationality, Sexuality, and Gender. In W. Lubiano (Ed.), *The House That Race Built* (p. 154). New York: Vintage.

Young, J., & Braziel, J. (2006). *Race and the Foundations of Knowledge.* Chicago: University of Illinois Press.

Yuval-Davis, N. (2006). Intersectionality and Feminist Politics. *European Journal of Women's Studies, 13*(3), 193–209.

Zambrana, R. E., & Logie, L. A. (2000). Latino Child Health: Need for Inclusion in US National Discourse. *American Journal of Public Health, 90*(12), 1827–1833.

Zambrana, R. E., & Holton, J. K. (2007). Disparity/Inequity, Knowledge Production and Public Policy. *Journal of Ethnic and Cultural Diversity in Social Work, 16*(3/4), 169–178.

CONTRIBUTORS

L. JANELLE DANCE holds a joint appointment as associate professor in sociology and the Institute for Ethnic Studies at the University of Nebraska at Lincoln. She received a Ph.D. in sociology from Harvard University. Dance's areas of interest include the sociology of education, urban sociology, youth cultures, U.S. race and ethnic relations, intersectional and critical theory, and qualitative methods (with an emphasis on ethnographic research). Most recently, Dance has been nurturing a new interest in immigration studies. In her most recent research project she conducted ethnographic work at two Swedish high schools as part of project titled, "The Children of Immigrants in Schools," that is funded by the National Science Foundation (NSF), and directed by Professor Richard Alba. She has also received a Spencer Postdoctoral Fellowship to conduct research on site at two inner city schools in Philadelphia, Pennsylvania. Dance published the book titled, *Tough Fronts: The Impact of Street Culture on Schooling* (2002) and is working on two additional manuscripts: "At Risk Near Harvard U.: Working Class Teens and Teachers They Love," and "Black Strawberries: Teenagers, School Reform, and Urban Change in North Philly."

BONNIE THORNTON DILL is professor and chair of the department of women's studies and founding director of the Consortium on Race, Gender and Ethnicity at the University of Maryland. She is formerly founding director of the Center for Research on Women at the University of Memphis. Her research focuses on intersections of race, class and gender with an emphasis on African American women and families. She has published articles in *Signs*, *Feminist Studies*, *Journal of Marriage and Family* and her work has been reprinted in numerous edited volumes. Her most recent articles include: "Disparities in Latina Health: An Intersectional Analysis" with Ruth E. Zambrana in *Gender, Race, Class, & Health*, edited by Amy J. Schulz and Leith Mullings (2006); "Future Directions of Feminist Research: Intersectionality" with A. McLaughlin and A. D. Nieves in *Handbook of Feminist Research: Theory and Praxis* edited by S. Hesse–Biber (2007); and "Between a Rock and a Hard Place: Motherhood, Choice and Welfare in the Rural South," in *Sister Circle: Black Women and Work* edited by Sharon Harley and Black Women and Work Collective (Rutgers University Press, 2002). She has won

291

two awards for mentoring—one from Sociologists for Women in Society and a second from the University System of Maryland Regents. She also received the Jessie Bernard Award and the Distinguished Contributions to Teaching Award both given by the American Sociological Association. In 2001–2002 she received the Eastern Sociological Society's Robin Williams Jr. Distinguished Lectureship and served as vice president of the American Sociological Association from 2005–2008.

LORRIE ANN FRASURE is an assistant professor in the department of political science at the University of California–Los Angeles. Her fields of study include American politics and political economy, with areas of interests in immigrant and ethnic minority politics, suburbanization, state and local politics, public policy and research methods. Her current book project examines post-1980 immigrant and ethnic minority suburbanization and the responsiveness of state and local institutions to changing suburban demographics. Frasure was a post-doctoral associate at Cornell University (2005–2007), and a Ford Foundation Dissertation Fellow (2005). She holds a Ph.D. in government and politics from the University of Maryland–College Park (2005) and a Master of Public Policy from the University of Chicago (2001).

MARY GATTA is director of the Sloan Center on Innovative Training and Workforce Development (ITWD) at Rutgers University. Dr. Gatta's work is focused on providing intellectual, technical, and financial support and leadership to ensure that low-wage workers have access to the education and skills training that are tied to high-wage, high-demand jobs. Central to this is the belief that educational and workforce development and policies must be crafted so that they attend to the life and work needs of individuals. This project provides technical assistance and resources to states to scale up a New Jersey pilot project of online learning for low-wage workers throughout the country. Her book on this project, *Not Just Getting By: The New Era of Flexible Workforce Development* was released in December of 2005. In addition, Dr. Gatta is the director of Workforce Policy and Research at the Center for Women and Work at Rutgers University. Her areas of expertise include gender and public policy, low wage workers, earnings inequality, and sex segregation studies. Her earlier book, *Juggling Food and Feelings: Emotional Balance in the Workplace* was published in 2002.

DEBRA HENDERSON received her Ph.D. from Washington State University in 1996 and is currently an associate professor of sociology at Ohio University. She is a faculty fellow at the Voinovich Center for Leadership and Public Affairs and a past associate editor of *Rural Sociology*. Her research interests focus primarily on rural poverty and the impacts of structured inequality on culturally diverse individuals and families. She has published in journals such as *The Journal of Children and Poverty*, *Family Relations*, *Affilia*, and *Social Psychology Quarterly*.

ELIZABETH HIGGINBOTHAM is currently a professor in the department of sociology at the University of Delaware. She is a native New Yorker who completed her Ph.D. at Brandeis University. She was one of the founders of the Center for Research on Women at the University of Memphis. Higginbotham is the author of *Too Much to Ask: Black Women in the Era of Integration* (2001), coeditor of *Women and Work: Exploring Race, Ethnicity, and Class* (1997), and *Race and Ethnicity in Society: The Changing Landscape,* 2ed. (2008). Her articles appear in *Gender & Society, Women's Studies Quarterly,* and many edited collections.

AVIS JONES-DEWEEVER is the former director of Poverty, Education, and Social Justice Programs at the Institute for Women's Policy Research (IWPR) and recently joined the National Council of Negro Women as Director of the Research, Public Policy, and Information Center for African American Women. She is continuing her connection to IWPR as an affiliated scholar. Her work examines the causes and consequences of poverty on the well-being of low-income women and families while identifying effective programmatic strategies that result in poverty reduction. Dr. Jones-DeWeever has authored or coauthored numerous publications including "When the Spirit Blooms: Acquiring Higher Education in the Context of Welfare Reform," "Saving Ourselves: African American Women and the HIV/AIDS Crisis," and "The Women of New Orleans and the Gulf Coast: Multiple Disadvantages and Key Assets for Recovery." A highly sought-after speaker, Dr. Jones-DeWeever's policy perspectives have been distributed through a variety of media outlets including CNN, ABC News Now, National Public Radio, BBC Radio International and the *New York Times.* Her areas of expertise include poverty in urban communities, inequality of educational opportunity, and the impact of welfare reform on women and communities of color. Dr. Jones-DeWeever received her Ph.D. in government and politics from the University of Maryland–College Park and currently serves on the board of directors of the Women's Voices.

VICTORIA-MARÍA MACDONALD's research examines how historical legacies impact contemporary policy, access, and equity of Latino and African American students into high quality educational institutions at all levels. She is the author of *Latino Education in the United States: A Narrated History, 1513–2000* (2005) and has written numerous book chapters and articles. She is currently visiting associate professor in minority and urban education at the University of Maryland–College Park. Professor MacDonald received her doctorate from the Harvard Graduate School of Education, and is a former Spencer Foundation postdoctoral fellow.

TIFFANY MANUEL is assistant professor in the political science department and the public policy Ph.D. program at the University of North Carolina–Charlotte. Her Ph.D. was earned at the University of Massachusetts–Boston. An expert on social welfare and labor policies, her interests include the integration of work, family, and community demands by low-wage workers; the dynamics of social support, employment interruptions due to care giving obligations, and earnings; and the conditions under which informal and formal flexible employment policies develop. She has also worked as an economic development consultant in the areas of program evaluation, comparative regional economic analysis, cost-benefit analysis, industrial cluster analysis, and social welfare and labor policy analysis. She is the author of several articles, book chapters and reports including "Keeping Jobs and Raising Families in Low-Income America: It Just Doesn't Work" with Lisa Dodson and Ellen Bravo.

AMY MCLAUGHLIN is former associate director of the Consortium on Race, Gender and Ethnicity at the University of Maryland. Her research agenda uses an intersectional lens to analyze social inequality in many different areas. She has analyzed the symbolic role that violence plays in women's lives, studied how large universities practice diversity, and pursued theoretical, methodological, and pedagogical insights into intersectionality. She received her Ph.D. in sociology from the University of Maryland. Currently, Dr. McLaughlin is analyzing the benefits of housework firsthand as she takes time out of the paid labor force to raise her two children.

SANFORD SCHRAM teaches social theory and policy in the Graduate School of Social Work and Social Research at Bryn Mawr College. He has published research articles in *The American Political Science Review*, *The American Sociological Review*, *The Social Service Review*, and other journals. He is the author of a number of books including *Welfare Discipline: Discourse, Governance, and Globalization* (2006) and *Words of Welfare: The Poverty of Social Science and the Social Science of Poverty* (1995), which won the Michael Harrington Award from the American Political Science Association. He is currently completing a coauthored book tentatively entitled "The New Poverty Governance: Devolution, Discipline and the Color of Welfare Reform."

ANN TICKAMYER received her Ph.D. from University of North Carolina–Chapel Hill in 1979 and is a professor of sociology and chair of the department of sociology and anthropology at Ohio University. She is a past president of the Rural Sociological Society and a past editor of the journal *Rural Sociology*. Her research focuses on rural poverty and inequality, gender, work and development, and social welfare provisions in the United States and Indonesia. Her work is published in leading journals and she is coeditor of two books, *Communities of Work: Rural Restructuring in Local and Global Context* and *The Sociology of Spatial Inequality*.

LINDA FAYE WILLIAMS, professor of government and politics at the University of Maryland, died in October 2006. A former Texan who fought for justice, decency, and human rights all her life, she specialized in illuminating the roots of injustice and racism in the United States and its politics. Prior to coming to

Maryland, Williams held faculty positions at Howard, Cornell, and Brandeis Universities. She also served as the head of the Congressional Black Caucus' Research Group and held the position of associate director of research at the Joint Center for Political and Economic Studies. Her last book, *The Constraint of Race: Legacies of White Skin Privilege in America* (2003), received the Michael Harrington Best Book Award, the W.E.B. Du Bois Best Book Award and was named the Best Book of 2004 on Public Policy and Race and Ethnicity by the American Political Science Association's Organized Section on Race, Ethnicity, and Politics. She was also author of *The Long Struggle for Black Political Empowerment* and coauthor with her husband Ralph Gomes of the edited book *Exclusion to Inclusion: The Long Struggle for African American Political Power.*

RUTH ENID ZAMBRANA is professor in the department of women's studies, director of the Consortium on Race, Gender and Ethnicity, and interim director of the U.S. Latino studies Initiative at the University of Maryland–College Park and adjunct professor of family medicine at University of Maryland–Baltimore, School of Medicine, department of family medicine. Her work focuses on the intersections of gender, race/ethnicity, socioeconomic status, and other contextual variables in the provision of public health, education, and human services with an emphasis on Latino women and children. Her emerging scholarship is on inequalities in racial/ethnic women's health and the intersections of disparity, knowledge production, and public policy. Two of her books include *Health Issues in the Latino Community* (coeditor, 2001) and *Drawing from the Data: Working Effectively with Latino Families* (2003). She is currently working on a book to synthesize the scholarship on Latino families including sections on girls to women and boys to men. She has published extensively in her field, has served on several editorial boards including *The American Journal of Public Health* and *Journal of Health Care for the Poor and Underserved.* She has served on several national and state boards and committees and recently served as a member of the Centers for Disease Control and Prevention Agenda Committee, Office of Public Health Research, Health Information Services and Health Equity Champions Work groups (2005), and the State of Maryland Governor's Transition Task Force on Higher Education (2006). She was honored by Hispanic Business Magazine as 2007 Elite Woman of the Year for her commitment and dedication to improving the Hispanic community through her service and scholarship.

INDEX

Italicized page numbers refer to figures and tables.

CPSIA information can be obtained
at www.ICGtesting.com
Printed in the USA
LVOW12s2031220416
484898LV00002B/127/P